Entrepreneurship and Small Business Development: Text and Cases

Entrepreneurship and Small Business Development: Text and Cases

George R. Forsyth
Joan Mount
J. Terence Zinger

This book has, from its conception through to publication, been a collaborative, team effort, with each author playing a vital role. Therefore, authorship is presented in alphabetical order.

Prentice-Hall Canada, Inc. Scarborough, Ontario

Canadian Cataloguing in Publication Data

Forsyth, George, 1933–
  Entrepreneurship and small business development:
text and cases

Includes bibliographical references and index.
ISBN 0-13-282641-0

1. Small business – Management. 2. Small business –
Management – Case Studies.   I. Mount, Joan.
II. Zinger, J. Terence (James Terence), 1951–
III. Title.

HD62.7.F67 1991   658.02′2   C90-095421-3

© 1991 Prentice-Hall Canada Inc., Scarborough, Ontario

Prentice-Hall, Inc., Englewood Cliffs, New Jersey
Prentice-Hall International, Inc., London
Prentice-Hall of Australia, Pty., Ltd., Sydney
Prentice-Hall of India Pvt., Ltd., New Delhi
Prentice-Hall of Japan, Inc., Tokyo
Prentice-Hall of Southeast Asia (Pte.) Ltd., Singapore
Editora Prentice-Hall do Brasil Ltda., Rio de Janeiro
Prentice-Hall Hispanoamericana, S.A., Mexico

ISBN 0-13-282641-0

Copy Editor: Chelsea Donaldson
Production Editor: Kelly Dickson
Production Coordinator: Florence Rousseau
Cover Design: Derek Chung Tiam Fook
Page Layout and Design: Derek Chung Tiam Fook
Cover Image: Geoffrey Gove/The Image Bank Canada
Typesetting: Q Composition Inc.

1 2 3 4 5 WL 94 93 92 91 90

Printed and bound in Canada by Webcom Limited

Table of Contents

● ● ● ● ● ● ● ● ● ● ● ● ● ● ● ●

Preface

Few small businesses, at any of the early stages, are organized in ways that fit the conventional wisdom propagated in most small business courses. This text is structured around the typical phases of development faced by most small businesses. The text and cases examine the factors which have an impact on success and failure in each phase and suggest how these can be managed. We will also examine ways of managing major strategy changes and major organizational changes as the business moves through the phases. This approach is largely driven by the following consideration: dividing small business studies into functional areas may be a convenient way to conduct research and train students, but rarely is this an accurate depiction of small business practice. The reader will find that the book provides a coherent, pragmatic approach to the issue of small enterprise management.

This book can be utilized in a variety of course settings. The book's "decision-making" focus calls for a previous course in financial accounting as well as some understanding of the basic concepts of marketing and financial management, conceivably in corequisite courses.

The wide array of post-secondary course offerings in the small business field (Small Business Management, Entrepreneurship, New Business Development) attests to the popularity of the subject area. However, the selection of materials available for use in these courses is still rather limited; certainly the case studies that have been aimed at the small business market are often one-dimensional, well defined problem situations, and hence not at all indicative of the multifaceted issues that typically confront the entrepreneur. The cases developed for this text cover a diverse range of small business settings within Canada and are meant to appeal to a broad audience. For instance, the analysis of certain cases will lend itself to a fairly detailed examination of financial data or operating procedures; the focus of other cases is such that little, if any, quantitative analysis is required. Similarly, some of the cases emphasize external factors and the long term direction of the organization, while for others, the issues will be more immediate and the possible courses of action somewhat limited.

The first three chapters act as the book's theoretical foundation. Chapter 1 provides an overview of small business management and outlines the basic themes of the book. Chapter 2 is devoted to a discussion of the phases of small business development and how this concept can provide a general framework for managing the small enterprise. Chapter 3 introduces the business plan as an integral aspect of both the initial startup and the ongoing operation of the business.

The small business cases contained in this book are organized in modules according to the developmental phase to which they best apply. However, given the dynamics of the subject enterprises, there is inevitably some overlap across phases, since not all facets of the business will necessarily develop at the same rate.

With the exception of a single case in Chapter 3, all of the case studies are positioned in Chapters 4 through 7. Each of these four chapters includes text material designed to provide some conceptual underpinning to the cases. This "Notes and Cases" approach provides an effective portrayal of the problems and opportunities characterizing the different phases of the small business growth cycle. However, being able to recognize the problems and opportunities that accompany a particular phase, and structuring the organization accordingly, is only part of the challenge of operating a small business successfully.

One must also be familiar with the basic tools of management and how they can contribute to the effective acquisition and utilization of resources. These tools, i.e. the traditional management functions (Marketing, Operations, Finance, Personnel, Accounting, and General Management), are presented in Part 2 (see Figure p-1).

This structure provides the reader with a handy set of optional materials, which can be used as background for different case studies. Also, the functional orientation of Part 2 will be quite valuable in courses where students may have had very little previous exposure to the various techniques of management. In

Figure P-1

Text
Arrangement

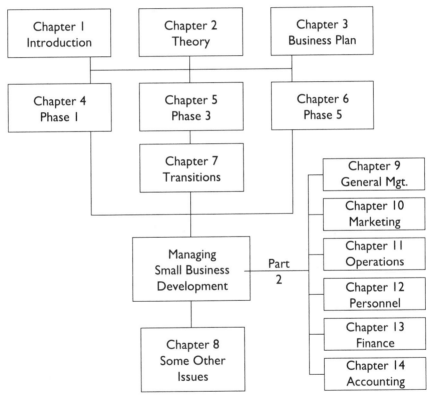

other, more advanced settings, these chapters can be omitted without detracting from the book's primary focus.

There are also two appendices which should be useful as background material: **Case Analysis** and **The Business Plan Format**.

Chapter 8 deals with a number of other issues which have an impact, in varying degrees, on the small business sector. For many readers, this chapter will act as a useful reference point, since the topics outlined may provide a focus for issues that emerge from particular cases.

· · · · · · · · · · · · · · · · ·

Acknowledgments

We wish to extend our thanks to the various small business owners who allowed their companies to be used as case examples for this text. Many of these entrepreneurs devoted considerable time to this project, knowing that they would derive very little in the way of tangible benefits in return. The ongoing development of good case materials depends on the contributions of people such as these. In addition, we are indebted to a number of businesspeople who provided case leads.

We are grateful to a number of external case-writers who contributed the following case studies:

Dr. Paul W. Beamish
(Univ. of Western Ont.)—*Kolapore, Inc.*
Prof. R. Mulholland
(Laurentian Univ.)—*Lizards Actionwear*
Phoenix Airmotive
Dr. David C. Shaw
(Univ. of Western Ont.)—*Eclipse Golf Ltd.*
Prof. Ian Spencer
(St. Francis Xavier Univ.)—*Perfect Pace*
Dr. Louis Zanibbi
(Laurentian Univ.)—*Valley Potatoes*

We also wish to express our appreciation of the efforts of those individuals listed below for their work on the following:

Shauna White—*The Perfect Pace*
David Porter—*Eclipse Golf*
Lola Ranger—*Joe's Service Station*
Terry Lang—*A Business Plan Format*

Colleagues at other colleges and universities have made valuable suggestions and we would like to acknowledge these reviewers: Raymond Kao, John Chamard, Dorothy Derksen, Megeed Ragab, and Ian Hayglass.

Special thanks are also due to the staff at Prentice-Hall Canada, Inc. who have provided valuable guidance during the development of this manuscript: Ruth Bradley-St Cyr, Yolanda de Rooy, and Jean Ferrier. We must also acknowledge the contribution of our copy editor, Chelsea Donaldson.

1

The Phases of Small Business Development: Entrepreneurship and Management

1

Managing Small Business Development: An Introduction

Introduction

The focus of small business, particularly in the academic setting, has frequently been on the pre-startup or startup phase. Such a focus provides a rich and fertile arena for classroom projects, hands-on developmental experience, and even some live examples where student projects emerge as small businesses. Governments have devoted considerable effort to creating seed money for startup, and a whole industry of business plan writers and small business consultants has concentrated on new business development. And yet, the statistics on new business and small business failures remain virtually unchanged over the years: even though the data will vary from industry to industry, most studies reveal a failure rate in the 50 percent to 70 percent range with 5 years of startup. Governments and lending institutions often fund startup business plans and research as a precondition to grants and loans. Yet as small businesses grow, it becomes extremely difficult to get funding for investments that could lead to increased employment, improved stability and, ultimately, the profitability essential to insure the business remains viable in a changing and competitive economy.

This text not only covers the topic of business startup and the many facets of successfully coping with the hazards of that process, it also looks closely at the less attractive and certainly less fashionable problems of "growing the business." Later phases of development receive equal attention here as part of a conceptual framework which makes the task of running and growing a small business as exciting, educationally, as starting that business.[1]

What is a Small Business?

There is no generally accepted definition of what qualifies as a small business. First, there is no consensus on what dimension to measure. To categorize business by size, government and financial agencies typically select a working definition that uses any one of sales revenues, total assets or number of employees as a measure. Further, what constitutes the upper limit on small is also arbitrary. For instance, according to Industry, Science and Technology Canada, a manufacturing company is small if it employs fewer than 100 people, whereas the cutoff for non-manufacturing companies is only 50 employees. Alternatively, in order to qualify for monies under the terms of the Small Business Loans Act, an enterprise's annual sales cannot exceed $2 million.

This definitional problem is complicated by the phenomenon of intra-industry comparisons on a scale that is relative to the industry being considered. The SAAB automotive division is a small organization in comparison with its General Motors' counterpart, but it is a big organization relative to the biggest local machine shop. However, the proprietor of that machine shop undoubtedly refers to his shop as big when comparing it with other shops that he knows. Such issues breed confusion over what really is a small business.

The strategies for growth and development chosen by some small enterprises require an extensive resource and skill mix, while other businesses, with more limited strategies, have fewer needs. Because of these differences, measuring size by employee numbers, sales volume or net income rarely reflects the real differences between large and small. Statistically convenient measures may satisfy governments' needs for reporting, but they do not address the problems of managing a small enterprise. Many of the details and differences among various levels of enterprise are obscured when a large and growing part of the economy is classified as small business. (Some 98 percent of Canada's 880 000 businesses are below the aforementioned 100 employee threshold.)

The activities that together constitute managing—planning, organizing, directing and controlling—are as crucial in running small businesses as large. Many small businesses embrace all or most of the basic functions (production, marketing, personnel, accounting, finance) associated with big business, and these are every bit as vital to the health of the small enterprise. Those functions not performed in-house by the small organization are often sought externally. Of course, purchasing services outside is not limited to small organizations; big businesses typically engage advertising agencies, market research firms, and other outside agents such as subassemblers to assist them in some aspect of their operation.

Small Business and the Business Life Cycle

Beyond the factors which make small businesses distinctive as a group, there are fundamental differences among small businesses themselves. Small businesses develop according to a particular progression, from owner operated, to owner managed, to functional organizations. This life cycle pattern provides a means of describing and classifying small organizations. The principles which apply to the development and management of small business will vary according to how far the enterprise has evolved. The problems encountered and the resources available in the early phases of development seldom resemble those associated with the later phases. Only when one has identified the phase in which a small business finds itself, is it appropriate to develop solutions for managing within that phase. Thus, a life cycle framework, besides being a descriptive tool, is also a vehicle for prescription.

Not all small businesses will become large; nor will all enterprises that remain small develop to the same extent. The evolutionary process often ceases at some point, in some cases due to market conditions and in other cases as a result of a conscious choice on the owner's part. Indeed, many firms go through some measure of development, growth, consolidation and perhaps decline without ever moving out of a particular phase of development.

The rate of development will not be uniform. However, for the business that does proceed from small to big, the progression will follow a certain sequence. Generally, by the time it stabilizes in the final phase of the pattern, the business will no longer be small even by conventional quantitative definitions.

The proposed life cycle framework captures the evolution of business enterprises as they expand from small owner-operated entities into more complex organizations, with several layers of management and a number of functional areas. This progression requires major organizational and strategic changes as the business proceeds toward a functional organization that encompasses the marketing, production, research and development, and other activities required for it to grow, compete, and/or achieve some desired level of specialization.

This life cycle perspective is very different from the standard approach employed in studying small business, whereby the enterprise is dissected into various functional components. In reality, it can be highly dysfunctional for the small business manager to attempt to resolve a particular problem by focusing on a narrow facet such as finance, personnel or marketing. For example, declining sales may appear to be a marketing problem when in fact the incentive plan discourages prospecting.

Outside Assistance

The small business is dependent to a certain extent on external parties to round out the basic skills of the enterprise (in essence, the proprietor's personal skills). This is particularly true in the earlier phases of its development. These external agents can provide a variety of services, such as legal, marketing research, product design, accounting, public relations and computer support, that are essential to the fledgling organization's survival and growth. Some of these are available at little or no cost from government sources, financial institutions and business schools. Unfortunately, small business managers may fail either to seek or to follow through on obtaining outside assistance; indeed, they may not know how to procure effective external skills and resources.

As the small business grows (with outside assistance as appropriate), it generally brings some of the needed skills in-house, thus fleshing out the existing organization and in many instances proceeding into a new developmental phase. Functional areas within the small enterprise will typically acquire in-house resources and skills at differing rates so that some functions may be highly evolved, while others remain far behind. A construction firm, for instance, might acquire full-time engineering and cost estimating expertise as demand for its services grows, but leave responsibility for financial reporting procedures in the hands of outside accountants.

Entrepreneurship

What about entrepreneurship? *Funk and Wagnalls* defines an entrepreneur as:

> One who undertakes to start or conduct an enterprise usually assuming full control and risk.[2]

The growing interest in entrepreneurship represents a shift in our basic values. Bulloch explains this change by suggesting that more Canadians are questioning the rewards of a career in a large institution or corporation, and instead choosing the personal development, freedom and independence they associate with running their own business.[3] While it is widely held that all small business owners possess some degree of entrepreneurial spirit, entrepreneurship and small business management are not simply interchangeable terms.

Deaver Brown, in *The Entrepreneur's Guide*, sets forth what he feels best describes an entrepreneur, and contrasts that description with the characteristics most often exhibited by successful corporation executives:[4]

> Enthusiasm and Endurance—Irrepressible enthusiasm and endurance seem to be crucial entrepreneurial trademarks. . . . This powerful conviction radiates confidence to employees, suppliers, lenders, and customers who often remain loyal and supportive despite overwhelming reasons to desert the enterprise. . . . Professional executive training and experience totally undermines this crucial talent. Corporate experience carefully dismantles dreamers and turns them into cautious curators . . .
>
> Conclusiveness—Conclusive decision-making is imperative since the new venture must move to survive. . . . Without a decisive nature, the founder will fold under the relentless pressure to act.
>
> Leadership—I have yet to meet an entrepreneur who was not a natural leader . . . They can ignite their followers . . . [and can] inspire devotion and loyalty, mustering excellent performances from average people.
>
> Product Pride—Few characteristics distinguish the executive from the entrepreneur more clearly than product pride. The executive world promotes a cool, detached posture; to fall in love with your own products is to sacrifice dignity, objectivity and judgement. The entrepreneur believes in a totally involved attitude; not to love your product is to settle for mediocrity, complacency, and boredom.
>
> Marketing Skills—Entrepreneurs with a marketing background usually have the best chance of success since marketing and sales are the crucial functions in a new enterprise.

Nerve and Shrewdness—Enterpreneurs must have the nerve and shrewdness to put the whole company together and keep it alive . . . to persuade people, companies, suppliers and customers to do business with your shaky new enterprise. Each outsider must be sized up carefully. Nerve and shrewdness will be your primary tools in dealing with them.[5]

The classic entrepreneur identifies quite closely with the business, which for him is much more than an economic venture.

Notwithstanding the efforts of some to subdivide entrepreneurs into several different categories, this text takes the approach that entrepreneurship *per se* is a form of management, one that has as its hallmarks creativity and risk taking.[6] We further argue that the entrepreneurial bent associated with bringing the business into existence in the first place can also propel the enterprise onwards through the life cycle. Entrepreneurship may seem less crucial to the business in the later phases, but it should not be stifled in the interests of "managing" the organization. (See Figure 1-1. Note, however, that the figure is somewhat oversimplified insofar as it is confined to individual entrepreneurship and does not deal with the notion of collective entrepreneurship. This distinction is described in Chapter 8 and depicted in Figure 8-1.)

Indeed, for businesses that move beyond the initial phase(s), a problem that often arises is the inability to get the business operating in an entrepreneurial fashion once again. Continuous innovation is an essential element in the success of most small businesses. Entrepreneurship should not be regarded as a process or mindset that pertains only to the early phases (or for that

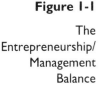

Figure 1-1

The Entrepreneurship/ Management Balance

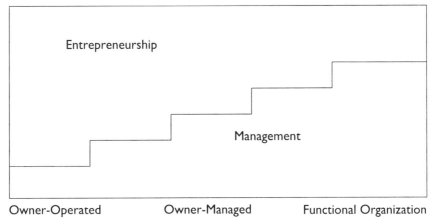

matter only to smaller organizations). The cultivation of an entrepreneurial atmosphere contributes to an organization's flexibility and allows it to adjust its course as circumstances change.

How Experience Shapes Decisions in Small Organizations

In contrast to decision-makers in large organizations, the owner-operator of a small business in the earliest phases, or the owner-manager of a more evolved small business, must generally make decisions in the relative absence of hard data and without recourse to computer-assisted analysis. He or she is also typically the sole agent in the decision-making process. As a result, the analysis leading to the decision may seem shallow, and to a large extent may be attributable to a broad-based feel for the business setting, including some degree of awareness of present and potential opportunities and threats; some appreciation of the key success factors in the particular business domain; and perhaps an idealistic perception of the organization's internal resources and constraints.

When faced with a decision, the owner-operator or the owner-manager tends to place considerable faith in a fluid blend of direct experience, recalled information, and extrapolated generalizations. From this experience base the decision-maker can derive propositions that apply to the analysis of novel situations, and can use these propositions with some degree of confidence because they are based on experience. The propositions may even be converted into decision criteria against which to assess alternative courses of action. For instance, a retailer who is considering extended hours because of competitive pressure, may elect not to make the change primarily because she has had poor experience, albeit in a different setting, with part-time labour.

As the business evolves into a functional organization, the manager, now normally the General Manager, is called on less often to examine new decision-making situations within the context of past experience, and more often to weigh the merits of conflicting viewpoints expressed by others—a process that often involves testing the assumptions behind the arguments mounted by in-house specialists in particular areas. Thus, the single decision-maker's dependence upon experience lessens as the organization develops. However, many entrepreneurs find it difficult to rise above their experience and to assume a role that involves sharing authority.

Summary

This text, in dealing with the opportunities and problems facing the small business manager, examines the factors which can help determine success or failure as the small business develops. The primary management activities—planning, organizing, directing and controlling—are different at each point in the progression (quite often these differences are revealed by external forces, such as the need for financing or a shift in the marketplace). It is crucial that the small business person, in carrying out these activities, take into account the status of the business in the life cycle.

In many situations the manager of a small organization faces decisions similar to those faced by counterparts in larger business situations, but with fewer resources and skills available. As a result, the range of decision options is constrained and the time horizon for formulating and implementing decisions differs from that in an organization where resources and skills are more abundant. The cases presented in this text not only involve the reader in the decision process of the small enterprise, but also cover the dynamics of managing within the context of the business life cycle. These cases cover a wide range of small business settings: retailing, manufacturing, service industries, franchises (Old Country Furniture (C)), family businesses (San Linde Bakery, Kampro, Inc., Fraser Inn), and enterprises owned and operated by women entrepreneurs (Lizards Actionwear, Computer Coveralls, and The Perfect Pace).

List of Key Words		
(Small Business) Development		Management
Enterprise		(Small Business) Phases
Entrepreneurship		Startup
Experience		

Questions for Discussion

1. What general factors do you feel explain the high failure rate (from 40–60 percent within 12 months of startup) for new small businesses?

2. a) Although outside experts can be invaluable to a small enterprise, particularly during its infancy, what are some of the dangers in relying too heavily on such assistance?

   b) For many people the term "outside assistance" implies professional consultants and contractual agreements. Discuss some of the less formal alternatives that are often available to the entrepreneur in need of business advice.

3. A large proportion of small businesses in Canada are family owned. Here, too, external advisors have a valuable role to play. As one member of a family business remarked: "They help us understand the value of each others' strengths and weaknesses, and building bridges instead of walls" (*Financial Post*, May 14, 1990, p. 36).

   Nonetheless, fewer than 30 percent of family owned ventures survive into the second generation, and approximately 10 percent reach the third generation. Do these businesses have their own unique set of problems?

4. Do you see *salesmanship* as an integral component of *entrepreneurship*? Explain your answer.

Selected Readings

Burch, John G., "Profiling the Entrepreneur," *Business Horizons*, September–October 1986, pp. 13–16.

Cook, James R., *The Start-Up Entrepreneur*. Toronto, Ont.: Fitzhenry & Whiteside, 1986.

Drucker, Peter F., *Innovation and Entrepreneurship: Practice and Principles*. New York: Harper and Row, 1985.

Shapero, Albert and Lisa Sokol, "The Social Dimensions of Entrepreneurship," in *Encyclopedia of Entrepreneurs*, eds. Kent, Sexton and Hall. Englewood Cliffs, N.J.: Prentice-Hall, Inc., 1982.

Stevenson, H.H. and D.E. Gumpert, "The Heart of Entrepreneurship," *Harvard Business Review*, 63, no. 2 (March–April 1985), pp. 85–94.

Welsh, John F. and Jerry F. White, "Growing Concerns: A Small Business is not a Little Big Business," *Harvard Business Review*, 59, no. 4 (July–August 1981), pp. 18–32.

Endnotes

1. Paul Hawkin, *Growing a Business* (New York, N.Y.: Simon and Schuster, 1987)

2. *Funk and Wagnall's Standard College Dictionary: Canadian Edition* (Toronto, ON: Longmans Canada Limited, 1963, p. 443). This definition, while similar to many others, tends to be more general than that suggested by many users of the term. Some suggest that size is relevant (small), others that ownership is essential, etc. The *World Book Dictionary* (Chicago, IL: Thorndike-Barnhardt, 1970, p. 697) defines an entrepreneur as "a person who organizes and manages a business or industrial enterprise, taking the risk of not making a profit and getting the profit when there is one."

3. John Bulloch, "Entrepreneurship and Development," *Journal of Small Business and Entrepreneurship*, 6, no. 1 (Fall 1988), 3–7.

4. Deaver Brown, *The Entrepreneur's Guide* (New York, N.Y.: Ballantyne Books, 1980). See "The Entrepreneurial Profile," pp. 7–20.

5. Brown, *The Entrepreneur's Guide*, pp. 7–20.

6. Vesper has identified 11 different types of entrepreneurs and these are discussed further in Chapter 2. Norman Smith (*The Entrepreneur and His Firm: the Relationship between Type of Man and Type of Company*, East Lansing, Michigan State Univ. Graduate School of Business Administration, 1967) propagated the notion of two types of entrepreneurs: the craftsman-entrepreneur and the opportunistic-entrepreneur. Later, Russell Knight (*Small Business Management in Canada: Text and Cases*, Toronto, Ont: McGraw-Hill Ryerson Limited, 1981) developed the concept of three levels of entrepreneurial activity: the inventor/craftsperson, the promoter, and the general manager.

2

Patterns of Small Business Development: A Working Concept

Introduction

As Chapter 1 suggests, small business definitions abound. Most encompass a wide range of small business types; few adequately describe the complexities of managing in the small firm setting. The range of activities involved, even under the most limited definition, is unwieldy.

Figure 2-1 presents the five phases of small business development (owner-operated, owner-managed, and functional organization, with two transition phases) used as the coordinating theme for this book. Startup activities are portrayed as an umbrella for the various phases, since not all businesses begin in phase 1. While it is difficult to avoid some use of size criteria, the primary focus of our model is on the phases of development of small business and the management problems and opportunities encountered in each. This allows us to avoid the problems of oversimplification that can result from a more general approach to small business issues.

The study of small business in its various

Figure 2-1

Small
Business Growth
and Development

STARTUP	ACTIVITIES			
Phase 1	**Phase 2**	**Phase 3**	**Phase 4**	**Phase 5**
Owner-Operator	Transition to Owner-Manager	Owner-Manager	Transition to Functional Management	Emerging Functional Management
Owner as Operator		Owner as Manager		Functional Management
			Emergence of the General Management Role	

phases permits a closer look at the anatomy of change and the factors associated with small business development. The phase breakdown is designed to accommodate both the descriptive analysis and the prescriptive action central to managing the variety of situations that confront small business.

To provide a context for our own five-phase model, we will first describe the major components of management theory as they relate to the practical needs of each small business stage, and examine several models of small business development that have been proposed by other theorists. We will then show how our five phase model attempts to incorporate the essentials of both these topics.

As we shall see, each of the phases discussed has unique resource and organizational issues associated with it. In subsequent chapters, we will explore some of the unique dimensions of managing the small firm through its development phases, point out the differences evident in each phase, and suggest ways to deal with the impact of these differences on the way small firms manage their growth and development.

Managing the Small Business

Growth and development in the small firm come, at least in part, from effective management in each phase. Since we stress small business management throughout the chapter, it is important to look at the components of management before offering a working model for this text.

The Activities of Management

While there are a number of opinions on what constitutes management, most agree with Koontz and O'Donnell[1], and Drucker[2], that it involves planning, organizing, directing and controlling. Simply put, **Planning** involves determining the direction (objectives and strategy) for the firm.[3] **Organizing** involves the marshalling of resources required to meet plan needs. **Directing** involves the actions, including motivation, essential in using available resources to allow the firm to run according to plan. **Controlling** involves the performance measurement activities necessary to assess and adjust the objectives, strategies, and actions essential to achievement of the plan. Figure 2-2 presents the functions of management as part of the five-phase model.

Implicit in the model is the suggestion that the tasks or activities of management differ from phase to phase. For example, planning in the owner-operator phase is designed to organize day-to-day activities, is of a very short-term nature, and involves limited detail and a strong internal focus. Planning in phases 2 and 3 involves providing direction in acquiring and allocating skills and resources. There is an emerging need for an outward focus to provide guidelines, a lengthening time frame to allow for the growing complexity of

Figure 2-2

Management Activities: An Organizational Approach to Small Firm Growth and Development

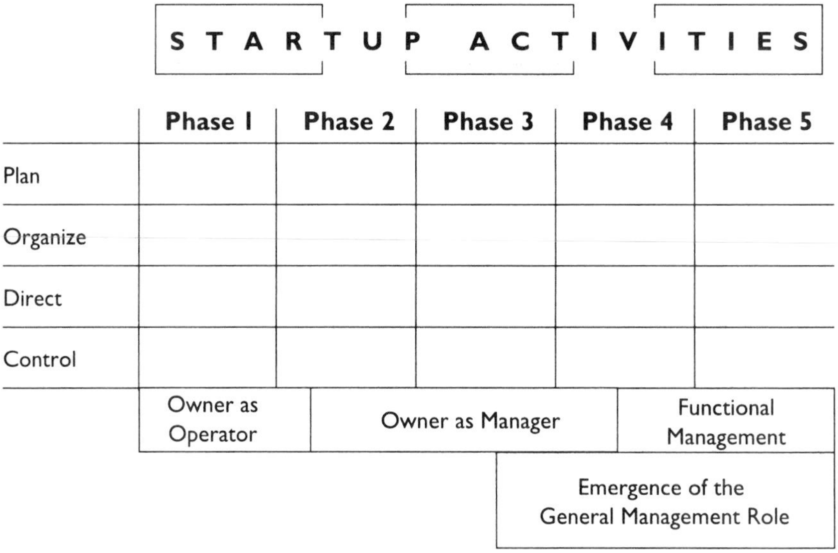

STARTUP ACTIVITIES				
Phase 1	**Phase 2**	**Phase 3**	**Phase 4**	**Phase 5**
Plan				
Organize				
Direct				
Control				

Owner as Operator	Owner as Manager		Functional Management

Emergence of the General Management Role

the organization, and an increased emphasis on detail to meet inside and outside needs. In phases 4 and 5, planning provides direction, but also requires that managers be able to communicate their plans effectively to a growing organization, in which the responsibilities of management are being delegated to others.

In other management areas, such as organizational design, communications and information systems, the phase is a factor in determining both the design and the use of appropriate management techniques. The same is true of organizing and directing; as the organization develops, different techniques and skills are required for the management tasks essential in the evolving small firm.

Functional Management

Most management texts use the term "functional management" to include the management of marketing, operations, personnel, finance and accounting. Even before a functional organization emerges it is convenient to use these divisions. The convenience arises because much of the research and the writing on management is done by specialists in these functional areas. As well, these divisions have provided a useful shorthand for dealing with outsiders. Thus, one speaks of marketing plans and marketing programs, production plans and financial plans even though in the early stages of growth these are all developed and implemented by one person. Figure 2-3 presents these additions to the text model.

Early in the new firm's development, one person, usually the proprietor, generally assumes responsibility for marketing, operations, personnel, finance

Figure 2-3

Functional Management: An Organizational Approach to Small Firm Growth and Development

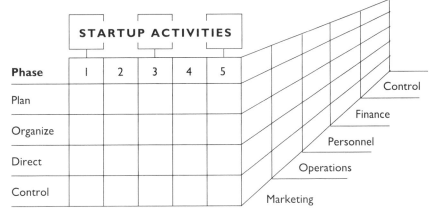

and control as day-to-day needs dictate. As the organization grows, running the operation often increasingly involves managing the activities of others. Eventually the responsibilities for managing expand beyond the capacity of the owner-manager, and some sharing of management responsibility takes place. Early authority/responsibility sharing seldom occurs along well defined functional lines. In phases 4 and 5, key activities such as marketing and operations may emerge as full-time jobs requiring specific skills. With these changes, the need for a general management role emerges as a distinct and separate activity.

Concepts of Small Business Development

The problem of reducing the mass of small business to useful subgroups has challenged a number of authors. Susbauer proposed a framework which divided small businesses into four groups in terms of increasing success. These included:

1. Survival firms,
2. Attractive growth potential firms,
3. Underachieving firms, and
4. High-success growth firms.[4]

Vesper grouped small businesses into "economic categories" as follows:

1. Solo, self-employed entrepreneurs,
2. Workforce builders (typical service companies),
3. Product innovators,
4. Unutilized-resource exploiters,
5. Economy-of-scale exploiters,
6. Pattern multipliers (franchise entrepreneurs—McDonald's, etc.),
7. Takeover artists,
8. Capital aggregators, and
9. Speculators.[5]

In both cases the authors sought to classify groups of small business and to describe some of the characteristics of their growth strategies, but they made no attempt to discuss the process of management or organizational development. Nevertheless, the need to classify in an effort to better understand meaningful differences among small firms is well documented.

Business Growth Cycles

An interest in business growth cycles has been with us for some time. Chandler, in his book, *Strategy and Structure: Chapters in the History of American Industrial Enterprise*, was among the first to study the development of corporations.[6] Subsequently, Scott[7], Salter[8], and Thain[9] offered and developed a concept proposing three distinct stages of corporate development:

- Stage 1, the entrepreneurial/owner-operated organization,
- Stage 2, the functional organization, and
- Stage 3, the divisional or decentralized organization.

Scott emphasized the life cycle approach to corporate development but, unfortunately for those interested in small business, stage 1 organizations received little attention except as a starting point for business development. Further complicating the issue was the wide variety of business firms and situations that were lumped into this stage 1 group. Finally, none of these theorists who wrote about the stages framework dealt with the transition between stages 1 and 2 and stages 2 and 3, critical turning points in the growth and development of most firms.

Cooper proposed a three-stage scheme to expand our understanding of small business activities within the entrepreneurial or owner-managed stage.[10] His three stages included:

- Stage 1, startup,
- Stage 2, early growth, and
- Stage 3, later growth.[11]

The startup stage included the decision to found the firm, to position it within a particular industry, and to use a particular competitive strategy. The early growth stage featured the development and testing of a product market strategy and direct control over all activities by the owner-manager. The later growth stage featured some additions to functional management, the delegation of decision-making, some diversification for manufacturing firms and the addition of multiple sites for some retail and service businesses. While other typologies have been proposed, Cooper's schema remains the most common approach to explaining the growth patterns of small firms. Others have used the Cooper framework to study a variety of small business management activities, including planning.[12]

Figure 2-4

Stage
Comparisons
Between the
Scott and
Cooper Models

Scott[1]		
Stage 1	**Stage 2**	**Stage 3**
Owner Managed	Functional	Divisional/ Decentralized

Cooper[2]		
Stage 1	**Stage 2**	**Stage 3**
Start- up	Early Growth	Later Growth

1. Scott, B.R., *op. cit.*
2. Cooper, A.C., *op. cit.*

When one compares Cooper's and Scott's typologies, it is evident that Cooper's three stages partially overlap Scott's stages 1 and 2. Those writing about corporate stages spend little time exploring stage 1 and make no mention of the problems of startup. Although Cooper identifies the startup stage as a beginning for most small firms and the later growth stage as the beginning of a functional organization, neither Scott nor Cooper addresses the issues and problems of transition where firms are moving from one stage to the next. Figure 2-4 compares the Scott and Cooper typologies and their respective concerns. While the individual schemes consider a number of different factors, each suggests that those who look at growth and development in both large and small firms see some significant merit in depicting development as a staged process.

Both Salter and Thain offer elaborations on Scott's work. Thain's discussion of the Scott framework sets forth some of the key differences in management, planning, etc. evident across the stages.[13] Of particular interest is Thain's recognition of the management characteristics unique to Scott's stages. His characterization of organization structures, ownership/management styles, decision processes and financing structures as they vary between stages of corporate development provides useful insights for a similar breakdown within the stage 1 (owner-managed) small business situation. In our approach we break Scott's stage 1 into five growth and development phases and look extensively at the characteristics of managing in each. Once the firm has entrenched a functional organization it has moved by Scott's definition to stage 2. Our phases parallel those offered by Cooper although we use different descriptive parameters. As well, we have added two transition phases.

Finally, in an article entitled "The Five Stages of Small Business Growth," Churchill and Lewis offer a five-stage model.[14] Their experience, review of the literature and empirical research suggest the following five stages:

- Stage I, existence,
- Stage II, survival,
- Stage III, success,
- Stage IV, take-off, and
- Stage V, resource maturity.

The stage descriptions were based on "an index of size, diversity, and complexity, and described by five management factors: managerial style, organizational structure, extent of formal systems, major strategic goals, and the owner's involvement in the business.[15] The authors suggest that earlier models were tied too closely to size and growth, while their model considers a range of factors. However, in their model, it seems that small businesses that are owner-operated or owner-managed cannot succeed, since stage III, "success," involves a functional organization and stage IV, "take-off," is characterized by a divisional organization.[16] In our model, existence, survival and growth are possible in each of the five phases. At issue, however, may be the definition of small business.

Scott, Cooper, Churchill, and Lewis all portray each stage as a discrete situation. Thus, movement from stage 1 to stage 2 in the Scott model results in a sharing of managerial decision-making as the boundary is traversed. The problems of developing even the beginnings of a functional organization while still operating in an owner-managed stage are not discussed. Cooper's treatment is similar in this respect. Yet, in practice, a large number of companies spend significant time in between the stages. For example, we may find multiple sites and diversification, yet also find that there is little delegation of decision-making or authority. The characteristics in periods of transition are often some mix of the characteristics evident in both the preceding and following stages. These situations pose special problems and opportunities for small business managers. Thus, as an approach to managing the small firm, we use a five-phase model (see Figure 2-1).

Development Phases

We start from the premise that each phase in small business development has some unique features and requirements. These, in part, dictate or determine the management role and how it is carried out.

Startup

Many authors refer to the beginning phases of a new business as pre-startup; we have combined the activities of pre-startup with those of startup, since the dividing line is difficult to discern.[17]

Not all new businesses begin with the owner as operator. In fact, many new businesses begin as owner-managed companies and some begin with a full functional management in place. Of course, the startup activities at all levels share common elements, but because the requirements for businesses in each of these phases are different, the startup activities are also different. Moreover, as we will discuss in Chapter 3, different startup activities require different business plans. Thus, in our model startup is treated as a phase-related activity.

Many small businesses begin without much planning, often simply as an extension of existing activities. For others, the activities of the startup are a major factor in the early functioning of the new firm. Some participation in pre-startup activities, even when outsiders are not involved, saves time and frustration later.

While there are many important facets to the startup activities, the focus is on developing a business plan. Often these develop as a result of attempts to obtain outside financing. More than at any other time in the life of a small firm, outside involvement dominates startup. At this time the ability to find ingenious ways to obtain, but not necessarily own, needed resources is a survival skill.

However, the plans prepared to convince outsiders of the business's viability may be of little use in the early phases of business startup. Business plans prepared by accountants or consultants for investors or bankers often go well beyond the real needs and capabilities of startup operators and managers.

Phase One: The Owner-Operator

The owner-operated phase is characterized by the owner or owners "doing everything." Here, as well as in the transition to the owner-managed phase, the owner finds little to manage and is almost totally immersed in the welter of daily detail, performing activities that will eventually be done by others as the owner-operator becomes owner-manager. In many small firms the role of the owner as operator continues to exist well into phase 3.

Phase Three: The Owner-Manager

Here, the owner's role as manager begins to take form. While early in the phase management is not a full-time activity, success in phase 3 does require a move to some specific management activities, as well as the continued performance of some of the operating activities performed in phase 1. Planning, organizing, directing, and controlling become somewhat separated from the operating role of the owner.

Growth and development in phase 3 require planning which goes beyond that done for startup and, as a result, a greater need for control emerges. Certainly, if there is to be a comfortable sharing of authority and responsibility, these activities must begin in phase 3 and continue to develop in phase 4.

Phase Five: Emerging Functional Management

Throughout most of phase 5 the functional organization is likely to be a hybrid, since some of the functional management roles will not require full-time attention. There is a tendency to create the first management positions around those tasks that the owner cannot or does not like to perform. Thus, a sales or operations manager may be saddled with a wide variety of tasks not directly related to his or her functional assignment. (As well, the new functional organization often lacks the infrastructure to permit an easy transfer of both responsibility and authority.) Tight restrictions on management data and information may make functional management difficult and ineffective. For instance, performance records and accounting data necessary in a functional organization, particularly those relating to costs and profitability, are often kept confidential by owners who believe that such information is not essential for management decisions.

Transition Phases

The transition phases (2 and 4) deal with the activities and problems faced by small firm managers as they move their firms from owner-operated to owner-managed and, again, from owner-managed to functionally managed.

Phase Two Transition   In phase 2, the transition is from a series of plans and ideas prepared for outsiders (and sometimes *by* outsiders) to raise the capital and resources needed to start the company, to plans for the direction and survival of the company. Often the owner is skilled in one of the functional areas (marketing or operations) and the transition requires the development of a broader range of functional skills, as well as some capacity to manage. This can be a particularly difficult period insofar as the range of skills required of the owner is extremely broad. During this period there is a tendency for owners to manage on demand and to make use of external help (accountants and consultants) to do the work, rather than provide the skills and training needed for the move to phase 3. These problems, and some possible guidelines for dealing with them, are discussed in Chapter 7.

Phase Four Transition   The transition from phase 3 to 5 begins with a serious threat to the essential skills of stage 3, where all management authority and responsibility have been in the hands of the owner. The addition of specialists requires a sharing of both responsibility and authority, which can pose difficult problems for successful owner-managers. As well, the initial moves toward a functional organization often result in peculiar organizational arrangements which can complicate short-term decision-making, and under-utilize newly acquired skills and experience. There is a need to commit resources to new overhead activities to facilitate communication, control, and performance evaluation so that new managers can work effectively in the organization. It is not unusual for first and some subsequent attempts at developing a functional organization to founder, for a variety of reasons which we discuss in Chapter 7.

Small Business Growth and Development

As companies move through each phase it becomes essential to invest in the overhead of the next phase to foster development continuity. For example, it is clear that the information needs of a functional organization (phase 5) are substantially different from similar needs in earlier phases where one person performs the management tasks. Likewise, organization growth (phases 3, 4 and 5) requires that personnel functions such as hiring, training, and performance appraisal become somewhat more formalized than in earlier phases.

For some small firms growth is not a primary objective, certainly not if it means loss of control or ownership. Being in control, even to the extent that there is little sharing of management authority or responsibility, means that many firms cannot develop beyond the owner-managed phase. Other owners may desire growth but, without some sharing of management, will not be able to attain it. A few may move to a functional organization and still have very limited growth objectives. While growth and development are often related, development within a particular phase as opposed to development for the purpose of growing out of a phase is also a legitimate objective. An example of such development might be the addition of a computer system that substantially extends the capacity or capability of the owner-managed company to grow in terms of sales and revenue without any loss of owner-manager control.

Similarly, we should note that not all firms proceed through all phases. Some companies, because of skill limitations or personal objectives, remain in phase 1 (owner-operated). For some owner-operators the task of managing rather than doing is one for which they have little experience. Other owners, for a variety of reasons, choose not to go beyond phase 3, the owner-managed small company. Or, having chosen to be in a particular kind of business in a particular market, the limited need for management may constitute a role easily handled by the owner-manager. Others may attempt to move from phase 3 to phase 5 but find that a successful transition (through phase 4) requires management changes that conflict with personal and ownership objectives. Also, limited management skills may prevent the transition to a successful functional organization. The key to the stage 4 transition is less the exhibited skills of planning, organizing, directing, and controlling than the skill of delegating responsibilities for these management functions. The skill of delegating emerges as one of the key activities for the owner-manager as the firm moves through phase 4. As professional managers (functional specialists) are added to the firm's organization, the need to delegate becomes paramount. Where it is not in conflict with the owner's objectives, there is a natural shift to the management sharing role, particularly if the owner can move comfortably into the role of a general manager.

Other businesses, such as some available from franchisors, may move the new operations to either a phase 3 or phase 5 type operation immediately upon start up, as part of the contractual arrangement. With the support, training and the infrastructure that are passed on as part of the franchise package—the development of business plans, the acquisition and training of shift or department managers, and the reporting and control systems—the franchise operation can often begin at stage 5. Thus, we argue in subsequent chapters that there are a number of ways that an organization can grow and develop. Some franchise operations are designed to eliminate the need for an owner-manager, preferring to build franchisor support around the role of an owner-operator. In these situations the roles of planning and organizing are embedded in the franchise system, and the owner-operator simply follows some highly structured procedures (directing) to operate the firm. The control function is performed using a performance measurement system and on-site inspections to assure that the requirements of the franchise contract are being met. In return for this role (limited responsibility and authority), the management skills of the franchisor minimize the risks of business failure.

From the franchisor's point of view, such a system allows the sale of franchises to owners who can raise adequate funding but who may not be capable of managing in a non-franchise form of organization. In some non-franchise organizations, accountants and various consultants play a similar role, although such involvement usually is not part of the formal infrastructure.

Summary

The variety of situations encompassed by most definitions of small business includes a vast, heterogeneous group that renders any but the most general analysis misleading. We have taken a life cycle approach, dividing the growth and development of small firms into five phases. In each phase, the small firm exhibits different needs and different characteristics. Categorizing small businesses by phase offers an improved opportunity to describe, analyze and prescribe meaningful solutions tailored to meet real needs.

List of Key Words

Control	Plan
Franchise	Pre-startup
(Managing) Development	Startup
Marketing	Strategy
Organizing	Transition Phases

Questions for Discussion

1. How does the book's focus on the phases of development as a key discriminant for studying small business differ from the approach whereby small enterprises are differentiated according to size?

2. Discuss the treatment of business startups in this text and how it differs from the more standard approaches.

3. Outline the unique aspects of the transition phases.

4. "For some small firms growth is not a primary objective . . . " Why is this strategy appropriate in certain cases? Give some examples.

5. In general, how do stage or phase concepts enhance the understanding of entrepreneurship and small business development?

Selected Readings

Coltman, Michael M., *Franchising in Canada*. Vancouver, B.C.: International Self Counsel Press Ltd., 1985.

Facts about Franchising. Toronto, Ont.: Ontario Ministry of Consumer Affairs and Commercial Relations, 1985.

Griener, Larry E., "Evolution and Revolution as Organizations Grow," *Harvard Business Review*, July-August 1972, pp. 37–46.

Seigel, William L., *Franchising*. Toronto, Ont.: John Wiley and Sons Canada Limited, 1983.

Steinmetz, Lawrence L., "Critical Stages of Small Business Growth: How to Survive Them," *Business Horizons*, February 1969, p. 29.

Endnotes

1. Harold Koontz and Harold and Cyril O'Donnell, *Principles of Management: An Analysis of Management Functions*, 5th ed. (New York, N.Y.: McGraw-Hill, 1972).

2. Peter F. Drucker, *Management: Tasks, Responsibilities, Practices* (New York, N.Y.: Harper and Row, 1974).

3. Here we depart slightly from the commonly accepted definitions of strategy and planning. We take the approach that in the small firm the planning task encompasses the development of strategy as a direction and a context within which the firm's activities are carried on.

4. J.C. Susbauer, "Commentary" in D.E. Schendal and C.W. Hofer, *Strategic Management: A New View of Business Policy and Planning* (Boston: Little, Brown and Company, 1979), pp. 327–332.

5. K.H. Vesper, "Commentary" In D.E. Schendal and C.W. Hofer, *Strategic Management: A New View of Business Policy and Planning* (Boston: Little, Brown and Company, 1979), pp. 332–338.

6. A.D. Chandler, *Strategy and Structure: Chapters in the History of American Industrial Enterprise* (Cambridge, MA: M.I.T. Press, 1962).

7. B.R. Scott, "Stages of Corporate Development," 9-371-294, BP 998, Intercollegiate Case Clearinghouse, Harvard Business School, 1971.

8. Malcolm S. Salter, "Stages of Corporate Development," *Journal of Business Policy*, Spring 1970, pp. 23–27.

9. D.H. Thain, "Stages of Corporate Development," *The Business Quarterly*, Winter 1969, pp. 33–45.

10. A.C. Cooper, "Strategic Management: New Ventures and Small Businesses," in Schendal and Hofer, *Strategic Management: A New View of Business Policy and Planning*, pp. 316–326.

11. Ibid, pp. 316–326.

12. R.B. Robinson and J.A. Pearce II, "Research Thrusts in Small Business Planning," *Academy of Management Review*, January 1984, pp. 128–137.

13. Thain, "Stages of Corporate Development," p. 37.

14. Neil C. Churchill and Virginia L. Lewis, "The Five Stages of Small Business Growth," *Harvard Business Review*, May-June 1983, pp. 30–50.

15. Ibid, p. 31.

16. Ibid. see Exhibit IV., p. 38.

17. Few of the major authors who deal with the growth and development of the firm (See Cooper and Scott for example) separate out a pre-startup phase. Typically, pre-startup discussions emerge in the academic setting or in seminars developed to promote the business plan activities. In this text we recognize the value of proper planning for the new business, but treat it as part of the startup activities rather than as a separate phase. Raymond Kao in *Entrepreneurship and Enterprise Development* (Toronto, Ont.: Holt, Rinehart and Winston of Canada Limited, 1989, pp. 127–174) devotes a chapter to pre-startup activities.

CHAPTER

3

The Business Plan

Introduction

All small enterprises, no matter how wide their initial scope or how substantial their resources, evolve out of some type of conceptual plan. Usually the fledgling company undertakes a number of activities prior to becoming operational. These include:

1. Generating and evaluating new product and service ideas;
2. Analyzing demand and identifying market opportunities;
3. Determining physical resource needs; and
4. Projecting financial requirements, calculating break-even levels, and providing for financing.

Along with other elements, these comprise the **business plan** required of most new ventures, particularly if they wish to attract shareholders or other forms of outside financing. Thus, the business plan plays a specific role, mainly financial, and comes into play at startup, or when a firm requires major infusions of new capital. The business plan is a key element in the resource acquisition process.

There is a second kind of plan, used to guide the company in its day-to-day functioning. Called a working plan or **operating plan**, it is designed to deal with the ongoing resource allocation process of the functioning organization.

Chapter 3 is about business planning, both special purpose business plans (e.g., startup, refinancing) and operating plans. (Figure 3-1 provides a graphic look at the chapter content.)

As a basic premise, we have argued that the management of the small company varies with its phase of development. Understanding the management differences associated with each of the phases permits more relevant problem description and, subsequently, more meaningful prescriptive action in operating the small business. Appropriate planning, a key management task, responds to the same rationale. The content essential for the startup and operation of an owner-operated company is different from what one expects to find in a phase 3 (owner-managed) or phase 5 (functionally managed) company. This chapter is about those differences, and its objective is to foster useful and appropriate business planning for the small firm. As well, we look at the special problems of planning for the transition from one phase to the next.

Figure 3-1

Business Planning in the Small Business

Development Phases	1	2	3	4	5
Business Plan Resource Acquisition	Startup		Startup		Startup
Operating Plan Resource Allocation					
Marketing		T		T	
		R		R	
Operations		A		A	
		N		N	
Support Services Personnel		S		S	
		I		I	
Finance		T		T	
Control/Information		I		I	
		O		O	
General Management		N		N	

The Business Planning Process

Business planning has received a great deal of attention, both in practice and in the literature. This attention has resulted in a proliferation of planning terms (long-range planning, strategic planning, marketing planning, production planning, etc.) and a diversity of focus (business plans, small business planning and corporate planning, etc.). As a result, there are a variety of options for both small and large companies and institutions to choose from. We will look at some of the variations in small business plans, and try to develop an approach that is appropriate to the growing small firm. We have organized our discussion to include both special purpose business plans and working plans, and we will approach these activities in terms of the needs of owner-operators, owner-managers, and functionally managed small companies.

Finally, we focus on the small business plan as an integral part of management and not something separate and apart from getting things done. It should be a project-oriented process that takes place periodically; one that is flexible, and designed to facilitate change. It should provide a context for the exploration of options, and a cost-effective way of assessing a particular choice before resources are committed.

Why Plan?

While many small business owners are encouraged to develop a formal or systematic planning process, most find the task difficult to perform and the rewards questionable. Studies indicate that most firms do not engage in systematic planning,[1] and that when the activity does take place it is "informal, sporadic, and frequently only a mental activity of the owner-manager."[2] Golde noted that small business planning was done on an *ad hoc*, problem oriented basis, with owner-managers tending to rely on the advice of acquaintances, often with less skill or experience than themselves.[3] Not all the evidence suggests that formal planning in the small business really works.[4] Robinson and Pearce, in a study of banks, found no significant differences between those who engaged in strategic planning and those who did not.[5] So why invest time and resources in planning?

To begin, there is much evidence that a formal planning process in small business offers numerous benefits, including the facilitation of performance and success.[6] Goldstein concluded that a lack of formal, systematic planning was a major reason for small business failure.[7] Potts found that the use of outsiders played a key role in the success of small firms, noting that successful manufacturers made much more extensive use of outside accounting and financial services.[8] Robinson, studying the use of outsider-based planning, concluded that it led to significant improvements in profit, sales growth, employment and productivity.[9] In a study of small business strategic planning, Sexton and Van Auken divided the 357 companies studied into five groups based on levels of planning. Among their many findings were some that strongly support the need for strategic planning by small firms.

> The highest percentage of failures (20 percent) occurred among firms at the lowest strategy level; the lowest percentage (7.9 percent) occurred among firms at the highest strategy level. Strategic planning appears to help many firms survive in a competitive market.[10]

Further, Sexton and Van Auken note that their findings suggest a link between strategic planning and success over time, and concluded by stating that:

> Strategic Planning appears to be a scarce, fragile commodity in the business environment. Most small firms do not engage in true strategic planning at all, and the rest may do so only sporadically or temporarily, despite the evidence that strategic planning can help firms survive and prosper.[11]

Finally, Robinson and his colleagues produced research indicating that "basic planning activity has a positive impact on small firm performance."[12]

For many small business managers, the *process* of planning may be more important than the creation of something an outsider might term a formal plan. In many owner-operated and owner-managed businesses, where the need to communicate with others is minimal, less formal planning may be adequate. A planning format which encourages small business managers to think about future direction (objectives, strategy, and resource acquisition) and action (resource allocation and strategy implementation) without requiring the creation of a formal plan may better suit the real needs of the situation.

Different Needs, Different Plans

While there are many types of plans, the formats for small business usually include only two:

1. The business plan, and
2. The operating plan.

The Business Plan

Typically, business plans involve startup situations or other points in the firm's development where major changes (in direction, growth rate, market, or facilities expansion) are contemplated. Fry and Stoner suggest that:

> Financial or investment plans are constructed to appeal to those who may become stakeholders in the firm through either debt or equity capital. These plans are undertaken mainly to gain funding from an outside source, and only secondarily to improve one's competitive position in the marketplace.[13]

These special purpose plans, whether for startup or for subsequent financial infusions, follow a great deal of research, information gathering, and discussion. In order to determine whether his business idea is worth processing, the entrepreneur must consider the various aspects of product feasibility, marketing feasibility and financial feasibility.

It is useful, before getting too far into the development of one's small business ideas, to look closely at what a good plan for implementing a specific small business idea requires, and why. While it is important that the eventual reader of the plan be considered, this should not alter the content of, or the approach to, business planning. After all, it is also important to minimize the risk to one's own investment in time, money, and reputation.

Developing Business Plan

Why Prepare a Business Plan?

Unlike the operating plan, prepared by management for internal use in the belief that such an activity can help a small firm function more effectively, the business plan has become an essential tool in dealing with outside stakeholders. In preparing a business plan, it is important to recognize that it should demonstrate the following:

1. Product/service feasibility,
2. Realistic market identification,
3. Adequate access to funds,
4. Clear objectives,
5. A viable business strategy, and
6. Managerial ability.

Simply stated, the business plan must convince lenders and shareholders that the business can be started and operated successfully. While a good business plan cannot insure success, it can go a long way toward insuring that owners and investors clearly understand both the potential risks and returns of the venture.

In addition, the business plan can serve as a road map for the process of beginning a new business, in that it outlines a list of activities that are central to the business startup.

Who Should Prepare the Plan?

The logistics of venture initiation have received widespread attention, and nowhere is that more evident than in the proliferation of business plans and planners. Government agencies, private lenders, potential stockholders and creditors all expect detailed business plans as an essential ingredient in the startup process. As a result, business plan writing has become a growth industry. Consulting firms, accounting firms, and a variety of individuals and companies specialize in the creation of business plans. Unfortunately these plans, while impressive to the lenders, may provide little guidance to the startup owner who, too often, is only marginally involved in the preparation process.[14]

The plan should be prepared and understood by the person or persons responsible for its implementation. Clearly, the ability to prepare a good business plan says a great deal about how well the firm will be managed. Moreover, while many aspiring entrepreneurs require technical help (product design, engineering, accounting, marketing and planning, etc.) such assistance should come within the parameters of a business plan that has been developed by the manager(s) responsible for its implementation.

When Should the Business Plan be Prepared?

Some suggest that the business plan should be the last step before setting up a new firm. We take a slightly different view, depicting business planning as an ongoing activity. We are concerned that the business plan be designed not only to convince the outsiders essential to the firm's startup, but that it also provide guidance and direction for the insiders who must implement it. Often business plans are long on justifying investment and short on insuring that startup resources, once acquired, are used to achieve the business plan objectives. By placing undue emphasis on getting started, management can overlook the need for survival planning. The low survival rates of small enterprises in the early years provide ample testimony to this weakness in many business plans. So, while the completed plan may be the final and most crucial step in securing the funds needed to transpose a business idea into reality, the business planning exercise should provide guidelines for, and document all of the steps taken by the entrepreneur in developing the new business. The document itself should be a reporting of what has been done and what will be done to insure that the new business is a success. A good business plan should provide a blueprint for starting the new business. While the process of development need not be a part of the actual report, such documentation can provide detailed background for the working plans essential to subsequent operations.

Not all new businesses begin as simple owner-operator firms, and the business plan should reflect this reality. The business plan needed to convince the bank to grant a loan where the owner's personal assets provide the security is much less detailed than the one needed to gain the approval of shareholders, venture capitalists and other high-risk lenders. The marketing component of a business plan for an owner-operated startup will be different from that needed by a new enterprise established by the senior managers of a well established company, who are capable of organizing as a functional organization. In this chapter we look at the needs of companies that start out as owner-operated, owner-managed, or functionally managed firms.

What Should be in a Business Plan?

There are numerous ideas about what should be contained in a business plan. Many of the differences involve presentation and format. However, the content will also differ, depending on the phase into which the firm was launched. For example, the importance of management ability increases greatly for those firms entering phase 3 or phase 5. Here we will discuss important variations that are part of startups in each of three phases:

- Phase 1 startups—owner-operated firms,
- Phase 2 startups—owner-managed firms, and
- Phase 3 startups—functionally managed firms.

Yet, there is an accepted core for all business plans, so before considering these phase-related differences, we will look at the general concepts of the business plan that are applicable to all startups, regardless of the phase to which they relate.

Firms in all phases of development must, at a minimum, answer some basic financial questions. These include:

1. Why are the funds required?
2. What use will be made of the new funds?
3. How much is required?
4. How much will come from increased equity?

The Business Plan Format

Appendix B outlines the logistics for putting together a business plan and is accompanied by a software program written in dBase III. For now, we need only remark on the importance of adhering strictly to a general format. Otherwise, the business plan will likely lack focus and fail to address the real concerns of potential investors. Some new ventures, particularly high risk endeavours, must address areas of potential concern in some depth; other areas require less attention, and still others may not be relevant to the proposed business.

How Long Should it Take to Develop a Business Plan?

There is no set answer to this question. How long should it take to develop and start a new business? The answer obviously varies with the situation surrounding the new business and the owner's particular circumstances. Some entrepreneurs take a very long time, while others, with single purpose, traverse the process quickly. Less important than the time it takes, although this may be a factor in exploiting particular product or service ideas, is the process involved. Cursory attention to critical steps in the startup process can result in time consuming and costly adjustments later. Clearly, the process of investigating and testing ideas on paper generally offers an effective way for the entrepreneur to put the new business in perspective. This is the essence of business planning.

Walter Good, in adapting Siropolis' work, has provided a list of suggested steps for developing a business plan.[15] The flow diagram in Figure 3-2 presents a sequencing of these steps. While Siropolis suggests a sixteen-week time frame, it is evident that these steps can vary in complexity and, as a result, the time frame could be much longer. Moreover, the process does not factor in the time and cost of convincing others of the business plan's viability. In some cases this can take much longer than the time required to prepare the plan and may result in compromises which can jeopardize the eventual success

Figure 3-2

Flow Diagram: Developing a Business Plan[1]

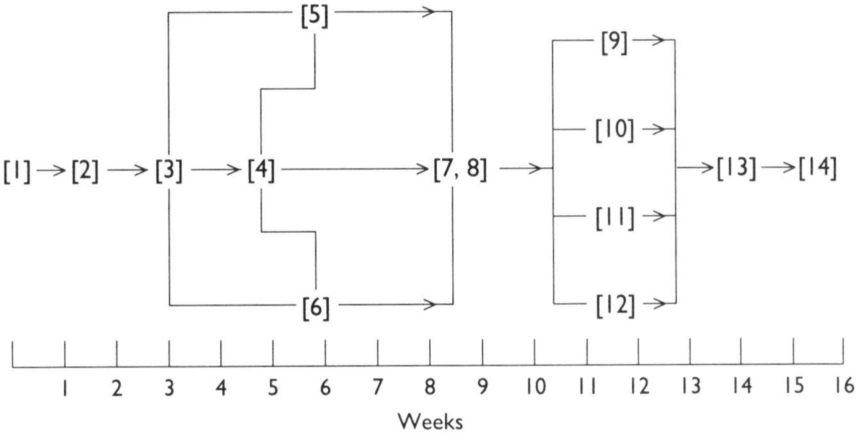

Key

1. Decide to go into business
2. Analyze yourself
3. Select product or service
4. Research market
5. Forecast sales revenues
6. Choose site
7. Develop production plan
8. Develop marketing plan
9. Develop personnel plan
10. Decide business form
11. Explain record needs
12. Develop insurance plan
13. Develop financial plan
14. Write summary overview

1 Adapted from Good, Walter S. *Building a Dream: A Comprehensive Guide to Starting A Business of Your Own* Toronto, ON: McGraw-Hill Ryerson, 1989, p. 143.

of the business. If the plan involves equity or venture capital, the time horizon might be much wider. George Fells has suggested that one of the rules for finding risk capital is "start early and be patient . . . raising money takes two or three times as long as your worst guess."[16]

Nonetheless, target dates for completing each step in the process are essential. While the sequencing suggests a step-by-step approach, most of the listed activities overlap, and work takes place in a number of these areas simultaneously. As well, when potential investors require outside studies (e.g., market research), the time horizons for steps dependent on such information may take much longer than indicated.

Business Planning in the Phase One Startup

The growing use of a particular format for business plans means that businesses of all sizes end up using a similar approach. However, there are facets that are uniquely important in owner-operator startups. Businesses that are at this stage of development operate most effectively within relatively defined boundaries. The business plan should be narrowly focused, taking advantage of owner-operator strengths. Business plans in this phase should highlight the skills of the owner-operator and their relevance to the success and growth of the firm. To the extent that needed skills (e.g., product development, financial control) are weak or missing, the plan should build in outside assistance.

In later phases the diversification of markets, products, and facilities may be viewed as a way of minimizing risk. However, for the owner-operated business, diversification is likely to result in a lack of focus, which can hamper the effective use of limited resources. Expanding the enterprise's range of products and markets inevitably increases the complexity of production, distribution, administrative, and control processes, all of which can make premature demands on the management skills of the owner-operated company.

Business Planning in the Phase Three Startup

The business plan for a phase 3 startup moves the focus from the owner's operating skills to the owner's management skills. These skills (planning, organizing, directing, and controlling) are balanced in phase 3 by the continued need for the owner to be heavily involved in day-to-day operations. The balancing of roles poses special problems and the business plan must deal with these difficulties. The need and ability to generate and use both external and internal information must be evident in the business plan. The plan must also provide evidence of the need to integrate special skills into the management process. Many of these are first obtained in the form of outside assistance (such as legal services, accounting services, and product design support) and evolve into in-house activities in response to their more and more frequent use. The business plan for phase 3 startups must convey the owner's ability to manage in an increasingly complex organizational setting.

Business Planning in the Phase Five Startup

The business plan for phase 5 startups broadens the focus to include a general management role, and to report on functional strengths in the areas of marketing, operations, and the support activities (personnel, finance, and control). The ability to delegate emerges as an important consideration. The need for, and the effective use of, information, communications and control systems are important considerations to those reviewing the business plans for phase 5 startups. In this phase, the ability to build and use an organization is added to the core needs of business plan documentation. In addition, there must be a commitment to the process of long-term planning, whereby management periodically assesses not only the strengths and weaknesses of the enterprise, but also the competitive environment. Hence, at this level the business planning process will also provide for the modification, for instance, of such fundamentals as the product/market focus, the organizational structure, or the performance evaluation system.

The Operating Plan

As mentioned earlier, Fry and Stoner investigated the differences between working plans and investment plans.[17] They note that

> one type of plan is not 'better' than the other—they merely serve different purposes. . . . The fundamental purpose of the working plan is to provide information and guidance for making operational decisions about the firm. Revised periodically, it prescribes objectives, goals and targets, and it delineates steps to be taken to achieve those goals.[18]

In fact, the analysis and detail necessary to structure a comprehensive and meaningful working plan will automatically provide much of the detail necessary to prepare the more specialized investment plan.

Why Prepare an Operating Plan?

The careful management of the firm's resources is as important as their acquisition in the first place. At this level, planning is concerned with the effective use of available resources. Unfortunately there is not the same onus on most small business managers to have a good operating plan as there is to have a good business plan. Lenders and investors tend to focus on the business plan and often do little to monitor the firm's progress until it is time for new financing or, alternatively, when the new firm fails to meet its commitments under the original financing package.

Drawing up an operating plan can provide both inside and outside payoffs for management. On the outside the plan facilitates communications with lenders and shareholders, and allows realistic comparisons of performance to plan. Internally, the process of generating the plan can focus the allocation of scarce resources, assuring that the crucial needs of the growing firm are met. In general, this process allows management to consolidate its thinking, and provides a means for keeping the enterprise on track.

Who Should Prepare the Operating Plan?

While it is possible to have special purpose business plans prepared almost totally by outsiders, the operating plan requires significant management involvement. In fact, most such planning in small firms is carried out by the owner-operator and owner-manager for inside use. As a result, there is a strong tendency to formulate operating plans in an informal manner and to believe that such planning is adequate for most small business needs.

Cohn and Lindberg report that effective planning is one of the most difficult functions that small business managers perform, so it should come as no surprise that many small business managers simply avoid the task.[19] The high incidence of small business failures might be reduced substantially if resource commitments were regularly reviewed as part of an ongoing planning process.

When Should the Operating Plan be Prepared?

In many larger organizations an operating plan is prepared annually as part of a broad process which may involve budgeting, financial planning, and a variety of activities that are part of the planning process. In smaller firms this exercise can result in planning for the sake of planning and may produce little benefit for the real needs of day-to-day operations. (Chapter 14 reviews some of the procedural aspects of budgeting from a small business perspective.)

The most useful planning approach for small firms is likely the "living document" approach, involving short-term plans supplemented by a periodic review of the firm's long-term needs. This approach to planning in the small company makes the plan a vital part of its day-to-day activities—in effect, a map for guiding operating decisions, and a low cost means of assessing potential resource commitments.

What Should be in an Operating Plan?

There is no standard length for an operating plan; it should be designed to meet the needs of the firm in question. Its major purpose is to provide direction, information and guidance for making various operating decisions.

As such, it should deal with objectives, consider the implications of possible alternative courses of action to achieve these objectives, and set forth the steps essential to implementing the chosen option and the controls for measuring performance. The plan should be thorough and realistic, and since it is not primarily a vehicle to convince outsiders, it should focus on weaknesses as well as strengths; both are important to the success of the plan. The form is not important as long as it facilitates implementation. As the organization grows, the plan can be both a communications and a motivational tool.

The Operating Plan Format

As with the special purpose business plan, firms in different phases of development have different planning needs. Vozikis and Glueck found that the stage of development was an important factor influencing the formality and implementation considerations of strategic planning.[20] Hofer stated that: "The most fundamental variable in determining an appropriate business strategy is the stage of the product life cycle."[21] The research seems to suggest that the nature of the planning process in general, and business plans in particular, is contingent on the firm's stage of development. Finally, Lindsay and Rue concluded that development stage and firm size were important contingent variables in the planning process.[22]

There are numerous planning models available, some simple, others extremely complex. Most share some common elements:

1. An environmental scan, which identifies the opportunities and risks facing the small business;

2. A company profile which describes the company's strengths and weaknesses;

3. A clear set of objectives which can provide direction, specific goals, and a basis for performance measurement;

4. A strategy for acquiring and allocating the resources essential to achieving stated objectives;

5. A working plan which describes in detail the timing and degree of resource allocations, the contribution of these allocations to the achievement of objectives, the timing of specific activities and the identification of those responsible for implementing the plan;

6. The development of controls that will tie the complexities of the operating plan to the needs of day-to-day implementation; and

Figure 3-3

Preparing
a Small Business
Operating
Plan

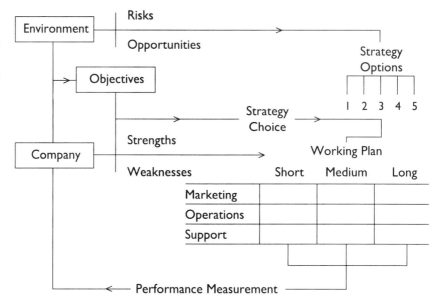

7. A time frame which recognizes that most decisions will have short-, medium-, and long-term implications for resource acquisitions and allocations.

Figure 3-3 presents a flow diagram of the process entailed in preparing an operating plan. It shows that implementation of an operating plan is a dynamic process, which demands a strong commitment from the small business manager. In Chapter 9, we further develop the idea of strategy formulation, implementation, and measurement.

The Operating Plan in Phase One

The evidence suggests that few owner-operators plan, and those that do plan in informal and intermittent patterns. Since the communication and motivation aspects of planning are minimal at this level, the plan can be a simple document that has just three concerns:

1. That there is a set of objectives to provide some direction for the firm's development as a small business;

2. That day-to-day decisions are consistent with the direction established when the firm's objectives were defined; and

3. That short-term decisions do not require medium- and long-term resource commitments which go beyond the firm's ability to generate new resources.

Major decisions (such as facilities expansion, or new product and market additions) should be handled using a business plan approach, and likely should involve outside help.

The Operating Plan in Phase Three

In the move to phase 3, management becomes part of the owner's activities, and this signals the need for more attention to management concerns. Larger and longer-term resource commitments, and the risks attached to these commitments, increase the need for communication with outside shareholders. Furthermore, generating an operating plan for phase 3 provides a basis for encouraging continued outside support for the business, as well as translating broadly stated objectives into tasks that can be assessed in support of management's performance. Internally, the planning process provides the owner-manager with a way of assessing decision choices and their implications for the firm without making premature resource commitments.

As the firm grows, the demand for scarce resources makes the resource allocation process more critical, and short-term changes in resource commitments becomes more difficult and more costly. The flexibility of the earlier phase comes at a very high cost, and can only be achieved by insuring that the "dead-end options" are eliminated in the planning process.

The Operating Plan in Phase Five

The operating plan in phase 5 assumes three additional roles beyond those of the earlier phases. With some growth in the management organization, communication, motivation, and control become important components of the plan. As well, the process becomes more formalized, as rules and conventions are developed in order that the task of planning can be shared. During its development, the operating plan provides a way for managers to share objectives, as well as performance expectations. The general manager uses the process to share his or her expectations with the staff. The plan can also help delineate new divisions of authority and responsibility as well as control mechanisms essential to effective management.

Questions for Discussion

1. Why does the chapter suggest that planning is affected by the phase of development?

2. a) Outline the basic differences between a business plan and an operating plan.
   b) Why is the periodic updating of the operating plan a worthwhile exercise?

3. What are the pros and cons of owner involvement in the development of the business plan?

4. In an interview with the *Financial Post* (May 14, 1990, p. 35), Bernie Nisker of Coopers & Lybrand management consultants remarked that: "When I send clients away to prepare a business plan, more than three quarters don't come back." Why do you think entrepreneurs have such an aversion to this task?

Selected Readings

De Geus, Arie P., "Planning as Learning," *Harvard Business Review*, 66. no. 2 (March-April), 1988, 70–74.

Harrison, Frank E., "The Concept of Strategic Gap," *Journal of General Management*, 15, no. 2 (Winter 1989), 57–72.

Hosmer, Larue T., and Roger Guiles, *Creating the Successful Business Plan for New Ventures*. New York, N.Y.: McGraw-Hill, 1985.

Larson, E., "The Best Laid Plans," *Inc.*, 9, no. 2 (February, 1987), 60–64.

Luther, William M., *How to Develop a Business Plan in 15 Days*. Englewoods Cliffs, N.J.: Prentice-Hall, Inc., 1986.

Orpen, Christopher, "The Effects of Long Range Planning on Small Business Performance," *Journal of Small Business Management*, 23, no. 1 (January 1985), 16–23.

Szonyi, Andrew J., *The Business Plan Workbook*. Scarborough, Ont.: McGraw-Hill Ryerson, 1988.

Tregoe, Benjamin B. and Peter F. Tobia, "An Action Oriented Approach to Strategy," *The Journal of Business Strategy*, January-February, 1990, 16–21.

Endnotes

1. T.W. Still, "An Exploratory Investigation of Strategic Planning Behavior in Small Businesses" (unpublished doctoral dissertation, Florida State University, 1974).

2. *Ibid*, p. 385.

3. R.A. Golde, "Practical Planning for Small Business," *Harvard Business Review*, 42, no. 5 (September-October 1964), pp. 147–161.

4. R.B. Robinson Jr. and J.A. Pearce II, "Research Thrusts in Small Firm Strategic Planning," *Academy of Management Review*, January 1984, pp. 128–137.

5. R.B. Robinson and J.A. Pearce II, "The Impact of Formal Strategic Planning on Financial Performance in Small Organizations," *Strategic Management Journal*, 4, no. 3 (July-September 1983), pp. 197–207.

6. See, for example, R.B. Robinson, "Forecasting and Small Business: A Study of the Strategic Planning Process," *Journal of Small Business Management*, July 1979, pp. 19–27; and V.K. Unni, "The Role of Strategic Planning in Small Business," *Long Range Planning*, April 1981, pp 54–58.

7. K. Mayer and S. Goldstein, *The First Two Years: Problems of Small Firm Growth and Survival* (Washington, D.C.: Small Business Administration, 1961).

8. A.J. Potts, "A Study of the Success and Failure Rates of Small Businesses and the Use or Non-Use of Accounting Information" (Ph.D. dissertation, George Washington University, 1977). Cited by Donald L. Sexton and Phillip Van Auken, in "A Longitudinal Study of Small Business Strategic Planning," *Journal of Small Business Management*, 23, no. 1 (January 1985), pp. 7–15.

9. R.B. Robinson, "The Importance of 'Outsiders' in Small Firm Strategic Planning," *Academy of Management Journal*, 25, no. 1, 1982, pp. 80–93.

10. Donald L. Sexton and Phillip Van Auken, "A Longitudinal Study of Small Business Strategic Planning," p. 13.

11. *Ibid.*, p. 15.

12. R.B. Robinson, J.A. Pearce II, G.S. Vozikis, and T.S. Mescon, "The Relationship Between Stage of Development and Small Firm Planning and Performance," *Journal of Small Business Management*, April 1984, p. 52.

13. Fred L. Fry and Charles R. Stoner, "Business Plans: Two Major Types," *Journal of Small Business Management*, 23, no. 1, January 1985, p. 6.

14. *Ibid*, pp. 1–6. In this article Fry and Stoner distinguish between "financial plans" prepared primarily with a view to gaining access to external funding, and "working plans" involving a detailed assessment of the environment and the organization's fundamental strengths and weaknesses; the latter are intended for internal use to guide decision making. We argue, despite agreement with the foregoing dichotomy, that very few actual business plans fit the latter category. In fact, more attention to the "working plan" concept in the business planning process might insure fewer failures during the early years of the new firm's life.

15. Walter S. Good, *Building a Dream: A Comprehensive Guide to Starting a Business of Your Own* (Toronto, Ont.: McGraw-Hill Ryerson Limited, 1989), p. 143. Adapted from Nicholas C. Siropolis, *Small Business Management: A Guide to Entrepreneurship*, 2nd. ed. (Boston, MA: Houghton-Mifflin Co., 1982), pp. 138–141.

16. George Fells, President of SB Capital, quoted in Tina Powell, "A Case Study in Good Relations," *Canadian Business*, October 1989, p. 120.

17. Fry and Stoner, "Business Plans: Two Major Types," pp. 1–6.

18. *Ibid.*, p. 6.

19. T. Cohn, and R.A. Lindberg, *How Management is Different in Small Companies* (New York, N.Y.: American Management Association, 1972).

20. G.S. Vozikis, and W.F. Glueck, "Small Business Problems and Stages of Development," *Academy of Management Proceedings*, 1980.

21. C.W. Hofer, "Toward a Contingency Theory of Business Strategy," *Academy of Management Journal*, 18, no. 4 (1975), pp. 31–40; and C.W. Hofer and D.H. Schendal, *Strategy Formulation: Analytical Concepts* (St. Paul, MN: West Publishing Company, 1978).

22. W.M. Lindsay, and W.L. Rue, "Impact of the Organization Environment on the Long Range Planning Process: A Contingency View," *Academy of Management Journal*, 23, no. 3, 1980, pp. 385–404.

Boatlift Products

W hen George Ibert retired in 1986, he turned his weekend fishing trips into a full-time occupation. Unfortunately, many of his fishing buddies were not available during the week, and so he spent much of his time fishing alone.

Handling his boat had become a real task, and to deal with the problem Ibert developed a simple mechanism that allowed him to "single-hand" the aluminum boat to his car top. The mechanism attracted a great deal of attention wherever he went and several people had copied it for their own use. By 1988 he had discussed the mechanism so often that he began to believe it might be a saleable commodity. Over the winter, he had the local machine shop produce 50 units. These were painted red and packaged. The box, part of an overrun, was only an approximate fit, but it was adequate for the trial sale planned for the 1989 Toronto Sportsman's Show.

During his ten days at the show he sold 134 units at a retail price of $34.95 (plus tax and shipping where applicable). Since many buyers preferred to have the unit mailed, Ibert had an adequate inventory for the show and returned home with 11 units.

Commenting on his experience at the Sportsman's Show, Ibert made a number of observations:

> The show sales certainly exceeded my expectations. I went with 50 units expecting to sell those and then make some assessment about future production and marketing. Once there, I discovered that many buyers were happy to pay the mailing charges, and since most didn't plan on fishing until May or June, the four-week delivery time posed few problems. I sold well over a hundred units and certainly paid for my time in Toronto, but now I am faced with some problems I didn't anticipate. I need to order almost 100 units to meet booked sales but that would leave me with a very small inventory. Currently, the unit price up to 100 units is $12.70. Add to this the other parts and packaging, and the price totals $15.90. MacDonald (the machine shop owner) has given me prices on 250 units ($11.20 per unit) and 500 units ($9.80 per unit), but I'm not sure what I would do with them since I had not

planned to do any marketing beyond the Sportsman's Show. I enjoyed the Sportsman's Show and wouldn't mind attending those things all across the country. It would be a way to combine business, travel and a little bit of fishing as well.

Ibert felt that the biggest benefit he derived from attending the Sportsman's Show was the large number of dealer contacts he made. He accumulated over 200 business cards from prospective dealers and planned to do a mailing on his return to Leamington.

The Company

Ibert had contacted the Department of Consumer Affairs and registered the names Boatlift and Boatlifter. A friend had developed the *BOATLIFT* and *BOATLIFTER* logos. He had not yet decided to incorporate the company. On the advice of his accountant he was operating the business as a proprietorship.

Several weeks before the Toronto Show Ibert had approached his local bank manager about a credit line. Because he was well secured, the credit he requested was readily available. However, the bank manager suggested that a business plan should be prepared as part of the loan request. Such a plan would allow Ibert to look at the total financial requirements for a startup. As well it would assist him in sorting out some of the decisions that had to be made before the company could begin functioning effectively. Ibert agreed to talk with his accountant, and would consult others to prepare a business plan for their next meeting.

The Product

The product was produced using steel pipe and fabricated sheet metal. (See Exhibit 1.) It was designed to be mounted on the rear bumper of an automobile, usually welded or bolted to a trailer hitch. Ibert had developed several simple devices for attaching the boatlifter but these were not yet being produced. So far the product was manufactured in only one model and in one colour (red), although his supplier thought the unit should be produced using rustproof aluminum paint.

The Market

The market, as Ibert saw it, included all those who cartopped boats and canoes, and particularly those who did it alone. While Ibert had no estimate of how large the market was, he did know that the various aluminum boat manufacturers sold over 100 000 units per year. Estimates placed the number of small boats in Canada at over a million units, although a large number of these were never moved. Other boaters used small trailers.

Sales to date were made almost exclusively to Ontario customers, although many of the dealer contacts Ibert had made were out-of-province. Since the units could be mailed or sent by small package anywhere in Canada, the market was not restricted to Ontario.

Marketing   Ibert had made few plans beyond attending the Sportsman's Show. He felt it would take most of 1989 to make the business arrangements if the 1989 show suggested there was a market for Boatlifter. He would kick off his business startup with the 1990 show. In the meantime there were a number of decisions to be made before he could sell the product.

Distribution   As the result of attending an FBDB Marketing Seminar on Small Business, Ibert had learned of a number of possibilities for distributing Boatlifter. These included one or more of the following choices:

1.   Show distribution,
2.   Retail dealers,
3.   Mail order, and
4.   Show/mail order combination.

He wasn't exactly sure which would work best for the product and for him. After some discussion with retail friends, he concluded that most retailers would not want to be involved if he was considering mail order or heavy price discounting at camping, sports, and hardware shows. On the other hand, he felt the company could get a lot of marketing mileage out of the 35–50 percent markup that most dealers would want to handle the product. As well, there were inventory, accounts receivable, and credit implications for each choice.

Advertising and Promotion   Ibert was currently having a printer prepare a promotional brochure and a revised instruction sheet to cover assembly and installation of the Boatlifter. Whether he went the dealer route or decided to market through a variety of shows, these materials would be useful.

Ibert was aware that there were a number of fishing, hunting, and sporting magazines that could be used to advertise the product. He had been a long time subscriber to some of these magazines, as had many of his friends. He felt that the audiences for most of these publications would include many who might be prime customers for his product.

Marketing Plans

While the company was to be incorporated under the name "Boatlift Products," the product would carry the name "Boatlifter."

Ibert favoured a marketing plan that would involve camping, boating, sporting, and hardware shows where he could sell and promote his product to the public. As well, he would use mail order and would promote the product in fishing, hunting, and boating magazines. Although he had no experience in this kind of marketing he felt that his fishing and boating experience would allow him to sell to customers who would not even look at the product if it were just displayed in a retail store. He admitted that this preference had no research behind it, and he knew that the bank and others would expect something in the way of data to support the approach.

Product Pricing

The product was offered in only one model and had been sold at the Toronto Sportsman's Show for $34.95. That price had been calculated as shown in Table 1.

Discussions with various friends had resulted in a wide variation in suggested retail prices. The range went from $19.95 to $59.95. Ibert

Table 1	Boatlift (3 pieces)	$12.70
Boatlift Products	Clevis Pin	.44
Suggested	Instructions	.16
Retail Costs	Packaging	1.10
and Pricing	Subtotal	$14.40
	Contribution to Other Costs	6.60
	Subtotal	21.00
	Federal Excise Tax (12%)	2.52
	Subtotal	23.52
	Contribution to Marketing Costs	11.43
	Selling Price	**$34.95**

decided on an introductory or show price of $34.95, with a suggested retail price of $39.95.

Others thought that the price should reflect user utility, and since there were few alternatives those with a real need for the product would find a $59.95 price reasonable. Ibert leaned toward a mark-up on actual costs and chose his suggested retail price on that basis.

Manufacturing

The Boatlifter was manufactured to order for Ibert. He did not plan to alter that arrangement in the short term. He felt the pricing was reasonable and knew with increased order sizes he could lower the price. MacDonald had offered to quote on quantities of 1000 and 2400 with four to twelve releases a year from inventory. On that basis the machine shop would produce the product when it suited its work schedule.

Inventory control, order quantities, and delivery would be Ibert's responsibility. While he had made some sales projections, these had not been translated into deliveries. The machine shop could deliver an order in six weeks. If Ibert ordered the larger quantities, there would be a factory inventory to call on for immediate delivery. Ibert needed about one week to package and ship the product. If he decided to attend a number of shows across Canada, some other arrangements for packing and shipping would have to be made.

As a result of his discussions with the bank manager, Ibert had prepared some preliminary sales projections (see Table 2). These were based on a combination of show and mail-order sales and were projected on the basis of units and dollars.

Exhibit 2 presents an income statement for Ibert's appearance at the Toronto Sportsman's Show. Exhibit 3 presents a beginning balance sheet for Boatlift Products.

Table 2

Boatlift Products Sales Projections

Product	Selling Price	Projected Sales—Units		
		1990	1991	1992
BLPROMO	34.95	400	750	900
BLRETL	39.95	250	750	1200
Product	Selling Price	Projected Sales—Dollars		
		1990	1991	1992
BLPROMO	34.95	$13,980	$26,213	$31,455
BLRETL	25.96	$6,490	$19,470	$31,152
Totals		$20,470	$45,683	$62,607

Boatlift Operations

Currently the product was received on pallets from the manufacturer. The parts were stored in the pallet boxes until assembled and packed.

Ibert had rented space in a small industrial building. Here he kept his records, inventory of parts and goods for shipment, packing materials and tools. Twice a week he made deliveries to the Post Office. For the sales at shows, Ibert intended to load up his van and trailer and take up to 100 units with him. If he decided to do the shows further afield, he could have additional units shipped to the show sites.

Commenting on what lay ahead for Boatlift Products, Ibert noted that:

> A lot of things are happening because of the boat show and I'm not ready to handle them at this time. I had originally thought that we could start this business in 1990 but everybody is encouraging me to take advantage of the contracts and the momentum from this year's show.
>
> I don't really need the bank loan, although it would be comforting to have the line of credit in place. My problem seems to be one of developing the business plan and thinking my way through how this business should be operated. There is a lot of pressure to just take some orders and start shipping. Perhaps if I did a little advertising and hit a few of the shows I could keep this thing going. In my spare time I could develop a plan for the bank and have the advantage of a little more experience to make the plans and projections more realistic.
>
> I have to deal with the immediate problem of filling the outstanding orders, and in the next few days I have to make a decision about additional inventory.

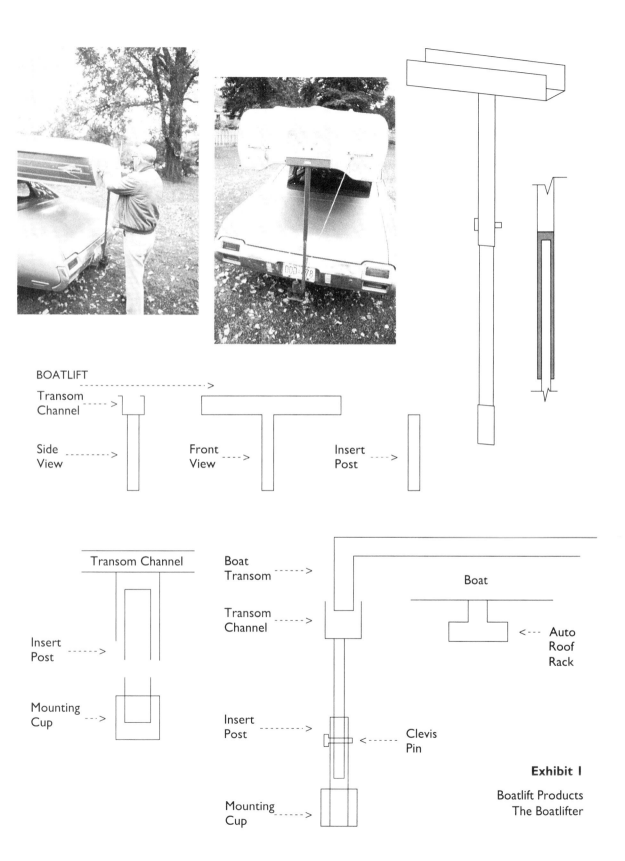

BOATLIFT

Transom Channel

Side View

Front View

Insert Post

Transom Channel

Insert Post

Mounting Cup

Boat Transom

Transom Channel

Insert Post

Mounting Cup

Boat

Auto Roof Rack

Clevis Pin

Exhibit 1

Boatlift Products
The Boatlifter

Sales		4,681
Cost of Goods		1,929
Gross Profit		2,752

Expenses

Space Rental	340	
Promotion	124	
Display	86	
Lodging	426	
Meals	289	
Travel	462	
Miscellaneous	128	
	1,855	1,855
Net Profit		**897**

Exhibit 3

Boatlift Products
Balance Sheet–
July 1, 1989

ASSETS

Cash	7,150
Inventory	1,260
Equipment	
Office	670
Dodge Van	12,340
Total Assets	**21,420**

LIABILITIES

Accounts Payable	1,420
Shareholder Loan	20,000
Total Liabilities	**21,420**

C H A P T E R

4

Phase One: The Owner Operated Business

Introduction

Two prominent features of a phase 1 enterprise are its reliance on one person, generally the proprietor, and on one main product. Usually few, if any, employees are involved, and the running of the business depends much more on the non-managerial skills (e.g., technical, selling) of the owner-operator than on management ability. The focus is on action. Since many small businesses begin in the owner-operator phase, one finds, at least initially, that a number of these individuals display a strong entrepreneurial spirit. Indeed, many owner-operators are classic entrepreneurs, with their personal identities closely tied to the business (see Chapter 1). A sense of self-actualization and the social recognition of owning their own small business are the rewards which make them willing to shoulder the risks, long hours, and "brinkmanship" that beset many small, and particularly new, ventures. Further, for many, the joy of independence—being one's own boss—offsets the negative features.

The options open to a small business are linked as much to the personality traits and skills of the owner-operator as to the external circumstances surrounding the venture. In establishing a new company, the entrepreneur may or may not be interested in building a business that will grow beyond a relatively modest level. Many companies are organized as proprietorships or partnerships and never expand beyond a limited offering of products or services, restricting their scope to a particular geographic territory. (Note that our definition of the phase 1 organization can extend to companies that might be considered relatively large by virtue of the revenue, asset, or total employee yardsticks.)

The notion of continuing as an owner-operated enterprise for an extended period of time can easily be overlooked in the study of small business management. Yet for many businesses the owner-operator format, where the owner essentially "does everything," is appropriate on an ongoing basis because it fits desired objectives, strategies, and markets (e.g., an art dealer). In a fast changing business setting such as fashion design, the flexibility of such an organization can provide a valuable competitive advantage. Alternatively, it may be an appropriate response to unfavourable economic conditions or to specific product/market limitations. Certain personality traits of the owner-operator, such as aversion to risk, resistance to change, or lack of ambition, may act as impediments to moving beyond phase 1. Also, there may be skill deficiencies, such as an inability to delegate authority or a reluctance to deal with nonroutine matters. Sometimes, too, the enterprise is unable to marshall some critical resource, such as the necessary financing or suitable labour.

Essential Traits of the Phase One Organization

Those organizations that can be described as owner operated must deal with problems distinctive to this phase of development. Most small organizations face two conspicuous handicaps: the limited range of skills and resources at their disposal, and the daily deluge of tasks that generally permits the owner-operator little time for reflection or innovation. The constraints faced by the four-person printing company would resemble those of the four-person independent accounting firm more closely than those of a competing printer with several locations, a dozen employees, and a wider array of services. Likewise, the vulnerability of the two smaller enterprises would likely be greater if a major customer were lost.

In general, the phase 1 enterprise tends to be characterized by recurring operations that place a premium on efficiency and attention to detail. Some of the tasks undertaken in the course of executing these operations may require a considerable measure of discernment and even flair; nonetheless they fit within the framework of a predictable pattern of operations. The need to execute these activities, for instance hiring temporary staff to meet seasonal demands, arises on a regular basis. Consider for example, fitness facilities, speciality clothing retailers, local cartage companies, single office architecture firms or local theatre centres. Notwithstanding different degrees of volatility in the business setting, all tend to have a *modus operandi* wherein managing, if undertaken at all, is performed as part of regular day-to-day activities. Moreover, while these diverse activities will contain such elements of marketing, finance, personnel, operations, or accounting and control that the owner-operator deems appropriate, she normally does not organize her efforts in terms of the clearly distinct functions that characterize a more evolved enterprise. Figure 4-1 summarizes some of the critical dimensions along which enterprises differ in the three stable phases.

Planning in phase 1 is mainly about planning specific activities, with minimal emphasis on the planning of a context. By "context" we mean a domain within which a course of action will unfold, involving an external element—the business setting; and an internal element—the organizational structure. Generally the phase 1 business operates within a preplanned and established context.

This context constitutes the environment in which the small business person applies his experience. Experience is the backdrop for operating decisions in phase 1, but changes in the context may render this experience irrelevant. Either the business setting becomes difficult to interpret, or the organizational structure proves inadequate to the increasing magnitude or diversity of demands placed upon it, or both. For example, the need to modify some aspect of the product or the served market may mean that new skills are required. This condition can leave the owner-operator in a state of confusion, which may precipitate a series of quick, and often ill-advised, responses. When this happens the business may fail. Alternatively, the owner-operator may seek to make changes in order to carve out a different niche within which to focus action and utilize experience. The move to owner-manager is not always proactive: in some cases it is reactive. In a reactive situation the owner must try to find a new context within which to pursue his goals, having been obliged to respond to changes in the context of the phase

Figure 4-1

Checklist of
Dimensions
which Define
Phase
Differences

Dimensions	Phases		
	One	**Three**	**Five**
Entrepreneurial Impetus	High for startup	High for startup	High for startup
Reliance on Experience	High	Mixed	Low
Reliance on Outside Assistance	Often high	Moderate	Relatively low
Feeling of Ownership/ Control	Total	Moderate	Low
Ratio of Routine to Nonroutine	High	Moderate	Low
Managerial Focus	Low	Moderate	High
Functional Perspective	Peripheral	Increasing	Central
Succession	Very often an issue	Less often	Least often
Flexibility in Terms of Current Direction	High	Moderate	Low

1 operation. For such a move to be successful, the owner must have an opportunity to modify the organization, a desire to do so, and the ability to manage an expanded organization. Whereas routine activities dominate the sphere of the owner-operator, the owner-manager must relinquish many routine tasks to others and address non-routine matters. In some instances, although he recognizes that he can no longer cope alone, the owner-operator resists delegating responsibility to others in-house, as this would entail giving up control. Rather than moving directly to owner management, he may seek, by engaging outside assistance or buying a franchise, to maintain his owner-operator status and yet still accommodate growth and development. Both of these options will provide the organization with needed skills and services

while allowing the owner-operator to remain in phase 1, but both entail costs and a loss of autonomy in varying measure. These options will be discussed subsequently.

Characterizing the Activities of the Owner-Operator

The owner-operator is typically consumed by the various demands of the business—taking sales orders, negotiating suppliers' terms, scheduling deliveries, handling staff and/or customer complaints, etc. While routine activities exist in firms of any size, they tend to dominate in the owner-operated enterprise. Hence, the small-business person at this level is involved primarily in implementing, expediting, and supervising. Lack of resources generally imposes severe constraints on the owner's scope for action, and hence strategy devolves into exploitation of immediate opportunities, usually related to a narrow product/market niche. Whether the phase 1 company is an independent entity or a franchise operation, complex decisions or tough judgements are rarely called for. Instead, the owner-operator is constantly seeking solutions to short-term operating problems ("firefighting"), often in order to ensure survival. This translates into a "hands-on" approach to the business, and the need for management skills is minimal.

In addition, the specific skills and background the small-business person brings to the business play a pivotal role in determining the complexion of the organization. The enterprise's strengths and weaknesses are closely aligned with the personality, ability, contacts, and personal financial situation of this individual. Hence, the question of succession (who will carry the business after me) is often compelling.

As explained in Chapter 1, in most instances the owner-operator is highly dependent on past experience. In contrast to decision-makers in large organizations, she must often make decisions on the basis of relatively primitive financial data, and/or inconclusive observations within an unfamiliar business setting. The analysis leading to the decision is rarely "bounced off" any knowledgeable sounding board.

It is important that the owner-operator be aware of the potential costs of relying on preconceived perceptions of the market. While a certain degree of subjectivity is unavoidable, and may sometimes enhance creative thinking, too many ill-founded phase 1 decisions are attributable solely to the instincts of the small-business person. The owner-operator who can recognize the shortcomings of such judgemental decision-making is more likely to seek the advice of outside advisors—not only professionals, but also trade associations, small business groups, suppliers, family, and friends. Not only can these groups provide the individual with a fund of knowledge; but he or she can also benefit from their objectivity in evaluating opportunities and threats encountered by the business.[1] As a result, the owner-operator essentially can gain a position analogous to that of a general manager, who is able to draw on the inputs of functional managers.

Managing the Owner-Operated Organization

Startup in Phase One

As indicated in Chapter 3, business plans in this phase should highlight the skills of the owner-operator and their relevance to the success and growth of the firm. There is growing use of a standard business plan format favoured by lending agencies. Irrespective of form, the plan should be narrowly focused, taking advantage of owner-operator strengths, and building in outside assistance to cover weaknesses or to perform essential tasks for which the owner-operator lacks time or interest.

Planning

The evidence suggests that few owner-operators plan, and those that do, plan in informal and intermittent patterns. Generally, the usefulness of the operating plan as a motivational and coordinating device within the organization is minimal at the owner-operator level. In Chapter 3 it was suggested that the operating plan for a phase 1 company should be a fairly simple document which encompasses the firm's basic objectives, provides guidelines for day-to-day decisions, and ensures that adequate physical, human, and financial resources are in place. Typically, the firm's objectives will reflect the personal objectives that were part of the owner-operator's motivation for getting into business in the first place. In most cases expert opinion should be sought before expanding facilities, offering new products, or pursuing new markets.

There is overwhelming evidence to suggest that the notion of systematic long-range planning is not a popular one within the small business sector; we contend that the barriers to formal planning (e.g., lack of resources to undertake new activities, the propensity of entrepreneurs to be doers rather than planners, and their tendency to focus on immediate, task-oriented problems[2]) are formidable. Businesses at this level rarely allow the owner the uninterrupted periods of time necessary to attend to the planning function.

Also, as Cohn and Lindberg have found, for most small business owners " . . . a focus on operating problems can result in immediate pleasure with the obtained results, while activities such as planning have deferred feedback."[3] By definition, few owner-operators are imbued with the type of attitude that is a prerequisite to effective planning: a readiness constantly to evaluate the status of the business, and a concern about how future changes in the marketplace might impinge on the company's fortunes.

In summary, one can appreciate that the nature of the planning exercise envisioned within the framework of conventional management theory is not always applicable, and perhaps even undesirable in the phase 1 organization.

Organizing

For the owner-operator, organizing involves marshalling the resources necessary to meet the requirements of the startup plan and to sustain subsequent operations. Generally this entails some combination of activities geared to: securing a suitable market, establishing a production facility, creating an efficient order system, setting up a simple accounting system (usually supervised by an outside accountant), recruiting and hiring any needed personnel, and providing for short-term credit needs. No matter how good the plan, the business cannot operate effectively unless these elements are in place.

Directing (Coordinating)

Directing involves the actions, including motivation, essential to using available resources in such a way that the enterprise runs to plan. However, the phase 1 organization does not require a great deal of direction inasmuch as it has not acquired substantial physical, human, or financial resources. We suggest instead that at this level the operative activity is *coordination* of the actions taken to sustain daily operations. Much of the owner-operator's energies are devoted to this function as she typically turns her attention to the myriad details of day-to-day operations. The owner-operator makes decisions unilaterally and only involves others enough to ensure that these decisions are implemented. Personnel in an owner-operated enterprise generally have personal contact with the boss on a daily basis. The reward-punishment system is often informal, based on the subjective judgement of the boss.

Controlling

The management activities of planning and controlling are intertwined. Management control systems are normally based on a control cycle, consisting of the planning of various functions, implementation, and evaluation of the results, which is factored into the planning for future periods. Given that the typical phase 1 organization is characterized by standard operating procedures, its control requirements are best served by regular data that help the owner-operator determine whether or not specific tasks are being performed effectively and efficiently. These data are often most useful if provided in terms of pounds of material or labour-hours, for example, rather than solely in financial terms.

Owner-Operated Enterprises: Diverse Formats

There are three major versions of the owner-operated enterprise: the self-sufficient operator who seeks no outside assistance (e.g., an independent chartered accountant); the owner-operator who engages a variety of outside agents to provide assistance as an economical way of delivering services (e.g., a graphic artist who engages an agent, a bookkeeper, and perhaps a tax accountant); and finally the franchisee whose contract with the franchisor provides him with a bundle of management services and requires that the franchisee run the operation according to a prescribed pattern. Note that each type of phase 1 enterprise has a limited product/market and a negligible managerial component.

The Importance of Outside Assistance

The keys to a successful operation need not be complicated. For instance, there are any number of automotive service stations, restaurants, or hotel/motel businesses that survive largely as a result of a prime location. However, with limited resources and a narrow range of skills, the astute utilization of external expertise is often critical to the firm's survival. This issue was raised in Chapter 3 and can be of the utmost importance to the phase 1 organization. The nature and degree of assistance will depend on the owner's particular skills, the complexity of the market, and the needs of institutional lenders and silent partners. It can take the form of legal services, market research, financial accounting, product design expertise, or personnel recruitment and selection.

Unfortunately, the resistance of many owner-operators to sharing information with outsiders and their fear of incurring consulting expenses which may or may not yield immediate results means they are left to their own resources. The example of the Toronto shoe manufacturer that elected to fund its sales growth through relatives who had no interest in the affairs of the business is instructive. The company had been in operation for 18 years and was experiencing a severe cash shortage, but a fear of outside interference prompted the owner to reject a financial package involving $300 000 from two new shareholders in addition to an increased bank line of credit. The decision to rely on the hard-earned savings of relatives, while expedient at the time, did not address the company's ongoing funding needs. It was not long before the company was placed into receivership.

The Franchising Option

Many franchise operations are organized in a way that typifies the owner-operated enterprise. The franchise concept is an efficient way for the owner-operator to secure access to a wide range of external services in a single package. That is, in return for an upfront franchise fee and ongoing royalty payments, the franchisee is provided with a trademark, an initial training program, an operations manual, and access to inventory and equipment suppliers. The franchisor generally performs all the background activities necessary to get the business up and running (in effect providing the franchisee with a "turnkey operation"), develops an advertising program, and establishes specific budgeting and reporting procedures. In addition, the franchisor will usually provide some combination of the following services: lease negotiation, site selection, market research, store design, inventory control, centralized purchasing, and financing guarantees. Figure 4-2 provides a representative list of franchise operations and some comparative data from the respective franchise agreements.

The highly structured approach to running the phase 1 business is exemplified by the standard franchise arrangement. For instance, The Second Cup has a compulsory program of monthly promotions that must be implemented at the local level by the individual franchisees. However, as pointed out at the beginning of the chapter, the phase 1 entrepreneur places a high premium on independence. As a result, a certain segment of the owner-operator group is quite skeptical of the franchising option, despite its relatively low failure rate. For others, the security offered by the franchise is very attractive.

Figure 4-2

Representative
Franchise
Operations

	Baskin Robbins	Color Your World	First Choice	Mark's Work Wearhouse	Molly Maid	Rent -a- Wreck
Type of Business	ice cream	paint/ wallpaper	hair care	retail apparel	residential cleaning	car rental
Date of first Canadian Franchise	1971	1979	1982	1985	1979	1976
Current no. of Cdn. Franchises*	200	80	108	33	165	66
Franchise Fee $(000)	25	50+	25	50–99	11	30–50
Start-up Costs $(000)	120–150	125–225	55	50	3	100–200
Royalty Fee	0.5%	0.5%–7%	10%	7–8%	6%	6%
Advertising Fee	4%	6.5%	2%	none	2%	4%

* Figure does not include company-owned outlets. In some cases, there may be substantially more outlets than franchises. Only Canadian totals are given.

Source: *Financial Post Moneywise*, August 1989.

Diversification

Whether anxious about the future of a business that is tied to the life cycle of one product, attempting to achieve a higher return, or simply impelled by entrepreneurial vigour, many phase 1 owner-operators attempt to move beyond their initial product/market definition. Yet the strain on limited resources or risk of failure in the marketplace often prompts them to seek closely related products (goods or services) and/or markets. Successful small business people will often adopt a conservative approach, seeking diversification opportunities that evolve from present operations: for example, the fitness centre that also stocks sportswear. If diversification is successful, the payoffs may be growth, higher profits, and greater security. To ignore such opportunities can breed stagnation, which is anathema to the entrepreneurial spirit.

The hazards of diversification, however, cannot be overstated. It is in this phase than an organization is most vulnerable to financial failure. It is also in this phase that the owner-operator, often the sole decision-making agent, may be deluded by her own optimism. Too often the entrepreneur, basking in the success of the primary business, will forge ahead into a new market without adequate preparation, only to find that the factors that contributed to her previous success don't necessarily apply in the new operating environment. The sales task may be quite different, there may be a limited supply of trained personnel, or product standards may prove to be too rigid.

Poorly conceived diversification programs have been the undoing of small enterprises in all phases. (Indeed, this topic is addressed again in Chapter 6 in the context of the phase 5 organization.) Often incremental fixed costs prove to be too high to be supported by the increase in sales revenues. Resources, especially working capital, production capacity, and managerial capability may become overextended to such a degree that the new initiative fails to prosper and even "bread and butter" operations are jeopardized.

Summary

Certainly a large portion of the organizations that comprise the small business sector can be described as owner-operated. This chapter differentiates these enterprises from other small businesses by outlining the general attributes of the phase 1 company and the nature of the management task at this level. Nonetheless, this phase does encompass a reasonably wide range of business settings. In many of these situations some degree of external assistance is crucial to the success of the enterprise.

One of the most frequent pitfalls of phase 1 organizations is the adoption of poorly conceived diversification strategies. When successful, diversification can certainly provide a needed boost to some small businesses. However, adequate preparation and careful research are crucial.

Questions for Discussion

1. a) Provide an example, different from any of the ones mentioned in the chapter, of an actual small business that you would classify as *owner-operated*.

   b) Compare the basic characteristics of this company to those listed in Table 4-1.

   c) Is it possible for a company with as many as 30 or 40 employees to be a *phase 1* business? Explain.

2. Is a long background of relevant experience essential before one can be considered a self-sufficient-owner operator within a particular industry? Explain.

3. There is a tendency to think of proprietorships as phase 1 organizations. Can you think of any exceptions?

4. Give an example of a small company that has suffered as a result of diversifying into a new service or product area. What elements do you feel would have improved the prospects for this new venture?

Selected Readings

Brandt, Steven C., *Entrepreneuring: The Ten Commandments for Building a Growth Company*, New York, N.Y.: New American Library, 1982.

Fontaine, Stephen, "How to Win the Franchise Game," in *Readings in New Venture Development*, Walter S. Good. (Toronto: McGraw-Hill Ryerson Limited, 1989), 309–315.

Kreisman, R., "How Startup Franchisors Fail," *Inc.*, September, 1986, 106–18.

Endnotes

1. Outside assistance can be subdivided into two broad categories: it can be of an *opportunistic* or *correctional* nature, i.e., aimed at reducing costs or at improving productivity. See Harold H. MacKay, "Small Business and Advisors," *Proceedings of the Eighth International Symposium on Small Business*, Ottawa, Ont., October 19–22, 1981, p. 499.

2. See G.A. Steiner, *Top Management Planning* (New York, N.Y.: Macmillan, 1969), p. 112; and G.A. Steiner and J.B. Miner, *Management Policy and Strategy* (New York, N.Y.: Macmillan, 1977), p. 204.

3. T. Cohn and R.A. Lindberg, *Survival and Growth: Management Strategies for the Small Firm* (New York, N.Y.: Amacom, 1974), pp. 45–47.

The Perfect Pace

Early in March, 1986, Patricia Cameron, 25, sat at her parents' kitchen table reviewing the hectic schedule of the previous two months and beginning to map out what likely would be an even more hectic schedule for the two months ahead. Just after the New Year Patricia had returned to her hometown, Antigonish, Nova Scotia to open a fitness club for women. Since her return Patricia had created a name for the club; found a suitable location; contacted several equipment suppliers, local contractors and office furnishings dealers to obtain estimates or quotations; studied the Antigonish market; met with insurance agents, media reps, bankers, and government officials; and tentatively lined up two experienced instructors. In the weeks ahead Patricia knew that she would have to supervise or finalize all of these arrangements as well as develop in some detail a tentative programme of activities for members, price and sell memberships, and effectively promote the opening. The target date for the opening of the club was May 1.

Patricia had chosen Antigonish not only because it was her hometown but also because Antigonish had no fitness club to serve the needs of women. From her experience as the assistant manager of a fitness club in Truro, Nova Scotia, and as a teacher of fitness and aerobics classes at both the Halifax YWCA and Mount Saint Vincent University during the previous four years, Patricia believed that The Perfect Pace could achieve a membership base of 400 by the end of the first year. As she sat at the table Patricia realized that the longstanding dream of owning her own business would soon come true. She was excited. She was enthusiastic. And she was determined to succeed.

The Fitness Craze

In the mid-1970's the Participaction programme generated widespread awareness of a massive Canadian fitness problem. The average 60-year-old Swede, Participaction claimed, was fitter than the average 30-year-old Canadian. By the early to mid 1980's hundreds of thousands of Canadians had made a commitment to better physical health. Some did it on their own. Some did it through company or recreation department sponsored programmes. Some did it through television (The 20 Minute Workout) or books (Jane Fonda's or Christine Brinkley's plans). And some joined private fitness centres.

By 1985 all Canadian cities and most larger Canadian towns had one or more fitness centres that offered members workout gymnasiums, exercise mats and equipment, weight equipment for body building and muscle toning programmes, a variety of fitness and aerobics classes, fitness assessments, diet planning, saunas, showers and locker facilities. Some centres even had squash and racquetball courts, colour and beauty consultations, tanning beds, and child-minding services.

The Antigonish Market

Although the population of the Town of Antigonish was only 5500, the Antigonish trading area contained an estimated 35 000 people. Most families from Antigonish County (population 18 000) and Guysborough County (population 13 000) shopped in the Town of Antigonish with some regularity. As well, a minority of families from Richmond, Victoria, and Inverness Counties to the east and Pictou County to the west shopped in Antigonish. Antigonish County occupied the northeast corner of mainland Nova Scotia, about 250 km west of Sydney and 250 km northeast of Halifax. Antigonish was the home of Saint Francis Xavier University, which generated an annual influx of 2300 students each September to April. The Antigonish Town Office had provided Patricia with age, sex and labour force profiles for Antigonish County. These are reproduced in Table 1.

Patricia had not conducted any formal marketing research but informally, from listening to her peers and some of her mother's friends, she sensed a strong interest in the idea of a women's fitness club. Patricia felt that they were tired of doing nothing, that many had been bored for too long, and that her club would be an ideal alternative for them.

As a further indication of interest, Patricia discovered that Linda Steeghs, one of the two qualified instructors she had approached about working for her, had offered fitness classes for women with great success during 1983 and 1984 through a franchise called Dance Fit. Linda had been unable to continue these classes after 1984 because the large and very inexpensive space that she had rented became unavailable when the building was sold and later torn down.

Patricia also discovered that the university posed some competition on two fronts. First, physical education students offered aerobics classes for a nominal fee to their fellow students. Second, the University offered

Table 1	Age Group	Male	Female	Total
	0–14	2 744	2 570	5 314
The Perfect Pace	15–24	1 760	1 725	3 485
Population and	25–34	1 399	1 398	2 797
Labour Force	35–44	957	944	1 901
Statistics for	45–64	1 354	1 444	2 798
Antigonish	65 +	812	999	1 811
County	**Totals**	**9 026**	**9 080**	**18 106**
	Labour Force			
	Population 15 +	6 282	6 510	12 792
	Labour Force	4 485	2 940	7 425
	Participation Rate	71%	45%	58%
	Employed	4 405	2 570	6 975

Source: Statistics Canada, 1981 Census

public memberships in a Fitness and Recreation Association. Patricia was not too concerned about this competition. The aerobics classes were taught by students just trying their hand at it. Thus, she reasoned, they were not qualified personnel. Further, the Fitness and Recreation Association offered no fitness classes and tended to be a do-it-yourself facility. Its main attraction for families was access to the only indoor swimming pool in the area. It also offered a weight room; squash, racquetball, handball and tennis courts and access to the university gymnasium. The only overlapping activities with The Perfect Pace that Patricia could see were the weight room, the sauna and showers. A family membership in the Association cost $195 and a single adult membership $160. To Patricia's knowledge there were no other organized fitness organizations in Antigonish but the ever-present risk that someone else might be planning to start one heightened the urgency of opening The Perfect Pace as soon as possible.

The Hectic January and February Pace

Patricia's first two actions in January were to see the family's bank manager and to decide on a name. The bank manager indicated that with favourable revenue and profit projections he could probably loan her up to 100 percent of the value of her equipment, repayable over five years, if the equipment were pledged as security. She would have to raise the balance of the initial investment privately. Patricia believed that with favourable projections this would be possible.

A few days later Patricia heard about some space available above a dry cleaning business just off Main Street at the east end of town. Substantial renovations and improvements would be required and available parking on the short side street would not always be easy for members to find. However, the room was large, had windows on three sides, a fairly high ceiling, a solid floor and a rent of only $650 per month plus utilities. Near the end of January Patricia signed a one-year lease with an option to renew for two years at a rent to be determined. Patricia's rough sketch for utilizing the space is reproduced in Figure 1.

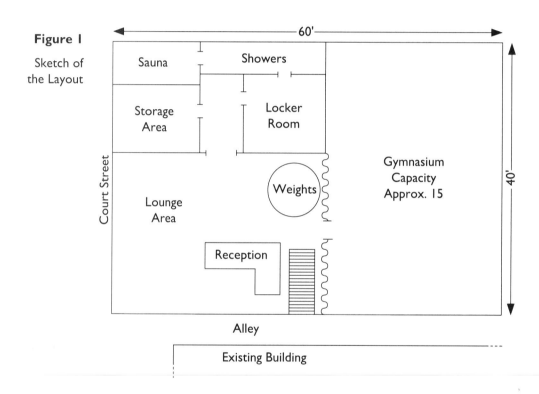

Figure 1

Sketch of the Layout

Patricia solicited cost estimates from several equipment suppliers, two general contractors, several tradesmen and two office furnishings dealers. By early March the file folder of estimates was thick and virtually complete. It appeared as though renovations and improvements including all electrical, plumbing, heating, insulation, carpentry, tiling, drywalling, and painting would total about $16 000. The fitness equipment including mats, bikes, benches, rowing machines, a central weight machine, a quality tape deck, and assorted hoops and balls would come to about $15 000. The office furniture and furnishings including carpeting, chairs, a table, a stool, locker room benches, a reception counter, planters and pictures would come to $6000.

With a little bit of assistance from a friend Patricia estimated that monthly operating expenses other than rent and interest on the loan would be about $3500. This figure included salaries, benefits, CPP and UIC, utilities, telephone, office supplies, maintenance supplies, instructional supplies, insurance, property taxes, and advertising. In developing the expense estimates Patricia had assumed that The Perfect Pace would be open approximately 70 hours each week from Monday to Saturday. As the membership wished or necessitated, these assumptions could change. The instructors would be paid on an hourly basis at a higher rate for teaching a class and at a lower rate for working at the reception desk. Patricia planned to act as both manager and instructor and expected to work 60–70 hours per week for the first year if necessary.

Patricia also had a file folder on the program of activities to be offered. The folder contained a summary of the Truro club's facilities and services and some of her own programming notions. The Truro club charged a membership fee of $325 per year. A membership bought unlimited access to all facilities and classes. The facilities available to members were a series of exercise machines, called the Nautilus System, on which an individual programme of body building of muscle toning could be developed, six stationary bikes, free weights, a sauna, two tanning beds, showers, a change area with hair dryers, and a lounge area with a television and a video cassette recorder. The two classes that were offered were introductory and advanced aerobics. Each class, including change time, warm-up time, cool-down time and class time, ran about an hour. Some days there were only a few classes and other days the exercise gym was booked solid. Patricia recalled that the average was about five classes per day. The Truro fitness club was open Monday to Thursday from 7 a.m. to 10 p.m., Friday from 7 a.m. to 9 p.m., Saturday from 9 a.m. to 5 p.m. and Sunday from 11 a.m. to 6 p.m.

Patricia planned to offer aerobics classes at the beginner, intermediate and advanced levels, weight toning and body building programmes and fitness assessments. In time, if demand seemed to warrant, The Perfect Pace would add a child-minding service to appeal to mothers. Patricia wanted The Perfect Pace to be known for quality instruction and quality service. Each member would be assured careful attention and guidance as she advanced in the programme. Patricia also wanted to ensure that members who were inexperienced did not injure themselves, become discouraged, or lose interest. She was highly committed to the proper education of every member.

The Hectic Pace Ahead

Patricia believed that 90 percent of the members of The Perfect Pace would be women from Antigonish County, including some of the students at the university. She felt that few women from the adjacent counties would travel the 50 to 100 km to take advantage of her fitness classes and facilities. Hence, in thinking about creating awareness and signing up members Patricia planned initially to focus on the town, the county within about 30 km of town, and the university campus.

The price of a Perfect Pace membership was a critical decision. Patricia felt that the Truro club's fee was a bit too high, while the university Fitness and Recreation Association's fee was a bit too low. She had thought about offering introductory memberships for three or six months in addition to the regular full-year memberships but she was unsure whether they would lead to a larger membership base or not. She had also thought about a user pay plan whereby someone could pay by the hour or by the activity but she wondered what the regular members might think of sharing the facility with casual users. Finally she believed that she should offer an eight-month student membership but had not determined an appropriate price.

Decisions on advertising and promotion also would be critical to the success of The Perfect Pace. From her discussions with the media reps Patricia had learned that the local newspaper had a weekly circulation of 8500 with most of these copies sold in Antigonish County. A very small ad one column wide and one inch high would cost $4, a one-eighth-page ad would cost $60 and a one-quarter-page ad $120. The local radio station had a total six-county reach of over 70 000 people each week. On average, the number of listeners during a quarter-hour time period between 6 a.m. and midnight was about 8000. The radio station would charge $15 for each 30-second commercial. Advertising in the campus newspaper would cost about half as much as the local newspaper while advertising on the campus radio station would cost about a quarter as much as the local radio station. Flyers could be printed and distributed for as little $.10 each for a one-colour , one-side only, 8 1/2″ × 11″ page. Larger four-colour flyers printed on both sides could cost as much as $2–3 each. To date Patricia had not done any detailed planning for the advertising, special promotions or publicity. In the operating expense budget, she had tentatively estimated advertising at $1000 for the first year.

As she began to mull over issues like pricing of a membership and advertising for the opening Patricia became a bit concerned. She certainly had not lost her enthusiasm nor her determination to succeed. However, the importance of these factors in motivating women to join The Perfect Pace coupled with the importance of making the right decisions really made her wish she had someone she could turn to for help.

CASE 4-2

Joe's Service Station

" How many more problems am I going to have to deal with?" muttered Joe Simard to himself as he deliberated what he was going to do about his business. Joe was the proprietor of Joe's ESSO, a full-service gas station and repair shop in Timmins, a small city (population 45 000) in Northern Ontario. He had been in operation at this location for 10 years (since 1973), and had built up a loyal clientele. But now it seemed he was being faced with numerous problems all at once.

The most recent of his problems arose because ESSO (Imperial Oil) had become involved in a rent disagreement with Joe's landlord. Joe realized this dispute could threaten the very existence of his business. In addition, ESSO had recently implemented a new system of payment for gas shipments.

As if all of this were not enough, Joe had just lost his fifth apprentice. After training these men and sending them to school to get their certification for a Class 'A' mechanics license, he was finding that the majority found employment elsewhere. It seems they were unwilling to be the jack of all trades kind of mechanic his business needed. How could he continue spending time and money to train these people, only to lose them before recovering any of his expenses?

Operations

Joe made it a policy to have all of his employees treat the customers as friends, giving them nothing but the best in service. He also provided complementary supplies such as oil, windshield washer fluid, lock de-icer, gas line antifreeze and regular antifreeze. There was always coffee available to those customers who wished to stop and chat, and Joe believed that the friendly atmosphere of his station was one of the main reasons for the loyalty of his clientele.

Along with operating four gas pumps, Joe repaired cars in the three bays attached to the service station. He was assisted by John Williams, a full-time mechanic. Parts and labour accounted for almost 15 percent of gross revenues, with an approximately equal split. Joe kept some small parts in stock such as air filters, oil filters, sealed beams, and other lights. Other items needed to complete a repair were ordered and delivered by local automotive distributors. This reduced the amount of inventory Joe carried and the cost of keeping bigger, slower moving inventory on hand. There was an average markup of 20 percent on parts sold at the manufacturer's suggested retail price.

The shop (service bays) was open weekdays from 7:30 a.m. to 5:00 p.m., and on Saturdays from 8:00 a.m. to 12:00 p.m. As for the gas bar, it was open from 7:00 a.m. to 9:00 p.m. daily except for Sundays when closing was at 5:00 p.m. This provided patrons with maximum access to Joe's services. One added feature for regular customers was a wrecking service.

Background

Joe Simard had attained his mechanics license at age 20 and had begun to work at the station he now owned. He gained ownership when the previous owner retired and offered him the business. He believed that someone had given him a break early in life, when he needed it, and he tried to do the same for others. This was one of the main reasons why he trained so many young mechanics and encouraged them to get their licenses. However, his generosity and patience were not always repaid in kindness, particularly of late.

Joe's ESSO had been profitable under Joe's direction, but in recent years Joe had watched profits steadily decline. This has been very disappointing since he had made no major changes in his operation. The changes were occurring externally, because of initiatives taken by ESSO. The financial trend was so bleak that continuance of the business had become an issue (Exhibits 1 and 2). Joe had consistently drawn about $25 000 to support himself and three dependants, and felt that he could not easily reduce this amount.

Joe was also faced with the possibility of relocation if ESSO and the landlord could not come to an agreement about rent. As it stood, ESSO rented from the landlord and Joe subletted from ESSO for $1300 a month. An ESSO inspector visited the premises twice yearly, often by surprise, to ensure that all company policies were upheld.

Location

The service station was situated on the city's main artery, which was also a major highway. The station was on a corner lot with plenty of parking and access from three sides, near the outskirts of the business and shopping areas, and accessible to both highway and local traffic.

Competition

The two major competitors were a Shell station and an independent station, both located on the same throughway and all within a mile of one another. The Shell was directly across from the independent, and both were situated one city block closer to approaching highway traffic.

The Shell outlet offered a car wash service and a self-serve gas bar. Rumour had it that the Shell was about to offer "split-serve," both self-serve and full service. The independent was a full-service gas bar offering no complementary line of products, but its gasoline prices were competitive with Shell's self-serve, and both were slightly cheaper than Joe's full-serve gas prices.

Besides the range and quality of services offered, gasoline prices were the main competitive tool. There hadn't been any price wars locally, although they had occurred in the other parts of the country as a means of gaining market share. If this were to happen, the proprietors would be the ones to absorb the price cut on the gasoline, and this would directly affect their profits, as the markup was normally only two or three cents per litre.

Future Opportunities

Recently, Joe had been approached by Texaco Canada. It had a service station up for tender, a facility very much like Joe's present station but with one less service bay and one less pump. Texaco had offered Joe the first opportunity to bid. The Texaco garage was located in the downtown core, away from the highway, as seen in Exhibit 3. Joe expected he would have lower gas sales at the new location. However, repairs contributed more to gross profits that gas (Exhibit 4), and the monthly rent would be $200 lower than Joe was currently paying. There was one other garage nearby, with a good track record for repairs but only one pump.

Joe wondered how many of his customers would follow him to the new location, and whether the new customer base would make up for the losses he might suffer. Joe knew that the present owner of the downtown facility had created a great deal of ill will with his pricing policy on repairs. He had assumed that the customers in the surrounding area would pay a premium price for the convenience of his location, even though premium pricing was not the practice of other garages in the area, who only charged the manufacturer's suggested retail price for parts.

A particularly attractive feature of this location was its proximity to automotive dealers in the area. The Texaco dealer claimed that some of his customers bought their own parts directly from these automotive dealers and then only wanted him to install them. He had been heard to argue that his prices on labour needed to be commensurately higher because he was deprived of any markup on parts. Joe reflected that this easy access to automotive dealers might be turned to his own advantage if he could pick up parts himself, especially when he needed them in a hurry. He knew, however, that there was a stigma attached to this station because of the present owner's pricing policy, and also because of his brusque manner. Joe realized that should he decide to act upon Texaco's proposal, he would have to overcome the station's negative reputation.

There were a few other issues to consider regarding Texaco's offer. One of the main ones was the time lag of three months between closing operations at ESSO and re-opening at Texaco. What would this mean to him, and more importantly where would it leave his customers?

Another concern had to do with the location of the station. It was in a highly populated area and the regulations were much stricter with regard to the handling of gasoline shipments. The lot itself was smaller, offering less parking space and only one point of access. Also, municipal taxes were higher in the business sector than in Joe's present location. In his present financial position he had to wonder whether this option was feasible.

The drawing card that enticed Joe was the method of payment used by Texaco. Texaco required payment for gasoline within seven business days of its delivery. This differed from ESSO's newly implemented consignment system, whereby the tanks were refilled automatically with payment due upon receipt. Each time that a tank was "topped up," the unused portion in the bottom was measured and Joe was given a refund at the current price per litre. Since prices had been falling, this procedure worked to his disadvantage—ESSO purchased the gas back at less than what Joe had originally paid for it.

With all this in mind, Joe knew that he had to come to a decision soon about the ESSO situation and the Texaco offer. He knew that to remain with ESSO he had to overcome the various obstacles before him quickly or face the possibility of losing money this year. Also, Texaco would not wait forever for a reply. If he intended to move he would have to do so quickly before he missed the opportunity.

"I expect to lose gas sales if I move away from the highway. On the other hand, it's the mechanical side that contributes the most to gross profits (see Exhibit 4), but right now this place has a reputation to live down."

	1983	1982	1981
ASSETS			
Current Assets			
Cash	$16,846	$18,615	$17,342
Accounts receivable	34,863	9,801	11,380
Inventory, at cost	6,215	17,711	16,128
Prepaid expenses	2,726	2,493	2,372
	60,650	48,620	47,222
Fixed Assets			
Equipment and vehicles, at cost	32,020	32,020	31,611
Less accumulated depreciation	21,177	18,896	15,773
	10,843	13,124	15,838
	71,493	61,744	63,060
LIABILITIES			
Current Liabilities			
Accounts payable	21,643	5,385	2,369
Loan payable	650	1,325	5,225
	22,293	6,710	7,594
PROPRIETOR'S CAPITAL			
Balance at end of year	49,200	55,034	55,466
	$71,493	**$61,744**	**$63,060**

Exhibit 1

Joe's Service Station Balance Sheet as at October 31, 1983 (Unaudited)

Exhibit 2

	1983	1982	1981
Joe's Service Station Statement of Income For the Year Ended October 31, 1983 (Unaudited)			
Sales	$831,078	$980,501	$930,142
Cost of Sales	706,806	834,819	783,980
Gross Profit	124,272	145,682	146,162
Sundry Income	361	310	331
	124,633	146,001	146,493
Expenses			
Accounting and legal	900	1,020	650
Advertising	2,610	2,937	2,443
Bad debt	1,328	320	1,456
Depreciation	2,281	3,123	4,190
Employee benefits	2,351	3,010	2,482
Insurance	3,657	3,170	3,064
Interest and bank charges	2,340	2,000	1,659
Laundry and uniforms	2,067	2,261	2,538
Light, heat and water	1,920	1,492	1,650
Miscellaneous	161	523	284
Office	2,703	1,984	1,982
Repairs and maintenance	1,889	1,232	2,656
Rent	15,593	15,491	14,049
Supplies	3,035	5,405	3,805
Taxes and license	753	564	306
Telephone	1,789	1,779	1,638
Travel and convention	1,076	728	2,058
Truck	11,132	8,964	7,715
Wages	50,518	64,625	57,074
	108,103	120,628	111,699
Net Income for Year	**16,530**	**25,373**	**34,794**

Exhibit 3

Joe's Service Station Location Map

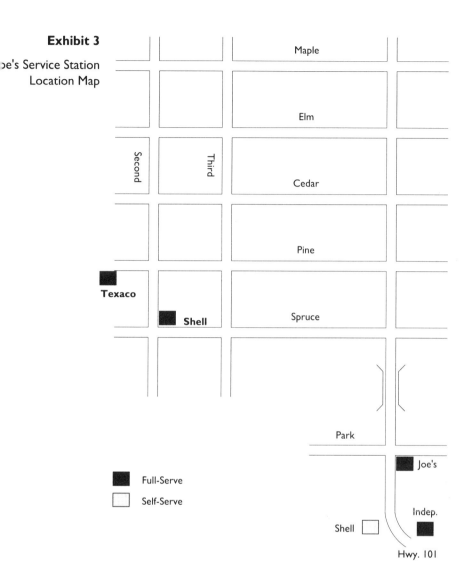

Full-Serve

Self-Serve

Exhibit 4

Joe's Service Station Gross Profit Breakdown 1983

	Gas	Parts and Service	Total
Sales	$719,024	$112,054	$831,078
Cost of Sales	660,829	45,977	706,806
Gross Profit	**58,195**	**66,077**	**124,272**

Lizards Action Wear

Introduction

Liz Upton sat at the desk of her basement office in February 1990. As she reviewed the financial statements of Lizards Action Wear, she considered the company's performance over its long startup period and wondered what the future would hold.

Located in Sudbury, Ontario, Lizards manufactured and retailed Lycra[1] stretch sportswear for athletes. The main products were high quality cross country ski suits and cycling jerseys and shorts which were targeted at teams and clubs up to the national level. Although the sales of her company had been increasing steadily, Liz felt the business had not reached its full potential. She had higher expectations for her level of income from the business and wondered if the current strategy required more time to develop or if she should take a different tack.

Company History

Lizards was initiated in 1984, as the result of several factors. The bankruptcy of her husband's construction business two years' previously led to Liz's return to the work force as the sole income earner in a family of four. Liz had a personal interest in cycling, and while pursuing this interest on a trip in Vermont she noticed the prevalence of Lycra cycling gear. Lycra was just emerging in the US as a sport clothing material. Its ability to stretch made it comfortable, and of particular interest to athletes was its ability to "wick" moisture away from the body. Liz was aware of a lack of Canadian-made Lycra cycling shorts and recognized this as a business opportunity. Coupled with her sewing ability and an interest in fashion design, this observation led to the launch of Lizards. At first, she maintained her day job as executive assistant to the director of a local hospital, and produced the cycling shorts with the help of friends. As interest in the shorts grew, Liz recruited two home sewers to make the product, but Liz kept her full-time job. She continued to cut all the fabric herself, as this was a critical aspect of achieving the desired quality and fit. As more shorts were sold, she reinvested in material inventory and equipment. The growth in product sales was encouraging, although with this growth came increased pressure on her, as training sewers, checking garments for quality, and administering the business required more and more of her time. By mid-1986 it was apparent that if the business was to continue to grow she would have to work at it full-time.

In the late summer of 1986, Liz began to investigate financing to expand the business to a full-time venture. Over a five-month period, she drew up a business plan to support her request for financing. She discovered quickly that conventional financing was not available, since she had no collateral and the business had only a limited track record. Instead, she approached the Sudbury Community Adjustment Project (SCAP), a local joint private/federal/provincial agency supporting secondary industry in Sudbury. After reviewing the Lizards' business plan, SCAP approved her application and granted her a forgivable loan over three years in the amount of $74 000.

This financing, which was received in January 1987, allowed Liz to begin to work full time at the business in order to develop it to a self-sustaining level of sales. The family recreation room, which had already become a work area, now also became a storage room for a large fabric inventory. Five additional home sewers were recruited, trained, and supplied with sewing machines and a full-time assistant/cutter was hired.

Marketing

Products   By this point the company was producing many types of Lycra sport clothing, including cycling shorts, jerseys, and one-piece suits, cross-country ski suits, triathlon suits, gymnastic suits, aerobic suits, and running tights. Liz was always looking for new applications and garments to be made from Lycra.

Promotion   Liz began to promote the business personally throughout the province by visiting retail stores, schools, and club teams wherever she could. She wanted to supply national-calibre athletes with her suits, but found the requirements of being a National Team supplier beyond the financial capabilities of her small company. She then tried and was successful in securing orders from a few provincial-level teams in cycling and cross-country skiing (see Exhibit 1 for a list of customers). This meant reducing her regular pricing, but she felt the exposure was worthwhile.

During the summer of 1987 Liz decided to attend the Colgate Games, a national track meet held in Toronto. She thought this would be an ideal setting for promotional activity, so she prepared several thousand dollars worth of product, rented a hotel suite near the track meet location, and then waited for customers to appear. She did not sell anything at this promotion which was, as she described it, "a humbling experience." Subsequently, she showed her wares at track-side out of the trunk of her car, which was only slightly more successful but much less costly. Liz learned that athletes come to meets to race, not to purchase gear. However, she felt that the exposure was worthwhile and important contacts were made, so she continued with this activity.

Liz tried a number of commission salespeople, but they were unable to generate enough activity to support themselves. Liz found that selling to retail stores was difficult, as her profit was reduced due to the retail margins demanded (30-50 percent on selling price); nonetheless she maintained a few stores as distributors. A direct mail campaign to cycling and cross-country ski clubs was marginally successful.

One of her most successful ideas was the introduction of a national toll-free telephone number which gave her ready access to the entire Canadian market by allowing customers to place orders free of charge. She also placed advertisements in a few selected regional sport magazines in Manitoba, British Columbia, Ontario, Alberta, and the Atlantic provinces, and in a cycling handbook produced by the provincial sport governing bodies of these same provinces. Lizards was usually granted a one-page advertisement in these publications in return for some level of sponsorship of the provincial team. This gave credibility and exposure to the product.

Athletes could also call for a free catalogue, which was mailed to them. It included fabric swatches, a colour photo depicting the appropriate sport and garments, style sheets, product sketches, descriptions, an order form, and a measurement form. (See Exhibit 2 for a partial catalogue.) The order and measurement form assured custom fit for each athlete and Liz checked on orders to be sure customers understood the measurement scheme.

Liz was always seeking orders from high profile athletes by attending competitions and speaking with them directly or sending them catalogues, although she could not afford to sponsor them outright. She was pleased to receive a large order ($4000) in 1989 from the Canadian Association of Nordic Ski Instructors (CANSI) for ski suits. The order, which was unsolicited, was the result of a CANSI member seeing the Ontario Cross Country Ski Team with Lizards' gear. She was pleased, as she felt that this type of order would increase the level of awareness for her product.

Table 1		Cross-Country Ski Suit	Cycling Suit
Lizards			
Action Wear	Retail Price	$170	$64
Product Pricing	Wholesale Price	110	41
	Material	35	13
	Labour	25	15

Pricing   Pricing of two typical products in the Lizards line was as shown in Table 1.

Markets   After some time Liz began to focus on small cross-country skiing and cycling clubs and teams (5-20 members), in Ontario and the western provinces, from high school age up to, but excluding, national level teams. This was accomplished using the combination of the above mentioned advertisements and the toll-free number. Additionally, Lizards' products were available in selected retail stores in Ontario and custom orders could be placed through those stores. Liz estimated that 80 percent of sales were to clubs/teams while 10 percent were to individual athletes and the remaining 10 percent came from retail. She further estimated that Lizards' sales represented less than 10 percent of the club/team market in Canada.

The market was small and specialized, as cycling, running, and skiing were performed on a recreational basis by less than 15 percent of the population. Elite or competitive participation in these sports was much lower.

Competition   To Liz's knowledge she had only one major competitor, Louis Garneau, a Québec-based manufacturer. His operation was a factory-style set-up for handling orders of a much larger size than Lizards could accommodate. Garneau supplied the national teams, provincial teams, and school and club teams as well as selling in retail stores. Lizards was able to make some inroads into the club and team market with its high quality and quick turnaround on orders, but Garneau controlled the bulk of the retail trade.

Two other western competitors, Domini and Sugoi, were beginning to emerge and Liz had won and lost small contracts in competition with each. She wanted to know more about them but had been unable to obtain any information.

Table 2		
	December	$12,200
Lizards	January	4,800
Action Wear	February	21,500
Sales by Month	March	5,500
December 1988	April	8,200
to November	May	5,700
1989	June	8,900
	July	9,500
	August	4,300
	September	2,400
	October	12,900
	November	28,600
	Total	**124,500**

There were a number of smaller competitors, but none were as well established as Lizards. Liz did lose a contract with the Alberta cycling team to a smaller Alberta competitor because of a problem with raw material quality. She secured an order with the cycling team in early 1989 and had already shipped it when it was discovered that this particular batch of Lycra did not have as much stretch as usual. The fit of these cycling suits was inferior and the athletes were dissatisfied. Liz did what she could to control the damage, recalling as many suits as possible and replacing them.

Sales   Predicting demand had always been a problem for Lizards, with sales ranging from $2400 to $28 600 per month. Table 2 illustrates the monthly variation in sales for the year ended 30 November 1989. Liz found this volatility quite stressful, in that cashflow was insufficient when orders were down, or alternatively, there was pressure to complete orders when it was a busy month.

Operations

Product Design   Orders were generally placed by phone or mail and a 50 percent deposit was required. Liz would discuss the colour and design of the product with the customer. Adding colours to any garment meant additional cutting and sewing of fabric. Liz designed all the product patterns with the help of her assistant and in consultation with customers.

Production   Lizards carried a large inventory of fabric, so material was usually in stock as needed. If not, the customer was notified and asked about substitute material or a longer delivery date. There were only two Canadian suppliers of Lycra, and Liz had an arrangement with one to supply her with less than the usual minimum quantities. Credit terms were 60 days. In 1988–89 there was a world-wide shortage of Lycra, which at one point was so severe that Liz had to order six months ahead of time for raw material. This was complicated by the fact that it was difficult to predict the colours athletes would choose for their gear. However, the Lycra situation had eased somewhat, allowing Liz to reduce the size of her inventory.

The material was cut by Liz or her full-time cutter, as this was a critical aspect of the construction of each garment. The fabric, along with any notions, was bagged and delivered to the house of one of 10 home sewers who lived up to 30 kilometres away. Once completed, the garment was picked up and checked for quality. The team or club name/logo was heat transferred onto the garment, which was then repackaged, and shipped by courier to the customer. Sewers were paid every two weeks on a piece-work basis for the work they had completed. Only two of these sewers regularly worked over 30 hours a week; the remaining eight worked up to 20 hours per week during busy times.

Quality Control   Liz trained each sewer and, as a result, quality control was not usually a problem. If there was a minor repair to be made or thread to be tied off, Liz or her assistant usually did it because of the time and effort involved in returning it to the sewer. Major faults were corrected on the sewer's time, but sewers were not charged for material wastage.

Finance

Lizards had been supported to date by a substantial injection of cash from SCAP and Liz had reduced her draw in order to build up inventory. She thought she could reduce her inventory to six weeks' worth of material because of an improvement in supply. There was little chance of further grant financing and she was unable to provide more money to Lizards personally. The bankruptcy of her husband's business in 1982 left her renting the family home with no equity to use as security for a loan. It also left her with an understandable aversion to debt. Before she would consider financing growth with debt there would have to be a clear plan which demonstrated realistic, achievable returns.

Cost Control

Because Lizards' sewers operated on a piece-work basis, controlling labour costs was simple, Once Liz had designed a garment, she and her assistant would make a few and decide what a reasonable allowance for labour was. The sewers were then paid this amount for each unit produced.

Since only Liz or her assistant cut out material, costs in this area were also easily controlled. Attention was given to pattern design so that efficient use was made of material. Lizards did not purchase enough raw material to command significant discounts, although the supplier did grant 60-day credit terms.

Current Situation

In 1989 Lizards sold approximately 3000 units and improved its profit position substantially over 1988 (see Exhibits 3 and 4). The 1988 season was also an improvement over 1987, which was really a partial year, given that operations did not get under way until late winter (November was usually the busiest month). Liz's decision to concentrate on the provincial, club, and school-team markets instead of general retail meant dealing with elite athletes, who tended to be very demanding regarding the fit and finish of their garments. However, Liz had set similarly high standards for Lizards' products: the company's motto was "Excellence in Action."

The Lizards logo had been trademarked in 1987 at a cost of $2000. The name was a derivative of Liz's own name and the image seemed to be appropriate to the function and feel of the garments. The trademark was small but conspicuously displayed on the chest of all suits and jerseys, and one leg of all pants and shorts.

Recently, Liz had expanded the product line to include winter warm-up jackets and pants made of Tasnyl, a breathable, yet wind-proof nylon material. They were lined with an insulating material and seemed to be popular with cross-country skiers and other winter sport athletes. Tasnyl was available from a different supplier who required COD payment terms. The jackets and pants were individually priced just below the cost of a cross-country ski suit. Liz was working on developing a similar product for cyclists and runners but planned to substitute the insulating layer for some lighter material.

The Future

Liz reflected on the strategy she should pursue in the future. She knew that her costs were too high to compete on a mass retail level, yet she thought she would like to capitalize on the awareness of the Lizards' name with athletes. Last year had been the final year the grant had affected her income statement and she wondered what level of sales was now required to show a profit. Liz was seeking a 25 percent increase in sales.

She was interested in a process called "sublimation," whereby the fabric could be printed in one operation with appropriate colours and a logo. This would save on the cutting and sewing of garments that had several colours—particularly on cycling jerseys and suits, where there would be a $6 decrease in labour per unit. She knew she could get the transfer designed, but the cost of a machine to heat press it onto the Lycra was approximately $4000. In addition, she would need to make leasehold improvements of $1000 for installation, wiring and venting, and she wondered if this was worth pursuing.

The market for teams and clubs in the areas of cycling and skiing still held potential, as there were over 35 colleges and universities and some 500 high schools in Ontario alone. Many towns had club teams in cycling and cross-country skiing which she had not yet approached.

Another opportunity lay with the network of home sewers she had established. She had not approached half the capacity available to her, and she wondered how she could make better and more profitable use of their skills.

All these thoughts ran through Liz's mind as the phone rang. It was a cycling team representative confirming a $6000 order to be delivered in one month. Liz put aside thoughts of the future and began to plan production.

Endnotes   1.   Lycra is a product of Dupont. It is a stretch fabric made of nylon and spandex.

Lizards®

ACTIONWEAR FOR THE SERIOUS ATHLETE.
DES VÊTEMENTS POUR L'ATHLÈTE SÉRIEUX.

Look who's wearing
Lizards...

Ontario Provincial Cycling Team
Ontario Provincial Cross-Country Ski Team
Nova Scotia Provincial Cycling Team
British Columbia "Champions" (Cycling)
Northwest Territories Cross-Country
    Ski Team
University of Western Ontario X-C
    Ski Team
Trent University X-C Ski Team
Queen's University Cycling Team
Porcupine Ski Racers
Soo Finnish X-C Ski Club
Northland Nordic X-C Ski Club
Laurentian/Adanac Alpine Ski Racers
Waterloo Nordic Ski Club
Sudbury Cycling Club
North Bay Knights Cycling Club
Sault Ste. Marie Cycling Club
Top Notch Cycling Team (Oakville)
Brampton Cycling Club
Brant Cycle Team (Burlington)
Training Wheels Cycle Team (Mississauga)
London Cycling Club
Cornwall Cycling Team
Grande Prairie Wheelers (Alberta)
Uli's/Rocky Cycle Club (Surrey, B.C.)
Leaside High School X-C Ski Team
Wingham High School X-C Ski Team
Lion's Head High School X-C Ski Team
Canadian Association of Nordic Ski
    Instructors
Barrie North Collegiate Gymnastics Club
Hopkins Academy Gymnastics Club
    (Victoria Cove, NFLD)
Levack Gymnastics Club
Owen Sound Cycling Club
Mississauga Cycle Club

Silent Sports Cycle Team (Thornhill)
Trinity College X-C Ski Team
Zippy Print Racing Team (Mississauga)
Red River Service Cycle Team
    (Thunder Bay)
Mowat Nordic Ski Club (West Hill, Ont.)
Crestwood Secondary School Track Team
    (Peterborough)
Thousand Island Secondary School Track
    Team (Brockville, Ont.)
The Tour du Canada (Leader's and
    Presentation Jerseys—four years)
The Fonthill/Niagara Classic Junior Stage
    Race (Leader's and Presentation
    Jerseys—two years)
N.W.T. Speedskating Team
University of Toronto X-C Ski Team
Carleton University X-C Ski Team
Lakehead University X-C Ski Team
Ontario Biathlon Team
Cycles Cartier (Dawson Creek, Alberta)
Wostawea Ski Club, St. John, N.B.
Ski de Fond d'Ullois (Chelsea, Que.)
Fonthill Cycle Club (Fonthill, Ont.)
'Fit Company' Ski Club (Toronto)
Husky X-C Ski Club (St. Quentin, N.B.)
Toronto Bicycling Network
Newmarket Cycle Club
Earl Haig S.S. X-C Ski Club (Toronto)
Kingston & Area Racing (Cycle) Team
Kingston Velo Cycle Club
Georgian Bay Nordic Ski Club
    (Wiarton, Ont.)
Chinguacousy Nordic Ski Club
Woodstock S.S. X-C Ski Team
Stratford Central X-C Ski Team

Put Lizards on your Team
Call 1-800-461-4833

Exhibit 2

Lizards
Action Wear
Price List

Box 16, Site 26, R.R. #4
Sudbury, Ontario P3E 4M9
(705) 522-5580
1-800-461-4833

1989-90 PRICE LIST—CYCLING & TRIATHLON WEAR

Cycle Jerseys

Lizards cycle jerseys are where we excel. Look at these features—zipper enclosed in collar preventing neck irritation; body-hugging design for wind resistance; European cut—low in back, high in front, and elasticized to stay put; double weight pockets to withstand loading. Available in 80-20 Canadian made lycra in 15 vibrant colours, and in white Coolmax.

	Short Sleeve	Long Sleeve
Style CJ-L6	$ 57.00	$ 67.00
Style CJ-L7, CJ-L8, CJ-L9I	$ 62.50	$ 72.50
Style CJ-L11 (printed stripe)	$ 62.50	$ 72.50
Style CJ-L88, CJ-L96	$ 65.00	$ 75.00
Style CJ-L9, CJ-L10, CJ-L95, CJ-L97	$ 69.00	$ 79.00

Skin Suits

Lizards aerodynamic skin suits incorporate the same fine features as our jerseys and 6-panel shorts. The long-sleeve version is available with standard cuffs or thumb straps.

Style SKS-L41, SKS-L16 (printed stripe)	$100.00	$110.00
Style SKS-L12, SKS-L13, SKS-L15, SKS-L91	$110.00	$120.00
Style SKS-L88, SKS-L96	$114.00	$124.00
Style SKS-L14, SKS-L95, SKS-L97	$118.00	$128.00

NOTE: *Discounts for Team Orders* (above items)

6–11 units	less *20% off list*
12 units and over	less *25% off list*

Cycle Shorts

Lizards cycle shorts are available in two-panel or six-panel models, and 7 distinctive designs. All Lizards shorts feature generous leg length, high cut back waist, non-roll waist (lies flat against the body without constriction), and gripper leg elastics. The durable 'ultra chamois' foam-backed padding has the look and feel of natural sheepskin but wicks moisture away from the body thereby remaining dry. 'Ultra chamois' provides a soft ride even after countless ridings and washings.

**Exhibit 2
(cont'd)**

Lizards
Action Wear
Price List

Box 16, Site 26, R.R. #4
Sudbury, Ontario P3E 4M9
(705) 522-5580
1-800-461-4833

Six-Panel Cycle Short

Style CS-L17-8	$ 64.00
Style CS-L18-8	$ 68.00
Style CS-L19, CS-L86-8 (not shown— 3-part stripe)	$ 70.00

Exhibit 2 (cont'd)

Lizards
Action Wear
Measurement
Chart

Lizards®
Measurement Chart

NAME _____ M ( ) F ( ) AGE _____

1) **NECK** (base)   . . . . . inches

2) **CHEST** (bust)   . . . . .

3) **UPPER CHEST** (women)   . . . . .
   (above bust)

4) **WAIST**   . . . . .

5) **HIPS** (widest part)   . . . . .

6) **BACK LENGTH**   . . . . .
   (measured while sitting on
   flat surface from neckbone
   to surface)

7) **UNDERARM LENGTH**   . . . . .
   (armpit to wrist)

8) **SLEEVE LENGTH**   . . . . .
   (centre BACK neckbone over
   shoulder to wrist)

9) **LEG INSEAM**   . . . . .
   (crotch to below ankle bone)

10) **LEG OUTERSEAM**   . . . . .
    (waist to ankle bone)

11) **THIGH**   . . . . .

12) **CALF**   . . . . .

13) **BICEP**   . . . . .

14) **HEIGHT**   . . . . . ft. . . . . . in.

15) **WEIGHT**   . . . . . pounds

Exhibit 3		1989	1988	1987
Lizards Action Wear Balance Sheet as at 30 November 1987, 88, 89	**ASSETS**			
	Current			
	Cash	$ 4,587	$ 9,484	$12,641
	Accounts receivable	12,273	12,345	4,459
	Inventory–at cost	15,472	11,338	12,173
	Prepaid income tax	0	126	160
	Total Current Assets	32,332	33,293	29,433
	Fixed Assets	5,642	7,522	13,656
	Total Assets	37,974	40,815	43,089
	LIABILITIES			
	Current			
	Accounts payable and accrued liability	15,560	12,967	5,694
	Other			
	Forgivable loan	0	15,330	26,930
	Advances from shareholder	26,205	18,504	18,395
	Total Liabilities	41,765	46,801	51,019
	SHAREHOLDERS' EQUITY			
	Capital Stock	1	1	1
	Retained Earnings			
	Balance at beginning of year	− 5,986	− 7,930	0
	Net income (loss) for the year	2,195	1,944	− 7,930
	Balance at end of year	− 3,791	− 5,986	− 7,930
		37,974	**40,815**	**43,089**

Exhibit 4		1989	1988	1987
Lizards	Sales	$124,489	$107,672	$35,509
Action Wear	Cost of Sales	75,938	65,680	26,601
Statement of	Gross Profit	48,551	41,992	8,908
Income				
Years Ended				
30 November				
1987, '88, '89	**Expenses**			
	Management salary	$ 18,863	$ 24,421	$22,374
	Office salary	10,558	13,197	2,228
	Vehicle and travel	8,404	9,213	5,558
	Telephone	9,202	8,365	3,193
	Advertising & promotion	6,356	7,585	2,859
	Professional fees	3,475	3,726	6,273
	Office and general	1,521	1,383	2,824
	Provision for depreciation	1,021	1,134	1,796
	Insurance	763	694	630
	Utilities	579	526	597
	Interest and bank charges	512	465	121
	Municipal taxes	433	394	357
		61,686	71,103	48,810
	Operating Income	(13,135)	(29,111)	(39,902)
	Other Income (SCAP)	15,330	26,930	31,775
	Wage Subsidy		2,741	
	Interest Income		1,384	197
	Net Income (loss)	**$ 2,195**	**$ 1,944**	**$−7,930**

Dav-Mur Communications Inc.

The sixty five thousand we're stuck with will come straight out of our hides. That's twice what we had to pay back last time we got stung. And we've got no more money lying around in '88 than we had in '85. It's going to hurt every bit as much. Why should we be good guys this time? What's to stop us from paying ourselves first?

It was November of 1988, and the debate raged back and forth between Dan Epton and Matt Turner, the owner operators of Dav-Mur Communications. TKP&P Inc., a promotional house that had subcontracted a project to them, had just gone out of business. They knew that Dav-Mur, their small advertising agency, would not get a red cent to cover the obligations incurred in doing its part of the project. They knew, too, that the major packaged goods firm that had initiated the contract had paid the promotional house in full.

Background

Dan Epton, an art director, and Matt Turner, a production manager, had worked together for a medium-sized advertising firm. When the firm closed in 1982, the two men decided to join forces and open a studio where they would offer "ad-wares" to small firms, and in particular retailers. Both were in their early thirties, and felt that they had gained the requisite skills and experience in design, copywriting, and production to offer advertising services to businesses that could not afford a full-fledged ad agency.

In February 1983 they opened under the name Ad-Craft. Dan created a logo and prepared a brochure for distribution, and Matt Turner assembled a prospective client list. Very shortly after opening, the partners received what they considered a break, when they were invited to move their small operation in-house at a large public relations firm in downtown Toronto. This arrangement would not only provide them with an on-going client and an opportunity to expand the scope of their work, but would permit them to establish credit with suppliers. The partners remained with the PR firm for a year-and-a-half. They were permitted to retain their identity as a separate business and to prospect for clients. In October 1983, they incorporated.

In December 1984 the partners struck out on their own. They established an independent studio, located in a renovated warehouse in a factory district of Toronto. Very shortly afterwards the small firm took on a job for a group of businessmen who held the license for a popular lottery, and who had also obtained a license to sell souvenirs of the Pope's upcoming visit. They asked Dav-Mur to do the on-site promotion.

When the Pope failed to attract the predicted crowds, the promoters were unable to pay Dav-Mur, and the small firm was left owing $30 000 to its suppliers. So as not to jeopardize their credibility in the industry, the partners decided to pay their creditors, and eventually were able to discharge all obligations.

In telling the story, Dan Epton mused reflectively,

> We were just getting started. We were very concerned about losing our credibility in the industry, and so we paid everyone back to the penny. With benefit of hindsight, it probably didn't make good business sense to pay up. There are so many suppliers that if we hadn't bothered probably most of them would never have known. And we could have hired a mechanical artist and a secretary at least a year sooner if we'd not been so forthcoming.

Fortunately, there were grounds for optimism, despite the unexpected need to pay out what for the small firm was a large amount of money. The client list was growing, and Dav-Mur was beginning to receive referrals of larger scale business.

At this point the firm was only billing art time, i.e., Dan Epton's time (see Exhibit 1), but both partners felt that the time had come to become accredited so that the company could buy media space (print and broadcast). Dav-Mur Communications would now perform all of the functions of an advertising agency: concept work, design work, production work, and media placement. The necessary steps were taken and accreditation was received in mid-1985. This meant that the firm now had the right to receive a commission from the media, normally 15 percent.

In the fall of 1987, having survived the growing pains of the first five years, the partners again took stock and decided to make a deliberate effort to develop an "upscale, downtown" image for the business. The three year lease which they had on their current premises was about to expire and this spurred them to seek a more prestigious location. In December, they moved to a highrise commercial building on the Avenue

Road boundary of Yorkville, a sophisticated centre-town retail district. Both the partners agree that this attempt to upgrade the firm's image by acquiring a fashionable address had been successful.

Current Situation

A few months after the move, Dav-Mur Communications was offered a major job by a promotional house, TKP&P Inc., which was under contract from a prominent packaged goods company. The subcontract involved the design and production of a promotional campaign for a well-known cereal. Before the job was completed, however, the contact person who had arranged the subcontract with the partners left TKP&P. The partners grew nervous when the promotional house claimed for a very long time after delivery of the final product that its client had yet to pay its bill. Dav-Mur Communications stood to lose $65 000. Then, under their very eyes, the partners watched the TKP&P company officers pay themselves handsomely out of revenues from the packaged goods account, declare insolvency a month later, sell off their assets and then rebuy them under a new name. A month later TKP&P, now calling itself NUW Corp., was back in business on exactly the same premises. The partners did not see a dime from the insolvent TKP&P Inc.

The partners soul-searched for weeks. Should they honour their accounts payable? They hadn't forgotten the struggle after the earlier loss associated with the Pope's visit, the deferral of plans to develop the business, and their personal belt tightening. And now they were looking at $65 000, not $30 000, at the very point when they were in the throes of leasehold improvements at their new site. They hadn't yet paid the invoice for creating the structure they used as a boardroom—a four-wall centre island of wood and glass block which enclosed a table and Italian chairs.

Should they fold and go their separate ways? Both of them had marketable skills and the economy was considerably more brisk than when they had gone into the venture together in 1982. And yet, more business was coming in the door every day.

Several small projects had just come their way and Matt had been talking to a large Toronto hotel/condominium developer. It was altogether possible that this firm would hire Dav-Mur Communications on a retainer basis. This would probably mean more art work than Dan Epton could do by himself. Fortunately there was a pool of freelance illustrators, copywriters etc. they could turn to. Matt Turner cast in a rueful aside:

If this deal goes through, there could be substantial outlays in salaries, and probably very large typesetting bills. Better not run into a situation again where the client refuses to pay. It's essential to avoid a recurrence . . . but how to safeguard ourselves is an open question.

Alternatively, the partners wondered if they should hire a lawyer and try to make deals with their suppliers. Dav-Mur Communications could threaten to declare insolvency, and offer to pay 50 percent of what was owing, so much now and so much later. The partners wondered if their suppliers would be willing to accept the terms presented. Would there be haggling? Would there be lawsuits?

Or should they follow TKP&P's example, fold, and try to set up under a new name? Dan Epton stated the case:

Why shouldn't we pay ourselves first before we pay our suppliers? If it were a big corporation, it would pay the Chief Operating Officer even if it then had to declare a loss. Surely we can find a lawyer and an accountant who can help us get fixed up without losing our assets. Like TKP&P we'd pay off the landlord and the equipment leases. We'd really like to stay at this address. Sure, there'd be some hassles in changing our name. We'd need to get new stationery printed. That will run us about $3000, and then there will be at least another $2000 to incorporate and cover other legal fees. A more serious consideration is the down time that would be involved. We'd have to figure out how to collect our other receivables, or else we'd forfeit those revenues too (see Exhibits 2 and 3). And if we close for awhile, we're sure to lose some of our present clients.

Exhibit 1

Dav-Mur
Communications
Inc.
Design Work
Sample

Exhibit 2

ASSETS

Dav-Mur
Communications
Inc.
Balance Sheet
(Unaudited)

	6 mo. ending Oct. 1988	1988	1987
Current			
Cash	$ 2,975	$24,884	$47,762
Accounts receivable	101,454	36,155	40,617
Prepaid expenses & sundry assets	2,325	2,325	360
Income taxes refundable	–	3,618	–
	106,754	66,982	88,739
Fixed–at cost less accumulated depreciation	39,256	21,712	748
Other–at cost			
Incorporation costs	955	955	955
Total Assets	**$146,965**	**$89,649**	**$90,442**

LIABILITIES

Current			
Accounts payable & accrued liabilities	$ 78,368	$42,841	$48,352
Income taxes payable	4,794	–	7,109
Due to shareholders	798	798	746
Total Liabilities	**$ 83,960**	**$43,639**	**$56,207**

SHAREHOLDERS' EQUITY

Capital stock	$ 2	$ 2	$ 2
Retained earnings	63,003	46,008	34,233
	63,005	46,010	34,235
	$146,965	**$89,649**	**$90,442**

Exhibit 3		6 mo. ending Oct. 1988	1988	1987
Dav-Mur Communications Inc. Statement of Operations (Unaudited)	Sales	$348,400	$511,504	$327,529
	Cost of Sales	253,000	379,130	209,568
	Gross Profit	**$ 95,400**	**$132,374**	**$117,961**
	Expenses			
	Management salaries	$ 37,000	$ 62,947	$ 55,888
	Rent	12,400	12,367	4,931
	Advertising, promotion & travel	8,620	22,354	11,949
	Office and general	3,810	5,583	2,058
	Bad debt adjustment	3,000	5,570	3,790
	Professional fees	2,070	2,119	1,870
	Telephone	1,426	2,082	1,460
	Equipment rental	1,377	–	–
	Insurance	964	2,007	–
	Business taxes	863	474	340
	Bank charges	208	276	78
	Depreciation			
	–equipment & furniture	1,054	1,245	187
	–leasehold improvement	819	593	–
		$ 73,611	$117,617	$ 82,551
	Profit Before Taxes	**$ 21,789**	**$ 14,757**	**$ 35,410**
	Taxes on Income	4,794	2,982	7,109
	Net Profit	**$ 16,995**	**$ 11,775**	**$ 28,301**

Blue Mountain Bookkeeping Services

n January 1988 Ralph Clymer was considering the purchase of his father's bookkeeping business. It was clear that he would have an uphill job rebuilding a business that had declined due to the ill health of Herb Clymer. During the last ten years the accounting services business had undergone marked changes in the Collingwood area. Many smaller firms had amalgamated and some of these had been absorbed by the larger firms, including those classified as the "big eight" accounting firms. As well, accounting firms had expanded the services they offered to include consulting, personnel placement and management services. All these changes confronted Ralph Clymer as he thought about rebuilding the family business. It seemed clear that he would have to develop a new approach to fit the changed conditions that had emerged in the industry.

Blue Mountain Bookkeeping Services

Blue Mountain Bookkeeping Services (BMB) had operated under the same management in the Collingwood area since 1959. As a result of his recent illness, Herb Clymer had substantially reduced his client involvement and was now only serving eight companies and professionals. While this did not make for a profitable business it was, Clymer said, "about what the doctor ordered," and since Clymer had adequate savings for his retirement, maintaining this level of business over the last few years had worked well for him.

In 1988, Herb felt that it was time to begin activating his retirement plan and he offered the business to his son Ralph. Ralph had graduated from university in 1985 with a Commerce degree. Following graduation, he worked in accounting for a Toronto construction firm. In January 1988, during a visit to Collingwood, Ralph's father had proposed that he take over and operate BMB. Although Ralph had never seriously considered the possibility, he now thought it would be the kind of job where he could make a decent living and exercise some significant control over his own future.

Herb Clymer suggested a July date to begin the transition with a formal change in ownership to take effect on January 1, 1989. Ralph and his father hadn't developed a formal purchase agreement, but it was understood that Ralph would pay for the business using future profits. Furthermore, Herb Clymer would be available on a consulting basis, and would continue to handle the present clients until 1990. During the two-year period, Ralph thought he could rebuild BMB as well as complete his Certified Management Accounting Courses.

At the time (January 1988), BMB was operating out of the Clymer home. With only twelve clients, revenues were approximately $24 000. Since there was little overhead almost all of it was taken in salaries and expenses paid to Herb Clymer. His wife, a former bookkeeper and employee of the company, helped on occasion, particularly when Herb Clymer was ill. This had not been recorded as an expense, since they considered it a family business. (See Exhibit 1.)

The method of operating was simple. BMB clients dropped off their invoices, sales slips and other transaction papers weekly. BMB created a general ledger, set up accounts payable and accounts receivable where applicable, and wrote out a list or prepared cheques to be issued to satisfy creditor claims. For two clients, payrolls were prepared, one bi-weekly and the other monthly. Month-end and year-end statements were prepared and income tax forms were completed, including the information for quarterly payments where these were required.

Ralph Clymer had worked part-time for BMB before his father's illness. He knew, at one time, the client base had included 52 business and professional accounts. These had produced revenues for BMB of over $200 000 in 1982. (See Exhibit 2.)

Many of the clients had been severed when Herb Clymer reduced his workload. Others left of their own accord because BMB had not kept pace with their needs. BMB under Herb Clymer had not attempted to automate any of the internal processes and often account statements were delayed because BMB's manual systems were overloaded. Herb Clymer had looked at one-write systems for some of his clients but, for a variety of reasons, had rejected these and stuck with the standard ledgers that were part of his background and training. Current clients got little in the way of analysis, although they appeared happy with the statements provided. Ralph Clymer's subsequent questioning of these clients indicated that few of them felt the statements were of much help in managing; they were essential because of the bank, the government, partners, shareholders, etc., and little used in the day-to-day activities of the business. He wondered if this could be changed. There were many possible reports that could help businesses make better and more timely decisions, but it was clear that these additional services would have to be sold.

The Management Services Industry

The accounting and management services industry in the Georgian Bay area included many small firms, as well as the offices of some of the "big eight" accounting firms. These firms had developed a wide range of services including tax specialties, consulting and planning (management advisory services), personnel placement, trustee and bankruptcy activities, and their mainstay, auditing and accounting services. More recently, some of these firms had begun offering computer training and accounting software programs as part of their accounting services. Access to the large staffs located in the major offices of these firms permitted the regional offices to specialize as well. For larger clients, this range of skills was often important. The existence of multiple office locations was also convenient for businesses that had different locations across the country. The presence of these big accounting firms had caused a number of smaller firms to amalgamate in an effort to remain competitive. This trend continued, making growth in the industry without acquisition or amalgamation difficult.

Recently some of the major firms had created special groups within the firm to specialize in dealing with the needs of small business. These offered consulting, accounting, tax and computer systems services designed to meet the needs of smaller firms. While it was not generally known how these services were priced for individual clients, the groups and services were designed to avoid the high hourly charges and overhead normally associated with accounting firms. Where they would succeed in expanding client bases with these services was not evident. Certainly, if priced right, they could attract new clients to the firm, and these could be profitable over the long term. A significant growth area over the past few years had been in the area of tax preparation. Firms such as H&R Block, Beneficial Finance and others had made considerable inroads into this area. And, to combat seasonality, some of these firms offered training courses, bookkeeping services and consumer loans as part of their product and service strategy.

It had been observed that tax services, general management advice, and computer consulting were emerging as the most popular services for small businesses. While the provision of bookkeeping, accounting, and management services was not specifically regulated, the provision of auditing services was limited to firms employing Chartered Accountants. Other professional accounting associations had questioned this monopoly, but it remained intact in Ontario.

Ralph Clymer had accumulated some figures from competitive sources, but their use for his purposes was limited. (See Tables 1, 2, and 3.) However, the figures did indicate that companies in management and

Table 1		No. of Partners	No. of Staff	Gross Revenues	Salaries	Operating Expenses*
Blue Mountain	A	7	86	$1,921,914	$1,052,640	$223,614
Bookkeeping	B	5	41	1,081,276	483,390	93,125
Services	C	4	33	816,734	467,610	62,175
Accounting	D	3	31	834,662	430,900	53,128
Office	E	6	43	1,198,806	497,510	126,340
Comparisons	F	5	60	1,128,288	710,400	96,321
	G	3	18	470,120	255,960	30,297

* Does not include partner salaries and bonuses

Table 2		1987	1986	1985	1984
Income Statement of a Typical Small Accounting Firm	Gross Billings	588,000	580,000	579,000	580,000
	Expenses				
	Salaries	305,500	300,000	290,000	270,000
	Staff Salaries	73,200	70,800	68,500	60,000
	Rent	77,500	68,300	62,100	45,000
	Public Relations	35,000	20,000	20,000	20,000
	Other	40,600	36,000	31,000	18,000
	Total Expenses	531,800	495,100	471,600	413,000
	Operating Profit	56,200	84,900	107,400	167,000
	Bonuses	56,200	84,900	64,850	60,000
	Income for Owners	**0**	**0**	**42,550**	**107,000**

Table 3		
Staff Member Time Analysis	Total Workdays (52 × 5)	260 days
	Vacations, Holidays	40 days
		220 days
	Training	20 days
		200 days
	Public Relations	25 days
	Available for Billing	175 days
	Actually Billed	150 days
	Slack Time	25 days

accounting services are labour intensive. Since available hours were limited and the elasticity of rates was somewhat constrained by competitive factors, firms were continually seeking techniques for achieving leverage in the business. The use of students, computers, and other systems to minimize input and clerical labour were important in cost control. Larger firms continued to diversify, seeking new areas in which professional expertise could be marketed.

In addition to the accounting services offered in the area, there were management consulting firms and companies offering bookkeeping services, computer accounting services, and farm management services. Another form of competition for management service suppliers arose from equipment, systems and software vendors. Major companies such as McBee and Nebbs sold one-write accounting systems, while some companies provided systems software packages designed for small business accounting. Declining hardware costs were to a large extent responsible for the increased incidence of automated systems in the small business sector and the concomitant demand for systems advice. In most of these situations some accounting and auditing services were still needed.

Some service segments were dominated by smaller firms. These included bookkeeping services for professionals and small companies, personal income tax services, and general accounting services for the smaller seasonal businesses that operated in the area. Some of the small farms in the region used bookkeeping and accounting services, while the larger farm operations tended toward specialized farm management services. The larger accounting firms also did bookkeeping and personal taxes, but their cost structures made this work unattractive and left many customers feeling that they had been overcharged. Thus it was difficult to apply to some of these services the same high hourly rates charged for auditing, tax, and other specialized services.

The Area and the Industry

The market served by BMB covered the area from Collingwood in the east to Wiarton in the west. Current clients were located mainly in the immediate vicinity of Collingwood. Ralph Clymer felt that he would have to serve the broader area again if the business was to be viable. He would concentrate on the area from Wasaga Beach to Owen Sound initially, expanding to Wiarton if the opportunity arose. (See Figure 1.)

The Georgian Bay area had a widely diversified economy including some small industries and a variety of mixed farming. Recent growth was largely in the tourist segment. The region also provided summer homes for a large number of people from Toronto and other points in Southwestern

Figure 1

Blue Mountain
Bookkeeping
Services
The Market Area

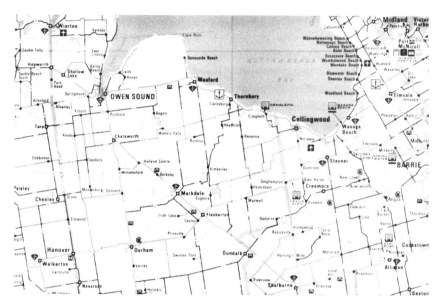

Ontario. Since 1982, the area had undergone a building boom with many new homes, condominiums and summer places springing up as part of new developments. And while some major industries (particularly ship-building) had declined, there had been a marked increase in services, retailing, and other small business development.

Area Survey

One of the first things Clymer did when he joined BMB was to attempt a survey of some small businesses and professionals in the Midland, Colling-wood, Craigleith, Thornbury and Owen Sound area. Part of this survey (see Exhibit 3) was based on contacts with 44 of the former clients of BMB. The results, Clymer knew, were a bit misleading since many of those contacted had said they would look at other bookkeeping services depending on the cost and services offered; however, since these were not specifically defined, it was difficult to tell from the survey data just how many of those contacted might be converted to new clients on the basis of different service packages. One thing he did discover was that even among those who were interested in alternative services there would be no quick conversions. "Until we contacted them few had problems nor had they thought much about alternate services, so our questions took many of them by surprise. Only two suggested that they would like to talk to a supplier of bookkeeping services in the near future."

One thing that surprised Ralph Clymer was the number of small firms and professionals that used outside services, and particularly the number who used bookkeeping services that had not been computerized to offer a more sophisticated service with faster turnaround time. He felt, on the basis of this information, that if he were going to find new clients the business would have to be built around a cost effective, computerized package. Such an approach would give Blue Mountain a marketing package that he felt would allow the company to differentiate its services from many of the more traditional services being offered by old-fashioned bookkeepers like his father.

Ralph Clymer's Concerns

Since his father's proposal had arisen without advance notice, Ralph Clymer had little background knowledge on which to base his evaluation of the proposal—if, in fact, it was a proposal. No price was discussed and Ralph knew his father would expect an offer. Since no investment was required, it was attractive as a starting point, but there were other considerations. Ralph didn't believe that he could achieve much growth simply by trying to sell more of the kinds of service currently offered by BMB. He felt he would have to develop a strategy that would give BMB some advantages over the competitive options currently available. He also knew that he needed some projections for sales and income in order to assess the business opportunity realistically. Yet despite Ralph's concerns over the market and the competition, his mind always came back to the family concern. He simply wasn't sure how it could be handled. An objective assessment was essential if he was going to take over BMB, but objectivity might strain family relations at a time when his father didn't need to be aggravated. He knew he could explain that he wasn't ready for the move and suggest that his father look to selling the business elsewhere. This might solve the family problem, but since he knew that eventually he wanted his own business, this opportunity warranted further investigation.

"And that's about it." said Ralph. "There is not much use going through BMB's statements since there isn't enough revenue to support me even if there were no costs. My problem is to find more clients and to sell each of them a wider range of services, if possible. There are many different configurations for the services offered by companies in this business, but it is not going to be easy to find a successful strategy, and there won't be any quick results."

Exhibit 1

Blue Mountain Bookkeeping Services Income Statement January 1, 1987– December 31, 1987

Revenue		
Sales		$24,000
Other		3,600
Total Revenue		$27,600
Expenses		
Rent	$ 3,000	
Salaries/benefits	14,500	
Office expenses	1,270	
Travel	3,400	
Depreciation	1,250	
Insurance	370	
Postage/telephone	1,280	
Utilities	1,375	
Miscellaneous	875	
Total Expenses	$27,320	27,320
Income		**$ 280**

Exhibit 2

Blue Mountain Bookkeeping Services Income Statement – 1982

Revenue		
Sales		$204,000
Other		3,000
Total Revenue		$207,000
Expenses		
Rent	$ 3,000	
Salaries/benefits	140,900	
Office expenses	5,420	
Travel	19,930	
Depreciation	5,670	
Insurance	3,040	
Postage/telephone	3,170	
Utilities	3,800	
Miscellaneous	1,670	
Total Expenses	$186,600	186,600
Income		**$ 20,400**

Exhibit 3

Blue Mountain
Bookkeeping
Services
Survey of
Small Business
Bookkeeping
Needs

	Contacts			
	Total		Former Clients	
	Yes	No	Yes	No
1. Are your bookkeeping activities performed by an outside service?	59	37	31	13
2. If supplied by an external firm are you happy with your current bookkeeping services?	52	7	27	4
3. Is any part of your bookkeeping computerized?	16	80	2	42
4. Is turnaround time in your statements important to your business?	79	17	36	8
5. In the area of bookkeeping would cost reductions or improved services for the same cost be of interest to your firm?	64	32	27	17
6. Would you be interested in discussing a change in bookkeeping services?				
−now	3	93	2	42
−in the future	24	72	8	36

Notes:

1. The sample totalled 110 telephone calls including calls to 44 former clients of Blue Mountain Bookkeeping Services. Ninety-six responded, 14 refused or provided too few answers to be of use.

2. Since the respondents had been guaranteed confidentiality questions such as #6 could not be used to generate specific names. Rather, it was meant as an indication of immediate vs. long-term interest.

CHAPTER

5

Phase Three: The Owner-Managed Business

Introduction

In general, the phase 3 enterprise is marked by less owner dominance, a more deliberate approach to decision making, a wider range of operating and marketing options, and a tendency towards shared authority. Typically, decisions involving the allocation of the company's resources will play an important role in managing the organization. At this level, the owner cannot afford to spend as much time on the operating activities discussed in the preceding chapter. Certainly the need to attend to day-to-day, task-oriented activities does not disappear, but by the time the company evolves into a phase 3 organization, there must be some delegation of these responsibilities.

Delegation gives the owner the freedom to take a broader view of the operation, spending proportionately more time dealing with the management functions of coordinating, controlling, and motivating. In other words, the owner-manager must focus on leadership, stimulating fresh ideas, directing the activities of the employees, and building consensus on key issues. Unfortunately, too many phase 3 entrepreneurs either regard the delegation of authority as a personal threat, or are unable to delegate effectively; some tend to monitor subordinates' activities too closely, refusing to give them the opportunity to make some mistakes.

The Business Environment

As the cases attached to this chapter will attest, the stability and limited horizons associated with phase 1 are displaced in phase 3 by a more dynamic set of operating variables. Perhaps the most significant of these is the external environment. The operating environment encountered by the owner-managed company may be quite challenging; survival may depend on the ongoing development of new products/services, close attention to employee training and motivation, or the cultivation of new sources of external funding.

While the environment is not something one manages, it certainly cannot be ignored; by phase 3 the entrepreneur finds himself responding to developments outside of the company itself.

The successful phase 3 ventures tend to be those with the ability to recognize and exploit technological opportunities, competitor weakness, changing consumer tastes, or societal demands. Of course, for many small businesses, the segment of the environment they operate in will be determined largely by their particular product/market focus at startup. As suggested earlier in the text, some enterprises might well emerge from the startup stage as phase 3 operations. Regardless of how the organization arrives at this phase, attention to planning will enable it to anticipate and evaluate external developments, rather than simply react to these forces.

Managing the Phase Three Enterprise

Planning

Despite the relative complexity of their operating environment, many owner-managers fail to plan beyond the immediate consequences of a particular decision. This behaviour is partially attributable to a common small-business mindset wherein planning is looked upon as an activity to be handled as expediently as possible so that one can get on with the real work of the business. The key for the owner-manager is to make a genuine effort to develop plans for the longer term, while giving others the freedom to plan and organize the more routine, operational activities.

Unlike a phase 1 business, the phase 3 operation will often be sufficiently secure in its market, and have adequate support, to allow the owner to plan for the future. In Chapter 7 we postulate that within the context of the small business life cycle, planning undertaken in phase 3 should be directed towards propelling the organization into phases 4 and 5. In all cases, future strategies must take into account the available resources, particularly personnel: for example, before launching a largely subscriber-based, weekly business publication, a community newspaper would have to be certain that it had the requisite sales, production, and editorial capability.

Organizing

Since the owner-managed entity uses more resources—machinery, materials, and people—than its phase 1 counterpart, organizing these resources is a critical activity. Many owner-managed organizations evolve beyond dependence on a single product or service or a single geographic region, and the owner is then faced with the challenge of organizing the business in an appropriate fashion. The manager is concerned here with obtaining the resources necessary to carry out the objectives spelled out in the planning stage. Moreover, she must provide a structure which will determine how to employ these resources. Subsequent chapters will describe the importance of effective communication at this stage.

In general, organizing involves such activities as determining the optimal asset mix for the operation, obtaining the necessary capital on favourable terms, deciding on the nature of the positions within the firm, and recruiting and selecting personnel.

Directing

A key aspect of managing the phase 3 company pertains to the coordination of the activities of employees. It is incumbent upon the owner to ensure that duties are assigned efficiently, that credit and sales personnel are not working at cross purposes, and that routine activities are carried out in a way that is consistent with overall objectives (such as timely delivery, generating greater repeat business, or improving customer relations).

To a large extent, directing relates to procedures for getting things done.

Through the scheduling of periodic meetings, the budget process, and other reporting mechanisms, the owner must attempt to ensure that each employee is aware of the duties of others in the company. Effective coordination can be achieved by encouraging the flow of information within the organization and by getting people to talk to each other as a matter of course. While the owner-manager may still be able to direct the operation in a fairly informal manner, the close attention to operating details and reliance on personal observation that characterize the phase 1 entity are no longer feasible.

Controlling

All businesses, to some degree, must identify the factors that are crucial to their success and closely monitor their performance according to these factors. For an owner-managed enterprise there would typically be a few key success factors; nonetheless, the task of tracking, say, product quality, response time, or the effectiveness of after-sale service can be very time consuming. In order to give proper attention to these issues, the owner-manager will have to delegate some administrative duties, such as order taking, scheduling, and inventory control.

While the importance of controlling as a management activity cannot be over-emphasized, many independent business people are somewhat deficient in this area. It is crucial to make the connection between planning, where many of the yardsticks for measuring performance are developed, and controlling, where the measurement actually takes place. The prime objective of both is to improve the *efficiency* of the operation. It is important for the owner to recognize that by phase 3, entrepreneurial innovation is a less important element of management than the need to utilize resources efficiently. (Figure 1-1 provides an illustration of the entrepreneurship/management dichotomy.)

The owner-manager must also undertake more regular and perhaps more extensive financial evaluations than would be appropriate at phase 1. (The various financial measures that are available are presented in Chapter 13.) Each business should have a set of key indicators that it can follow closely to identify adverse trends or variances from plan before they develop into major problems. As the small business progresses to phase 3, the importance of monitoring product line, department, or employee performance will become apparent, and relatively systematic measurement and feedback procedures should emerge. Performance targets can be determined by the overall objectives and an effective feedback process can be used to help indicate where deficiencies are occurring, and who is responsible for taking corrective measures. As a final point, it is worth noting that it is often appropriate to supplement standard quantitative measures (sales volume, hours billed, units spoiled, pounds processed), with less tangible objectives, such as customer complaints, facility maintenance or employee safety.

In phase 3 franchise operations, the responsibility for control is left largely to the franchisor. The control system offered by the franchisor will have been developed by identifying the specific factors that are critical to success in that industry, what performance measures are most appropriate, and what monitoring devices are most effective.

Outside Expertise

The reluctance to rely on external assistance is as prominent among owner-managers as it is in the earlier phases. However, the phase 3 business *requires* the owner to develop, or acquire, additional functional skills. Indeed, by late in phase 3, the organization may require market research, advertising, information system support, or recruitment and training services on a fairly regular basis.

The firm's requirements for outside expertise often arise from the owner's inability to cope with operational and conceptual problems simultaneously. The company may elect to hire consultants as a sounding board for major strategic decisions. Alternatively, situations can arise where employees cannot devote the necessary time to a project.

Entrepreneurs are becoming increasingly aware of the different ways in which external assistance can pay dividends. "You can hire a specialist for just about every strategic obstacle a growing company faces, such as selling equity, introducing technology, finding experienced managers, or developing a stream-lined organization . . . bringing in an expert saves time, effort and money learning your own lessons."[1]

As pointed out in Chapter 4, such assistance can take a variety of forms and must not necessarily be accepted without careful scrutiny. At the same time, the owner-manager should not sacrifice the entrepreneurial instinct that so often plays a key role in the success of the small business.

Summary

The owner-manager label probably applies to the largest portion of Canadian small businesses. Some enterprises move directly to this phase after startup, and only a small minority ever reach the next development phase. The threats to these businesses can be overwhelming, given an often quite volatile operating environment, their limited internal resources and competence, and funding arrangements that are typically inadequate. While some of the difficulties encountered by phase 3 companies are due to uncontrollable factors, the management approach prescribed in this chapter will certainly enhance the chances of success at this level.

List of Key Words

Direct
External Assistance
Owner-Manager
Organizing

Performance
Training
(Managing) Resources
Startup

Questions for Discussion

1. Describe how the typical small business will suffer if the owner-manager devotes most of his attention to routine, day-to-day tasks.

2. Outline some of the specific responsibilities of the owner-manager and contrast these with the nature of the tasks that must be undertaken by the owner-operator.

3. For the small enterprise at the phase 3 level, it seems clear that the principal must take time to plan for the future, while also ensuring that the operation stays on track. However, these activities are often beyond the capacity of the owner-manager. What particular advantages are offered by franchises with respect to this need for ongoing planning and reliable control mechanisms?

4. A family-owned, 18-hole public golf course is situated on the outskirts of a large suburban area. This operation also includes a driving range which has a second layer of elevated tees. The business has thrived during its first six years, in large part because of the seemingly insatiable demand for golf in the local area. However, only 20 percent of the users at any given time hold club memberships.

   Players must reserve tee-off times one day in advance. When they arrive at the course, their reservations are confirmed by the cashier in the pro shop and the appropriate green fee is paid. No receipt is provided and the players are simply directed to the "starter's hut." Here, they are organized into groups of four and put into play on a first-come first-served basis.

   A large parking lot separates the clubhouse/pro shop from the driving range area, where there are no staff members stationed. Users of the practice range must also pay at the pro shop and then carry their bucket of balls across the parking lot.

Evaluate the control system at this facility and recommend some procedures to improve the situation.

Selected Readings

Alcorn, Pat B. *Success and Survival in the Family-Owned Business.* New York, N.Y.: Warner Books, 1982.

Ward, John L. *Keeping the Family Business Healthy.* San Francisco, CA: Jossey-Bass Publishers, 1987.

Endnote   1.   Randall Litchfield, "Growth Gurus," *Small Business*, 9, no. 6 (June 1990), p. 62.

The Fraser Inn

I t was early in May, 1989 and for the past 10 months, the Anderson brothers, Brian and Jason, and their cousin, Stuart, had been working tirelessly at restoring a large, riverfront property on the outskirts of Chilliwack, B.C. However, the time was quickly approaching when some important decisions would have to be made with regard to the day-to-day operations of this proposed restaurant/entertainment lounge. The three young entrepreneurs were well aware that the long-term viability of their new venture could hinge on the decisions, both tactical and strategic, that were taken during the next few weeks. While they had already made significant progress towards the actual startup of the business, the fact that they had never before undertaken a project of this magnitude left them wondering if there were additional areas that should be addressed.

The principals had been reasonably successful with other business ventures, but none were as ambitious as the current one. Nearly a year ago in June, 1988, they had negotiated the purchase of a spacious, neglected 45-year-old building that had most recently housed an indoor tennis/fitness club. The property encompassed 1.5 acres of commercially zoned real estate, and became available at a bargain price when the club was petitioned into bankruptcy. The Andersons' objective was to transform the structure into a large-scale dining/entertainment facility. As the refurbishing phase neared completion, they were confronted with a number of pressing issues, including the hiring of key personnel and the arranging of a financial package.

Background

Brian, at 29, was the oldest of the group. He had left high school at 19 to apprentice as a carpenter for a large Vancouver construction company, and seven years ago had returned to Chilliwack to establish his own small contracting business. He hired his younger brother Jason and cousin Stuart, who were both 18 years of age at the time, as part-time employees.

By virtue of his activities as a contractor, Brian became well acquainted with the local real estate market. Through a series of timely "flips" of small residential and commercial income properties, he eventually amassed a considerable personal net worth, despite the limited profits being generated by his various construction and renovation jobs. During this time Jason and Stuart were allowed to supervise the remodelling and subsequent administration of a downtown mini-mall containing a convenience store, video outlet, and delicatessen. After a brief period this building was sold off at a small capital gain. Shortly thereafter the Andersons elected to wind up the affairs of the contracting enterprise as they moved on to establish Chilliwack's first 24-hour full-service restaurant, the All Ours Diner. The business operated as a partnership, and was housed in leased premises in a central location. The diner concept proved very popular with the college and high school market and enjoyed a record of steady profits, which to a large degree was attributable to the partners' efficient, hands-on approach to management. They discovered they had a natural affinity for the hospitality business and the success of this small restaurant whetted their appetite for something bigger. It was with little hesitation that they sold the All Ours Diner after 20 months, and devoted their efforts to their newest venture, which they christened The Fraser Inn.

Initial Financing

The purchase price of this property, which was located in an idyllic setting overlooking the Fraser River, was $315 000. The building itself was a local landmark, with a storied past that included a stint as a dance hall during the post-World War II era. The downpayment of $50 000 was well within the Andersons' means. They saw this venture as an opportunity to capitalize on their proven contracting expertise and entrepreneurial flair.

The balance of the original funding consisted of a Trust Company first mortgage in the amount of $225 000 supplemented by a private second mortgage of $40 000. The private financing was renewable after one year, while the first mortgage stipulated a fixed rate of interest over a five-year period and was closed to any prepayment. These monies were provided on the basis of the value of the real estate *per se*; the lenders felt comfortable that their funds were well margined, given the attractiveness of the site and the fact that their financing was based on a distress sale price that hardly reflected the property's real value in the marketplace.

The principals subsequently injected an additional $45 000 of their own cash to cover the cost of renovations, so their equity position now totalled $95 000. Their remaining cash resources were not nearly adequate to accommodate outstanding bills for subcontractors, orders for furniture, fixtures, and equipment, and other contingencies. Table 1 provides a

Table 1	Sources		Uses	
The Fraser Inn	First Mortgage	$225,000	Purchase Property	$315,000
Sources and	Second Mortgage	40,000	Renovations	85,000
Uses	Shareholders' Equity	95,000	($40,000 unpaid)	
of Funds		360,000	Purchase Furniture	
(10 months			& Equipment	106,000
ending	Shortfall	168,000	Initial Inventory	12,000
April 30, 1989)			Contingencies &	
			Miscellaneous	10,000
	Total	**$528,000**	**Total**	**$528,000**

breakdown of the various expenditures and shows the extent of the financing shortfall.

Operating Plan

The facility had two levels and was immense. The operating plan called for three separate areas, the largest of which would function as an entertainment hall/beverage lounge with seating for up to 325 people. The Andersons had installed a 75-foot-long bar in this room and planned to build a portable stage for the entertainment acts they hoped to attract. Given the size of the area, they were considering some rather interesting bookings, ranging from gymnastics displays to dinner theatre performances.

Also located on the main level would be a room set aside for fine dining. The remodelling program allowed seating for 60 people here, and the objective was to develop a posh supper club atmosphere that would provide competition for the various upscale establishments in the Greater Vancouver/New Westminster/Chilliwack vicinity. While there was a wide selection of quality dining facilities in this populous region, the Andersons' experience suggested that a need for such a dining room existed in the immediate Chilliwack area. They agreed that they should operate this room on a "reservation-only" basis, from 5 p.m. until midnight, seven days a week.

On the upper level there would be a licenced light dining area. The plan was to provide seating for approximately 120. However, since this part of the complex was to be situated a floor above the kitchen area, the menu would be somewhat limited. The section was located on a mezzanine, and afforded a good view of the main hall below. The Fraser River flowed within 200 feet of the back of the building, and was also visible from some seats in the mezzanine. There would be a separate bar in this area, and the principals felt that operating hours of noon until 10 p.m. would be appropriate for the business and student markets they were targeting.

Current Status

Despite their youth, the Andersons recognized the hazards of moving ahead with a small business on the basis of inadequate planning. Since acquiring the facility, they felt they had accomplished a good deal more than a physical transformation of the building. A number of preliminary decisions had already been made, based primarily on the Andersons' familiarity with the Chilliwack area, their previous restauranting experience, and a good measure of intuition.

Attributing a certain value to the reputation they had cultivated, the principals felt that for the first several months of operation a very limited advertising budget would be in order. The idea was to ease into the market by relying on word of mouth to promote the facility. Also, the owner/managers felt that this approach would give them the flexibility to put together an advertising campaign built around the most popular features of the establishment, while perhaps countering any competitive reaction. The Andersons expected that the large entertainment hall would inevitably emerge as the main drawing card of the Fraser Inn. If they were able to bring in some popular entertainment acts, Brian believed they should widen the geographic scope of their target market. Accordingly, the business's marketing plan would have to be expanded to include potential customers from Vancouver and possibly as far away as Seattle.

The company that had been incorporated to carry on business as the Fraser Inn was given a June 30 fiscal year-end and shares were distributed as follows: Brian 46 percent; Jason and Stuart 27 percent each. Brian and Stuart, who were both single, planned to live on site.

Each of the three partners had assumed a distinct area of responsibility. Brian's duties included control of the marketing program, purchasing activities, and the administrative function. Jason, who was in the process of completing a bartender's training course at the local community college, would take charge of liquor operations, inventories, and floor management and security. Stuart's area of responsibility was the physical upkeep and maintenance of the building and grounds. For now, each would be responsible for making the hiring decisions for his respective area of control.

Potential employees were readily available by virtue of a large local pool of university and community college students who were naturally interested in part-time and seasonal positions. However the question of full-time staff was still unresolved. The Andersons were pleased with the three recruits they had recently brought on board, but until the business was operational, they could not be entirely certain of their staffing needs. Nonetheless, with the opening only a month away, it was crucial that they secure the services of a competent head chef quickly. Two prospects had already been interviewed for this pivotal position, but neither was deemed to be suitable.

The principals had been quite successful at minimizing the costs of the refurbishing program. There was no price attached to the labour they each contributed, and they managed to acquire fixtures, furniture, utensils, and sundry decorative items at bargain prices through bulk purchases and auctions.

They had also taken great pains to ensure that their remodelling efforts would provide for smooth operations: for example, their plans had allowed for such details as the efficient movement of food and accessories from the kitchen to the different dining areas and the proper placement of lighting and sound equipment.

External Support/Additional Funding

As the time to mobilize the organization's resources drew near, it was quite apparent that substantial outside funding would be required. The Andersons' huge cash contribution underlined their total commitment to the venture, but they were hesitant to inject any more equity themselves. They preferred to retain their personal liquidity as a hedge against any operating losses that the business might incur during the startup period, rather than exhausting their resources to cover outstanding capital expenditures. Secondly, they had so far been able to avoid personal borrowings and Brian in particular was adamant about keeping his personal indebtedness to a minimum.

In February, 1989, a loan application for $150 000 had been submitted to the local branch of a major chartered bank. This bank had a large presence in western Canada, and Brian had been impressed by its recent promotions featuring lending programs for independent business. He felt that the amount requested would be adequate to cover the completion of the renovations as well as working capital needs for the first year of operation. However, it was now clear that due to certain overlooked items and cost overruns in other areas, even further financing would have to be arranged.

At about the same time as the loan request was prepared, Brian had enlisted the services of an old high school friend, Bob Van Pelt, to put together an accounting system. Bob was a junior member of a large Vancouver C.G.A. firm, and helped the Andersons assemble the *pro-forma* financial statements detailed in Exhibits 1 and 2. When the bank had expressed some doubts about its ability to approve the $150 000 loan, Bob referred Brian to the Federal Business Development Bank. This institution, which specialized in financial assistance and advisory services for small business, was generally recognized as being more liberal in its lending policies. Though he lacked an in-depth knowledge of this particular venture, Bob was reasonably confident that the FBDB represented a much more appropriate source of funding. In fact, by May the Fraser Inn had been given an undertaking that provided for $200 000 in FBDB term financing based on the following conditions:

1　$40 000 of this amount would be used to retire the second mortgage;

2　The Andersons would be obliged to inject $15 000 in additional equity and each would be required to provide a personal guarantee in the amount of $35 000;

3　Half of the principal would be repaid monthly over a five-year term, with the remainder due and payable at maturity;

4　The company's current ratio must not fall below .8:1;

5　The loan would carry a fixed interest rate of 14.5 percent (in May of 1989, the prime rate stood at 13.5 percent as opposed to 10.75 percent one year earlier);

6　Total shareholder remuneration (whether via salary or dividends) would not exceed $90 000 per annum; and

7　In any year that revenues totalled more than $850 000, there would be a bonus payment to the lender in the amount of 10 percent of the revenues in excess of that figure.

None of the principals was pleased with items 2 or 5, and while they could live with 7, its intent left them feeling somewhat uncomfortable. Accordingly, they had as yet taken no action on this offer and were considering the merits of canvassing other potential funding sources.

Bob had also tried, albeit unsuccessfully, to interest the Andersons in retaining consultants with hospitality industry experience. He felt that such assistance could be invaluable, since it would allow the owners to focus on completing the renovations and seeing them through the initial operating stages. He was also concerned that, outside of the hiring of a permanent part-time bookkeeper, there hadn't been enough effort to shore up the company's in-house financial capability.

For his part, Brian saw the ability of the owners to work together effectively as a key strength of the enterprise; but given the various unresolved issues, he was beginning to question the wisdom of continuing to go it alone. As a group, the Andersons placed a great deal of faith in the "school of hard knocks" approach to their development as managers and they shared a clear idea of the direction they wanted the business to take. Nonetheless, there was a growing concern among them as to whether the traits on which they had always depended—diligence, enthusiasm, attention to detail—would enable them to meet the challenge of starting up an operation of this scale. Brian explained:

> Without a doubt we were very pumped up by the success of the All Ours Diner. Close control is important to us and it was our feeling that we could handle something like The Fraser Inn without a lot of outside interference. With the way this facility is shaping up, I still believe that securing the required funding won't be a major problem, even though the bank seems to have lost interest in us. We've enhanced one of the choicest pieces of property in town and I've already been approached by three different people interested in buying into the business. I'm just not sure that a silent partner wouldn't end up creating more problems for us than he/she solves.
>
> If we can just settle our main staffing issues, we should be able to open up sometime in June. Once we're up and running, we'll have a better idea of the level of financial and managerial support we'll require.

Exhibit 1

The Fraser Inn
Pro Forma
Income
Statement
for Fiscal Year
Ending June 30,
1990
(000's)

Revenue		
Food	$470	
Liquor	190	
Total	660	660
Cost of Goods Sold		
Food	200	
Liquor	64	
Wages	185	
Total	449	449
Gross Profit		211
Other Income (Cover Charges)		80
		291	$291
Operating Expenses		
Heat, light & power	20	
Maintenance supplies	10	
Insurance	7	
Telephone	4	
Legal & accounting	7	
Laundry	4	
Advertising	3	
Property tax	12	
Entertainment costs	45	
Vehicle expense	4	
Depreciation	34	
Management salaries	75	
Interest	49	
Miscellaneous	3	
Total	277	$277
Earnings Before Tax		14	$14
Income Tax (@ 23%)		3.2	
Net Profit		**10.8**	**10.8**

Exhibit I
(cont'd)

Notes To
Income
Statement

1. The forecast of food sales is based on the following details:

	Average Cheque Per Person	Daily Turnover Mon-Wed	Thur-Sat	Sun	Weekly Volume
Light Dining (120 seats)	$ 6.00	.67	1.25	.5	$4,507
Fine Dining (60 seats)	$14.00	.5	.8	1.5	$4,536
					$9,043

2. Liquor sales are projected as 40% of food sales.

3. "Other Income" consists of cover charges for special entertainment events and is estimated on the basis of 30 events attracting an average audience of 375 (includes mezzanine level seating) at $7.00 per admission.

4. For illustration purposes, the F.B.D.B. financing package has been used to determine interest expense, repayment requirements and capital structure:

	Loan Amount	Interest Rate	Total Installments Year #1	Interest	Principal
First Mortgage (20 yr. amort.)	$225,000	9.75%	$25,269	$21,444	$ 3,825
Other Long-Term Debt	200,000	14.5 %	47,500	27,550	19,950

5. With two of the principals taking up residence at the complex, management salaries are expected to be relatively modest.

Exhibit 2

The Fraser Inn
Pro Forma
Balance Sheet
as at
June 30, 1990
(000's)

ASSETS

Current

Cash	$ 3	
Inventory	20	
Prepaid expenses	3	
		$ 26

Fixed

Land & buildings—at cost	$400		
(Less: depreciation)	(11)		
		389	
Equipment, furniture & vehicles—at cost	130		
(Less: depreciation)	(23)		
		107	
			496
			$522

LIABILITIES

Current

Current portion— Long-term debt	$ 24	$ 24

Long Term

Realty mortgage	217	
Term loan	160	
		377

SHAREHOLDERS' EQUITY

Common stock	110	
Retained earnings	11	
		121
		$522

Kampro Inc.

Kampro Inc. (KI) began operations in 1984 in the small Lake Huron town of Forest, Ontario. The business was owned by Irene and John Kubiak. It had grown out of Irene's industrial sewing experience, John's welding and machine shop experience, and their avid interest in camping. In five years the small firm had expanded to include six full-time and six part-time employees. Sales for 1989 reached $550 000 and were expected to exceed $1 million by 1992.

The product line included two small tent trailer units and a cartop unit. As well, KI produced canvas products for farm and industry, and a line of small utility trailers for two major retailers. The camping products were designed for those who wanted to camp overnight as opposed to longer-term campers. Quick setup and low prices were the main features of the Kampro units. The Kubiaks had tested the two basic models extensively and had sold a number of the early prototypes by displaying them at sports and camping shows in Sarnia and London, Ontario.

The Industry

Since the Second World War, camping in North America had grown into a major industry. The proliferation of products and services had created a number of specialized markets. The emergence of the compact car opened a market for downsized equipment to serve beginning campers, as well as those who wanted lightweight equipment in order to both camp and travel.

The large increase in the number of government run campgrounds, as well as the growth in the number of private campgrounds, had encouraged the practice of summer camping. With more available camping space had come a wide array of camping equipment, ranging from tents through tent trailers to mobile homes and recreational vehicles. The campsites had also evolved, from spots in the wilderness to fully serviced lots for the camping home-away-from-home.

Forest, Ontario

Located near Lake Huron in southwestern Ontario, Forest was a community with a population of 2600 residents. While primarily involved in serving the surrounding farming community, Forest was also involved in the tourist trade and had a small but growing light-industrial base. During the summer months, large numbers of campers and cottagers used the town's commercial services.

The Company

Kampro Inc. had been started by Herbert Kubiak as the Kubiak Machine and Welding Service in 1949. It provided a variety of services to the surrounding farm community until Herb Kubiak retired in 1984. At that time the business was put up for sale, but there were no takers. As a result, John Kubiak, Herb's son, decided to return to Forest and take over the family business.

John had been trained by his father as a welder and had worked for a manufacturing firm in Toronto as a maintenance supervisor. Irene had also been employed in the Toronto area, as an industrial sewer working with canvas products. She had previous experience as a sailmaker and as a tent and awning designer, and before leaving Toronto was supervising a small operation which produced canvas and fabric products for the military and heavy industry. Both had considered starting a small business in Toronto but had never pursued the interest. The need to deal with the family business provided an opportunity, which they decided to act on in 1984.

While John operated the machine shop for a few months, it was not the Kubiaks' intention to continue that business. Through some Toronto contacts John managed to negotiate a contract for the production of utility trailers, so early in 1984 the Kubiaks leased some additional space and began to produce the order. Irene's skills in the area of canvas design and production provided the impetus for manufacturing a camping version of the utility trailer. This was produced during the summer of 1984 for display at the fall and winter camping shows. Production began early in 1985 and the first units were delivered in March of that year.

The company's involvement in canvas products began with the production of awnings and miscellaneous products for farmers and campers. In 1985, Irene designed special canvas covers for a large firm of long distance truckers, and this resulted in additional orders from both Canadian and US companies. Farm equipment covers, grain storage covers, and custom canvas products had also generated a growing volume of business for Kampro.

In July of 1984 the Kubiaks incorporated Kampro and moved to new facilities. While the plant was larger than they required, the Kubiaks were able to negotiate a lease for part of the space with an option on additional space as required. By 1988, the business had expanded to fill the entire facility.

Marketing

The three major product groups were all marketed differently. Canvas products were produced and sold direct from the factory. Utility trailers were manufactured under contract and sold to two chain-store buyers. The camping trailers were sold through dealers, although some orders were taken by company representatives at sport and camping shows and fall fairs (where the products were promoted to dealers). In each product group Kampro was considering some changes. KI planned to add a version of the utility trailers to the camp trailer line and offer these for sale through a variety of recreational vehicle dealers. As well, KI had approached some rental equipment operators and this had resulted in the development of a special utility unit for rental use in the London area. Kubiak planned to mail promotional materials to rental equipment operations across Canada.

In the area of camp trailers the plan was to display at all the major shows in both eastern and western Canada in 1990–91. John hoped to increase their dealer complement to 150 by the end of 1991, up from the 31 dealers now used in southern Ontario.

With respect to canvas products, sales would continue to be factory direct. KI was considering the addition of new cutting equipment and some additional sewing machines to produce industrial products. Irene planned to quote on some of the business that her former Toronto employer had dropped since her departure.

Products

Started as a local machine shop, the company also produced a variety of products for local needs. However, since taking over, the Kubiaks had increased their emphasis on the Kampro line. To keep Irene and her staff busy in the canvas shop they also produced a variety of custom-made canvas products.

Camping Products   Kampro produced a cartop tent unit and two camping trailers for use with compact cars and motorcycles. The major differences were in wheel sizes (8″ and 12″). The trailer units featured a simple fold-up tent with mattress and storage space for camping equipment. Unlike the more elaborate family models, which featured built-in storage, cooking, refrigeration and heating equipment, the Kampro units were designed for the travelling camper, particularly those who owned small cars or motorcycles. The units could accommodate two adults.

The cartop unit, designed for compact cars, slept two and folded flat when not in use. It was sold with a cartop carrier and could accommodate up to 300 kg. The unit, weighing 30 kg, could be set up quickly and removed from the car top when not in use.

Canvas Products   The major canvas products were designed for farm and industry sales. Machinery covers, temporary storage units, truck and trailer covers, canopies and awnings were manufactured for a variety of customers. About 50 percent of these products were sold through retailers, and the balance were sold direct as part of contract quotations. All canvas products were sold from the factory, with commissions allowed where orders were placed by equipment dealers. Since much of the work required custom manufacture, the commissions were limited to 10 percent. Orders for five units or more were quoted and the buyer established the retail selling price. KI maintained minimal finished goods inventories for its canvas products.

The major new product, planned for 1990, was a canvas carport. While there were competitive units on the market, John Kubiak felt that his design would result in lower prices and easier setup. The units were designed for cottagers and for winter storage of cars and recreational vehicles.

Utility Trailers   Kampro produced utility trailers for two major retail chains. Total production exceeded 800 units in 1989 and was broken down over four models (see Table 1). The trailers were designed with a steel frame and featured a marine plywood box and floor with reinforced steel corners. The model variations included two wheel sizes (8″ and 12″) and two box sizes (4′ x 4′ and 4′ x 6′).

The trailer models, premium priced in the marketplace, were designed to handle 250 kg (8″ wheels) and 500 kg (12″ wheels). For the heavier weights and longer trips, KI recommended the models with 12″ wheels. All units were finished with rust-proof red paint and guaranteed against defects in manufacture for up to one year from the date of purchase. Guarantees for the running gear (wheels, axles, bearings and tires) were provided by the manufacturers of this equipment.

Projections for 1990 and 1991 utility trailer sales called for approximate

Table I		1986	1987	1988	1989
Kampro Inc.	Utility Trailers	$ 61,644	$ 73,002	$131,885	$193,017
Sales by	Camping Units	35,470	59,690	94,800	229,630
Product Line	Canvas Products	99,670	121,340	118,660	121,927
	Miscellaneous	62,221	54,970	27,690	12,430
		$259,005	$309,002	$373,035	$557,004

increases of 5 percent in each year (see Exhibit 1). Currently, Kampro was looking at the possibility of distributing units through their camping equipment dealers, but thus far these distribution proposals were only in the planning stage. Kampro had also sold a number of units to rental equipment dealers and was exploring this market for future sales.

Markets

Kubiak, a motorcycle enthusiast, had developed the original prototype to use when he and Irene went camping. Subsequently, more as a result of customer interest, his market interests broadened to include camp trailer units for very small cars. Later, he had added a cartop camper to meet the needs of travellers who wanted to camp but did not want the inconvenience of an elaborate, time-consuming setup. Canvas products were sold by tender, contract, or through agents, while utility trailers were handled on a contract basis with large distributors such as Canadian Tire and Home Hardware.

Distribution

In the fall of 1989 Kampro had 31 dealers, most of whom were camping and recreational equipment dealers located in southern Ontario. Two were motorcycle dealers, one located in Detroit, Michigan and the other in Winnipeg, Manitoba. In both cases these dealers had seen the product in southern Ontario and had contacted Kampro. The Kubiaks had not attempted to sell the product line outside of southern Ontario.

Pricing

Kampro priced on the basis of cost estimates. Competitive products, where they existed, provided some guidelines, but in the main the company sought product niches where there was no direct competition and then priced to make a reasonable profit. Currently, the camping products had no direct competition. The utility trailers were priced above the lightweight metal models sold by most retailers. Canvas products were priced on the basis of cost, although Irene felt that some of the military and industrial contracts they were looking at would have to be priced to meet the Toronto competition. She reasoned that such contracts would provide sewing work during the fall and winter when camping sales were slow and products had to be priced lower.

Advertising and Promotion

Kampro did only a limited amount of advertising. Much of the cost of advertising and promotion arose from printing brochures for the camping line. These brochures were distributed free of charge to dealers who stocked the line. As well, they were distributed at trade and sports shows as part of the product promotion. Some local advertising was done as a community support activity. Kampro also advertised in some camping publications and maintained listings in the Yellow Pages. The company did not advertise their canvas products or their utility trailers, although some brochures and information had been printed for use in a direct-mail campaign they were planning.

Marketing Plans

While Kampro had no formal planning, the Kubiaks had a list of things they wanted to do. Among these was a plan to round out the product line currently offered to camping and recreational dealers. This line would include small utility trailers similar to those sold to the chain retailers, as well as the tent trailers and the cartop units. After some consideration of trade show costs, John Kubiak had decided to use established agents to sell the line outside of Ontario. Many of these agents attended regional shows and could exhibit the Kampro line along with their related products.

Currently, canvas products were sold mostly by contract, with some custom orders sold from the shop. The Kubiaks were looking for some lines that were not seasonal, in an effort to maintain stable employment in the canvas shop over the winter months.

Finally, the shop continued to provide welding and machine shop services to local customers. John Kubiak doubted that this work was profitable and knew it interfered with the other production activities but, so far, had not made the decision to stop.

While Kampro speculated about future sales growth, no specific projections were made. As a result, sales were missed, deliveries were late, and costs of production were higher than necessary. Without sales projections, both purchasing and operations activities were hindered and cost control was non-existent. Kubiak's accountant had suggested installing a standard cost system for the volume products, but no action had been taken.

Operations

Despite increasing run sizes, Kampro continued to produce on a job lot basis in both the machine and canvas shops. There was very little finished goods inventory, since all units were produced against firm orders. It was John's plan to change this in 1990. Camp trailers and cartoppers would be produced for inventory. Utility trailers would be run monthly as part of the chain orders, and some of these would be inventoried for independent sale. Sales patterns suggested that inventories could be built up during January, February, March, and April, maintained in May and June, and allowed to decline during July, August and September. A similar pattern was reflected in the delivery schedules negotiated for utility trailers.

Since the camp trailers and utility trailers shared some common parts and assembly operations, production orders could combine these units to increase run sizes. Since utility trailers were released for delivery on a predictable schedule, most of the production planning in the shop was structured around the delivery of these units. Unfortunately, the planning was *ad hoc*, and typically was done around the crises created by late deliveries. John knew that he could reduce his manufacturing cost by ordering larger quantities of wheels, axles and structural steel, since all of these were sold with substantial quantity discounts.

There was no one person assigned to control quality. Each welder, assembler, or sewer took responsibility for the quality of his or her units. John Kubiak and Vera Franklin (from the machine shop) did a cursory inspection of each unit before it was shipped, but this was mainly to ensure that the appearance met acceptable standards. There had been few reported problems with any of the products, and those that had arisen were with the utility trailers. Without exception these had been traced to overloading or misuse of the vehicles by the user.

Delivery had been a problem in 1988, and a major problem in 1989. Since the company maintained only minimal inventories, the large sales increases in camp trailers and cartoppers in these years created major difficulties. Dealers complained that three- and four-week delivery times meant lost sales. Since most buyers did not plan these purchases in advance, and the camping season was short in Canada, there was a need to deliver off the lot. Dealers complained that Kampro was not providing adequate support. It was a problem that had to be solved if Kampro was to expand beyond the southern Ontario market.

Inventories were not controlled in any formal way. Kubiak ordered when the physical count suggested a need. As a result, deliveries created production bottlenecks since the large suppliers shipped from scheduled production runs and kept only small inventories.

Manufacturing Facilities

Kampro moved into leased facilities in 1984. The building had been vacant for a number of years and required some investment to upgrade its electrical and heating services. Further investment in leasehold improvements was planned, but until the facility was close to capacity these plans were delayed.

Both the canvas shop and the machine shop provided clear space and permitted efficient equipment and material handling layouts. The building was well lit and adequately insulated. The plant had access to major highways and to suppliers in London, Toronto, Sarnia and the US. Figure I presents the plant and office layout.

The facility included 25 000 square feet of covered manufacturing and storage space and 3000 square feet of office space, broken down as follows:

- Machine Shop: 15 000 square feet,
- Canvas Shop: 6 000 square feet,
- Storage: 4 000 square feet, and
- Office: 3 000 square feet

The office space was located on the second floor of the main building. This space had not been used by Kampro and was not included in the first five-year lease.

Personnel

While there was no personnel department as such, the Kubiaks kept a separate file cabinet for all matters related to personnel. Both had experience in union shops and while Kampro was not unionized, they recognized the value of good employee records.

The company had an extensive application form which it required new applicants to complete. Stella Connors, the bookkeeper, checked references and kept all employee files up to date. Every year, each

Figure 1

Kampro Inc.
Plant / Office
Layout

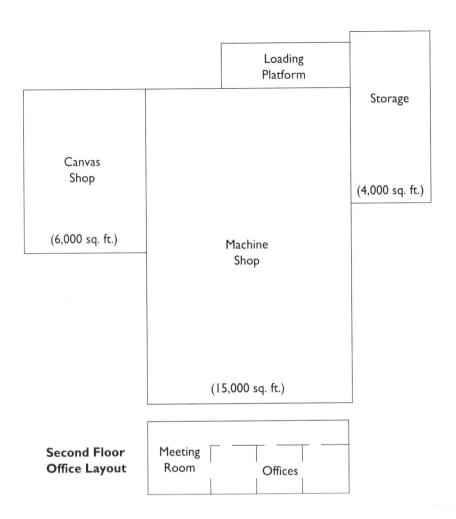

employee file was reviewed and a letter commenting on a variety of job-related activities (skills, absenteeism, etc.) was given to the employee, with a copy placed in the file.

Job safety had also received a great deal of attention at Kampro. All employees attended annual training programs put on by the Ontario Accident Prevention Association. The Kubiaks were proud of the company's safety record, which now included three years without a lost-time accident. This performance was reflected in Kampro's Worker's Compensation rates.

The company offered the two-week vacation period required by law, as well as the eight statutory holidays that were legislated in Ontario. The company also closed down for two weeks over Christmas and New Year's.

Most employees worked voluntarily on Saturdays during the fall so that they would be paid a regular salary during the Christmas shutdown.

The Kubiaks published a small handbook outlining company rules and such policies as were in place to meet company and government regulations. Even though relations were informal at the plant, the Kubiaks insisted that each employee adhere to the "company rules."

Typically, employees worked a 40-hour week, although some overtime was required. Overtime rates (1.5 times the regular rate) were paid when an employee was required to work more than eight hours per day, or more than 40 hours per week. Bankrolling Christmas hours was a voluntary activity and these were worked at straight time.

While there was no particular need for a formal organization chart, John Kubiak had drawn one up as part of his presentation to the bank. It was, he pointed out, part of the long-range plan and was not yet fully in place. Figure 2 presents Kampro's planned organization. In 1989, John and Irene Kubiak filled all of the management positions except that of bookkeeper. John supervised the machine shop and looked after purchasing and sales. Irene supervised the canvas shop and looked after the personnel function. As well, John had appointed Vera Franklin assistant supervisor, primarily to run the machine shop in his absence. Financial matters usually involved John, Irene, and the bookkeeper, and, when required, the company's accountant. The bookkeeping job was filled by Stella Connors, on a part-time basis until September 1989, and full time after that.

The Kubiaks had some difficulties with the organization chart. Both felt that their skills cut across some of the boundaries suggested by the

Figure 2

Kampro Inc. Organization

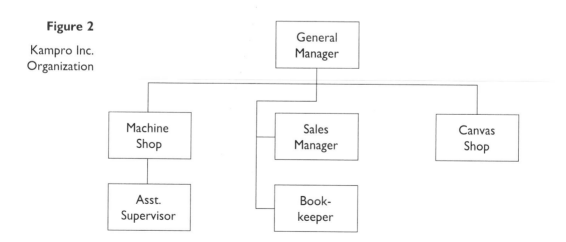

proposal, and both wanted to revise the proposal to better reflect their job interests. As of September, 1989 nothing had been done about this.

Finances

Kampro began in 1984 with a family investment of $60 000 for equipment, inventories, and supplies. Early in 1985 the original building and property were sold and a newer, larger facility leased. Proceeds from the sale were invested in Kampro and these monies, along with a $100 000 bank line, provided the company with its capital base.

Although there were small losses for the first two years, Kampro turned profitable in 1988 and increased those profits in 1989. (See Exhibits 2, 3 and 4.)

In 1986 Kampro had signed a five-year lease on its present building, with an option to buy at the end of that period. During the first three years the company had a net/net lease at $.70 per square foot of space. The rate increased by $.05 in each year of the five-year lease. During the first three years (through 1989) Kampro only paid for the space it used; during years four and five the rate included all but the office space.

The options clause provided Kampro with two choices:

1. A five-year net/net at $1.00 per square foot per year, or
2. Outright purchase of the land and building for $300 000.

Accounting and Control

Although the business had grown dramatically, little had been done in the area of accounting. Year-end statements and income tax returns were drawn up by a local accounting firm. The company's bank did not require an audit. Since the Kubiaks were involved in all operations at the plant, they felt little need for operating figures, although both felt that the time for a more formal accounting system was at hand. Cost control was informal, with prices being adjusted on an annual basis. Labour rates were reviewed annually and appropriate competitive increases were made each January 1.

Beyond those required by legislation, only two fringe benefits were paid: a 50-percent contribution to the employee's OHIP (Ontario Hospitalization Insurance Program), and an annual bonus based on profits, contributed to a RRSP (Registered Retirement Savings Plan). The bonus required an equal contribution from the employee and was locked in for five years. The minimum contribution was $500 for each full-time employee with a minimum of two years' service. Since the company did not have a pension plan, employees were encouraged to participate in this program, although how many would actually leave their money in the plan had yet to be seen as the plan had only been in effect for 3 years.

While costs for each product were revised annually, or at the time of new quotations, there was no cost accounting system in place. Periodically the Kubiaks would track individual orders or runs through the factory to check costs, but this was not done in any systematic way. Each employee completed daily additions to a production card accompanying each lot. This card indicated the date, operations, and number of hours assigned to the job lot. While these job cards were kept on file, there was no regular use of the information.

Wages and salaries were paid every second Friday and were based on hours reported through the previous Thursday at 5 p.m. The bookkeeper prepared few reports except those required by provincial and federal governments, and for the preparation of year-end statements. John Kubiak and Stella Connors prepared an aged summary of accounts receivable each month for the bank. As well, some reports were prepared from time to time for credit agencies and the small business organizations in which Kampro had memberships.

John Kubiak, commenting on the company's growth and future, observed that:

> We're doing all we can to keep Kampro's growth on track but both of us are finding that more and more things are just not getting done. It seems as though we simply move from one crisis to another. So far sales have not been a problem; it's in production where we are experiencing most of our difficulties. Later this year, when things slow down a bit, we hope to spend some time looking at the whole operation. Hopefully, we can rearrange some of the work so that it can be done by others. I've talked to a number of people, including my accountant, and some good suggestions have been made. But all of them seem to involve bringing new people into the organization—specialists, Harvey (the accountant) calls them—to help with marketing and production. I'm not sure, though, that we want a company where we can't be involved in everything. I don't think I could manage these specialists and then just sit in my office to wait and see if things would happen.

Exhibit 1			**Units**	**Retail Price**	**Dealer Price**	**Total Sales**	**Annual Sales**
Kampro Inc. Utility Trailer Sales/Pricing	1986	8–40	$120	$319	$175	$21,054	
		8–80	0	399	219	0	
		12–40	200	369	203	40,590	
		12–80	0	449	247	0	$61,644
	1987	8–40	150	329	181	27,143	
		8–80	0	409	225	0	
		12–40	220	379	208	45,859	
		12–80	0	459	252	0	73,002
	1988	8–40	170	339	186	31,697	
		8–80	100	419	230	23,045	
		12–40	240	389	214	51,348	
		12–80	100	469	258	25,795	131,885
	1989	8–40	220	349	192	42,229	
		8–80	200	429	236	47,190	
		12–40	280	399	219	61,446	
		12–80	160	479	263	42,152	193,017
	1990*	8–40	230	359	197	45,414	
		8–80	210	434	239	50,127	
		12–40	295	409	225	66,360	
		12–80	170	479	263	44,787	206,688

* Projected

Exhibit 2

	1986	1987	1988	1989
Gross Sales	$259,005	$309,002	$373,035	$557,004
Federal Excise Tax	21,386	25,514	39,968	59,679
Net Sales	237,619	283,488	333,067	497,325
Cost of goods*	172,400	197,978	227,656	339,888
Gross Profit	65,219	85,510	105,411	157,437
Expenses				
Facilities	2,440	3,059	3,160	3,345
Salaries	44,650	51,230	50,500	67,890
Benefits	6,698	7,685	7,575	10,184
Taxes	1,890	1,975	2,124	3,221
Telephone	2,105	3,270	3,480	4,310
Travel	2,560	2,950	3,140	5,120
Advertising	2,680	3,860	4,763	7,120
Depreciation	1,720	2,290	2,650	3,090
Interest	2,210	2,480	2,565	4,452
Freight	2,629	2,439	4,120	3,120
Membership	2,140	2,276	2,460	2,590
Maintenance	1,204	1,091	1,127	1,503
Utilities	690	734	1,260	2,210
Supplies	1,264	1,160	1,009	1,720
Bad debts	2,340	0	990	2,270
Leaseholds	1,000	1,400	1,600	2,000
Promotion	2,210	3,560	4,760	7,980
Total Expenses	$ 80,430	$ 91,459	$ 97,283	$132,125
Net Profits Before Tax	−15,211	−5,949	8,128	25,312
Taxes	0	0	0	4,556
Net Profits After Tax	**−15,211**	**−5,949**	**8,128**	**20,756**

Kampro Inc. Income Statements 1986–1989

Exhibit 3

	1986	1987	1988	1989
Materials	$ 65,512	$ 78,003	$ 111,618	$ 137,315
Labour	70,684	80,973	114,394	140,713
Overhead				
Facilities	18,960	19,651	24,560	23,446
Utilities	9,808	9,130	12,357	13,458
Supervision	2,000	4,000	6,000	12,000
Miscellaneous	5,436	6,221	8,727	12,956
	$ 36,204	$ 39,002	$ 51,644	$ 61,860
Cost of Goods	**$172,400**	**$197,978**	**$277,656**	**$339,888**

Kampro Inc. Cost of Goods Summary

Exhibit 4

	1986	1987	1988	1989
Interest	$3,600	$3,693	$5,924	$ 8,490
Insurance	1,230	1,690	1,870	2,240
Maintenance	340	590	760	1,689
Miscellaneous	266	248	173	537
	$5,436	$6,221	$8,727	$12,956

Kampro Inc. Miscellaneous Overhead Breakdown

Valley Potatoes Inc.

Introduction

In the spring of 1989, Collette and Jean-Marc (J.M.) Tremblay were preparing for significant changes to the family business. In order to remain competitive and become better off financially, they were about to increase capacity and install new equipment in their potato packing operation.

Background

Valley Potatoes was a family business that was managed by the third generation of the Tremblay family. It had begun as a potato farm in the valley area close to Sudbury, Ontario. This particular area within the Sudbury basin contained soil conditions ideal for growing potatoes. In addition to farming, later generations added a packaging process which packed potatoes for delivery to supermarkets. While originally used for only the family farm's crop, the packaging operation began providing services to other farms in the area.

Encouraged by the success of the packaging operation, the family decided to branch out into yet another area. The farm happened to be located on a busy regional road—ideal, they felt, for a garden centre. This, too, had proven to be a successful venture so that now Valley Potatoes was comprised of a potato farm, a potato packaging plant and a garden centre. The business employed 12 full-time and 13 part-time employees. Two full-time and three part-time employees worked in the garden centre; the remaining employees all worked in the potato packaging operation.

The Tremblays had been the owner/managers of Valley Potatoes for the last eight years. Collette primarily managed the garden centre and J.M. managed the potato growing and packaging operation. J.M. was more aggressive than the previous owners and was continually looking for ways to expand and develop the business. Although the business had done well, he felt that, for the work involved, he should be receiving greater financial rewards. In his words: "If I can't live comfortably off the land, then I don't want it."

It was this approach to the business that prompted him to cast about for ideas on how to increase the level of operations and generate more cash flow. The loans officer at the regional office of the Eastern Bank suggested that Tremblay invite an agronomist that the bank retained at head office to review the operation. On the basis of his visit and discussion with Mr. Tremblay, the agronomist suggested that the potato packaging operation was both too small in scale and too labour intensive to be financially lucrative.

Markets

While the garden centre served a local market, the bagged potatoes were delivered to stores within about a 125-km radius. Three chain stores, Dominion, IGA, and Red and White were the primary customers. In addition, Valley Potatoes served a number of restaurants in the Sudbury district, as well as National Grocers, a wholesale food distributor.

Valley Potatoes owned and leased trucks for delivery. Each truck required two men since there were no forklift trucks at the retail stores and they had to be unloaded by hand. There was no charge for delivery.

Mr. Tremblay had tried to break into other chain stores but had met resistance from store managers, who argued that they could get the potatoes cheaper from the south, since trucks from Toronto made daily deliveries anyway. They reasoned that the potatoes had no delivery cost since halting deliveries of potatoes would have no effect on the cost of sending trucks to Sudbury every day.

Prices were determined by the market (which meant the large chain stores) so that Valley Potatoes really had no influence in this regard. Prices for potatoes had been distressingly low for the past four years.

The Expansion

Improved efficiency, improved product quality, and greater capacity were the main reasons for the proposed expansion. Since a lot of southern potatoes that were in the stores were washed, J.M. considered it important that the perceived quality of the Valley Potatoes product be improved by implementing a washing and grading operation. As well, the following additions were contemplated:

New packaging line	$175,000
New building	125,000
Renovated storage	42,000
Diesel truck	69,500
Total Additions	$411,500

Mr. Tremblay was to take charge of the expansion program. He would retain contractors and oversee the progress of the expansion himself.

Operating Characteristics After Proposed Expansion

Mr. and Mrs. Tremblay's home, the potato packaging operation, the garden centre, and the farm occupied 70 acres of land, and they rented an additional 300 acres of land. Currently, 200 acres were committed to potato growing with an approximate yield of 4 million pounds of potatoes per year. Total production was limited by the storage facilities at the farm.

In addition to its own potatoes, Valley also bagged potatoes from other local farms and potatoes purchased in bulk from the United States. The breakdown of volume after the expansion was to be:

from the potato farm:	4 million pounds
from other local farms:	1 " "
from the US:	5 " "
Total packaged	10 million pounds

Currently, all the packing operations were done by hand, and there was no washing or sizing of potatoes, which lowered their perceived quality. The new packaging operation involved the following steps: The potatoes arrived at the operation in boxes. The boxes were emptied into a continuous auger which delivered the potatoes to a washing device. After the potatoes were washed, they were dried and delivered on a conveyor to a grading station. The grading operation involved at least three people who removed culls from the batch. (About 25 percent of the potatoes at this point were culls. Valley paid only for the good potatoes.) After grading, the potatoes went to an automatic sizer, which sorted the potatoes by weight into three categories: small, medium and jumbo. An automatic bagging machine produced 10 lb and 20 lb bags. Fifty-pound bags were packed manually by one person who took the bags off and tied them.

The packed bags were piled onto pallets and delivered by a forklift to a stack room for storage. J.M. Tremblay was unhappy with the current situation, because the stack room could handle only about two trailer loads of potatoes. In addition, the room was not refrigerated, which meant that storage time was limited. From here, the potatoes were ready for delivery to customers.

Financing

The agronomist met with the commercial loans officer of the regional branch and developed a financing strategy that took advantage of government programs. The branch was certain that the following financing would be available:

1. A Department of Agriculture Northern Grant of $20 000;
2. A Northern Ontario Development Corporation (NODC) loan of $60 000, which would be forgivable over a five-year period if the owners remained in the business;
3. A new truck loan, financed separately by a finance company with payments of $1471 monthly over a five-year period; and
4. The remaining $262 000 would be provided by the Eastern Bank as an increase in the outstanding demand loan.

Financial Assessment

The government departments and the bank were so positive about the expansion, Mr. and Mrs. Tremblay thought that the financing package was complete. At a social event, J.M. related the story to a local business consultant. The consultant agreed that, with the parties involved, the project was sure to go ahead. However, when the consultant asked if a financial analysis of the impact of the expansion had been undertaken, J.M. had to admit that he had certainly not conducted one himself and he was unaware of any other analysis being done.

The consultant suggested that the two men spend a couple of evenings collecting data and doing the financial assessment. Mr. Tremblay agreed that it would not hurt to do so. The only financial information available was that provided by Valley Potatoes' accountants. This consisted of an Income Statement (Exhibit 1), Balance Sheet (Exhibit 2), a Statement of Changes in Financial Position (Exhibit 3), and Notes to the Statements (Exhibit 4). The consultant noted that these were interim statements for the first 8 months of 1988. Mr. Tremblay stated that the year-end statements were not normally provided by the accountants until May or June. Therefore, these statements were the only ones available for analysis.

The consultant proceeded to develop forecasts for the new operation with the help of Mr. Tremblay. The results of these efforts are provided in Exhibits 5 to 8. Finally, the consultant assembled data pertaining to potato purchases and sales over the last three months in order to determine the spread between the cost of bulk potatoes and the selling price for packed potatoes (shown as Exhibit 9). The consultant was somewhat surprised to hear from J.M. that no increase in price would be secured as a result of having the potatoes washed. Therefore, the most recent spread between cost and selling price was used for forecasting purposes.

While Mr. Tremblay was working with the consultant, he received a phone call from the bank's agronomist. Since he would be in Sudbury the following day, the agronomist thought that it would be an ideal time to finalize the expansion plans. He indicated that he was quite willing to accompany J.M. to the regional branch of the Eastern Bank in order to secure the financing. Mr. Tremblay indicated that he thought he would be able to give the agronomist his decision some time the next day.

Exhibit I

Valley Potatoes Inc. Statement of Income for the 8 Months Ended August 31, 1988 (Unaudited) and Year Ended December 31, 1987

	Potatoes	1988 Garden Centre	Total	1987 Total
Sales	$679,559	$330,928	$1,010,487	$992,057
Cost of Sales (Note 6)	496,554	262,778	759,332	584,066
Gross margin	183,005	68,150	251,155	407,991
Expenses				
Advertising & business promotion	–	11,151	11,151	32,182
Electricity	2,593	2,259	4,852	3,861
Equipment leasing	–	3,717	3,717	3,717
Heat	2,128	2,378	4,506	2,590
Land rental	2,620	–	2,620	2,139
Plowing & harvesting	2,155	–	2,155	1,773
Repairs & maintenance				
–buildings	7,711	243	7,954	12,941
–equipment & vehicles	26,533	–	26,533	15,546
Taxes				
–realty	487	486	973	1,129
–business	100	100	200	176
Vehicle expenses				
–gas & oil	16,351	–	16,351	13,055
–insurance	2,265	–	2,265	1,994
–licences	1,013	–	1,013	802
–leasing	10,710	–	10,710	12,248
Wages	127,603	62,076	189,679	188,518
	202,269	82,410	284,679	292,671
	(19,264)	(14,260)	(33,524)	115,320
Administrative Expenses (Note 7)	77,945	35,434	113,379	99,319
	(97,209)	(49,694)	(146,903)	16,001

	Potatoes	1988 Garden Centre	Total	1987 Total
Other Income				
Crop insurance proceeds	–	–	–	14,217
Potato subsidy	1,000	–	1,000	1,000
	1,000	–	1,000	15,217
Earnings (loss) before taxes	(96,209)	(49,694)	(145,903)	31,218
Income taxes				
–current (recovered)			(2,008)	2,008
–deferred			(5,175)	1,800
			(7,183)	3,808
Net Earnings			**$ (138,720)**	**$ 27,410**

Exhibit 2		1989	1988	1987
Valley Potatoes Inc. Balance Sheet (Unaudited)	**ASSETS**			
	Current			
	Cash	$ 15,218	$ 1,926	$ 700
	Accounts receivable	57,498	58,641	69,678
	Inventories	155,500	214,849	155,188
	Prepaid expenses	4,069	1,343	2,510
	Income taxes receivable	2,008	–	5,050
		234,293	276,759	233,126
	Fixed (Note 2)			
	Land, buildings and equipment	744,635	319,206	214,872
	Less: Accumulated depreciation	139,050	107,071	80,827
		605,585	212,135	134,045
	Other			
	Deferred finance charges	10,436	1,925	3,273
	Deposit	500	500	500
	Incorporation costs	651	753	502
	Goodwill	5,750	6,750	7,750
		17,337	9,928	12,025
		$857,215	$498,822	$379,196

LIABILITIES

Current

Bank advances	–	–	19,498
Bank loans (Note 3)	463,199	122,000	141,000
Accounts payable and accrued charges	156,032	159,944	95,473
Income tax payable	–	2,008	–
Current portion of long-term debt	21,570	11,235	11,235
	641,801	295,187	267,206
Long-Term Debt (Note 4)	156,106	43,722	56,287
Deferred Income Taxes	–	5,175	3,375

SHAREHOLDERS' EQUITY

Capital Stock (Note 5)

Issued and fully paid

7,500 preference shares Class A	75,000	75,000	–
4,810 preference shares Class B	48,100	–	–
200 common shares	200	200	200
	123,300	75,200	200

Retained Earnings (Deficit)

Balance at beginning of year	79,538	52,128	38,787
Net income (loss) for the year	(138,720)	27,410	13,341
	(59,182)	79,538	52,128
Deduct: Dividends declared	4,820	–	$379,196
	(63,992)	79,538	
	$857,215	**$498,822**	

Exhibit 3

Valley Potatoes Inc. Statement of Changes in Financial Position for the Eight Months Ended Aug. 31, 1988 and Twelve Months Ended December 31, 1987 (Unaudited)

	1988	1987
Sources of Working Capital		
Operations		
Net income for the year	–	$ 27,410
Depreciation and amortization	–	27,347
Deferred income taxes	–	1,800
Amortization of deferred finance charges	–	1,348
	–	57,905
Disposal of equipment	–	1,354
Issue of preference shares	48,100	–
Total sources	48,100	59,259
Uses of Working Capital		
Operations		
Net loss for the year	137,233	–
Depreciation and amortization	(31,594)	–
Amortization of deferred finance charges	(2,777)	–
Deferred income taxes	5,175	–
	108,037	–
Additions to fixed assets	445,429	105,689
Less: Long-term financing	(159,229)	(75,000)
grant proceeds	(20,000)	–
	266,200	30,689
Reduction of long-term debt	46,845	12,565
Incorporation costs	–	353
Deferred finance charges	11,288	–
Dividends	4,810	–
Total uses	437,180	43,607
Increase (Decrease) in Working Capital Position	(389,080)	15,652
Working Capital Deficiency at Beginning of Year	18,428	34,080
Working Capital Deficiency at End of Year	**$407,508**	**$ 18,428**

Exhibit 4

Valley Potatoes Inc. Notes to the Financial Statements for the Eight Months Ended Aug. 31, 1988 (Unaudited)

NOTE 1: Summary of Significant Accounting Policies

a) Inventories are stated at cost.

b) Fixed assets are stated at cost. Depreciation is provided on the diminishing balance method at the following annual rates:

Parking area   – 8%
Buildings   – 5% and 10%
Equipment   – 20%
Automotive equipment – 30%

c) Incorporation costs and goodwill are stated at cost, less accumulated amortization. Amortization is provided at 10% per annum on a straight line basis.

d) The company accounts for income taxes using the deferral method of tax allocation, under which income taxes are provided in the year transactions affect net income regardless of when such items are recognized for tax purposes. Timing differences giving rise to deferred income taxes relate to depreciation—where the cumulative amounts claimed for tax purposes exceed the amount of depreciation booked.

NOTE 2: Fixed Assets

	1988		1987		1986	
	Cost	Accumulated Depreciation	Cost	Accumulated Depreciation	Cost	Accumulated Depreciation
Land	75,835	–	75,835	–	–	–
Parking area	15,187	1,987	10,484	839	–	–
Buildings	258,538	30,608	78,213	20,516	68,775	14,358
Machinery & equipment	284,535	66,337	113,635	55,921	105,058	41,493
Automotive equipment	110,540	40,118	41,039	29,795	41,039	24,976
	$744,635	**$139,050**	**$319,206**	**$107,071**	**$214,872**	**$80,827**

NOTE 3: Bank Loans

The bank loans are secured by an assignment of inventories, a general assignment of book debts, an assignment of crop and fire insurance policies, a mortgage on real property, machinery, and equipment and a floating charge debenture payable on demand.

Exhibit 4
(cont'd)

NOTE 4: Long-Term Debt

	1988	1987
Mortgage payable, $610 monthly including interest at 9.3% per annum (secured by a first chattel mortgage on equipment and automotive equipment)	–	34,160
Loan payable, $326 monthly including interest, secured by lien on equipment	11,467	15,383
Loan payable, $1,471 monthly including interest, secured by lien on vehicle	69,978	–
Loan payable, Province of Ontario	60,000	–
Advances from shareholders	36,231	5,414
	177,676	54,957
Deduct: Current portion	21,570	11,235
	$156,106	**$43,722**

NOTE 5: Capital Stock

The authorized capital stock of the company consists of 2,000 Class A, 7%, non-voting, non-cumulative, redeemable preference shares with a par value of $10 each, 15,000 Class B, 10%, non-voting, non-cumulative, redeemable preference shares with a par value of $10 each and ranking in priority to the Class A preference shares, and 10,000 common shares without par value.

During the year, the authorized capital stock was increased by $150,000 and 4,810 Class B preference shares were issued.

Notes to the Financial Statements for the year ended December 31, 1989 (Unaudited)

NOTE 6: Cost of Sales

	1988			1987
	Potatoes	**Garden Centre**	**Total**	**Total**
Inventory at beginning of year	36,078	178,771	214,849	155,188
Purchases	379,044	177,823	556,867	551,308
Freight, customs, and packaging	98,996	14,184	113,180	92,419
Fertilizers, pesticides	29,936	–	29,936	–
	544,054	370,778	914,832	798,915
Deduct:				
Inventory at end of year	47,500	108,000	155,500	214,849
	$496,554	**$262,778**	**$759,332**	**$584,066**

Exhibit 4
(cont'd)

NOTE 7:   Administrative Expenses

	1988			**1987**
	Potatoes	**Garden Centre**	**Total**	**Total**
Bad debts	–	1,456	1,456	5,007
Capital tax	459	459	918	1,084
Depreciation & amortization	26,284	6,797	33,081	27,347
Dues and fees	170	425	595	1,066
Employee benefits	5,199	2,561	7,760	7,282
Interest and bank charges	24,750	15,661	40,411	24,772
Interest on long-term debt	4,785	–	4,785	5,195
Insurance	7,356	464	7,820	6,768
Life insurance	951	951	1,902	1,091
Office	2,383	2,383	4,766	5,282
Professional fees	2,016	1,650	3,666	8,313
Telephone	2,127	2,127	4,254	4,103
Travel	965	–	965	2,009
Directors' fees	500	500	1,000	–
	$ 77,945	**$ 35,434**	**$113,379**	**$ 99,319**

Exhibit 5	Dues and Fees	$ 1,200
	Seed Potatoes	25,000
Valley Potatoes	Fertilizer	25,000
Inc.	Pesticides	14,617
Forecasted	Green Manure	3,810
Potato Growing	Labour	32,451
Costs, 1989	Land Rental	2,620
	Custom Work	2,155
	Property Tax	616
	Fuel (Gas and Diesel)	2,678
	Repairs and Maintenance	15,000
		$125,147

Yield: 200 cwt/acre × 200 acres × 100 lbs/cwt = 4,000,000 lbs.

Salable Potatoes (less 25% losses) = 3,000,000 lbs

Cost/lb Salable Potatoes = $125,147 / 3,000,000 = $0.0417/lb.

Exhibit 6	**Variable Costs**	
	Bags (.00631/lb.)	$ 63,100
Valley Potatoes		
Inc.	**Fixed Costs**	
Forecasted	Labour (1 shift basis)	78,624
Packaging Costs,	Fuel (drying)	4,095
1989	Electricity	3,861
	Propane	1,512
	Repairs and maintenance—equipment	7,148
	Lease on towmotor	3,840
	Repairs and Maintenance—building	7,711
	Labour—delivery	44,834
	Gas and oil—delivery	15,181
	Vehicle: insurance	2,265
	license	1,013
	leasing	26,160
	Insurance: building and equipment	8,216
	Heat	2,234
	Total Fixed Costs	**$206,694**

Exhibit 7	Sales	$331,000
Valley Potatoes Inc. Forecasted Operating Results, Garden Centre, 1989	Gross Margin (33%)	109,230

Fixed Costs:

Advertising	$ 11,151
Equipment leasing	3,717
Repairs and maintenance—building	243
Wages	62,076
Total Fixed Costs	**$ 77,187**
Operating Profit	**$ 32,043**

Exhibit 8

Valley Potatoes Inc. Overhead Expenses, 1989 Forecast

Cash Expenses

Bad debts	$ 1,500
Capital tax	1,000
Life insurance	1,902
Office	4,766
Professional fees	3,660
Telephone	4,411
Travel	1,000
Director's fees	1,000
Taxes: business and realty	557
Total	**$19,802**

Depreciation and Amortization

Class	Rate	Cost	1989 Depreciation
Land	0	75,835	0
Parking	8%	15,187	1,056
Buildings	6%	258,538	13,676
Machinery & Equipment	20%	284,535	43,640
Auto	30%	110,540	21,127
			$79,499

Exhibit 9	Potato Sales				Purchases	
	Month	**Cash**	**Charge**	**Total**	**$**	**lbs.**
Valley Potatoes						
Inc.	Jan.	$4,273	$31,359	$ 35,632	$23,694	631,860
Potato Sales	Feb.	3,527	33,159	36,686	19,703	314,655
and Purchases	Mar.	3,200	32,774	35,974	18,229	375,740
to Mar. 31, 1989	**Total**			**$108,292**	**$61,626**	**1,322,255**

CASE 5-4

Dynamic Satellite Systems

D ynamic Satellite Systems (Dysat) had not yet been formally incorporated. It was about to be formed by Gordon Taft, who was negotiating the sale of his current company, Dynasound Ltd. "You know," Taft said,

I thought when we formed Dynasound we had undertaken a tough job. We didn't have much money and the banks wanted a detailed business plan. So, with my accountant, we pulled together four or five pages, put the family home up as collateral and we were in business. We leased in a new mall, advertised the product line and built the business one step at a time as our money allowed. Twice we expanded the Chatham store and then added outlets in Sarnia and Wallaceburg. Our first business plan was our last. This new business is a whole different ball game, and this time I don't even need bank money to start it. In fact, the financing seems to be the easiest part. I'm faced with a whole lot of choices and I don't think it is feasible to go at it a little bit at a time. This time I need some kind of plan just to get a total picture of my new proposal. I'd like to think that I should be able to lay it all out before I make the first major commitments, but it isn't coming together. I do need a business plan for the bank manager but, even more, I think I need one to ensure that I've thought my way through this new business startup; and I'm finding that it is a major undertaking. Given that I am considering manufacturing, wholesaling, retailing, and financing the retail paper, it is a much more complicated business than Dynasound.

Dynasound Ltd. (DL) sold a full range of sound equipment in southwestern Ontario. During the last ten years the company, or more correctly its sole shareholder, Gordon Taft, had dabbled in the sale and installation of satellite systems out of the Chatham store. While this particular aspect of the sound business had resulted in less than $40 000 in sales in 1987, Taft was convinced that it could be developed into a profitable business. As well, it would offer him an opportunity to invest in a growth area, as opposed to leaving his money in the more mature areas of the sound business. The increasing number of franchise dealers and the increasing emphasis on price competition made the high service areas of the business more attractive to people like Taft. It was his intention to sell DL without the satellite communications systems. He thought if the prospects justified it that he would invest in a new company to build, lease/sell and install satellite communications systems. That new company would be called Dynamic Satellite Systems.

The Satellite Dish Industry

While satellite systems had been sold in the area around Chatham for some time, Taft believed that the market had only started to develop. The competitors, though numerous, were not well organized and seemed to be mostly part-time participants, few of whom had made a serious commitment to the business. The major competition came from the expansion of cable systems, but as the cost of satellite systems came down and the cable operators raised their prices for comparable packages, Taft felt that satellite systems could now be sold on a sound economic basis; even in the cities, prices would be competitive with cable systems operators. The rural market was largely untapped, and here, too, there was an immediate opportunity to sell satellite systems.

Recently, some large producers such as General Instruments and Anden had been recruiting dealers. Both offered excellent equipment and some dealers in the area had begun selling these lines. Taft felt that these manufacturers should be considered before he made a final decision on his product line. Both offered premium price equipment. (For a summary of technical specifications, regulatory policies, and local regulations, see the attached appendix.)

Gordon Taft and Dynasound Limited

Dynasound Ltd. began its operations in Chatham, Ontario in 1968. In 1970, Jim Taft opened a second outlet in Wallaceburg, Ontario and in 1976 Dynasound opened in Sarnia. From 1976 through 1982 high interest rates and a sluggish economy resulted in limited growth and some unprofitable years. Products such as video players, equipment rentals, and CB radios sustained the operations. From 1982 through 1987, Dynasound experienced tremendous growth in both sales and profitability. Early in 1988 Taft decided to sell Dynasound and concentrate on the manufacture and sale of satellite dishes. (See Table 1 for unit sales of satellite dishes through Dynasound.)

Table 1

Dynamic Satellite Systems Unit Sales by Dish Size

Size	Unit Sales				
	1983	1984	1985	1986	1987
4 ft.	0	0	4	9	12
6 ft.	0	0	2	2	2
8 ft.	0	0	0	0	0
10 ft.	2	4	5	7	11
Total	2	4	11	18	25
Revenue (000)	$3.4	$7.7	$17.5	$27.7	$37.8

Dynasound had been selling satellite dishes since 1983. All of the sales were handled by Taft and, as a result, most were made out of the Chatham store. (See Tables 2 and 3.) He recommended aluminum mesh in the ten-foot size, although sales of the smaller dishes had increased since 1986. Since 1983 (1983–1987) Dynasound had sold 60 units. Sales in both Wallaceburg and Sarnia were referred to Taft in Chatham. He then contacted the customers and provided quotes for the required equipment. This procedure, in Taft's opinion, was not very effective; he was able to close only one sale in 20 requests, a rate far below that experienced in Chatham. This factor would be important in the plans for his future company, particularly if his marketing was to include Dynasound as an agent.

Gordon Taft enjoyed selling and prided himself on his product knowledge in the sound and electronics business. He felt that his selling skills were particularly relevant in the satellite systems area, since it was a significant purchase and the range of product, price, and specifications was confusing for most customers. Taft's experience, however, was mostly in

Table 2

Dynamic Satellite
Systems
Unit Sales
by Store

	1983	1984	1985	1986	1987
Chatham	2	4	9	14	20
Wallaceburg	0	0	2	4	4
Sarnia	0	0	0	0	1
Total	2	4	11	18	25

Table 3

Dynamic Satellite
Systems
Dollar Sales
by Store

	1983	1984	1985	1986	1987
Chatham	3,440	6,720	14,310	21,560	29,400
Wallaceburg	00	00	3,180	6,160	5,880
Sarnia	00	00	00	00	1,486
	3,440	6,720	17,490	27,720	36,766

These figures do not include installation. Taft was considering the use of dealers such as Dynasound. They would sell the satellite systems for a commission, Dysat would install and service the units. He also wanted to consider direct sales, using an 800 number and his own sales personnel.

the retail setting. He realized that selling satellite dishes over a three-city area would require a different approach.

Dynamic Satellite Systems (DySat)

Throughout the negotiations to sell Dynasound, Taft protected the small area involving satellite dish sales. It was agreed that Taft would retain the inventory and equipment related to satellite dishes for his new venture. It was also agreed that the Dynasound stores would act as agents for Dysat if that fit into Taft's marketing plans, but it was not an important factor in the sale and thus far Taft had not decided how he would approach the satellite systems market after the sale was complete. It would not be an exclusive arrangement for Dynasound since Taft was also interested in direct sales from his planned factory.

Taft expected that 1988 sales of Dysat would total 30 units and exceed $50,000 (see Table 4). Taft could only speculate on the profitability of the satellite dish sales since the costs had never been separated from those of the retail stores.

The sale was to take effect on December 31, 1988. As currently planned, it would be a cash deal and, apart from agreeing not to go back into the sound business in the Chatham-Sarnia area for three years, there were no other restrictions on Taft's business activities.

Table 4

Dynamic Satellite
Systems
Projected Sales

Unit Sales	1989	1990	1991	1992	1993
Chatham	30	36	42	48	56
Wallaceburg	12	16	20	24	30
Sarnia	15	20	28	32	36
Total	57	72	90	104	122
Revenue	$85,500	112,320	144,000	170,560	213,500
Installation	$11,400	15,840	21,600	27,040	34,160
Total $	$96,900	128,160	165,600	197,600	247,660

The Market

Generally speaking there were two broad markets: household and commercial. These were further subdivided according to whether or not the area was served by cable. Within the areas served by cable were a number of small towns where the cost of cable was spread over a small number of households and, as a result, was high.

The commercial market—including hotels, bars, and restaurants—was saturated in many areas, although new locations provided new opportunities. Satellite systems were used to acquire specialized programming such as sports or music. As well, satellite units were used by schools and some business operations.

For many households, the accessiblity of cable systems had been a barrier to the development of this market. However, as satellite system prices had dropped, more interest had arisen in cities and towns where cost differences with other options were minimal and program variety beyond that offered by the cable systems was desired by the subscriber. Expected price decreases and improved technology, which would result in better picture quality, would likely make satellite systems more attractive in urban areas, particularly with cable service costs increasing.

The Competition

Many competitors were small operations specializing in satellite dishes; others were sound and television stores who, like Dynasound, were involved only in the sales of satellite units. Typically they bought parts from the whole-salers and manufacturers and performed the assembly on an order-by-order basis. Prices varied widely, and there was a lot of turnover in the business, making customers wary of new operators.

The Chatham-Wallaceburg-Sarnia area had a number of dealers, but few large ones. Several dealers in the larger cities in the area, Windsor and London, offered services throughout southwestern Ontario.

There were few barriers to entry. Some technical skills were required, particularly for the installation of larger systems. Parts and complete systems were readily available from a variety of wholesalers and many competitors in the area handled the same equipment.

Direct Competition   The direct competition included approximately 12 retailers who sold and/or installed satellite dishes in the market area. Over the course of his involvement with dish sales Taft had encountered only seven competitors who had been around for more than three years.

Indirect Competition   Indirect competition in the area came from the cable systems, videos, various antennae able to access the border stations and, of course, from the networks that provided regular commercial broadcasting in the market area. Both cable and video use had grown substantially over the past ten years.

Cable and Pay TV   As cable operations expanded, more households were added. As well, cable operators continued to upgrade and expand their offerings. With these changes, rates for both basic services and the special packages were increased.

Video-VHS   Originally used to copy selected material from commercial TV, VHS had become a major entertainment option. With the advent of home movie rentals at very reasonable prices, many people chose this option over the acquisition of movie channels. The equipment was still used extensively to record programs for later viewing. The units were part of the equipment used by both cable and satellite dish users.

The Consumer

Canadians own and use televisions extensively. They expect both the variety and volume of programming available to US viewers, despite living in a market that cannot easily support such options. They spend heavily on sophisticated equipment and the services necessary to use it. Census figures indicate that multiple TV ownership is common. Typical purchasers of satellite systems did not have access to cable systems, although cable price increases were contributing to increased dish sales in urban, cable serviced areas. Channel variety, picture quality, initial costs and service costs, as well as service and seller's reputation were important factors in the purchase.

Since the purchase was technical and expensive, the buyer would usually shop around, and was dependent on the skills and knowledge of the sales person. This reliance on the seller's reputation and integrity was complicated by the poor reputation of many industry participants. Since many dealers handled only one type of dish, this was a factor in the consumer's choice of a supplier. Once satisfied that the dealer was credible, the customer would look to price, since most buyers seemed to believe that the products offered by different dealers were homogeneous.

While most dealers could get all types of satellite dishes, each seemed tied to one material or another and every effort was made to convince the customer to buy this model. Most firms would only install the units they handled. One firm in the market area offered a range of materials and sizes and was prepared to acquire what the customer wanted.

Advertising

Since many of the companies participating in the satellite dish market were small, budgets for advertising were limited. Most used the Yellow Pages to attract customers who did comparison shopping before buying. Those satellite sellers that were part of the stereo and television business did in-store promotions and made reference to the product in their regular advertising. Few, however, made it an important part of the business. Flyers, advertising in TV magazines, and some TV advertising was used, but were not a big factor. Most dealers spent their advertising dollars in September and late December.

Installation Services

All competitors offered installation, some using their own service people, others employing contractors. For the larger dish installations service was essential, but most customers used the dealer only as an installer. The cost of installation was extra and varied widely depending on the situation. Some dishes were mounted on rooftops, some on poles anchored to the house or building, and others were bolted to concrete pedestals. Finally, some dealers included service and maintenance contracts as part of their service approach.

Operations

Although Taft had done no fabrication and only limited assembly work when the satellite dish operations were part of Dynasound, he was interested in considering an integrated approach for Dysat. He had space for storage, assembly and some limited fabrication (Figure 1), and after considering the costs and some of the advantages of being involved in the assembly process, he felt the investment could be justified. In addition to providing better delivery and service, the involvement would make it possible to hire two or three full-time people to assemble, service, and install the satellite units. The investment in equipment was between $30 000 and $50 000, exclusive of the office equipment. Because the inventory would be in parts, this investment would be lower than if Dysat simply inventoried ready-to-ship units. Taft made some estimates of the costs of assembly, noting that these costs would decrease with improved skills and increased volume. (See Table 5.)

Although the Dynasound stores had been located in leased mall space, Taft used a small warehouse he owned for storage of his inventory of sound equipment. Since this building was not included in the Dynasound sale, he planned to use the building for his new venture. It was a fully insulated steel structure with a small loading and shipping dock. The space was open, and Taft thought he could install a curtain wall and some office

Figure 1

Dynamic Satellite Systems Plant Layout

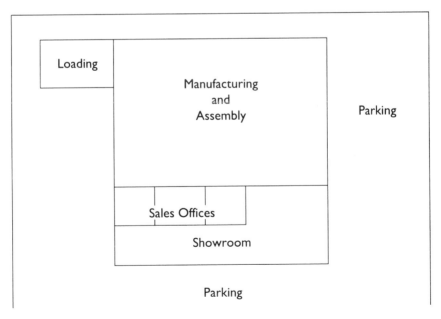

Table 5			
	Materials	18%	
Dynamic Satellite	Labour	17%	
Systems	Overhead	11%	
Cost and Profit			
Estimates—			46%
Assembly	Profit	14%	
Operations	Taxes	5%	
			65%
	For Dysat Marketing		35%

partitions to use the building for both manufacturing and sales. The cost of these renovations, complete with some lighting and electrical changes, was estimated at $15 000. The cost would be divided between the sales and manufacturing operations, with between $9000 and $10 000 of this total pertaining to operations and the balance to sales.

Using these figures, Taft projected manufacturing revenues based on the sales projections of Dysat. The resulting figures (Exhibit 1) indicated that he could expect to make additional profits on assembly if sales projections could be met.

Financial

Despite the fact that Taft felt he would have no trouble financing the business from the proceeds of the Dynasound sale, he wanted the company to be set up on a sound financial basis. Taft had discussed the proposal for Dysat with his banker and the Federal Business Development Bank. Before developing detailed figures Taft advanced the investment proposal outlined in Exhibit 2.

Finally, Taft projected Dysat sales and income along with his best estimates of the costs of selling satellite dishes through Dysat. (Exhibit 3.)

There was another financial matter to deal with, although Taft wasn't sure how, or if, it should be put together with Dysat. As part of the sale of Dynasound, Gordon Taft incorporated Taft Financial Services (TFS). He had two things in mind: first, TFS would hold all of the shares of Dysat; second, since TFS would have over $400 000 in cash when the sale was complete, Taft intended to use this money to finance the retail sale of satellite dishes.

Instead of using bank or finance companies to finance his sales, Taft would use TFS. TFS would hold title to the equipment until payments were completed and, if payments ceased prior to the completion of the contract, Dysat would recover the goods, refurbish them, and resell them to recover the unpaid amount.

Taft felt that he could issue such paper bearing 15 to 18 percent interest, be competitive with most consumer lenders, and get a much greater return on his money than if it were invested elsewhere. He also felt that the loans would be secure since TFS would own the equipment and these mortgages would be registered in order to protect its ownership. As well, Taft had been advised that the bank would lend up to 80 percent of the value of this paper at the prime rate plus one percent, so that TFS would be able to manage in excess of 4 to 5 million dollars in consumer loans if the need arose. TFS had offered to consider financing some of the sales of Dynasound and, while nothing had been finalized, the new owners had expressed an interest in this arrangement.

Taft was uncertain how much consumer lending TFS would take on, but to get some idea of the profitability of such a venture he made some projections (Exhibit 4). As well, he calculated the return he would get on the $400 000 if he simply invested it at a pre-tax return of 10 percent. He realized that this type of investment would be safer than operating his own finance company, but the difference in return seemed to justify his proposed financial services company (Table 6).

Returning to his opening concerns, Taft realized that there was a lot of work to be done before he could move ahead. Half jokingly, he remarked,

> You know, I'm really not sure of how to go about this. I sometimes think I should start with a part of the business, get it going, and then work into the subsequent parts. In a general sense I feel comfortable with the total proposal, but getting it together as a functioning unit is still not a really tight concept in my mind.

Taft had created a small decision tree to indicate the general process he had gone through, but as yet had not worked out all of the details (Figure 2).

Table 6		1989	1990	1991	1992	1993
Dynamic Satellite	Opening Balance	400	440	484	532	586
Systems	Interest (10%)	40	44	48	53	59
Investment of		440	484	532	586	645
Dynasound						
Proceeds						
(000's)						

Figure 2

Dynamic Satellite
Systems
Decision Criteria

Nor had he decided how Taft Financial Services would fit into the total plan.

Is there a step approach to these decisions and, if so, what are my options? Should I begin with selling only, selling and installation, selling, installation, and assembly, or selling, installation, assembly, and manufacturing? Should I wholesale? Should I do it inside or outside of the immediate market area? And there are more questions where those came from.

Exhibit 1

Dynamic Satellite Systems Manufacturing Revenues—Based on Dysat Projections

	%*	1989	1990	1991	1992	1993
Materials	.18	23,677	31,104	39,877	47,232	59,123
Labour	.17	22,362	29,376	37,662	44,608	55,838
Overhead	.11	14,469	19,008	24,369	28,864	36,131
	.46	60,508	79,488	101,908	120,704	151,092
Net Profit	.14	18,415	24,192	31,015	36,736	45,985
Taxes	.05	6,577	8,640	11,077	13,120	16,423
Manufacturer's Selling Price	.65	131,538	172,800	221,538	262,400	328,462
For Dysat	.35	85,500	112,320	144,000	170,560	213,500
Installation Revenue		11,400	15,840	21,600	27,040	34,160
Less: Costs		7,524	10,296	13,608	16,224	19,812
Installation Profit		3,876	5,544	7,992	10,816	14,348

---

* See Table 5

Exhibit 2	**Sources:**	Personal Investment	$ 40,000	
Dynamic Satellite Systems		Operating Loans	40,000	
		Long-Term Loans	40,000	
General Financial Requirements		Total Funds	$120,000	$120,000
Projected Funds— Sources and Uses	**Uses:**	Inventory	$ 15,000	
		Accounts Receivable	10,000	
			25,000	25,000

Expenses			
Manufacturing	24,000		
Installation	22,000		
Office	12,000		
Other	4,000		
Leasehold Improvements	15,000		
	77,000	77,000	
		102,000	
Not Allocated		**$ 18,000**	

The commercial bank agreed to finance approximately 50% of the inventory and receivables to an approved maximum of $40,000 (Taft's request). As well, there would be a personal guarantee secured by the owner's building.

FBDB financed the long-term loan for startup capital equipment requirements, to a maximum of $60,000. This loan would be secured by chattel mortgages against purchased equipment.

Exhibit 3		1989	1990	1991	1992	1993
Dynamic Satellite Systems Projected Income Statement	Sales	85,500	112,320	144,000	170,560	213,500
	Installation	11,400	15,840	21,600	27,040	34,160
	Total Sales	96,900	128,160	165,600	197,600	247,660
	Cost of Goods					
	Materials	29,312	34,654	41,400	47,424	55,574
	Labour	11,870	13,957	3,974	4,268	20,803
	Overhead	21,318	28,195	36,432	43,472	54,485
	Total Cost of Goods	62,500	76,806	81,806	95,164	131,012
	Gross Profit	34,400	51,354	83,794	102,436	116,648
	Expenses					
	Selling	2,400	2,750	5,000	6,000	8,000
	Advertising	5,500	6,000	7,500	8,500	10,000
	Telephone	1,800	2,400	2,750	3,200	3,600
	Travel	3,600	4,000	4,200	4,400	4,500
	Postage	640	700	750	750	750
	Utilities	2,150	2,240	2,300	2,400	2,500
	Wages	15,000	16,000	20,000	24,000	26,000
	Benefits	2,250	2,750	3,000	3,200	4,000
	Membership	200	200	200	300	300
	Interest	1,500	1,500	1,500	1,500	1,500
	Taxes	440	480	500	520	550
	Depreciation	4,500	4,000	3,600	3,600	3,600
	Lease	3,600	3,600	3,600	3,600	3,600
	Miscellaneous	750	1,000	1,000	1,000	1,500
	Total Expenses	44,330	47,620	55,900	62,970	70,400
	Net Profit	**(9,930)**	**3,734**	**27,894**	**39,466**	**46,248**

Exhibit 4		1989	1990	1991	1992	1993
Dynamic Satellite Systems Taft Financial Services Credit Sales Projections (000's)	Average Credit	700	1,400	2,100	3,200	4,000
	Revenue	105	210	315	480	600
	Expenses					
	Interest	42	84	126	192	240
	Sales & administration	24	30	36	40	44
		66	114	162	232	284
	Net Profit before Tax	39	96	153	248	316
	Opening Balance	400	439	535	688	936
		439	**535**	**688**	**936**	**1,252**

Regulatory Policies—Satellite Systems

In Canada, satellite receiving systems were controlled and licensed by the federal government. Recent technological developments had added to the difficulties encountered in controlling this and other means of receiving radio and television signals. As a result the controls, once enforced, appeared to be in limbo while the CRTC (Canadian Radio and Television Commission) struggled to develop new policies and rules to implement its mandate.

International Regulations Radio communications services, including direct broadcasting satellite services, were coordinated internationally by the Radio Regulations of the International Telecommunications Union (ITU). These regulations required that domestic services be designed to use the technical means available to prevent signal spillover, shaping the broadcast beam to correspond with national boundaries. Despite these rules, spillover from the US market provided a large number of Canadians with a wide range of signals. This programming represented a major selling feature for the satellite dish industry.

Individuals were not yet regulated by the CRTC. However Canada, along with a number of other countries, was reviewing policies in this area. With the spillover increase, the CRTC had expressed major concern over the impact of such programming on the cultural sovereignty of the nation.

National Regulations Canada's broadcasting policy is stated in Section B of the *Broadcasting Act* of 1968. It set up operating rules for the communication of radio and television signals, but did not anticipate satellite communications systems.

The CRTC and Canadian Broadcasting For some time, the CRTC had struggled with the need to adapt a cultural and social mandate to the rapidly changing technology of the communications industry. Maintaining a vigorous Canadian presence within the broadcast industry in the face of foreign programming had always required a balancing act. Now video, cable services, and satellite communications systems were adding to the complicated process of applying outdated regulations. The CRTC mandate, which sought to ensure Canadian control over cultural sovereignty, had two possible strategies. The policy-makers could increase regulation and limit or prohibit the use of US signals, or they could deregulate the industry to create a more competitive environment, leaving the choice and the cost to the industry and its customers.

The growing number of unlicensed distributors of US programming did not live up to Canadian content requirements. Attempts had been made to prosecute offenders using satellite technology, but the impact was minimal. Recently, the Commission had suspended these activities while it went about the difficult task of developing policies to permit the development of satellite technology while supporting Canadian program production. New initiatives (1983) promoted:

1. the expansion of cable as the most effective way to expand the viewing choices of Canadians,
2. the establishment of a Broadcast Program Development Fund to assist private production,
3. policies to allow the CRTC to issue legally binding directives on matters of policy, and
4. changes to abolish all satellite dish licensing requirements.

Local Regulations   For the most part, local bylaws covering satellite antennas were concerned with the location of the equipment. Control was exercised through the use of building permits. A typical local bylaw suggested that "no satellite antenna or dish can be installed in an 'exterior yard.' (see Figure 3). These bylaws were not always enforced, and many installations were done without permits.

Competitive Services

Satellite receiving systems had emerged as the most recent addition to the technology of receiving radio and television signals. Volume and design improvements had resulted in decreasing costs, making a variety of satellite receiving products available. The increased number of satellite transmissions and the locations of the satellite transmitting vehicles also helped lower costs and increase the range of offerings.

Cable Operations   Cable operations had expanded dramatically since their inception in the 1960s. Recently, cable operators had been aiming to

Figure 3

Dynamic Satellite
Systems
Interior and
Exterior Yards

Illustration of Interior
and Exterior Yards

Interior Yards

Exterior Yards

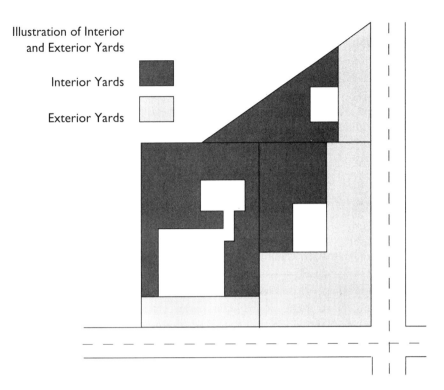

reduce the number of operators and substantially increase the size and clout of cable operators. Product offerings had greatly expanded, to the point where few customers lived with only the basic services. Movie channels, sports channels, and special interest channels devoted to children, religion, public affairs, etc. allowed cable operators to offer a variety of program options and prices. Statistics from a number of communities indicated that between 50 and 65 percent of households subscribed to cable where service was available. As well, about 10 to 15 percent of cable subscribers also subscribed to pay-TV. This market represented the growth area for most cable companies. With the transmission lines in place, increased program offerings provided attractive returns to most operators (see Table 7 for sample rental costs).

Broadcasters Many Canadians who lived close to the US border could access a wide range of channels (both US and Canadian) without the need to install expensive receiving equipment. However, to insure good picture quality, most sets were tuned to cable or antennae of various types. The major channels in Ontario (CBC, CTV, Global, and TV Ontario) were

Table 7

Dynamic Satellite
Systems
Sample Cable
Rental Costs

	Cable	Cable with Pay-TV
Installation*	$ 30.00	$ 30.00
Monthly Charge	14.00	14.00
Monthly Pay-TV Charges**	–	20.00
Annual Cost	**$168.00**	**$408.00**

----

 * This is a one-time charge

** Rates differ from system to system. As well, some offer a wider variety of Pay-TV
   and prices vary with customer choices. Annual increases of approximately 6% have
   been approved by the CRTC.

available with minimal aerial installations. US channels—including ABC,
NBC, and CBS—were also available, although quality could be a problem
without good receiving equipment. These broadcasters followed a wide
range of strategies to maintain market shares. The growth of cable, satellite
systems, and videos continued to fragment the viewing market, making it
difficult for the networks to improve profitability.

Video Cassettes   The advent of the video cassette system and the
subsequent cost reductions had resulted in a major move to the use of
this equipment. More recently, competition in the area of movie rentals
and movie sales had made this form of entertainment a major competitive
factor in the television viewing market. VCR equipment ranging from
$249.00 to $500.00, and movies that rented for $1.00 to $3.00 a day had
made the viewing of video cassettes a major business. The system promoted privacy, personal choice of time and content, and major savings,
particularly for families. The ability to copy and view network programming
at a later, more convenient time also made the system attractive.

Satellite Systems   Government initiatives in 1983 suggested that the
satellite dish licensing requirements should be removed, providing new
impetus for the sale of satellite dish systems. Rural sales, in the absence of
suitable alternatives, were the mainstay of dish sales. The removal of
licensing requirements placed the dish in direct economic competition
with cable systems, and this could result in new marketing approaches to
the sale and installation of satellite systems.

Offsetting the relaxed rules by government was the growing use (or
threatened use) of scrambled signals. The purchase of decoders and the

payment of royalty and license fees would add to the cost of using a dish and decrease the ability of satellite systems to compete in cable markets. Some pay-TV signals were scrambled, and accessing these signals cost between $10 and $15 per month each.

Satellite Systems Technology

Three basic functions were performed by the satellite antenna system: collection, amplification, and translation of the satellite signal. The receiving dishes were constructed from several materials and were designed to collect and concentrate the signals at the feed horn, in the centre of the dish. The quality of the picture was a function of the size and surface of the dish and, to a lesser extent, the material from which it was fabricated. Dish design featured two major materials: aluminum (solid and mesh) and fibreglass. Each had advantages and these are summarized in Exhibit 5. Environmental conditions (wind, snow, and acid rain) often determined which material best suited the buyers' needs.

The feed horn (see Exhibit 6) would take signals concentrated by the dish, and pass them to the low noise amplifier, which boosted the signal, enabling translation by the satellite receiver. These components, available in a wide variety of packages, determined the number and quality of the pictures received. Dealers tended to mix and match these components, seeking to optimize program availability and picture quality. The satellite receiver would take the signal from the LNA and transform it into a standard television frequency.

Several optional features were also available, including a power driven actuator, remotely controlled. Digital trackers facilitated satellite switching, and an LNB or "blockbuster" permitted the user to view different channels at the same time. Dish sizes, ranging from four to twelve feet, were chosen on the basis of geographic location and signal separation requirements.

Exhibit 5

Dynamic Satellite
Systems
Satellite Dish
Design and
Material
Comparisons

Material	Advantages	Disadvantages
Fibreglass	Does not rust Does not dent	Hairline cracking Resists wind
Aluminum	Double spun–adds to life	May dent or warp Corrosion susceptibility Requires extra support
Aluminum Mesh	Less wind resistance Fewer ice and snow problems	May dent or warp Requires extra support

Systems range in size from 3 to 16 feet and can be installed as fixed or portable
equipment.

Exhibit 6

The Satellite
Dish

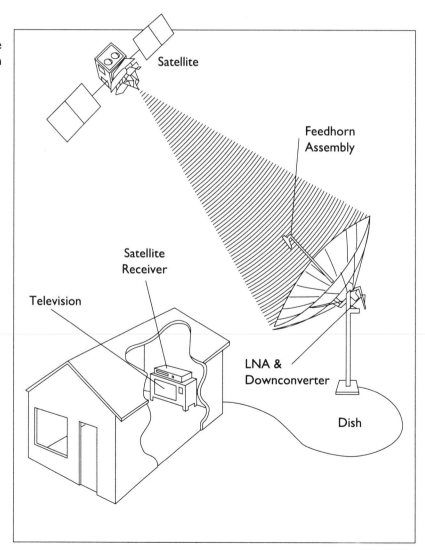

C H A P T E R 6

Phase Five: The Functionally Organized Business

Introduction

A phase 5 enterprise is characterized by the presence of a management team comprised of functional specialists and a general manager. No longer is there a single manager coordinating the activities of employees as in phase 3, but rather a general manager directing the activities of a functionally specialized team. While there is no set formula for the functions represented in this phase, the traditional areas are marketing and production, which we view as the *operating* functions, and finance, control, and personnel, which we regard as *support* functions. In phase 5, the small business has developed to the degree that it must bring on board one or more functional experts to deal with the complexity and risk entailed in the decisions it faces.

As sales grow and product lines expand, specialization develops in advertising, sales promotion, market research, etc., and often in the production and delivery of the product itself. The accounting system becomes more complex, as the control system must be adapted to functional decisions and problems. The expanding workforce calls for the implementation of formal policies for hiring, firing, training, and promoting. However, while the complexity of the organization will reflect the scope and size of the company, relatively few phase 5 companies will have experts in all of these areas.

Requirements of the Phase Five Enterprise

The phase 5 organization has three basic requirements. One of these involves the sharing of authority and responsibility from the top; the second entails the effective exchange of information in both directions; and the third centres upon effective team planning so that the company management group can synchronize its efforts. Let us examine the implications of each of these requirements.

The concept of top management delegating authority and responsibility means that the managerial activities of planning, organizing, directing, and controlling are not exclusively the mandate of the general manager (who may or may not be the owner); these same management activities are also performed by functional experts within the context of their particular units. Within the roster of management activities, the general manager places relatively greater emphasis on planning and organizing, leaving a certain amount of responsibility for directing and controlling to the next level of management.

The need for internal communication, and the facilities to ensure an accurate and timely information flow, represent a considerable fixed cost to the organization. Yet the phase 5 organization, *because* it has developed and grown successfully, has now reached a size and scope—of sales volume, product lines, markets served, or number of employees—which make expenditures on management information systems essential. To be competitive, the firm must develop an infrastructure that is efficient in the face of high-volume production and distribution. The sheer volume of information to be managed defies manual processing. (There is a discussion of automated information processing systems in Chapter 14.) Moreover, no longer is there merely a single individual with a need to know. As discussed in Chapter 7, the addition of functional specialists means that information must be assembled and shared if these people are to manage in their respective areas and, equally important, coordinate their endeavours successfully with those of other units. In short, the business has evolved to the point where the free flow of information between its different units is critical to its success.

The third requirement of the phase 5 organization is effective team planning. For the business to prosper in a competitive environment (mounting gross profits will invite competitive encroachment), it must formulate a strategy that permits it to develop or maintain some competitive advantage. This need typically calls for close attention to the particular markets it pursues, and the particular products it offers. Thus, a fundamental preoccupation of the general manager must be with the general thrust of the firm in selecting its markets, and with the way it defines itself in these markets through the combination of products and ancillary services it offers. Clearly she will need the best information, on both internal and external dynamics, that can be obtained.

Once these issues have been evaluated, broad objectives can be developed. However, these objectives, and the resultant allocation of resources, must be translated into functional plans and programs complete with tasks, resource requirements, responsibilities, and deadlines. It is the functional manager who is generally in the best position to link the strategic direction of the company with day-to-day operating activities in a given area. He must have a keen awareness of the company objectives and priorities communicated from the top. This is best achieved by establishing a process whereby specific performance objectives are arrived at on a joint basis. Thereafter, it is the responsibility of the general manager to assemble an overall plan to amalgamate these objectives. The document or plan should include targets for the time period covered, underlying assumptions, budgets for the different units, and measures for monitoring and controlling performance.

A plan that evolves from a group is generally more sound than one produced by a single individual. Without broad participation, key assumptions may not be fully articulated and reviewed, and essential information about opportunities, capabilities, and market responses may be overlooked. Moreover, collective involvement builds collective commitment—a crucial factor in an organization with a number of disparate functions and subfunctions. The effectiveness of a strategy depends upon consistency of action, and since the number of people in the organization generally precludes informal systems at this stage, coordinating the implementation of the strategy is all important. Moreover, planning at the phase 5 level must encompass external developments to ensure a good fit between the company's environment and what it has to offer. (Chapter 9 provides a perspective on the small business environment.)

Emergence of the General Management Role

From the foregoing profile of the needs of the phase 5 organization, it is clear that the general manager must be willing to share authority and responsibility with other managers. However, there is often a reluctance to share power in this fashion on the part of small business owners, who by this point have grown accustomed to exercising a large measure of control over the firm's activities. Not only have they been in charge of directing and controlling the firm, but they have generally maintained a day-by-day hands-on involvement with many of these activities. The profile of the phase 5 general manager may be utterly foreign to them. Now they must contend with experts who expect to share in the decision-making, and indeed to exercise a large degree of latitude within their areas of specialization. A computer system may have usurped the boss's status as the primary source of information within the organization. Given the sophistication of the issues and the degree of risk, the proprietor can no longer rely on experience and intuition to guide her decisions. It falls to her to screen the often conflicting viewpoints, expressed by the functional specialists, and to negotiate some consensus regarding a final course of action. It is little wonder that a number of small business owners find the transition to functional management highly uncomfortable. Indeed, they may be unable to move their companies beyond the owner manager category without substantial direction from outside specialists—to conduct market research, design and implement an information system, or perhaps locate sources of venture capital. Those proprietors who are successful can bring to the role of general manager the knowledge, contacts, and perspective that come with founding and developing the enterprise, and may even continue to imbue the organization with an entrepreneurial spirit otherwise frequently lacking in phase 5.

Managing the Functional Organization

Startup in Phase Five

As discussed in Chapter 2, the ability to build and use a functional structure is central to a successful phase 5 startup. Information, communication, and control mechanisms are crucial, regardless of the capital investment involved. In addition, there must be a commitment to long-range planning and to modification of such basics as the product/market focus or the internal structure, as needed. Periodic assessment of company strengths and weaknesses, and of the external business setting, constitutes an integral part of such planning.

Since the phase 5 organization does not enjoy the flexibility of a less evolved enterprise, careful attention must be paid to internal efficiency. This concern is all the more compelling when one considers that a phase 5 startup business is almost inevitably entering a competitive marketplace in which earlier entrants will generally have the advantage of experience. Many phase 5 organizations adopt a niche strategy (see Chapter 10), determining where the strengths of the company can be brought to bear. For instance, during the 1980s, a number of Ontario micro-breweries were able to establish a position in a market that had traditionally been dominated by two industry giants: John Labatt Ltd. and Molson Breweries of Canada Limited. Small enterprises such as Brick Brewing Co. Limited, Creemore Springs Brewery Ltd., and Upper Canada Brewing Company built a loyal following by producing a preservative free, premium priced product which was marketed to the upscale segment of the market.[1]

Drucker[2] delineates the hazards associated with spreading any organization over too wide a spectrum, and endorses the notion of concentrating the company's efforts on those particular activities that have the potential to produce the most significant results. The importance of this advice for the small enterprise cannot be overstated. In Chapter 4 the problems that can stem from ill-conceived expansion and diversification were introduced: an inordinate number of entrepreneurs tend to embrace new markets, services, or activities as a response to problems that arise in their original line of business. Alternatively, they jeopardize their main business by using it as a springboard to launch and support new ventures that may have questionable merit or be in unrelated areas. In general, the phase 5 small business is well advised to maintain a narrow focus—i.e., the smallest number of products, markets and distribution channels that will yield the greatest revenue.

Planning

By the time the organization reaches phase 5, planning can be subdivided into strategic planning, which pertains to the company's long-term direction, and operational planning, which involves less judgement and has a more immediate focus. The former is conducted by the general manager and involves such questions as What are our basic goals?; Should we be introducing new services?;

What resources will be required? Operational planning, on the other hand, is the preserve of the unit or department managers: What specific programs position us to attain our targets (for example, higher sales per invoice, number of new accounts) while making efficient use of our resources?

Interestingly, the foregoing dichotomy reflects the common belief that while entrepreneurship requires creative, long-range thinking, "management" entails a more structured, concrete, performance-oriented approach. However, as suggested earlier, entrepreneurship, while less of a factor here than in earlier phase situations, is still an important element in the development of fresh ideas designed to help the business thrive as conditions change.

For the general manager, planning in this phase encompasses two separate areas: the business environment (external) and the organizational structure (internal), which coalesce to provide the context for a selected course of action. The breadth of perspective required of the general manager has been described above. Her principal concerns lie with exploiting business opportunities and addressing problems, and with expanding or rationalizing resources, in response to the dictates of the environment. This focus on the environment places a premium on familiarity with the marketplace, and an ability to interpret its signals. This notion was introduced in Chapter 1 and is elaborated on by Peterson. The latter suggests that, as the entrepreneur gains more experience in the business, he tends to

> ... remove certain types of opportunities from his *action set*, because they do not match his ambitions, abilities or resources. The *action set* contracts over time ... but the entrepreneur never stops being reactive. He only becomes more astute at recognizing opportunities by pursuing them relentlessly.[3]

For the functional manager, planning centres largely on specific activities incorporated into a program or project. In this regard, the planning task of the functional manager resembles that of the owner-operator of a phase 1 business. However, in addition to aligning endeavours with company objectives, the functional manager must synchronize these endeavours with those of other functional managers.

Organizing

Prior to phase 5, the issue of formal organizational design rarely warrants attention. However, as the firm grows, "a logical basis for organizing human efforts and material resources must be formulated."[4] Many phase 5 companies find themselves faced with such decisions as whether or not to open a branch in a new region, how many staff should be assigned to each supervisor, whether to add or drop a night shift, or whether or not to add wholesaling activities to a retail operation. All of these choices have implications for the organizational chart.

Organizing in phase 5 also involves determining the systems needed by the firm to support an expanding number of functions. Defining the management information requirements of the company generally calls for intensive consultation between the general manager and the functional experts involved.

Another area of concern is sometimes referred to as "the channel." Once the basic business definition has been established, attention often shifts to the manner in which the product is distributed to the chosen markets. More specifically, how do we get the product to the end user? What distribution intermediaries are appropriate? And what margins should be offered? These issues, while linked to the marketing function within the firm, have major long-term consequences, and therefore warrant the attention of the general manager.

Directing

While the general manager does not normally direct the day-to-day operations of the firm, he fosters consistency of action within and between functional units by generating a commitment to shared objectives. This consistency can be engendered, for example, through training programs, regular personnel meetings, budget discussions and accepted norms for analysing and approving capital projects.

The general manager communicates objectives and priorities, vetts functional area plans, negotiates resource allocations, and approves performance goals. Directing specific programs and projects falls within the purview of the functional managers; however the degree of self-direction granted to the sales manager, accountant, production supervisor, etc., will depend on the nature of the organization as well as the individual's capability and need for autonomy. Typically, the functional manager would have the authority, for instance, to choose between overtime and multiple shifts, or repairing versus replacing machinery.

Controlling

At this level, control continues to encompass three basic components: the establishment of performance standards, a way of measuring actual performance against these standards at regular intervals, and the clear assignment of responsibility for corrective action to address any unfavourable variances. However, the general management role that the owner must assume in the phase 5 organization precludes involvement in this exercise in the direct fashion that is often possible prior to phase 4. In addition, keeping the organization on track in accordance with the overall plan can be difficult given the relative complexity of the functionally structured small enterprise. The principal of the business must become adept at reviewing the performance of the different units (e.g., the purchasing department, or the branch sales office), verifying that decisions are consistent with stated policies, and providing feedback in a timely and positive way. The functional or unit managers, who are held accountable for the performance of their assigned unit, will in turn exercise control in much the same way as an owner-operator, by ensuring that duplication of effort is avoided, proper procedures are followed, and record-keeping is accurate and up-to-date.

There are two other aspects of control that merit the attention of the small business person. First, no matter what business one engages in, and regardless of the reliability of one's control system, not all deviations from plan are controllable and it can be counter-productive to attempt to assign all such items to an individual or department. It is important that control activities are carried out in a constructive manner, so that employees are not threatened and managers are not constrained. Second, control is an activity that should be subjected to normal cost/benefit analysis (i.e., do the costs of developing a new reporting system and collecting and analyzing the information justify the benefits in terms of improved control over operations).

A detailed treatment of management control systems is beyond the scope of this text; however, Chapter 14 in Part 2 does describe some of the basic elements of the control process.

Summary

Regardless of the industry setting, effective management of the phase 5 organization depends on three primary factors: sharing of authority, effective lines of communication, and coordinated planning. The management activities of planning organizing, directing, and controlling must be adapted to the specific needs of the functionally organized business. It is only in the latter stages of this phase that the organization will have developed the ability to operate effectively within a functional structure.

The phase 5 company will have survived the extreme vulnerability of the early years, weathered the lean profit years generally associated with growth of sales, and established some relatively sustainable defence against competitive attack. Indeed, an organization that has evolved to this degree is frequently on the brink of developing, often by diversification or vertical integration, into an enterprise that can no longer be classified as a small business.

List of Key Words

Capital	Marketing
Communication	Organizing
Control	Performance
Department	Personnel
Direct	Production
Entrepreneurship	(Managing) Resources
(Business) Environment	Responsibility
(Business) Functions	(Organizational) Structure

Questions for Discussion

1. The phase 5 organization will almost certainly have a certain number of "unit" or "department" managers. Why is such departmentalization necessary at this level?

2. Rather than establishing, for instance, a marketing unit, an administrative unit, or a customer service unit, some small businesses adopt a structure whereby all of these functions have a presence in each of the company's main geographic regions. List the advantages and disadvantages of the territorial form of organizational structure.

3. a) What role should the annual budgeting process play within the control function as outlined in this chapter?
   b) Are there steps that can be taken to ensure that the budget does not end up being perceived by employees as little more than a pressure device?

4. In the earlier phases of small business development, experience can often play a significant role. Does this continue to be a major factor for the phase 5 enterprise?

5. There are a number of prerequisites to effective planning in any small organization. For instance, the principal(s) of the company must be prepared to set aside certain periods of time for the express purpose of planning. In addition, even though teamwork is an important element in the success of many businesses, the chances that there will be adequate time to plan are lessened considerably in those situations

where managers are constantly interfering in the assigned duties of their various staff members.

Outline some of the other factors which you feel are crucial to successful planning in the phase 5 situation.

6. As pointed out in this chapter as well as in Chapter 4, a poorly planned or executed diversification program can often be the undoing of the enterprise. Nevertheless, there are many success stories built on the entrepreneur's decision to change the direction of the business and commit resources to a new product, process or market.

Explain why this latter strategy is less feasible for the phase 5 organization than for other small businesses.

Selected Readings

Blanchard, Kenneth, Patricia Zigarmi and Drea Zigarmi, *Leadership and the One Minute Manager*. New York, N.Y.: William Morrow, 1985.

Clifford, Donald K. Jr. and Richard C. Cavanagh, *The Winning Performance: How America's High Growth Midsize Companies Succeed*. New York, N.Y.: Bantam Books, 1985, pp. 1–16.

McConkey, D.D., *How to Manage by Results*. New York, N.Y.: Amacom, 1976.

McMullen, W. and Wayne A. Long, *Developing New Ventures: The Entrepreneurial Option*. New York, N.Y.: Harcourt, Brace, Jovanovich, Inc., 1990, pp. 340–46.

Pearson, Andrall E., "Six Basics for General Managers," *Harvard Business Review*, 67, no. 4 (July/August 1989), pp. 94–101.

Szonyi, Andrew J. and Dan Steinoff, *Small Business Management Fundamentals*, 3rd ed. Scarborough, Ont.: McGraw Hill Ryerson, 1987.

Endnotes

1. Daniel Stoffman, "Beer: An Industry in Ferment," *Challenges*, 3, no. 2 Spring, 1990, pp. 29–35.

2. Peter F. Drucker, "Managing for Business Effectiveness," *Harvard Business Review*, May–June 1963, p. 56.

3. Rein Peterson, "Determinants of Small Business Success," *Proceedings of the Eighth International Symposium on Small Business*, Ottawa, Ont., October 19–22, 1981, p. 314.

4. Richard M. Hodgetts, *Management: Theory, Processes and Practice* (Orlando, Fla.: Academic Press, Inc., 1986), p. 139.

Mattawa Knitwear

" " **W**ell, I think it's fair to say that all the legwork is finished. I can't see us requiring any more data before we decide whether or not to proceed." This was how, in December 1983, Donald Atkinson summed up the situation facing the sponsors of a proposal to start up a garment manufacturing operation in the small town of Mattawa, Ontario.

Atkinson's comments prompted Angela Wilson, another member of the group, to remark:

> I agree. We've been provided with a good deal of background information on this industry and I think we are now well aware of the risks involved. There are a number of different ways of organizing this kind of business. Maybe we should examine these more closely and on that basis figure out if the business has a realistic chance of success. We must satisfy ourselves that this is more than just another "make-work project" before we actually put the business in motion.

Background

The impetus for Mattawa Knitwear had come from a group of five local citizens, who were concerned with the high unemployment rate in the area. Mattawa, with a population of 2800, was located 65 km east of North Bay at the junction of the Ottawa and Mattawa rivers. Recent commercial development and the increasing popularity of local ski operations helped reduce the town's traditional dependence on lumber and hydro-electric resources.

This group of business people and community activists had come together in early 1983. One of the members, Bill Leblanc, had some experience with a small sweater manufacturing concern operated by the Inuit in the Frobisher Bay area of the Northwest Territories. After exploring a few other business concepts, the group decided to promote a similar operation in Mattawa. Accordingly, the sponsors applied through the Sudbury office of Employment and Immigration Canada for seed monies under the Local Employment Assistance Program (LEAP). Their request was granted and developmental funding of $26 000 was advanced to defray the costs of gathering information on the feasibility of the proposed business. (LEAP had been set up by the federal government to funnel financial support to new small businesses that were organized expressly to create employment opportunities for one of four designated target sectors: youth, handicapped, women, and Native peoples. In the case of Mattawa Knitwear, women were the target group.)

The next step was a consulting study to investigate the viability of the Mattawa Knitwear venture. While the study's conclusions were generally supportive of the idea, the sponsoring group felt they should thoroughly evaluate the proposal once more before committing themselves to the next stage—LEAP "infrastructure funding," which was typically advanced to assist with such expenditures as equipment, leasehold improvement, and recruitment and training.

The Knitwear Industry

Industry statistics listed 45 Canadian sweater manufacturers. In addition, there was a fairly well established cottage industry segment producing a wide array of hand-knit items. More importantly, foreign suppliers represented a major source of competition in this market.

The most useful way of segmenting the market was according to price. At the lower end—under $100 retail price—the prospects for a new competitor were particularly bleak. This segment was very price sensitive and hence tended to be dominated by mass-producers, both domestic and foreign, most notably from the Far East.

Positioned in the higher price ranges were a handful of Canadian competitors, several "at-home" producers, and some well-known British, French, Italian, and US manufacturers. Among the more popular Canadian brands were Bonda and Tundra, which were heavy Arran-type knits in the $100–$200 bracket, and Parkhurst, a line of moderately priced cashmere sweaters mass produced by Dorothea Knitting Mills. Bonda enjoyed a good reputation for quality products, but its location in the Maritimes put it at a geographic disadvantage in the major markets of central Canada. The Tundra line was manufactured by Standard Knitting of Winnipeg.

In general, the individual at-home operators found it difficult to line up large retail accounts, given their low production capabilities, reputation for inconsistent quality, and tendency towards designs that were either too bland or too exotic. This group of competitors was also hampered by the fact that volume production was essential to yield the economies of scale necessary to be price competitive in the knitwear industry.

Perhaps the strongest competition for higher end garments was provided by foreign concerns. Retail buyers in Canada tended to look to Italian brands for the more stylish cotton and silk knits, while heavy Arran knits and mohair and cashmere styles from the British Isles were also very popular. With their wide variety of styles and established designer labels, these importers were particularly dominant at the top end of the market. Canadian producers seemed to be at a bit of a disadvantage, since domestic designers were not noted for being imaginative or progressive. The Mattawa Knitwear sponsors were encouraged, however, by indications in the feasibility study that various retail buyers would be receptive to promoting more high quality Canadian lines. There was not a great deal of retail volume at the highest levels ($250–$350); the annual market for sweaters retailing for more than $100 was estimated at 3.2 million units, with the majority of sales in the $100–$200 range.

Distribution channels were another key consideration in the knitwear industry. The method of distribution depended on the type of retailer: major department stores and specialty store chains generally had centralized purchasing departments which bought directly from the manufacturer, while independent clothing stores quite often deal with distributors or manufacturers' agents. Few of the independent owner/operators could afford the time to attend fashion shows, where the department and chain stores ordered most of their inventory for the upcoming season. These shows were held twice a year during the peak buying seasons in industry centres such as New York, Montreal or Toronto, and provided an opportunity for retail buyers, designers, and producers to cultivate valuable contacts and keep abreast of style changes. For the most part, imported sweaters were handled by distributors, but in many instances Canadian producers also took on the role of distributor in order to supplement their lines with foreign brands.

At the retail level, the major department stores accounted for a large share of sweater sales, carrying a mixture of national lines, designer labels, and their own private brands. An example of the latter would be Sears' Boulevard Club sweaters. There had been a marked trend towards more private-brand merchandising over the past few years, particularly within the independent specialty store sector, with some reporting that as much as 40 percent of their sales were private brands. In the smaller centres, these independent retailers carried a fairly broad range of apparel items, while in major cities some operated as boutiques, offering a more limited selection of knitwear lines and sometimes employing in-house designers.

Local Market Area

The immediate trading area extended as far east as Sudbury, which had a population of 160 000 in the metropolitan area. While Sudbury's economy had benefited from diversification efforts in recent years, it was still somewhat dependent on the vagaries of the nickel and copper markets.

North Bay, the "Gateway to the North", was the closest urban centre, and while the economy here was less volatile, with a healthy mix of light industry, a large Canadian Forces base, and a strong tourist trade, the population base totalled only 50 000. To the extent that it was considered desirable for Mattawa Knitwear to create a name for itself among the region's independent retailers, it seemed clear that the target area would have to include Ottawa in order to be viable, even though this market was located some 300 km from Mattawa.

Selling and Promotion

New manufacturers attempting to break into the knitwear business would initially proceed via direct sales calls on small retailers, presenting a sample line of merchandise for consideration. If the styling, price, and quality were deemed acceptable and the sales presentation was effective, the retailers would place a trial order. The size and frequency of repeat orders depended on the timeliness of deliveries and, ultimately, on consumer demand. Once a stable manufacturer-retailer relationship developed, the producer would usually bring in a sales agent, particularly in the case of more distant markets. It was fair to say, however, that even the most stable relationship could be jeopardized by the presence of flawed or defective merchandise. In the higher price segments, no producer could afford shoddy workmanship.

Another important element in effectively servicing this "high fashion" segment was the selection of retail outlets consistent with the desired image. It was important for the manufacturer to have its sweaters prominently displayed. Brand loyalty was another key factor in influencing the consumer; however, for higher priced knitwear, it was widely accepted that brand loyalty could not be directly influenced by effective advertising. Nonetheless, as a new entrant, Mattawa Knitwear expected to devote substantial resources to its advertising and promotional activities. Included in these expenses would be print ads (in local newspapers and Canadian fashion magazines), logo development, brochures, hang tags, packaging materials, display posters, and photographs of models wearing the company's proprietary designs. Under normal industry practice, a large order from a retailer would merit an advertising allowance in the form of a five-percent rebate. The retailer and manufacturer would typically share the costs of major promotions equally.

Staffing

The business plan called for the hiring of 10 employees in total. While the regular complement of knitters would be five, the consultants had recommended bringing an additional three trainees on-stream a month or so after the original five had started. The three backup knitters would initially be on call to cover absences due to illness and the like, and would serve as a hedge against potential turnover. One supervisor would be responsible for the training, scheduling, and evaluation of these personnel. All employees would report to the general manager.

The duties of the general manager would encompass three distinct areas:

1. Operations management, with an emphasis on quality control;
2. Sales and marketing (the consultant had raised the possibility of attaching showroom/retail space to the plant to accommodate local walk-in clientele, including tourists, and offering the general manager a five-percent commission on these sales); and
3. Office administration and financial control.

Day-to-day office procedures would be handled by a secretary/bookkeeper. The advertising manager would organize the advertising campaign, develop display materials, maintain industry contacts, and represent the company at the major fashion shows. The final position, that of designer, was perhaps the most pivotal in the organization. Among the skills required would be familiarity with research and styling directions, a proven creative flair that would yield original design ideas, and a certain cost consciousness. Rather than working in-house for a manufacturer, most designers either worked for one of the large fashion design companies or were self-employed (perhaps operating their own retail boutique). Regardless of employment status, most qualified designers expected a royalty fee for garments bearing their designer label.

External Support

This venture was somewhat unique in that the group initiating and organizing the business would not be actively involved in managing the enterprise.

The sponsors would assume the role of a board of directors, meeting monthly to review such items as budget variances, proposed expenses, sales targets, and design ideas. While they hoped eventually to become conversant with the salient aspects of the knitwear industry, it was agreed that the organization would need some dependable outside assistance in the short term.

The consulting firm responsible for the feasibility study had recently submitted a proposal to continue providing guidance during the startup phase. This support would encompass the review of a broad range of activities including pricing, designer submissions, the performance appraisal process, purchasing procedures, quality control programs, promotional ideas, staff selection and training, and financial control procedures. The consultants were willing to maintain weekly phone contact with the general manager in an effort to resolve crises, evaluate new information, and provide an outside perspective on various issues.

The sponsors realized that if they decided to allow the enterprise to proceed to the next stage of development, events would unfold very quickly and the plethora of tasks requiring attention could easily overwhelm the management team (see Exhibit I for a schedule of key activities). Solid candidates had already been lined up for the general manager and supervisor positions and the consultants had provided some valuable leads with respect to the advertising manager and designer positions. The consensus was that given the dynamic nature of the market, the type of active involvement being proposed by the consulting firm could prove to be invaluable over the next two or three years, as the organization attempted to find its niche in the marketplace.

Financial Outlook

From a strict financial perspective, the immediate prospects for the business were not at all promising. Based on its analysis of the market, the consulting firm had identified high, low, and average potential volume levels for Mattawa Knitwear for the next three years (see Exhibit 2). Projected income statements (Exhibit 3) and cash flow statements (Exhibit 4) were then prepared by a small, Toronto-based C.A. firm on the basis of the average forecasted volumes. While all the interested parties were concerned with the dismal financial picture that emerged from these forecasts, they still had a great deal of faith in the longer-term viability of the business. They reasoned that the startup period was normally painful for small enterprises and that they would have to have a good deal of patience if Mattawa Knitwear was to establish itself as a legitimate competitor. The feasibility study indicated that the firm would reach a breakeven level of operations by the fourth year (1987). Indeed, all parties found encouragement in the relatively modest volume required to reach the breakeven point (see Table 1), given the magnitude of the high fashion market being targeted.

The Employment and Immigration officials, who had been involved with the project from the outset, continued to be quite supportive and did not appear to be overly concerned about the funding requirements outlined in Exhibit 4. And the consultants were unquestionably in favour of the business moving ahead:

> There is a significant opportunity for a good quality knitwear factory in today's market. There appears to be an upswing in demand and, while there are many small producers, there are only a few professionally organized competitors . . . It is our opinion that the Mattawa Knitwear Project has good potential to become a viable business.

Table 1			
Mattawa Knitwear Breakeven Analysis (Based on 1986 Cost Factors)	Average Unit Selling Price		$95.00
	Unit Variable Costs		
	Materials	$27.60	
	Direct labour	28.30	
	Royalties	1.50	
	Commissions	4.75	
	Bad debts	2.85	
	Delivery	1.90	
	Shipping supplies	.50	
		$67.40	$67.40
	A. Unit Contribution Margin		$27.60
	B. Total Fixed Costs: $155,000		
	C. Breakeven Level $\frac{(\text{B})}{(\text{A})}$: 5,616 Units		

Summary

As the five sponsors assessed the status of their venture, it was apparent that there was general agreement on several issues. First of all, they readily accepted the recommendation that Mattawa Knitwear develop its lines to sell in the $100–$200 bracket. This translated into factory prices averaging

$65 per sweater for 1984. This price level precluded the use of cottons and silks, materials upon which many foreign competitors had built their reputation; instead, it was decided that the company should deal in high quality woollen yarns and wool blends. The company would keep three months' of raw material inventory on hand (worth approximately $20 per unit in 1984), but given their intention to produce to specific orders wherever possible, finished goods inventory would be minimal. Also, since the required production equipment was considered somewhat expensive, the group agreed that the major items—five knitting machines and two sewing machines—should be acquired through lease contracts. The sponsors had tentatively selected a 2700-square-foot facility that was capable of housing the company's operations and was available on a net/net lease basis. As a result, capital expenditures would be limited to less than $25 000 during the first year, and would be only nominal in the subsequent two years.

Bill Leblanc had very little difficulty in convincing the others that if Mattawa Knitwear was to have any hope of surviving the startup phase, the marketing focus should be on independent retailers:

> Let's start small, develop our direct sales efforts in the local area, and get our foot in the door with some of these small independents. The department stores and clothing chain stores are only interested in buying in volume and I just don't think we will be set up from either an operations or a marketing standpoint to go after that market.

Another member of the group, Carole Fortin, was quick to support Leblanc's suggestion:

> I have to agree with Bill. We can use direct selling for promotional purposes as well, and it will be important for Mattawa Knitwear to control how its lines are presented to retail buyers. I'm also wondering if there is an opportunity here to pick up some of the private branding business that these independents are turning towards.

These comments prompted a question from Don Atkinson:

> Private labelling might seem like a convenient way of boosting our volumes, but my concern is that we are already committed to putting out our designer's proprietary designs. Isn't there a threat that by moving into private brands the company will spread itself

too thin and possibly compromise its ability to, as the consultants have stated, "produce a compact line of high quality products with relative simplicity of manufacturing requirements?"

"I think those are all valid concerns," remarked Angela Wilson,

but before we can even consider them, we need to decide whether or not we should give this venture our blessing. I'd feel more comfortable if, before addressing that issue, we first give some thought to what steps might be taken to improve the short-term profit picture. Let's not forget that within three years this business will be expected to stand on its own two feet, without the financial support of the LEAP program. I also think that it's important that we not move ahead unless we're all satisfied that the kinds of workers we require are available locally, can develop the skills that are necessary, and can be properly trained within the time frame envisioned by the consultants.

"Maybe Angela is right in urging caution", responded Mr. Leblanc. "There may even be other factors the consultants haven't adequately covered."

This brought out an impassioned speech from Arnold McCullough, the fifth member of the group:

Let's not get too analytical here. After all, the consultants have told us what we wanted to hear and have even provided us with some basic direction for setting up the business. To be able to start up on the basis of a thorough, government funded study is a tremendous advantage! How many businesses enjoy that kind of edge? Don't forget that the government is paying the freight, and will likely continue to do so for the next couple of years. Why are we agonizing over whether or not we should go ahead? Let's get moving and give some of our citizens a chance to get into the labour force!

Exhibit I

Mattawa Knitwear Schedule of Functions— Year One	Function	1	2	3	4	5	6	7	8	9	10	11	12

Months

Function	Schedule
Prepare facility	(—)
Hire and train workers	(Contingency—)
Develop line (samples)	(————————)
Establish sales contacts	(————————)
Purchase yarns	(————)
Produce selling samples	(————)
Prepare and initiate promotion, advertisements	(————) (————)
Prepare costings	(————)
Develop M.I.S.	(————————————————————)
Conduct selling	(————————)
Purchase production supplies	(————————)
Begin production for 6 month delivery	(————————)
Test quality assurance	(—)
Marketing consultation	(—) (—)
Production consultation	(—) (—) (—) (—) (—
Design consultation	(————————) (—) (—)

Exhibit 2 **A. Optimistic**

Mattawa
Knitwear
Forecasts of
Unit Sales
by Quarter

Year	1st Qtr.	2nd Qtr.	3rd Qtr.	4th Qtr.	Total
1	nil	200	300	400	900
2	400	400	600	600	2,000
3	900	1,000	1,200	1,400	4,500

B. Pessimistic

Year	1st Qtr.	2nd Qtr.	3rd Qtr.	4th Qtr.	Total
1	nil	50	100	100	250
2	150	200	200	250	800
3	300	300	400	400	1,400

C. Intermediate

Year	1st Qtr.	2nd Qtr.	3rd Qtr.	4th Qtr.	Total
1	nil	100	150	250	500
2	250	300	300	350	1,200
3	500	600	700	700	2,500

Exhibit 3

Mattawa Knitwear Projected Income Statements

	1984		1985		1986	
Sales	$32,500		$96,000		$237,500	
	(500 units)		(1,200 units)		(2,500 units)	
Beginning Inventory	–		2,796		4,874	
Cost of Goods						
Manufactured	73,706		116,878		197,044	
	73,706		119,674		201,918	
Ending Inventory[1]	(2,796)		(4,874)		(5,870)	
	70,910	70,910	114,800	114,800	196,048	196,048
Gross Profit (Loss)		(38,410)		(18,800)		41,452
Selling and Administrative Expenses						
Design Consultant[2]	11,500		8,600		8,750	
Management salary	27,612		30,400		30,680	
Commissions	1,624		4,800		11,875	
Samples	1,864		2,052		2,236	
Advertising & promotion	18,000		24,000		12,000	
Freight	812		2,400		5,938	
Travel[3] & automobile	7,000		9,300		9,600	
Training	17,700		13,630		4,248	
Office salary & benefits	6,536		12,980		14,152	
Legal & accounting	3,000		5,000		5,500	
Consulting	25,000		15,000		7,500	
Telephone	3,600		1,800		2,400	
Office & general	7,640		4,020		5,400	
Bad debts[4]	975		2,880		7,125	
	132,863	132,863	136,862	136,862	127,404	127,404
Operating Loss		(171,273)		(155,662)		(85,952)

1. Figure is understated to the extent that the accountants in this case valued inventories using direct material and labour costs only.

2. Includes royalty payments of $3.00 per garment in 1984 and 1985, and $1.50 per garment in 1986.

3. Travel expense includes one sales trip per month to one of the major selling districts—Montreal, Toronto, or Vancouver.

4. Estimated as 3% of gross sales.

Exhibit 4

Mattawa Knitwear Projected Cash Flow Statement

	1984				1985	1986
	First Quarter $	Second Quarter $	Third Quarter $	Fourth Quarter $		
Receipts						
Accounts receivable[1]	nil	2,165	7,585	11,920	88,165	211,865
Disbursements						
Acquisition of fixed assets	24,600	–	2,915	250	550	–
Incorporation costs	1,000	–	–	–	–	–
Security deposits	1,000	–	–	–	–	–
Payments on accounts payable[2]	5,175	4,600	3,070	4,600	32,520	77,110
Direct labour	3,000	3,000	3,000	3,000	28,050	61,200
Employee benefits	540	540	540	540	5,100	10,965
Manufacturing overhead	13,365	13,365	10,440	10,440	54,040	57,540
Selling (net of sample costs)	17,153	15,940	16,333	17,122	79,500	78,843
Administrative	15,435	14,430	16,395	18,191	55,310	46,325
	$81,268	51,875	52,693	54,143	255,070	331,983
Financing						
LEAP Funds	81,268	49,710	45,108	42,223	166,905	120,118

1. Based on a 60-day collection period.
2. Based on a 30-day payment period.

San Linde Bakery Inc.

avid Lieberman stared out the window of his tenth-floor office at the city skyline, muttering:

What a mess. That business is running totally out of control. Put another $100 000 into it? If it weren't for family pressures, I'd let the whole operation run into the ground.

David Lieberman had just been talking to his father-in-law, a partner in the San Linde Bakery Inc., whom David had fallen into the habit of calling "the Baker." Usually the calls were to talk about one or more of the seemingly endless grievances that had plagued the partners of late, but this time the Baker had been almost beside himself for another reason. The president had hinted, the Baker informed his partner, that he intended to cancel the employees' annual Christmas bottle. The president argued that they did not deserve it. Even though business was booming, the factory had run at a loss in the 1984 fiscal year. The Baker, now an old man, was incensed that the tradition that had generated goodwill for him for so long was to be halted summarily. He wanted David to intervene. The Baker had seemed uncharacteristically worried, too, about the losses. He'd asked David point blank if he would put funds in yet again.

Background

The San Linde Bakery came into existence in a suburb of Montreal in the early 1950s. The formula was simple: bake in the back, sell in the front, and, since it was possible to produce a little more than moved out the front, do a small volume of wholesaling. In 1965, the business changed hands, but in 1966 it reverted back to the former owner. A new partnership was formed, consisting of the previous owner and two experienced bakers. The financing was heavily dependent on trade creditors; in an industry where seven days was the norm, several major suppliers agreed to extend credit up to 120 days. The product became recognized for its quality, and the business quickly expanded into five locations, with baking done at three. However, in 1967 the previous owner died suddenly, before the partners had struck a legal agreement. After some negotiating, the widow sold and the business was incorporated. Demand continued to be strong and the enterprise operated in a stable state for another seven years.

In 1974, an opportunity arose to purchase a 24 000-square-foot, semi-automated manufacturing facility at a distress price. Each of the partners put up 45 percent of the money, and David Lieberman, the son-in-law of one of them, put up the remaining 10 percent as a silent partner. San Linde was by then doing 80 percent of its business as a wholesaler. Its closest competitor, ABC Bakery, concentrated more on retail.

By this time one of the partners, known to be an inveterate pilferer (although never openly accused) was quietly encouraged to concentrate on the deli operation, which accounted for 7-8 percent of total sales revenues, while the other partner, the Baker, ran the bakery operation. The Baker's interest was not in the bottom line but in the product, and particularly in custom work. Yet the company was profitable, with favourable growth prospects. In 1980 Lieberman invested another $100 000 for plant expansion, increasing his stake to one-third.

In the late 1970s the partners had acquiesced to several requests from long-time employees to establish franchises. The terms were very loose: an upfront outlay of $3500 and an agreement to carry San Linde products. Beyond this there were no clear rules. San Linde was in a position to compete against ABC on price if need be, and to surpass ABC on quality and service, and the early franchises were highly successful. Demand for franchises was steady, and over time the franchise price escalated. Within six years it had reached $25 000. Proposed franchise locations were carefully screened by the partners so that they would not compete with one another or with the dwindling number of company-owned stores.

It was soon evident, however, that while franchisees did not balk at carrying San Linde goods, many were eager to deal with other suppliers who might offer a better price. Also, as the number of franchises increased, some did not do well. Ownership of a few reverted to San Linde, whose policy was to make each a subsidiary corporation. As requests had begun to come from outsiders, a general manager had been recruited to oversee the franchising operation. Unfortunately, the person selected, while creative and personable, was quite youthful looking and lacked the presence to wield the necessary authority.

In the summer of 1983, the business, with mounting accounts receivable, could not meet its payroll, and Lieberman injected $55 000 as a temporary loan to cover the shortfalls.

By 1983, the factory workforce consisted of more than 90 unionized employees of diverse ethnic backgrounds but predominantly Italian, Greek, Haitian, and Indian/Pakistani. The factory ran 24-hours-a-day, every day of the year, and had acquired a sales manager, production manager, and controller. That year the Baker was persuaded by Lieberman to hire a president, whose particular role would be to put a proper franchising system in place. The Baker was reluctant to bring in another outsider, but even he conceded that something had to be done about the franchises. Not only were there no satisfactory franchising agreements in place, but the constant demand for new franchises meant that someone had to qualify new franchisee prospects and vet proposed locations, an onerous task which fell mainly to Lieberman. He had never anticipated such a role, particularly since he had not intended to play an active part in the business.

Reflecting on the way the franchising operation had gotten out of hand, Lieberman did not hide behind the fact that the early franchisees, all close associates of the Baker, had lived up to the trust placed in them. He had known at the time that this was no way to do business. Once the partners were dealing with strangers, he should have insisted on tighter franchising agreements to protect the quality, the name, and the marketing terms. At least all new franchises could be properly managed.

The individual chosen for the position of president was a "fast track" banker from Alberta who was used to taking difficult decisions and applying tough measures to those who defaulted on agreements. The ex-banker was impressed by the ever increasing demand for the product and the very strong name recognition San Linde had developed. A survey to determine the appeal of the San Linde name for that type of product had been conducted nationally in 1981 by outside market researchers, and the results were highly positive. Astute enough to anticipate that succession would soon become an issue in this company, (afterall, the Baker was getting on in years), the banker saw the enterprise expanding across the country, with himself at the helm. He agreed to become president, but was not asked to assume an ownership stake.

Present Situation

In the fall of 1984, despite booming sales, the factory showed a substantial loss (see Exhibit 1). The friction between the president and the Baker was becoming intolerable. The president was used to working within a clearly defined hierarchy, whereas the Baker had always been a craftsman assisted by his "boys." No distinctions had ever been made within the cadre of workers. This changed, however, due to the president's decision that the firm's executive staff and key department heads (see Exhibit 2) should be entitled to the limited number of parking spaces adjacent to the factory building. In the executive suite upstairs the president had already dealt successfully with the franchises, and was now bent upon establishing computer-based control systems for the factory. The Baker was totally opposed to these initiatives. Lieberman suspected this stance stemmed from the Baker's feeling that his personal empire was being eroded. Certainly the old man was not averse to technology *per se*, and when exposed to various automated systems had displayed a ready grasp of their capabilities.

The only information system then existent in the factory was an order entry system, which had become fully automated the year before. Tighter control over the product exiting the factory had cut down on another problem: "bootlegging," whereby employees would deliver the product C.O.D. to retail outlets with no orders ever recorded, and simply pocket the cash. The president was convinced, however, that there was rampant pilferage on the shop floor which the present set-up failed to detect. Increased mechanization during the past year had made the factory operation more efficient, but the expected drop in cost of goods sold had failed to materialize.

The firm's selling expenses had risen drastically during the previous 12 months due to a decision to bring the selling function largely in-house. The product had previously been handled in large part by jobbers, but difficulties in collecting from these intermediaries had prompted San Linde to increase its own sales force, and to invoice directly on product still distributed by jobbers.

Labour unrest was also a problem. The local of the International Bakery and Confectionary Workers of America present in the factory had fallen into the hands of two extremists, who thrived on confrontation. They kept labour-management relations in turmoil with a constant flow of grievances. The situation became so threatening for Lieberman that he felt obliged to hire a bodyguard! Added to this problem was the frequent occurrence of racially inspired disputes, fist fights and even knifing incidents on the factory floor. Lieberman was also aware of the presence of a number of illegal workers who were able to rent a SIN card for $10 a week.

Although the income statement showed a loss, the cash flows were not unattractive, and the demand for the product was consistently on the rise. Should he call a meeting of all the principal players and lay the cards on the table? No cooperation . . . no investment. Should he fire the president? Labour relations certainly weren't the president's forte. But with him gone there would be no management whatsoever. The Baker was laissez-faire in the extreme where changes were concerned, yet very controlling in terms of daily detail. In Lieberman's words:

> Everyone on the floor knows not to move so much as a carton until the old man gives the nod. And the Baker isn't there more than four hours a day anymore. He arrives at 4:00 a.m., stays around until the office staff comes in at 8:00, and retires to his home, declaring himself "on call." Day staff never talk to the night crew. No one knows what has happened overnight. And the old man will never go for any kind of control system.

More and more, Lieberman had found himself drawn in to deal with the numerous and pressing labour problems. "I simply have to get out from under the burden of hands-on management. This has virtually become a second full-time job."

He was very aware that radical steps were in order but felt, as always, that he was in an awkward and sensitive position in dealing with his father-in-law. Indeed, the earlier decision to shift his father-in-law's original partner into the delicatessen operation, in the face of his fraudulent activities, was largely attributable to San Linde being a family business. Fortunately, product demand was strong and both the factory storefront and the C.O.D. wholesaling operation were generating positive cash flows. Lieberman was concerned about his problems with the union and was considering initiating talks with union headquarters. "Perhaps," he thought, "a deal can be negotiated higher up to put a check on the local rabble rousers."

Exhibit 1		1984	1983	1982	1981
San Linde Bakery Inc. Consolidated Statement of Earnings for the Year Ended September 30 (000's)	Sales	$5,694	$4,806	$4,277	$3,907
	Cost of Sales	4,485	3,778	3,466	3,045
	Gross Margin	1,209	1,028	811	862
	Franchise Fees	69	63	–	–
	Gross Earnings	1,278	1,091	811	862
	Expenses				
	Selling	698	225	165	233
	Administrative	670	783	531	450
	Depreciation	116	111	79	59
		1,484	1,119	775	742
	Earnings (loss) Before Income Taxes and Extraordinary Items	(206)	(28)	36	120
	Income taxes recovered (expense)	20	8	(4)	(30)
	Extraordinary items, profit (loss)	(7)	–	–	53
	Net Income (Loss)	**$ (193)**	**(20)**	**32**	**143**

Exhibit 2

San Linde Bakery Inc. Organization Chart

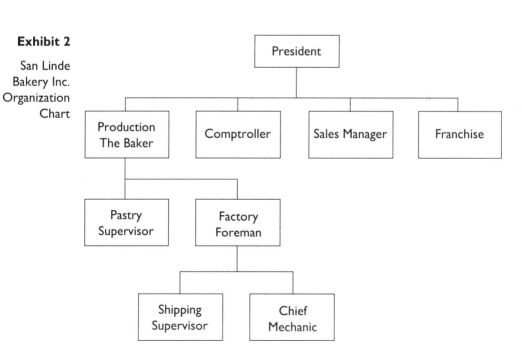

Marsden Compounding Ltd.

n November of 1978, William Jackson and Mitchell Cooper were attempting to arrange financing to purchase the assets of Marsden Compounding Ltd., a company which had been established in 1967 to produce thermo-plastic molding compounds for the plastic molding and extruding industry. Since 1973 the company had operated as a wholly owned subsidiary of Canadian Pacific Enterprises Ltd., which had an asset base of over $5 billion with interests in oil and gas, mines and minerals, real estate, agriculture, forest products, and steel. However, because of its failure to meet profit expectations, Marsden Compounding had been placed on the selling block by its parent corporation.

Jackson and Cooper both had extensive experience in the plastics industry and were well regarded for their business acumen. Together they had developed a number of specific strategies to improve Marsden's marketing and operational efficiency. However, the proposed purchase would involve a high degree of financial leverage, and consequently they were having difficulty securing proper financing for the venture. No chartered bank would provide them with adequate working capital or long-term financing, even though their investigation of Marsden had shown excellent earnings potential. Furthermore, both men were willing to invest all of their available personal resources in the purchase of Marsden.

The dilemma could only be resolved through the structuring of a financial package that took into consideration the perceived riskiness of the venture, and at the same time did not jeopardize the purchasers' position of control, debt serviceability, or financial flexibility.

Company Background

Marsden Compounding Ltd. was formed in 1967 by Elliott and Jason Marsden. The company produced thermo-plastic molding compounds for the plastic molding and extruding industry. Operations were located in Cornwall, Ontario and the company enjoyed a record of steady profits during its early years. In 1973 the Marsden brothers sold their shareholdings at a rather attractive price to Canadian Pacific Enterprises (CPE) Ltd., which at the time was in the midst of a program of diversification through acquisitions. CPE retained the Marsden brothers to manage the operation; however, as outlined in Exhibit 1, performance had been quite uneven since the takeover. (Also refer to Exhibit 2 for the most recent balance sheets.)

Elliott and Jason Marsden were 63 and 62 years of age, respectively, and it was apparent that since the sale of their stake in Marsden Compounding Ltd. they had been content to allow the company to find its own direction. As one industry observer commented:

> Marsden does excellent work, has very reputable personnel, and by virtue of its relatively small size has always been quite flexible from an operational standpoint. The curious thing is the complete lack of marketing push for the product line! Any success the company has had in recent years is due to favourable market conditions rather than good management.

Operations

As a manufacturer of thermo-plastic compounds, Marsden's basic function was the conversion of raw plastic resin into plastic pellets of specified colour, density, flexibility, and impact. The production process is illustrated in Figure 1.

Supplies of raw plastic were obtained both through primary suppliers such as Monsanto Canada Ltd. and Dow Chemical of Canada Ltd., and raw material traders. With the exception of colouring, the technology was quite straightforward. Subsequent to the blending stage, heat was applied under controlled conditions to produce a plastic mass with uniform chemical and physical properties. This mass was then extruded, cooled, and cut into thermo-plastic molding resin pellets. After packaging and shipping, the pellets were converted by the customer into finished plastic components. Customers included companies involved in injection molding, blow molding, and film, profile, and sheet extrusion.

To supplement its manufacturing activities, the company had also become involved in "trading". The firm would purchase natural resins such as styrene and polyethylene in large quantities and subsequently sell them in smaller lot sizes. Compounders such as Marsden had been able to enter this field simply because the large chemical firms had neither the time nor the labour-force necessary to market resins in the small quantities frequently required by extruding and injection molding companies. In fact, the large chemical firms, with their emphasis on volume, shipped product only in (rail) carload quantities. This practice opened up the trading market

Figure 1

Marsden
Compounding Ltd.
Process Flow
Diagram

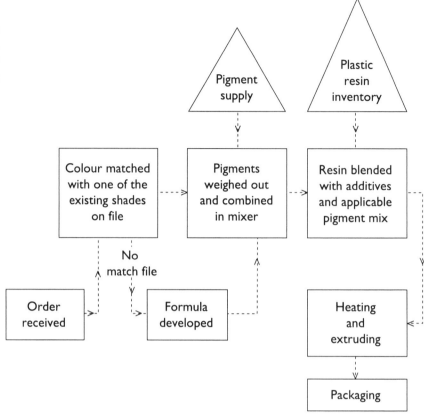

substantially for the compounders, giving them the opportunity to garner attractive returns by marketing the product in truckloads, boxes, and bags, in effect acting as a wholesaler.

The Marsden plant had three shifts, as the startup costs associated with the heating process were quite high. There were a total of 65 non-unionized labourers employed in the plant, which in 1978 was operating well under its capacity. The prospective purchasers felt that only nominal expenditures for plant refurbishing and streamlining would be necessary to meet their output projections for the next three years.

The Market

The company's traditional market was confined to the province of Ontario, which yielded approximately 200 potential customers for its products. Total annual demand was about 58 million pounds, and Cooper and

Jackson envisaged tremendous untapped potential in the automotive, communication, and appliance markets, which accounted for nearly 70 percent of the consumption of compounded products. It was their intention to exploit these sectors fully, since each had valuable contacts with various purchasing agents by virtue of their past experience in the industry. There were a total of 45 major users of thermo-plastic compounds in Ontario, each utilizing at least one million pounds per year; however, Cooper and Jackson could not understand why Marsden had only 20 percent of its 95 customers in this group.

The structure of the industry was such that the manufacturers who utilized plastic components in their production process tended to either operate their own molding facilities or control captive molding companies. For example, General Motors of Canada Ltd., the largest single Canadian consumer of molded parts, had molding plants in Oshawa and Windsor, while Canadian General Electric Co. and GSW Inc. had molding operations in Barrie and Cobourg, respectively. In addition, these operations were handling a greater proportion of their colouring needs in-house, especially for industrial components. However, extruders and molders were relatively unsophisticated in their colouring ability and consequently had no choice but to engage the services of a compounder when precise colour matching was important.

From the standpoint of the suppliers in this industry it had been observed that:

> Companies such as DuPont of Canada Inc., Dow Chemical of Canada Ltd., and Monsanto Canada Ltd., essentially regard themselves as converters of crude, producing the basic polymers in as large quantities as possible. If the end user requires some colouring of the product, the chemical company prefers to let a specialist do the job, insofar as it can take up to four days to change colours in an extruder. Monsanto is the only chemical company that is colouring or compounding to any degree, but only for lot sizes in excess of 10 000 lbs.

Another factor which impinged on the activities of the manufacturer of molding compounds was the restriction faced by independent extruders and molders on their sources of compounded plastic. This situation arose because buyers of plastic components often had a list of approved compounders that had to be observed. Consequently, the compounder's marketing effort had to be directed not only towards the independent extruders and molders, but also towards the end-user industries.

Jackson and Cooper saw the business of Marsden Compounding Ltd. as being relatively concentrated, with the 16 largest accounts comprising 70 percent of 1977 revenue. In their efforts to broaden the company's market base they looked with particular interest at the automobile industry. They had in fact researched this venture extensively and were convinced that Marsden Compounding Ltd. possessed the physical plant capacity, as well as the human resources and expertise, that would be required to service the plastic requirements of the automotive sector. Inexplicably, as of 1978, the company had absolutely no automotive activity whatsoever, although some competitors were doing as much as two-thirds of their business in automotive related areas.

With prime suppliers abandoning the compounding business, the compounding industry was enjoying a growth phase; given their extensive product and market knowledge, and well developed reputations in the industry, Jackson and Cooper estimated that they would ultimately be able to bring as much as 15 percent of the Ontario market with them if this acquisition were consummated.

Competition

The manufacture of molding compounds was a relatively close-knit industry with a limited number of participants and, according to one industry analyst, ". . . there are only a limited number of worthwhile compounders in the entire country!"

The strongest competitor, A. Schulman Canada Ltd., had been in operation for only four years. Annual revenues were in the $11 million range and the company's success had been attributed to raw materials buying power, close ties with the automotive market, and an aggressive marketing program. By 1978 this company's share of the Ontario compounding market stood at 35 percent.

Canadian Fiberfil Ltd., a division of Dart Industries Inc., had been established in 1971 and was generating sales of approximately $4 million. The company possessed valuable contacts with original equipment manufacturers in the electrical and communication industries, but was not considered particularly aggressive.

Argo Plastics Ltd., controlled by Noranda Mines Ltd., lacked knowledgeable personnel despite a long history in the compounding business. The company relied on two or three large accounts for most of its $3 million annual volume.

Another competitor, Aclo Compounders Limited of Cambridge, Ontario, was a wholly owned subsidiary of the American company, Crown Cork and Seal Limited. The smallest of Marsden's competitors, Aclo tended to concentrate on smaller accounts, did very little business outside of its immediate geographic area, and was saddled with an aging plant facility.

Jackson and Cooper regarded the Schulman and Fiberfil operations as the main barriers to any attempt to broaden the company's market base. However, they weren't sure whether their marketing plans would be perceived by these competitors as enough of a threat to warrant a serious response; they could recall no instances of price cutting among Ontario compounders in recent years.

The Proposed Acquisition

As already noted, Jackson and Cooper had examined every aspect of the business opportunity, and on the basis of long discussions with CPE had agreed on a purchase price of $1.2 million for the assets of Marsden Compounding Ltd. This sum would be apportioned as follows:

Land	135,000
Buildings	140,000
Machinery, Equipment & Furniture	220,000
Accounts Receivable	367,000
Inventory	338,000
TOTAL	$1,200,000

The real estate in question comprised nine acres of industrially zoned land. The main plant covered 125 000 square feet and was approximately 50 years old; it included a three-storey section of brick and stone construction, a one-storey brick section, and a two-storey brick and concrete block office area. In addition, there were two other free standing brick buildings and three large metal storage sheds. The property had been appraised at $225 000 in 1977.

The machinery and equipment consisted largely of sundry extruders, mixers, blenders, conveyor systems, and interior holding bins. These items were in a generally good state of repair. However, the marketability of such equipment was always questionable. An analysis of the company's receivables had shown that over 90 percent were current, i.e., less than 90 days past due:

1–30 days	189,640
31–60 days	132,620
61–90 days	41,465
91–120 days	11,950
over 120 days	17,250
TOTAL	$392,925

Marsden's inventory was comprised primarily of raw material. Jackson and Cooper were prepared to pay a good price for the resin, which could always be simply packaged and resold to those manufacturers requiring small quantities of uncoloured, non-compounded resin.

In addition to the actual purchase price, the purchasers were allowing a total of $25 000 for such items as legal, accounting, and financing fees, supplier liabilities, unfulfilled contracts, and minor housekeeping modifications.

Despite what they considered to be a well researched, fully documented loan proposal, which included a particularly attractive set of profit projections (Exhibit 3), Jackson and Cooper had not been able to convince any lenders to approve the level of financing required to complete this purchase. The principals were in a position to inject $35 000 each into the program. Even though they perceived this as a strong show of faith given their limited personal assets, the bankers they had approached seemed to be quite concerned over the extremely thin equity base on which the new entity would be operating. Moreover, the banking community seemed to focus on the fact that the collateral value of the underlying assets would be inadequate to support the level of funding being proposed. The National Bank of Canada had confirmed a willingness to provide credit line facilities, supported by receivables and inventory, with a ceiling of $425 000. In addition, the vendor, CP Enterprises Ltd., was prepared to finance up to $150 000 of the price by way of a subordinated debenture calling for equal principal installments over six years, commencing in 1980.

The real stumbling block to completion of the purchase was the $580 000 funding shortfall. There seemed to be no simple solution to this problem, but the principals were determined to find a source of funds to complement the commitments already in place, without impinging on the overall profit outlook, the operation's financial flexibility, or management's control position.

Irreconcilable Differences?

Both men had the utmost confidence in their ability to transform the company into a highly profitable operation. They were convinced that their profit projections were not, as various bankers had suggested, based on a highly idealistic perception of the operation's future prospects, but in fact reflected the strong performance that would be almost inevitable once their management policies were in place. Jackson and Cooper recognized that the purchase of Marsden Compounding Ltd. represented the type of opportunity that would not likely present itself again, but nonetheless were now on the verge of giving up in their attempts to find a lender that would look at the venture from their perspective.

Exhibit 1		1974	1975	1976	1977	1978
Marsden	Sales (Net)	$2,952	$2,578	$1,483	$2,358	$2,580
Compounding	Cost of Sales*	2,317	2,070	1,334	2,151	2,268
Ltd.	Gross Profit	635	508	149	207	312
Comparative						
Profit and Loss	Interest Expense	11	8	23	35	29
Statements,	Other Operating Expenses	221	149	103	131	205
1974–78	Provision for					
($000's)	Income Taxes:					
	Current	133	149	8	17	29
	Deferred	64	26	3	–	–
	Net Profit	206	176	12	24	49
	* Includes Depreciation Charges of:	**56**	**63**	**60**	**61**	**58**

	June 30 1976	June 30 1977	June 30 1978
Exhibit 2			
Current Assets			
Cash	$ 15	$ 87	$ 137
Accounts receivable	453	394	393
Inventory	368	392	401
Prepaid expenses	10	9	12
	846	882	943
Fixed Assets			
Property	479	448	397
Vehicles & equipment	464	477	502
Total Fixed Assets	943	925	899
(less depreciation)	(306)	(396)	(468)
Net Fixed Assets	637	529	433
Total Assets	$1,483	$1,411	$1,376
Current Liabilities			
Accounts payable	$ 265	$ 278	$ 233
Bank loans	59	35	41
	324	313	274
Long-Term Debt			
Advances from parent	504	419	374
Deferred income taxes	112	112	112
Equity			
Preferred shares	20	20	20
Retained earnings	523	547	596
Total Equity	543	567	616
Total Liabilities and Equity	$1,483	$1,411	$1,376

Marsden Compounding Ltd. Comparative Balance Sheets, 1976–78 ($000's)

Exhibit 3		1980	1981
Marsden Compounding Ltd. Projected Profit and Loss Statements, 1980 and 1981 ($000's)	Sales (Net)	$4,900	$6,850
	Cost of Sales		
	Opening inventory	475	670
	Raw material	3,135	4,260
	Direct labour	432	595
	Indirect labour	238	315
	Manufacturing overhead	300	415
	Depreciation	60	50
		4,640	6,305
	Ending Inventory	670	805
	Cost of Goods Sold	3,970	5,500
	Gross Profit	930	1,350
	Operating Expenses		
	Administrative salaries	123	148
	Advertising and promotion	31	58
	Selling salaries	56	83
	Office overhead	52	76
	Interest*	155	145
		417	510
	Operating Profit	513	840
	Provision for Income Taxes	110	180
	Net Earnings	**403**	**660**

* Interest expense estimates are based on the assumption that the $580,000 of outside funding is raised in the form of long-term debt.

C H A P T E R

7

Managing the Transition Phases

Introduction

In Chapter 2 we discussed two types of phases in the growth and development of the small business: first there were the operating phases (1, 3 and 5) in which the small business consolidates its resources, attends to profitability, and limits its growth to a level which can be supported by the stable phase structure. Second, there were the transition phases (2 and 4), which deal with the dynamics of moving between the operating phases.

The transition phases present special challenges to the firm's survival. Often, the move from one development phase to the next requires major structural changes to facilitate growth and task delegation in the small firm. For some, the transition to a more complex phase must be attempted several times, and for others, the transition is never completed. For most, the costs of transition are high.

In most small businesses, growth and development does not conform to any one pattern.

Typically, the shape of the firm is a function of the interests and skills of the owner, who will likely use a variety of approaches as the company seeks a viable growth path.

Chapter 7 discusses some of the problems encountered in the transition phases generally, as well as the particular difficulties that arise in the transition from an owner-operated firm to an owner-managed firm; and from an owner-managed to a functionally managed firm.

Growth and Development Objectives

A large number of small firms never progress beyond the owner-operated or owner-managed stage: some by choice, others because they are unwilling or incapable of adopting the organizational changes required. For instance, the cost of relinquishing control and/or management authority may make the emergence of effective functional management difficult or impossible, or the skills essential to the task of a general manager in a functional organization may not be readily available. At this point the owner-managed firm may become an attractive acquisition for firms with the required management skills, or an attractive sale for the owner-manager, if the value offered exceeds the return that can be achieved by continuing as a phase 3 company.

Phase Movement

What prompts firms to move from one phase to another? Growth often forces the small firm to move, simply because the size exceeds the management capacity of the owner-operator or the owner-manager. Development needs (technology, customer support systems, etc.) can force the move inasmuch as it becomes necessary to give specialist managers authority and responsibility for the development and use of new systems and procedures. Some moves arise from external forces, such as new business opportunities, new orders, new competitive realities, takeovers, or other pressures which alter the needs of the firm and its means of doing business effectively.

Movement through the development phases is usually more a continuum than a step-by-step process. In some cases, however, the company may make several unsuccessful attempts to move from one phase to another before completing the actual transition. Alternatively, part of the organization may be moved to the next development phase while major company functions remain entrenched in the earlier phase. This mixed-phase situation creates special problems for the small-business manager.

Successful phase movements are a function of the support that is in place before the movement of an operations or marketing activity can take place.[1] We refer to a negative phase movement as one where a productive activity is moved to the next phase without the support activities in place, and a positive phase movement as one where the support activities *are* in place.

Each phase requires different support systems to facilitate phase movement. The cost of such support increases as the firm grows. As with many management assets, the initial investment is high and the payoff, at best, long term. For this reason, many of the essentials of shifting from owner-operator to owner-manager, and from owner-manager to functional management, may be viewed as unnecessary frills by the characteristically self-sufficient small business owner.

Acceptable levels of profitability usually take place once the company has stabilized in one or another of the development phases. Profitability is not guaranteed in phases 1, 3 or 5, but is more likely to occur in these phases, when management seeks to take advantage of its investments in infrastructure, people, equipment, and systems. The nature of the transition stages almost insures that these periods in company development will feature reduced profits, and perhaps losses or even business failure. This has less to do with any theoretical definition than with the simple fact that transitions involve new investment in overhead and productive capacity. These costs, even when capitalized, appear in the financial performance figures long before any profits are realized due to the change. Therefore, planning and implementing phase movements are critical elements in company development.

Managing the Transition to Owner-Management

Making the transition from phase 1 (including startup) where the assistance of lawyers, accountants and other consultants may have had significant roles, to phase 3 requires that a number of activities be implemented. Although the cost of these services is high, they are variable and available as required. As the firm moves to phase 3 some of the activities provided by outsiders on a demand basis become essential parts of day-to-day operations and must be added to the permanent contingent of the firm. And a distinct, although limited, role emerges for general management.

The ability of the new owner to grow as a manager is extremely important if the firm is to develop. Typically, managing-by-doing is centred around the skills the owner brings to the firm at start up. For many small businesses this phase may continue for long periods of time. Management, as it is defined by most authors, goes beyond the needs of the firm at this stage. As the firm grows and management activities emerge as a necessity, the move to phase 3 begins.

While movement through this transition and into an early phase 3 position may still be guided largely by the ideas and direction presented in the business plan, the owner must now exhibit some management skills as well as operating skills.

This increased attention to the functions of management (planning, organizing, coordinating, and controlling) in turn requires increased communication, both internally and externally; increased information for such communication; and the facilities for processing increased information flows. The transition from owner-management to functional management accentuates these management needs while also requiring the sharing of responsibility and authority and a substantial increase in the need for effective planning and communications.

Managing a larger and more complex organization also forces the rearrangement of management time. In the early stages of development there is a tendency to invest little in planning and organizing and to focus instead on the coordinating function (that is, adjusting quickly to change as it happens). Because most small firms have limited investment in fixed-cost activities, they can make necessary changes relatively easily. As the organization grows, though, it becomes dependent on larger order quantities (volume), more efficient production and delivery systems, and an infrastructure that can handle high-volume activities effectively. This move marks the beginning of higher fixed-cost investments and the shifting of management attention to planning and organizing. The flexibility of the coordinating task, typical in the earlier phase, begins to erode with the need to operate more rigid facilities efficiently. As volumes increase, problems pervade both core functions (operations and marketing), and demand planning, communication, and control beyond that evident in owner-operated firms. Managers must not only invest in better information but must learn how to use it properly.

Planning in the Phase Two Transition

There are several major differences, as well as many similarities, between the operating phases and the transition phases. Perhaps the main difference is in the area of planning.

We would suggest that, in general, planning is not a major factor in transition management, but rather takes place in phases 1, 3, and 5. In these phases the need to plan for the transition becomes a significant consideration when the decision to move to the next operating phase is made. Thus, the planning components of phase 2, and the entry into phase 3, are appropriately part of phase 1 planning, while the planning components of phase 4 and the entry into phase 5 are rightfully part of the phase 3 planning activity.

The key management activities in the transition phases are those essential to getting from phase to phase expeditiously. There will always be a need for planning adjustments and these planning adjustments are the main focus of phase 2 and phase 4 planning. Since these adjustments (organizing and coordinating) take place on uncharted ground, the importance of sound planning increases as the business leaves phase 1.

When the need for increased management capacity becomes evident, planning for the transition assumes major importance. Since the next operating phase requires some structural change, plans for these changes must be undertaken to create structures capable of facilitating further growth and development. As part of this structural change there arises a need to plan for the people, skills, systems, and information essential to support new roles. Without a total package in place, many of the needs of the phase 3 operating system will not be met.

As the infrastructure grows (becoming less flexible in return for developing efficiency and capacity), the ability to reverse direction without incurring unreasonable costs is diminished. The need to commit more resources for longer periods increases the potential for greater losses if the commitment is ill-conceived. Planning can minimize the cost of choosing, and committing to, poor options, while allowing managers to explore options and risks. Thus, establishing direction and setting the limits for action are the key functions of phase 1 planning. Performing these activities effectively is one of the first steps in the growth of the owner-operator into an owner-manager.

Organizing in the Phase Two Transition

Since phase 3 requires more management time, several changes must be made by the owner-operator. Delegation, even in a small way, becomes a necessary skill, and involving other people, both inside and outside of the organization, becomes a major factor. Organizing depends on a need to understand the skills, the strengths, and the weaknesses of subordinates, and to develop communication processes that enable managers to monitor and to adjust the process. It also means more management decisions will have to be made on the basis of information feedback, as opposed to direct involvement.

Coordinating in the Phase Two Transition

In phase 1 the owner-operator is involved in a serial process: a little organizing, a little work, a little coordinating, and so on. The process is both dependent on, and limited by, the time and skills of the owner-operator. Since the owner-operator is central to all company activities, coordination is part and parcel of the organizing task.

Controlling in the Phase Two Transition

The controlling task in phase 2 is also affected by the total involvement of the owner-manager in all company activities. As a result of this involvement, the feedback of control information is immediate and the adjustment process continuous.

In summary, the total involvement of the owner-operator in all aspects of the company's operations blurs the distinctions typically associated with the management tasks of planning, organizing, coordinating, and controlling. However, in the phase 2 transition the owner must begin to develop an awareness of these activities in order to provide for the emergence of a growing management role in phase 3. This notion is illustrated in Figure 7-1, which shows, as an example, a negative phase movement, in which the operations function has reached a phase 3 level prior to the support functions.

Managing the Transition to Functional Management

Normally the phase 4 transition is complicated for owner-managers since it involves the sharing of both responsibility and authority. Further, bringing new managers onstream involves an investment in overhead, such as new systems to facilitate communication and measurements for control and performance evaluation.

The move through phase 4 (see Figure 7-2), where the addition of functional specialists means increases in the costs of information, communication, and control, can be extremely expensive. And the task of deciding which functional specialties should be added and in which order complicates the process.

Often, the early development of a functional organization begins with the

Figure 7-1

Transition Phase 2 - Moving to Owner - Management

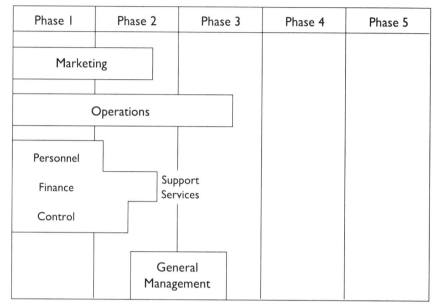

Figure 7-2

Transition Phase 4 - The Move to Functional Management

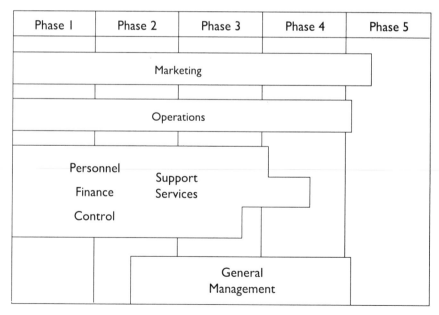

hiring of an additional manager to perform some of those activities that the owner-operator or owner-manager cannot or does not like doing. Evidence suggests that while some responsibilities *are* given up in order that the owner-manager can focus more time and effort on the role of general management, this transition seldom happens easily. The skills for this role are quite different from those practiced by owner-managers in phase 3, and the transition is characterized early on by a much greater shifting of responsibility than of authority and a penchant for intervention if a new manager does not perform to the owner's subjective expectations.

Many small firms do not have, and are not willing to invest in, the information systems essential to the needs of a functional organization. Typically, the owner-manager has not found such accoutrements necessary. On the other hand, new managers, with disparate backgrounds and limited knowledge of the firm, are unable to function properly if support for planning and decision-making are not part of the firm's information systems.

Planning in the Phase Four Transition

There is a significant difference in all of the management activities between the phase 2 transition and the phase 4 transition. While phase 1 and the early stages of phase 3 feature a serial process of management, the later stages of phase 3 and phase 5 require a parallel management process. In this changing setting the tasks of management become much more complex. There is a growing separation between management and operating activities, and hence a need to communicate and motivate within a process where the owner is less and less a part of the day-to-day operations. These activities must be integrated into the process and tasks of management. As well, the emergence of functional managers creates the need for a general management role.

In this phase, planning not only provides direction and a basis for action, it also provides a forum for sharing and integrating the skills of the new managers. Their participation in the planning process gives them a depth of understanding and greater motivation. In other words, effective communication in the planning activity directly affects the subsequent tasks of organizing and coordinating, and plays a major role in shifting some responsibility for the firm's growth onto non-owners.

Finally, planning in phases 4 and 5 becomes a two-step function: strategic planning takes place between the general manager and the functional managers, while operational planning focuses on the needs of functional managers and their subordinates. The same split becomes evident in each of the management tasks performed in this and subsequent phases.

Organizing in the Phase Four Transition

Organizing in phase 4 must adapt to parallel management processes where multiple management activities are taking place simultaneously, and often without the need for a central or controlling role by the owner. The growing time gaps between the acquisition and the allocation of resources, and the utilization of these resources within the company, puts a premium on the organizing tasks of management. Seldom will the resources available be adequate to meet the needs of company objectives but proper emphasis on the organizing task should insure that planned resource allocations are used effectively.

As with planning, organizing becomes a two-step process, in order to meet both the strategic and the operational demands of the firm. This split requires an increased attention to communications that was not as evident in phase 2.

Coordinating in the Phase Four Transition

While both the organizing and the coordinating tasks in phase 4 involve sharing authority and responsibility, the process is particularly acute in the coordinating/directing activity. Here, the functional manager is more or less alone with the responsibilities of the job. The general manager is less involved and has a growing dependence on performance information to determine if the planning and organizing of the company's strategic and resource allocation processes will pay off. While here, too, we see a two-step process, coordinating at this level is focused largely on operational, rather than strategic, issues. And, for the first time in the growth of the small business, the actual implementation of activities is in the hands of non-owner managers.

Controlling in the Phase Four Transition

Where the controlling function in phase 1 was minimal and oriented mainly to external communication, in phases 4 and 5 there is a marked change. The growing organizational span, coupled with the allocation of authority and responsibility to functional managers, makes the general manager dependent on a more formal control/information system. The information generated by the system becomes a central ingredient in both the planning and organizing tasks. The task of evaluating plans and the performance of managers, a role that was non-existent in phase 2, assumes a growing importance, and is dependent on a well developed control system that can provide timely and accurate information.

Survival, Vulnerability and the Transition Phases

Many factors affect the survival of small firms. There is strong evidence to suggest that until firms reach the five-year mark, they are particularly vulnerable to failure. Certainly environmental factors such as recessions, technological change, social change and competitive pressures challenge small firms. And, while all of these factors are common to most businesses, the phase of development of a small enterprise can exacerbate its vulnerability. Figure 7-3 portrays the changes in business vulnerability as the small firm develops and grows from phase to phase. The figure suggests that:

1. Areas of greatest profitability for most small companies exist in the mature periods of each phase, and
2. Major areas of vulnerability are faced by small firms attempting to move to a new phase.

Vulnerability is particularly high at the beginning of each phase and remains high throughout periods of transition. Figure 7-3 suggests that the management activities of planning, organizing, coordinating and controlling during these phases must be carried out as quickly as resources permit, minimizing the firm's exposure to high levels of risk.

Prescriptively, two implications are suggested. First, substantial planning for the transition should be undertaken in phase 1 before the move to phase 3 is attempted. Second, planning and the process of implementation should focus on making the transition as quickly as possible once the decision has

Figure 7-3

Business Vulnerability in the Transition Phases

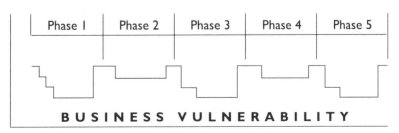

been made. Prolonged periods in transition can be costly, while failure to make adequate commitments to move may result in the need to retrench. These same problems are applicable to the move from phase 3 to phase 5.

The Role of Outside Services in the Transition Phases

As in most situations where change is a factor, time and investment requirements are tightly related. Once on the road to the next phase, the cost of failing to make the transition is particularly high. Because the transition will take the small firm into uncharted areas of activity, there is often a role for outside assistance. Such assistance can take many forms, including help in planning for the transition, acquiring new skills (particularly in management), designing new support systems, and training people to handle the expanded responsibilities that come with transition.

Despite their high cost, consulting services acquired on a one-shot basis can often provide the help necessary for transition without adding permanently to the overhead. Such assistance is particularly important when owner-operators or owner-managers are faced with decisions which involve them in areas foreign to their experience, or in situations where the time to do a particular job properly is simply not available.

The use of outside help in specialty areas (accounting, advertising and promotion) is accepted by many small businesses. However, few opt for such help when making growth and development decisions. This is unfortunate; since these moves and subsequent operating phase requirements introduce new variables for owner-operators, the use of outside assistance can be particularly effective. At a minimum, it can prevent a move destined to fail; at best, outside experience will assist company owners in a smooth transition.

Transition in a Franchise Setting

The problems of growth and development in the franchise organization are mitigated in large part because most franchise organizations begin and end in a predetermined development phase. Access to management and operating services is usually part of the franchise agreement. These services are provided on a variable-cost basis, making them both readily available and affordable. As a result, small franchise organizations seldom undergo phase evolution like that encountered in non-franchise organizations. The skills essential to entry at any particular phase are available as part of the franchise package. Growth objectives seldom require phase movement, since the franchise is tailored from the outset to exploit a well defined market. When the location served grows beyond the ability of the franchise to meet market needs, the company usually adds a new outlet. Again, the new outlet will be designed around an optimum location, facilities and infrastructure, and supported by the franchisor until the market is profitable.

Depending on the nature of the franchise, the operation may open and remain in any one of the operating phases. There are franchises designed to exploit the particular strengths of phase 1, such as tool distributors (Herbrand, Proto and Red Stallion), oil change operations (Quik Lube and Speedy Lube) and convenience stores (Mac's, Beckers, and Seven-Eleven). In these situations the business requires a minimum of management and a high level of owner-operator activity.

Phase 3, perhaps the most common slot for franchise operations, provides for a substantial increase in the management role. The owners of these franchises receive management training and function within a well structured management support system provided by the franchisor: examples include muffler shops (Speedy and Midas), car rental agencies (Budget, Avis and Rent-a-Wreck), and most fast-food franchises (Tim Horton's, Burger King, Harvey's and, despite the size of some outlets, McDonald's). Management is mainly involved with internal resources, since most franchises dictate the outlet's relationship with the external system. While many of the larger franchises adopt quasi-functional organizations, both the skills and the decision-making latitude are severely limited by the franchise agreement and the desire to make the owner-manager the only contact with the franchise system.

Phase 5 franchises typically involve master franchise agreements where the master franchisor sells and operates franchises within the allocated territory. Since most franchisors provide major functional services (marketing, accounting and control), franchises in phase 5 operate with only very limited or truncated functional organizations at best.

Only at startup do franchise organizations experience the vulnerability of transition. As long as the franchise concept remains viable, the organization will likely continue to function in its designated phase. Should the concept fail, most franchises become extremely vulnerable and disappear totally, or at least in many regions (Ponderosa and Red Barn). Figure 7-4 illustrates the issue of vulnerability in the franchise setting.

The strengths of franchising beyond startup (concept, location, facilities

Figure 7-4

Phase
Vulnerability
in a Franchise
Setting

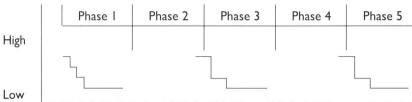

| | Phase I | Phase 2 | Phase 3 | Phase 4 | Phase 5 |

BUSINESS VULNERABILITY / COST

and operating procedures) include management systems, marketing assistance and control systems. Also, as part of the franchising agreement, the franchisee undergoes regular inspections of his facilities, product and services. All of these services are typical of the procedures of larger firms but are available to early phase operators because of the shared cost provisions of the franchise contract.

The weakness of the franchising system for most franchisees is the pressure to conform despite individual market differences. Change in these organizations takes place through franchisee committees, which meet periodically to lobby the franchisor. However, change requires consensus, thereby making it difficult for individual franchisees to deal with local problems.

List of Key Words

Acquisition
(External) Assistance
Communication
Controlling
Coordinating
Franchise

(Management) Functions
(Phase) Movement
Organizing
Plan
Vulnerability

Questions for Discussion

1. a) Why do many small firms have to attempt the transitions (phases 2 & 4) more than once? Why do attempts at transition often fail?
   b) Discuss the implications of positive and negative phase movement on the transition phases.

2. Explain how the transition to phase 5 can provide small business owners with an opportunity for divestment.

3. Explain how support activities can facilitate phase movement.

4. The text suggests that the risks of business failure increase during the transition phases. Why? What can be done to minimize these risks?

5. Why are franchise operations rarely affected by transition problems? Can the basic elements of the franchise setting be transferred to other small businesses?

Selected Readings

Beckman, Richard and Reuben T. Harris, *Organizational Transitions: Managing Complex Change*. Reading, MA: Addison Wesley, 1977.

Bulloch, J.F., "Problems of Succession in Small Business," *Human Resource Management*, Ann Arbor: University of Michigan Graduate School of Business Administration, Summer, 1978 pp. 2–6.

Charon, R., C.W. Hofer, and J. Mahon, "From Entrepreneurship to Professional Management: A Set of Guidelines," *Journal of Small Business Management*, 10 (January 1980), pp. 1–9.

Goodman, Jacob, "Franchisor-Franchisee Relation Requires Delicate Balance," *Marketing News*, February 17, 1984, p. 4.

Ibrahim, A. Bakr, "Is Franchising the Answer to Small Business Failure Rate? An Empirical Study," *Journal of Small Business and Entrepreneurship*, 3, no. 2 (Fall 1985), pp. 48–54.

Johnson, L. and R. Kuehn, "The Small Business Owner-Manager's Search for External Information," *Journal of Small Business Management*, 3, 1987, pp. 53–60.

Kao, Raymond, *Entrepreneurship and Enterprise Development*. Toronto, Ont: Holt, Rinehart and Winston of Canada Limited, 1989, pp. 320–40.

Morgan, John D., *Managing Change: The Strategies of Making Change Work*. New York, N.Y.: McGraw-Hill, 1972.

Endnotes

1. We have defined productive activities as those of producing or marketing the product or service of the business, and a support activity as one which facilitates the performance of the firm's productive activities.

CASE 7-1

Phoenix Airmotive

In September 1989 Mr. Dan Melanson, owner of Phoenix Airmotive, a helicopter repair and overhaul facility, was reviewing the firm's first two years and considering future options. Year two financial statements showed an eight-fold increase in sales, although the company was still operating at a loss. Summer was generally a slow period and Phoenix was entering the fall with a significant amount of trade debt.

Company Description

Phoenix was founded in September 1987 as an Ontario numbered company with Mr. Melanson as President. The business was initiated with a mixture of conventional and government loan financing as a venture in the helicopter/aircraft parts overhaul business. The maintenance of aircraft is governed by the Ministry of Transport (Canada). An Aircraft Maintenance Engineer (AME) must be licensed for each type of aircraft to be repaired. Phoenix is licensed to work on most light turbine and piston engine helicopters including the Bell 206, which makes up half of the Canadian fleet of 1300 machines. Within a 200-mile radius of Sudbury, there were approximately 40 helicopters operating, of which half were Bell 206's. The balance was split between Aerospatial A-Star, Bell 47, McDonnell Douglas MD500, and Bell 212 and 412. Phoenix could work on all these models except the Bell 212 and 412 which, as heavy machines, were in a different license category by weight.

The present site was in a rented space at the south end of Sudbury on property adjacent to a Canadian Helicopters (CHC) base. CHC is a national firm with over 200 helicopters; however, only a few were stationed at Sudbury. The Ministry of Natural Resources air base was just five minutes drive away on MacFarlane Lake. Both these firms were potential customers.

The various types of repair work performed by Phoenix include periodic maintenance, overhauling of dynamic, electrical, and hydraulic components on the basis of prescribed flight hour limits, non-destructive testing (NDT), helicopter salvage, refinishing, and rebuilding.

Mr. Melanson had 13 years experience in the industry, and contacts across the country. His career in aviation began in 1976 when he was hired as an Aircraft Maintenance Engineer (AME) with Okanagan Helicopters in British Columbia. He performed line and field maintenance in the High Arctic, the Northwest Territories, as well as in British Columbia, Ontario and Newfoundland. He remained with Okanagan Helicopters until April of 1981 when he was hired by Lakeland Helicopters, Sudbury, as Chief Engineer. In May 1984 he was appointed General Manager, Helico Canada, Calgary and was responsible for a fleet of 57 aircraft and 120 personnel at 22 bases across Canada. He returned to Sudbury in 1986 to set up his own maintenance facility.

The Industry

Helicopters have many applications, including transportation to off-shore and other isolated exploration and drilling projects; they are also used for mining claims and surveying, personal and air ambulance transportation, forestry, and forest fire suppression. Recent data indicated that the industry was in a state of growth. Following a decline in the early eighties which saw many smaller operators fold, the industry experienced steady growth, not only in hours, but also in the number of helicopters being flown. The local market gave every indication of increased activity, with new operators coming into the area and a general increase in the number of hours being flown.

There were approximately seven companies in the helicopter repair and service business in Ontario and 20 in Canada. The nearest competition for Phoenix was USCAN Aviation in Alliston Ontario, 320 km from Sudbury. The helicopter industry is a closely knit, small community. Reputation and contacts are key success factors in the industry.

Ministry of Transport regulations outlined the maintenance schedule for each type of helicopter based on manufacturer's specifications. All machines required daily inspections and 50- or 100-hour inspections, along with certain other requirements for parts/lubricant replacement. Major inspections and engine or other component overhauls were required at longer intervals of 600–2000 hours. Small operators (less than four helicopters) often did not employ an AME and were thus dependent on firms such as Phoenix for scheduled maintenance.

The salvage of crashed or damaged helicopters was a lucrative part of the helicopter repair business, as parts were expensive. Operators of executive helicopters in the southern markets did not, as a rule, buy parts from crashed machines, but northern bush operators often appreciated the value of used parts, which could result in their saving tens of thousands of dollars. Phoenix acquired three wrecks in 1988–89 and was actively pursuing this market. One problem with this business was that, as in automobile salvage, parts inventory is valued at the lesser of cost or market value, so that balance sheet inventory levels did not reflect actual saleable assets.

Company Operations

During the first year of operation, Mr. Melanson spent a considerable amount of time seeking the necessary approvals for working on aircraft. Sales were low for the first year ($36 000) as shown in Exhibit 1. During this time some helicopters were refurbished with paint and upholstery, but no mechanical work was done.

The second year saw a significant increase in sales, to $30 000 per month for the first five months. These sales were the result of increased maintenance activity and of the sale of salvage parts. A local investor who was interested in avaition was having a helicopter rebuilt for sale, and this provided a steady source of income for the shop over the winter months. However, the aircraft did not sell as expected in April 1989, and its presence in the shop began to hamper operations, both physically and financially: little billable time remained on the machine being rebuilt and new work could not be taken in because it was taking up shop space.

Sales for fiscal 1989 were $280 000, and Mr. Melanson felt that not selling the rebuilt helicopter had cost Phoenix two to three months in lost operating revenue. Net loss was $21 502. Cost of sales was made up mainly of parts and material purchases, with approximately $55 000 being wages. The cash flow situation was poor and Phoenix was in arrears up to six months with some trade creditors (Exhibit 2). One major supplier, which accounted for over $30 000, was willing to carry Phoenix because of the good relationship and prior history Mr. Melanson had established. This goodwill was a significant benefit of his reputation. Additional bank financing was not available, as the Northern Ontario Development Corporation held a charge against assets. This government assistance was a forgivable loan based on capital purchases and employment. No problems were anticipated in fulfilling the terms of the agreement. The current staff complement included Mr. Melanson, another engineer, several part-time apprentices, and a part-time bookkeeper. Mr. Melanson's duties included day-to-day engineering, any wreck recovery or salvage, all refinishing activities, and marketing.

Current Situation

In the early fall of 1989 Mr. Melanson faced a number of problems. After its second year of operation, Phoenix was still not making money. The facility was not an ideal one from an operating standpoint as the shop was too small. Several jobs had had to be turned away. As well, he found he couldn't turn some jobs around fast enough because of the necessity of dismantling a machine to get it through the door of the shop. To take advantage of increased activity in the market, Melanson felt a new facility was required. In addition, commercial and residential building around his facility was going to result in the heliport license[1] being revoked in the near future. Phoenix's landlord was developing another piece of property at the west end of the city, in an industrial area which had convenient access to the city on a major bypass. It seemed ideal for a new hangar and heliport. His neighbour, Canadian Helicopters, was under the same space constraints and heliport considerations, and they had signed a letter of intent to lease space at this new location. The property was on a lake (for float plane landings) and the adjacent land was suitable for development as a 3200-foot runway.

The concept of moving to a new facility was attractive. However, there would be an increase in overhead expenses from $7000 per month to double this amount. This fact concerned Mr. Melanson.

The potential facility presented a number of new options for the business. In addition to housing the helicopter service operation, the proposed hangar would be large enough for repairing fixed-wing aircraft (on floats), a market Melanson was somewhat familiar with. He knew that the two local fixed-wing (floats) maintenance facilities had sales totalling $700 000, while an additional estimated $150 000 went out of the city to Parry Sound and Sault Ste. Marie. This market was attractive, as fixed-wing maintenance was mainly carried out in the summer, while heavy helicopter maintenance happened in the winter time.[2] He would have to hire a fixed-wing AME and had someone in mind for this position. There were no negative implications of having fixed and rotary wing being worked on in the same hangar.

Refinishing of aircraft was something that Phoenix performed under less than ideal conditions currently, and he felt that the market for good-quality refinishing work was at least as large as current maintenance in dollar terms, based on requests he had from operators. The process of refinishing involved stripping all paint from the aircraft, repairing any body defects, and then repainting. With the purchase of additional equipment he could capture this market, as there were no local aircraft refinishing shops.

Fuel sales by Phoenix were proposed as a part of the new facility, since Canadian Helicopters was committed to moving there and they required fuel. Also, MNR had expressed an interest in basing its machines there. Their current consumption was about 350 000 litres/year at $.67/litre.[3] Fixed-wing fuel could be sold also and the market was estimated at 1.5 million litres ($.82/litre), although Melanson was not sure what portion of the fixed-wing market he could get. Phoenix was the logical choice to provide this service, although insurance to cover fuelling facilities was $15 000 per year.

The new facility would be a fixed base operation for aircraft, both fixed-wing and rotary-wing. It would provide service, maintenance, aircraft refinishing, fuel, storage, docking and tie downs for aircraft. This integration of services was a strong selling point for the facility, as aircraft operators were interested in one-stop shopping. Similar facilities did not exist north of Toronto. Mr. Melanson felt that in the new facility rotary-wing maintenance would account for sales of $30 000/month, fixed-wing $8500/month, and refinishing $24 000/month. Gross margin for these was approximately 25 percent. There would be additional revenue from storage and hangarage of aircraft of at least $2000 per month.

Mr. Melanson knew that financing would be required for capital purchases, leaseholds, fuel inventory, and working capital for two months' operation at the new facility. This amount totalled $200 000 (see Exhibit 3).

Mr. Melanson was in no position personally to inject additional equity, and he did not want to give up his majority share in the company, as he had previously suffered a bad experience as a minority shareholder. Because the company was not in a position to seek additional bank financing, he realized an investor would have to be found. Melanson did not have any idea what to offer an investor, or if he had other alternatives for financing. A potential investor had approached Phoenix because of his interest in aviation and because he thought it was good risk. The terms offered included a $100 000 injection and a $100 000 loan guarantee in exchange for 50 percent of the company. The investor was not interested in any operational position in the company.

The Future

As Mr. Melanson read his latest *Rotor & Wing* magazine (Exhibit 4) which forecasted continued growth[4] in the industry, he wondered what to do.

1. Ministry of Transport regulations require an eight-glide slope around heliports and other conditions which are affected by development on adjacent properties.

2. Helicopters on summer contracts are maintained in the field and all heavy maintenance is scheduled or delayed to the end of the season if possible.

3. Fuel had a 20 percent margin on sales.

4. The Canadian fleet mirrored US trends.

Exhibit 1		**1989**	**1988**
Phoenix	Sales	$283,055	$ 35,735
Airmotive	Cost of Sales	235,520	43,522
Statement of Income	**Gross Profit (Loss)**	47,535	(7,787)
For the Years Ended	Expenses		
September 30,	Rent	15,729	14,735
1988, 1989	Travel	12,152	3,130
(Unaudited)	Vehicle	11,369	4,761
	Telephone	5,180	2,505
	Insurance	4,636	2,675
	Interest and bank charges	3,841	4,104
	Office and general	3,766	5,808
	Utilities	3,761	3,886
	Professional fees	2,500	–
	Interest on long-term debt	2,101	1,875
	Advertising and promotion	1,675	3,595
	Bookkeeping	1,589	767
	Provision for depreciation	738	–
		69,037	47,841
	Income (Loss) from Operations	(21,502)	(55,628)
	Government assistance	–	24,570
	Net Income (Loss) for the Year	**$(21,502)**	**$(31,058)**

		1989	1988
Exhibit 2	**ASSETS**		
Phoenix Airmotive Balance Sheet as at September 30, 1988, 1989 (Unaudited)	**Current**		
	Accounts receivable	$ 33,975	$ 5,462
	Inventory	1,200	1,500
	Prepaid expenses	700	1,085
		35,875	8,047
	Fixed (Note 1)	5,113	–
		$ 40,988	$ 8,047
	LIABILITIES		
	Current		
	Bank overdraft	$ 21,987	$ 6,779
	Bank loans	19,800	–
	Accounts payable and accrued liabilities	49,817	8,531
	Deferred government assistance	–	8,695
	Long-term debt due within one year	5,263	3,437
		96,867	27,442
	Long-Term Debt (Note 2)	9,111	11,563
	Other		
	Note payable (Note 3)	11,470	–
		117,448	39,005
	SHAREHOLDERS' EQUITY		
	Capital Stock	100	100
	Retained Earnings		
	Balance (deficit) at beginning of the year as previously reported	16,594	–
	Prior period adjustments (Note 4)	(47,652)	–
		(31,058)	–
	Net income (loss) for the year	(21,502)	(31,058)
		(52,560)	(31,058)
	Dividends declared and paid	(24,000)	–
		(76,560)	(31,058)
	Balance at end of the year	(76,460)	(30,958)
		$ 40,988	$ 8,047

Exhibit 2
(cont'd)

Notes to
Balance Sheet

NOTE 1: FIXED ASSETS

Fixed assets consist of:

	Cost	1989 Accumulated depreciation	Net book value	1988 Net book value
Tools and equipment	$49,048	$11,665	$37,383	$33,798
Vehicle	3,051	458	2,593	2,547
Leasehold improvements	11,186	3,356	7,830	10,067
Government assistance	(57,434)	(14,741)	(42,693)	(46,412)
	$ 5,851	$ 738	$ 5,113	$ –

NOTE 2: LONG-TERM DEBT

Long-term debt consists of:

	Interest rate	Due date	1989	1988
Loan payable–Royal Bank of Canada	P + 1%	1993	$11,875	$15,000
Loan payable–Royal Bank of Canada	P + 3%	1991	2,499	–
			14,374	15,000
Principal payments due within one year			5,263	3,437
			$ 9,111	$11,563

The bank loans are secured by an assignment of inventory and a general security agreement on the assets of the company.

Principal payments required to retire the outstanding long-term debt are as follows:

1990	$ 5,263
1991	5,048
1992	3,750
1993	313
	$14,374

NOTE 3: NOTE PAYABLE

The note payable is unsecured, non-interest bearing and has no specified terms of repayment.

**Exhibit 2
(cont'd)**

Notes to
Balance Sheet

NOTE 4: PRIOR PERIOD ADJUSTMENTS

Retained earnings at September 30, 1988 has been adjusted as follows:

$(51,735)	Government assistance applied to purchase of fixed assets.
(8,695)	Government assistance deferred for application subsequent to year end.
12,778	Adjustment to depreciation.
$(47,652)	

Exhibit 3

Phoenix
Airmotive
Working Capital
Needs
(Two Months)

Working capital	$ 65,000
Fuel dispensing equipment	40,000
Special tools	20,000
Initial fuel inventory	20,000
Refinishing Equipment	40,000
Leasehold improvements	15,000
Total	**$200,000**

Exhibit 4

Phoenix Airmotive
FAA Forecast
of US Civil
Helicopter Fleet
1980-2000

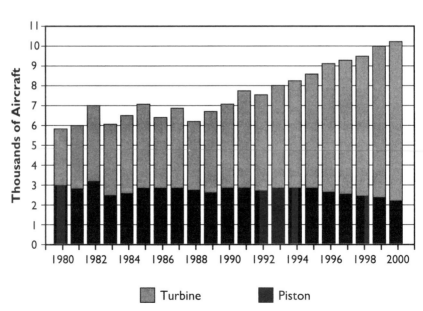

Choices Furniture

Michael Cecchetto, owner of Choices Furniture (CF) in Sudbury, Ontario, hung up the phone and took another sip from his coffee mug. He had just been listening to Heinz Dittman, part-owner of 3-H, CF's supplier of ready-to-assemble residential furniture, wax eloquent over the company's new line of office furniture. Cecchetto had already given his supplier's new line some thought, wondering if the time were right to introduce it into the store when it came on the market in January 1988. Cecchetto squinted reflectively into the late October sun. Dittman's closing remarks had taken him completely by surprise:

> Ever thought of getting out of the retail business? We need a 3-H distributor to handle both the new commercial line and our regular residential lines here in northeastern Ontario.

"Maybe that's the answer to my problems," thought Cecchetto.

Background

Choices Furniture was the first ready-to-assemble (RTA) furniture retail outlet in the Sudbury market when it opened in 1985. It was located in the Paris Plaza, a small strip mall in the south end of the city. After operating there for half of the three-year lease period, the proprietor of the mall offered to release CF from the agreement and also to provide a leasehold improvement as an incentive to relocate in another mall which he also owned. Now CF was centrally situated in Cedar Pointe, a strip mall visible to more people and well known to the majority of Sudburians.

Michael Cecchetto came from a prominent family in the Sudbury area. In 1972, he opened a home cleaning facility, his first business venture. After a year, which he described as "a good learning experience," Cecchetto decided to resume his studies at a local college. Graduating with a diploma in child care, he had not immediately found a suitable job and for two years had worked as a truck driver. In due course he took a position as a child-care worker with the provincial government which he kept for the next five years. Yet he was still attracted by the idea of being self-employed, and in 1985 he opened a ready-to-assemble furniture store in Sudbury, calling it Choices Furniture.

In late November 1985, a northeastern Ontario manufacturer, 3-H, began supplying a ready-to-assemble table line to two Sudbury retailers: CF and a downtown competitor, Eurokit, which had opened almost immediately after CF. Very soon CF took a decision to carry a full line of ready-to-assemble residential furniture, deciding to commit its resources to the 3-H make because of its premium quality. Cecchetto rounded out the store inventory with a few non-competing complementary lines. By the spring of 1987, 3-H had signed a letter of agreement granting CF exclusive rights to the Sudbury territory.

The Market

In the almost two years that he had been in this business, Mr. Cecchetto had observed that purchasers of the residential line of ready-to-assemble furniture were between the ages of 25 and 40, usually single. Both men and women purchased the furniture. In the limited radio and print advertising Cecchetto had undertaken so far, he had emphasized a "lifestyle" angle, focusing on style, quality and price.

CF had run into some difficulties trying to differentiate its ready-to-assemble product from the traditional format.

> It's not so much that Sudburians are "stick in the mud" conservatives. Most of them just never think of RTA and if they do, they think it's "cheap."

CF attempted to combat the image problem associated with this alternative by 1) carrying a high quality line and pricing it accordingly; and 2) offering free in-home decorating consultations. None of CF's advertisements had featured the ready-to-assemble aspect. CF also offered to deliver and set up the furniture in the client's home for a small fee.

Cecchetto was aware that although the dollar amount spent nationally on furniture, furnishings, and household equipment was increasing, Statistics Canada figures showed that the percent of total disposable income spent was decreasing. (See Table 1.)

Although he assumed that this trend applied to Sudbury, Cecchetto also knew that the store was now in the fastest growing city ward, close to a number of highrise apartments that were popular with singles.

At the same time, Statistics Canada data indicated that office furniture was a growing market, with a 12.31 percent increase in revenues from

Table 1

Personal Expenditure on Consumer Goods and Services: Furniture, Furnishing, Household Equipment and Operation

Year	Expenditures (000's)	% of Total Disposable Income
1977	$11,990	9.7
1978	13,006	9.5
1979	14,333	9.4
1980	15,494	9.1
1981	16,995	8.8
1982	17,356	8.3
1983	19,294	8.4

Source: *Market Research Handbook* 1985–86.

* Table to read: in 1977, $11,990,000, or 9.7% of the total personal disposable income was spent on furniture, furnishings, household equipment and operations.

1986 to 1987, and that different materials were preferred for different furniture items. For example, as shown in Table 2, wooden desks and metal chairs were more popular than metal desks and wooden chairs.

Thirty percent of the national furniture manufacturers were located in Ontario and Quebec in 1985. Cecchetto had recently read the transcript of an interview with Larry Blondell, an executive of the association of Ontario Furniture Manufacturers. Blondell stated emphatically that "the office furniture industry is booming" and estimated the current growth to be approximately 10 to 15 percent per year. He mentioned as well that only a few manufacturers supply the office furniture market nationally. In answer to a direct question, Blondell expressed the belief that a manufacturer in northern Ontario could be successful provided it offered competitive prices and good quality.

IKEA Ltd., a major player nationally in the ready-to-assemble furniture market, had entered the office furniture market in 1986. According to

Table 2

The Canadian Office Furniture Market

	1986	1987
Office Furniture ($000's)	617,124	693,515
Desks		
Wood	91,723	114,668
Metal	33,765	34,881
Chairs		
Wood	104,396	139,384
Metal	33,173	38,173

Judy Smith, manager of the IKEA sales office in Toronto, "People are attracted to ready-to-assemble even when it comes to office furniture. Price, quality, and service are three important features customers take into consideration when making a purchase decision."

Local Market for Commercial Furniture

In the spring of 1987, Michael Cecchetto had participated in a survey of area retailers and producers of office furniture. The survey had been conducted by a small business consulting group at the local university. The report had been made available to the participants, and contained the following information.

1. Office Product Distributors
   a) The local furniture market was growing steadily at an average rate of 7–10 percent annually.
   b) All the retailers surveyed carried ready-to-assemble wood and metal items to some extent.
   c) The majority of retailers agreed that wood items and wood appearing items were more popular than metal items.
   d) Most tended to agree that sales of ready-to-assemble products were increasing.
   e) Sales were high in early spring and fall.
   f) A majority of outlets reported an equal split in volumes between their sales force and catalogue sales. Two outlets, Simpsons Commercial and Muirheads, concentrated on catalogue sales.
   g) The price of an average quality office suite (which includes a chair, desk and filing cabinet) was $800.
   h) The four most important factors in the purchasing decision were price, quality, delivery and service.
   i) Fifty percent of the retailers agreed that they do get customers asking for something the manufacturers did not supply.

2. Distributors of Ready-to-Assemble Products

   The owner-operator of Eurokit (a ready-to-assemble retailer) indicated in the same survey that 80 percent of his business was in the residential market. He too had observed some resistance to this type of product, which in his opinion was due to a perceived lack of durability and problems with assembly. However, he stated that the lower price helped to stimulate an attractive level of sales.

3. Local Woodworkers

    With one exception, this segment reported receiving relatively few contracts to manufacture office furniture. Furthermore, the survey indicated that the majority of woodworkers did not actively pursue the office furniture market. In general, these enterprises were small in size and considered it beyond their ability and capacity to serve the commercial market.

Customers

As part of the same project, the university's Small Business Consulting Group had attempted to determine sales potential for office furniture by polling three distinct segments: 1) commercial businesses; 2) hotel/motel establishments; and 3) government institutions.

The survey revealed that commercial businesses spent approximately $100 to $500 per office per year, and after every five years completely refurnished the office. Further, 80 percent of the respondents indicated that they purchased their products from local office furniture distributors. However, these customers tended to comparison shop and did not always deal with the same supplier. Seventy-seven percent of the businesses stated that they tend to purchase products which are made in Ontario.

The hotel/motel segment was less attractive because virtually all the respondents reported that they dealt directly with the manufacturer when purchasing major items. Local distributors were contacted only when very few items were needed, or the items are inexpensive. They indicated that a) major items were replaced every five years on average; b) the cost for upgrading and maintenance included changing curtains, repairs of broken beds, dressers, etc.; and c) office furniture used in hotels and motels was replaced on average every five to ten years.

The institutional market (i.e., hospitals, government schools, etc.) seemed easier to target. The respondents reported buying office furniture on an ongoing basis, with average institutional furniture expenditures ranging from $20 000 to $100 000 per year, depending on the institution's size. The majority of institutional buyers indicated that they would rather buy northern-Ontario-made than Canadian-made, and some of the large institutions stated that they do purchase products from local companies. Attracted by credit and discounts, however, a number purchase directly from manufacturers located in southern Ontario. For example, Laurentian University reported receiving a 50 percent discount on bulk purchases from its southern Ontario supplier. Price was a major determinant for most of the organizations contacted, although quality and service were also mentioned.

The provincial government had just announced that the Ministry of Northern Development and Mines would be transferring a major part of its operations to Sudbury in 1990. Construction of a large cancer treatment centre was also slated for completion by the end of 1990.

Competitive Analysis

In the Sudbury area, CF competed directly against two other ready-to-assemble residential furniture retailers: Eurokit and Furniture Express. A third retailer, Muirheads, also sold a limited amount of RTA furniture (e.g., computer tables) suitable for home office use.

Indirect competitors included 33 furniture dealers-retailers, numerous department stores in the Sudbury area, three furniture designers and custom builders, and four furniture manufacturers that had the capability to produce similar pieces of furniture. Within the next year two large furniture franchises, The Brick and Leon's, would be opening in Sudbury. Already there had been a blaze of publicity in the media, creating advance public awareness.

Communications Programs

To date CF had no formal advertising budget. Advertising activity had been sporadic and *ad hoc*. Several direct mail campaigns in the form of a personalized letter and a brochure from the manufacturer, 3-H, had been aimed at the more affluent areas of Sudbury. However, the overall effectiveness of these initiatives was deemed to be minimal.

Attending trade shows to promote the product line seemed to be considerably more productive. CF had participated in the following local trade shows: Business Expo, Northern Wedding Show, The Home Show, and National Home Show Week. A number of orders were obtained at these events, and it was felt that public awareness had increased both for the product and for the CF name.

Present Situation

Michael Cecchetto's responsibilities included acting as a sales person in the store, soliciting new business for the residential line, and setting up in-store displays. He had a part-time employee who was prepared to work flexible hours so that he could leave the premises when required. Already pressed to provide the assembly service that the store offered, Michael knew that if he went into the office line he would have to hire someone full time whose duties would include organizing CF's exhibits at trade shows. He realized that there would have to be a lot of this kind of activity, and it would occur mainly on weekends.

Cecchetto was under no illusions: the Sudbury retail outlet was not doing well (see Exhibits 1 and 2). He'd given a lot of thought to what might be wrong and what he might do about it.

> Partly the idea of "ready-to-assemble" doesn't go with the image of high end. A lot of the people who come in to see our stuff are impressed but they want something cheaper. They weren't looking for this level of quality when they went out to buy RTA, and they aren't ready to pay our prices. We get to keep some of them by throwing in assembly as part of the package but a lot of these people head elsewhere for lower-priced options. And then there are probably a lot of people out there who are looking for this kind of quality but they'd just never think of "ready-to-assemble." It's those people we need to get a message to, but it's tough. Yet the competition seems to be doing pretty well.

Lately he'd been trying to think of cost-cutting measures. He was paying $2000 a month for his present quarters ($500 a month more than he had been paying previously) but he had started to wonder how much good this high visibility, high traffic site would actually do for the product, particularly if he went into office furniture. Sales in the past quarter had been 10 percent lower than in the corresponding period the year before. Although he felt that this slump might be because he had been organizing the move, with very little time for finding new clients, he wasn't altogether sure.

Cecchetto kept coming back in his mind to the office furniture option. The Sudbury retail outlet might suffer if it tried to focus on both the residential and the commercial lines.

Unless he hired another person immediately his energies would be diverted on an even bigger scale than they had been by the move. Of course, he could forego the possibility of running with the office line,

> ... but then 3-H will most certainly find someone else to carry its commercial line and CF might also lose the 3-H exclusive on the residential. It's obvious that 3-H really wants to flog office furniture. And with distinctive styling and the impeccable 3-H finish, this could be a valuable market opportunity. I'll be the only

guy in town to offer a full line of office furniture that one can take apart.

Cecchetto was convinced that the market appeal for this kind of furniture would have to come from its potential to create an office that makes a personal statement. He knew that most organizations furnish their offices with standard issue—uniform quality, price and design:

> Only a few people are permitted the luxury of differentiating their work places from run-of-the-mill office settings . . . key executives, lawyers, architects and other professionals. And of course a few people like psychologists need offices that make people feel comfortable.

He knew, too, that the people who bought the product would have to want an office setting "with a difference" strongly enough to forgo volume discounts. He suspected that because there would be no large volume discounts the price would be very comparable to that of the traditional format.

> And how much value-added incentive should we offer to the commercial market? Our competitors don't assemble the residential furniture when delivered; we're the only ones who do. Should we try to do the same for the commercial?

At the same time, Cecchetto wondered how well the ready-to-assemble concept for an office ensemble would sell. The notion of "knockdown" being cheap was proving difficult to overcome in the residential market. Maybe it would be even more of a problem in the commercial market.

> On the other hand, maybe some business people can be sold on this very feature . . . the fact that this format is so portable. Provided of course they can be convinced that 3-H offers durability.

Since he'd been contemplating the office furniture option in the past few weeks, it had occurred to him that portability might be an important feature missing from his present advertising strategy for the residential line:

> I've certainly not made anything of portability, but come to think of it, a lot of the people who do buy our furniture are highly mobile. Maybe I've been missing something here. And if I do focus

on this, I guess it makes sense to talk about 'knockdown' rather than 'ready-to-assemble'.

He found himself musing:

> If I were to move the store to less expensive space and really promote the portability of knock-down, I wonder if I could turn Choices around?

And now there was this new twist: he was clearly being courted to become a distributor. To go in this direction might mean the end of his retail venture—he'd either have to sell Choices or just shut down. He wondered aloud if he could negotiate exclusive rights to both the commercial and the residential lines for all northern Ontario. If he were going to be on the road again, he'd like to think he'd make a decent living. And if he did secure these rights, what resources would he need to do the job? Finally Cecchetto muttered to himself:

> Clearly if I can show a thriving business based on the marketability of the 3-H line, I can make a great case to others. How credible will I be as a distributor if the trade knows, or finds out, I couldn't make the 3-H line work at retail for me?

Exhibit 1

Choices
Furniture
Statement of
Income
Year Ended
September 30,
1987

Sales	$164,046
Purchases	134,084
Inventory at end of year	20,039
Cost of goods sold	114,045
Gross profit	50,001

Expenses:

Wages and employee benefits	38,245
Rent	22,727
Advertising and promotion	17,385
Utilities	7,523
Vehicle	6,757
Interest and bank charges	5,256
Professional fees	3,292
Repairs and maintenance	2,837
Office and general	2,435
Depreciation	1,040
Insurance	884
	108,381
Net loss	**$ 58,380**

Exhibit 2

Choices Furniture
Balance Sheet
September 30,
1987

ASSETS

Current assets:

Cash	$11,490
Accounts receivable	1,966
Inventory	20,039
	33,495
Fixed assets	12,221
	$45,716

LIABILITIES AND PROPRIETOR'S EQUITY

Current liabilities:

Accounts payable and accrued liabilities	$13,374
Customer deposits	2,657
Current portion of long-term debt	5,876
	21,907
Long-term debt	34,085
	55,992
Proprietor's equity	(10,276)
	$45,716

Computer Coveralls

F our years' training and two years in the clothing manufacturing trade seemed like a good start when Elaine Vasco embarked on her own venture early in 1989. But now, after five months, she recognized that there were many things involved in running her own business that had not been part of her apprenticeship in the Vancouver garment trade. And, interestingly enough, it was the success of her products in the marketplace that was creating major difficulties.

In September of 1988, at a family reunion in southern Ontario, Elaine and her father-in-law, Arthur Vasco, had discussed her desire to start a small business. It was during that discussion that the idea for Coveralls arose. His experience suggested that there was room in the microcomputer market for a line of diskette holders, preferably fabric, that would fit into the average briefcase. Also, he felt that her idea of brightly coloured computer-monitor, keyboard and printer covers might have a market in many modern offices where decor and colour were important.

With Arthur's help on sizes, and with general product specifications in hand, Elaine agreed to produce some designs and samples. Meanwhile, her father-in-law would undertake some limited market research to determine if the market potential justified the start-up investment in a small business capable of manufacturing and marketing the products.

By December 1, 1990, the designs were finished and some preliminary market research had been completed, cost estimates had been prepared, and tentative pricing had been submitted to several major computer and computer supplies retailers. There seemed to be strong support for the product. In fact, two large dealers offered to place orders for over 1000 units. At this time Elaine and Arthur agreed to draw up a business plan, discuss it over the Christmas vacation, and try to make a decision.

Over Christmas, they decided to go ahead with the business, and set target dates for getting the venture started. Elaine would leave her Vancouver job in February of 1990, and move to Victoria B.C. where the operation would be set up. They agreed that Elaine would be the only full-time employee, and responsible for all of the company's operations, while Arthur would be a silent partner, advancing the investment capital. Elaine would take a salary of $10 000 per year and the balance in shares. At the end of three years each partner would hold a 50 percent interest in the new company, and salaries would be renegotiated. Dividends, if there were any declared, would be determined by the partners at the annual meeting.

The Market

The original research had turned up several product and market possibilities. In the end, Coveralls decided to look at both the Canadian and US markets simultaneously, but planned to use different approaches in each. (See Table 1.)

The company decided to market the product through computer dealers, office supply houses and business stationers. These would be contacted by direct mail. Coveralls would also use mail order in the US and Canada, but would advertise only in US computer publications. Magazines such as *PC World*, *BYTE* and *Personal Computing* numbered among their readers many in the retail trade. The advertisements would be designed to attract individual mail-order customers but would specify that interested dealers should contact Coveralls directly. Product pricing would support dealer margins.

This approach was considered a cost-effective way to enter the market. It would, Elaine felt, provide adequate market exposure to meet the projections set forth in the business plan.

Table 1		Canada	USA
Computer Coveralls Market Entry Sequence	Dealer	1	2
	Mail Order	Based on US Advertising	3

The Products

Initially, three products were offered, in two sizes: the Diskpak 5, the Diskpak 3, the Briefpak 5, the Briefpak 3, the Execpak 5, and the Execpak 3. (See Table 2 for product pricing.) The three products were designed to handle the two standard disk sizes used on IBM, IBM Compatible, and Apple microcomputers. Each product was produced in a nylon fabric, and was available in five colours.

Table 2

Computer Coveralls Product Pricing, Retail/Wholesale

	Products		
	Diskpak	**Briefpak**	**Execpak**
Suggested Retail price per Unit*	$ 17.95	$ 24.95	$ 34.95
Dealer Cost (Qty. 6 units)	less 35%	less 35%	less 35%
Dealer Cost (Qty. 12 units)	less 35% less 5%	less 35% less 5%	less 35% less 5%
Dealer Cost (Qty. 24 units)	less 35% less 5% less 5%	less 35% less 5% less 5%	less 35% less 5% less 5%

Coveralls allowed 2%/10, net 30 on the payment of accounts. All first orders were cash only.

* Suggested retail prices were used as the advertised prices for mail order.

The products were described in the brochures as follows:

Diskpak–a durable fabric holder for storing and transporting diskettes. Each unit has room for 12 diskettes and can be securely closed with end flaps and a velcro fastener.

Briefpak–a lightweight fabric diskette holder meant to fit into the accordion folds of the standard briefcase. The Briefpak holds six 5 ¼" diskettes or eight 3" diskettes.

Execpak–The Execpak is in the form of a standard notepad holder. In addition to room for six diskettes (5 ¼" or 3") it includes a notepad, pen holder and calculator.

While other products were being investigated and developed, none was yet ready for production. Coveralls had been contacted by one large US chain of computer retail stores about private branding the existing Coveralls products as well as producing some other related products exclusively for the chain (computer monitor, keyboard, printer and other peripheral equipment covers). No action had been taken on these requests.

Sales

Sales orders came from two sources: dealer sales and mail order. These in turn were broken down into Canadian and foreign sales. Sales in the

Canadian market were aimed at dealers who handled computers and related equipment and supplies. Brochures were mailed to lists of office and computer suppliers across Canada.

Advertising and Promotion

Early expenditures for advertising and promotion of the product line were not viewed as an investment and, as a result, amounted to a relatively high proportion of Coverall's total expense budget. Much of the mail-order budget had been committed to advertising in major computer magazines. The budget for dealer sales was allocated to direct mail and to brochures.

At the end of five months, the direct-mail campaign had been launched in Canada, but not in the States. The full-colour brochures sent to prospective Canadian customers featured the three "pak" products, and included pictures, specifications, prices and discounts, as well as an order form.

Coveralls had also instigated an introductory mail-order offer aimed at retailers called "Meet the Pak." In Elaine's opinion it had been extremely successful, with over 80 percent of all dealer orders beginning with the "pak offer" and 69 percent of "pak offer" sales producing second orders. "Meet the Pak" was made up of five units: two Diskpaks (red and yellow) two Briefpaks (blue and grey) and an Execpak in black. These were priced at wholesale and shipped with promotional brochures. While "Meet the Pak" was a one-time offer, Elaine noted several dealers had requested additional shipments of the special. One retailer had ordered 54 "Meet the Pak" units, one for each of its stores.

During the first year, Coverall's plans included the purchase of mailing lists and a contract to have the mailings handled by a small firm which specialized in this business. No attempt had yet been made to assess the effectiveness of this approach. Nor was Coveralls making any attempt to develop internal mailing lists, although this was planned for the future. Table 3 presents the proposed advertising budget for 1990.

	1st Quarter	2nd Quarter	3rd Quarter	4th Quarter
Advertising				
Mail order	$2500	$4000	$5000	$5000
Dealer	3000	4500	4500	4500
Promotion	2500	2500	3500	3500

Table 3

Computer Coveralls Proposed Advertising Budget, 1990

To date, because of the large response from Canadian dealers via direct mail, little attention had been devoted to the mail-order part of the business. Only two advertisements had been placed (both in *PC World*), each at a cost of $250 (US). These ads have been undertaken mainly to test the mail-order market, and had resulted in 11 requests for information from US dealers. Five of these requests had so far produced orders for "Meet the Pak" units and two dealers had placed orders for 72 and 144 mixed-unit shipments.

Initial Results—The First Five Months

Unit sales for each product for the first five months of operations are shown in Table 4. Of the sales to retail outlets, 64 percent of the units were purchased by chain stores, while 36 percent were purchased by individual outlets not connected to the major chains or franchise operations.

Less than 15 percent of sales during the first five months had been mail order; half of these came from Canadian customers. This prompted some discussion of the need for a US mailing address but so far nothing further had been done. Arthur felt that it would take some time to develop the mail-order business and had committed Coveralls to run the small advertisement in *PC World* for 12 months.

Dealer sales, on the other hand, had exceeded expectations. As a result, Coveralls decided to withhold other planned magazine advertising and use the money to rent a booth at the office equipment show in Toronto later in the year. In the meantime, Elaine planned to focus on the supply side in an attempt to improve production. (See Exhibit 1 for sales projections.)

Table 4

Computer Coveralls Sales by Product

	January	February	March	April	May
Diskpak 3	54	102	112	340	470
Diskpak 5	170	242	367	590	840
Briefpak 3	22	71	112	204	226
Briefpak 5	20	54	234	340	420
Execpak 3	0	0	24	60	120
Execpak 5	0	0	56	78	242

Note: Units were usually sold in boxes of 6, 12 and 24. However, as part of the introductory "Meet the Pak" offer, individual units were sold to dealers. Most mail orders were also for individual units.

Pricing

Product pricing in Coveralls was based on the cost incurred (actual and projected). Prices quoted were retail with federal excise tax included, to facilitate mail-order sales. Discounts were allowed, as set forth in Exhibit 2.

Order Processing

All orders were shipped from inventory. When an order was received, a four-part invoice/shipping order was prepared. If payment was included, the invoices were marked paid and copy 1 was filed numerically by the accounts clerk. Copy 2 was held, later to be mailed to the customer. Copies 3 and 4 were sent to shipping where the order was filled, and an address tag prepared. When the order was completed, copy 4 was attached to the parcel as a shipping order. Copy 3 was returned to the office where, if prepaid, it was filed in the open customer file. If charged, it became part of the accounts receivable process and was filed by customer name in an open file until paid.

Some dealers required more than one copy of the invoice. In these cases the second copy was mailed and a photocopy of the invoice placed in the customer file. Elaine realized that some additional work on the paper flows was required, since this "one-write" package was already proving inadequate.

Also, the follow-up of accounts receivable and collections was not well organized. The company had a policy of not shipping new orders to customers with overdue accounts, but this policy had often been overlooked simply because the follow-up procedure was inadequate.

Mail and dealer orders were shipped parcel post except where size, weight and urgency dictated the use of a courier. The costs of shipping were paid by the customer, since all products were priced f.o.b. the factory in Victoria. Coveralls had contracted with a small local parcel-delivery firm to pick up shipments daily and deliver these to the Post Office.

Costs were determined based on estimates for materials, labour, and overhead. The overhead included a contribution to profits. (See Exhibit 2.)

Operations and Production

Early in the company's development it was decided that production operations would be located in Victoria. Since it was also decided that the company would use a cottage industry approach, only a small space was rented to house the office, cutting-room facilities and storage of raw materials and finished goods. (See Figure 1.) These facilities were located on the second floor of a small downtown commercial building and were reached by taking a freight elevator at the rear of the building. There was room for future expansion, and adequate parking for those picking up cut materials and dropping off finished goods.

The cottage-industry concept used by the company involved the use of home sewers to assemble and sew pre-cut parts provided by the company. The work was done on a piece-rate basis and the sewers were considered private contractors. Finished goods were inspected and, if acceptable, a receipt was issued and the contractor was paid for the goods seven days later. Rejected goods were returned to the contractor for

Figure 1

Computer Coveralls Facilities

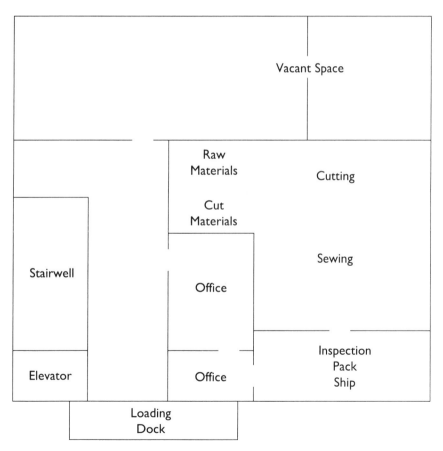

rework and repair. The reject rate was relatively low. Contractors who could not meet the standards were released.

The production process began with pattern cutting of the materials into "parts." These parts were bundled to make 24 finished units. Once bundled, the parts were stored for pick-up by the contractors. Goods returned by the contractors were inspected and stored for shipment.

Along with the cutting equipment, Coveralls had purchased two industrial sewing machines. These machines were used for product development, and for sewing the Execpak, which required the use of the industrial machines. Also, the machines were used to establish and check piece-rates, to produce samples for quality standards, and to test and train new sewers.

Material Control

The material control function included purchasing, production planning, inventory control, and shipping. Since most of the production work was done by contract sewers, controlling the ordering, use, and inventory of materials, both in-process and finished goods, was important. It took approximately six weeks to get raw materials, three weeks to produce the product and one week to inspect and inventory the product. As well, an additional two weeks was required to pack and ship the product. Material control was extremely important since Coveralls advertised one week delivery on its products. That period was currently running almost two weeks and still there were orders that had to be short-shipped, resulting in back orders that were subsequently shipped at Coverall's expense. To meet the targets, the company would have to build inventories around projected sales, but production had yet to catch up.

Inventory Control

At the end of each week the shipper took an inventory count of each product. (Products were numbered; for example, the Diskpak was coded 01 and the colour red was also shown as 01 resulting in a product code of "0101" and so on; other features such as diskette size were identified as /3 or /5: see Table 5). The inventory levels were reviewed weekly, outstanding orders were subtracted and the resulting figures provided quantities for the following week's cutting schedule. The process was causing some problems with stockouts, which, in turn, resulted in an excessive number of back orders. Back order costs were not recorded, but this item was high on Elaine's list of problems. Increasing sales volumes

Table 5

Computer
Coveralls
Product Codes

	Diskpak	Briefpak	Execpak
Red	0101/3	0201/3	0301/3
Red	0101/5	0201/5	0301/5
Blue	0102/3	0202/3	0302/3
Blue	0102/5	0202/5	0302/5
Yellow	0103/3	0203/3	0303/3
Yellow	0103/5	0203/5	0303/5
Grey	0104/3	0204/3	0304/3
Grey	0104/5	0204/5	0304/5
Black	0105/3	0205/3	0305/3
Red	0105/5	0205/5	0305/5

and a lack of past experience on which to base forecasts complicated the issue. Elaine estimated that 10 to 15 percent of dealer orders were delayed or shipped with back orders outstanding.

Inventory records were kept by hand. These records included a complete list of finished goods, work in progress, and both factory bundles and unassembled units in the contractor's hands. These were adjusted each time a shipment was made, and each time goods were inspected and placed in inventory.

Production Planning

Production planning assumptions were based on one-week turnaround from the sewers and a minimum of 48 units per sewer per week. Some sewers had produced over two hundred units per week, but the average among the experienced contractors was 144 units per week. Sewers were encouraged to return finished goods weekly and the payment for last week's work provided additional incentive to stay on this schedule.

Quality Control

Since the contractors produced most of the finished goods at home for a contract price paid on the basis of good parts, inspection of the finished goods was particularly important. Samples produced by factory personnel were used as standards. These were reviewed with the contract sewers before they started working for the company. These samples were also used during the training that preceded the contract work. When the sewer returned finished work it was inspected for defects. Early in the sewer's tenure completed goods were all inspected. After a short period and if the sewer's early work was acceptable, inspections were done on a sample of the finished goods.

For each of the "pak" products there were 12 inspection points. An inspection report was prepared for each sewer's work. This report indicated the quality of the finished goods. Defective products were returned to the sewer for repair. The report indicated defect levels, quantity of returned work and calculated a defect ratio (individual-order and running averages were kept for each sewer). When a sewer returned goods with defects in excess of 3 percent, or the running average exceeded 1 percent, a discussion was held to make sure the sewer was aware of the problem. Sewers who exceeded the 3 percent level more than three times in ten were retrained; if the 3 percent level continued, the sewer was released. Sewers whose running average exceeded 1 percent for more than one month were also released.

These quality reports were prepared by the inspector and summarized weekly by Elaine. When meetings were required with the sewers both Elaine and the inspector attended.

Two copies of the inspection reports were prepared. One was given to the sewer as a receipt for the returned finished goods. The second copy was sent to accounting and this was used to generate a cheque for payment to the sewer.

Elaine and the inspector had held several discussions about how the quality control process could be improved. Both wanted to look at some statistical sampling methods and better reports to track and analyze sewer performance. Not all defects could be repaired, and when goods were scrapped, Coveralls lost money on the materials, cutting labour and associated overhead. As well, both were aware that the statistical methods were less reliable given the relatively small lot sizes. These situations required 100 percent inspection. Finally, the inspector thought that the introduction of statistical sampling would mean that Coveralls would have to accept some reasonable level of defects and would have to share in the cost of correcting these problems. As volumes increased this would become a more pressing issue.

Accounting and Control

Elaine and the accounting clerk split the duties of bookkeeping and other record keeping. The factory and office payroll was done every two weeks. Sewers were paid weekly for the previous week's returns. Invoices were paid as they came due and Coveralls took discounts where available.

Accounts receivable were posted and a report on age of accounts prepared weekly. Overdue accounts were monitored and shipments were withheld where accounts were overdue, at least in theory. Both Elaine and Arthur Vasco were supposed to get involved when accounts exceeded sixty days, but as mentioned earlier, the procedure was difficult to maintain and shipments were being made to overdue accounts.

Taxes were collected for both provincial and federal governments. These included federal excise tax on manufacturers' selling price[1] and provincial sales tax on goods sold to individuals within British Columbia. Most dealers had sales tax licenses and were exempt from this tax. Payroll taxes were not collected, although gross incomes paid to the contract sewers were reported to the federal government. The collection of Unemployment Insurance and Canada Pension contributions was under discussion with federal tax officials, but thus far these had not been deducted and the sewers were responsible for reporting their own incomes for tax purposes. Coveralls did make all deductions for full-time and part-time employees. Thus far no other deductions were made, although some thought was being given to paying BC Health Care premiums for the full-time employees.

While Coveralls did not have much in the way of a bank loan, negotiating a line of credit resulted in the bank's request for a report on inventories and an aged listing of accounts receivable. These were due monthly. Thus far the company had not prepared monthly financial statements but Elaine was considering doing so. Arthur had agreed to spend a week in Victoria to help set up a bookkeeping system. Because there was already a large amount of paper moving about this small company, Arthur intended to contact a local consultant to determine if the bookkeeping, financial statements, inventory and quality records could be computerized. Mailing labels, mailing lists, purchase orders, and whatever else might be computerized would be part of the discussion.

A number of major problems required attention. Inventory records, quality records, and financial records required a more systematic approach. Both inventory management and production scheduling appeared to offer room for improvement.

All of these concerns were of some urgency, since Arthur Vasco intended to withdraw totally from the business.

Financial

At this point in the company's history financial issues were not critical. Arthur Vasco had provided the funds to start and operate the business. As well, he had negotiated a line of credit. Arthur would reduce his financial involvement at the end of the first year, allowing the business's operating requirements thereafter to be funded by the bank line. As Vasco noted,

> I agreed to help Elaine get this thing started and that is already nearly complete. Apart from some security for loans until the company is profitable, I will not have an active part.
>
> Elaine has done most of the work and is now running the company. Our agreement allows her to buy my shares and we are now negotiating that process. By year end it will be her company.

The company had not prepared formal financial statements, but Arthur and Elaine did pull together some figures for the first five months. These are presented in Exhibits 3 and 4.

Organization

As part of their original business plan, Elaine and Arthur had included an organization chart largely to indicate areas that would receive attention in the future. Coveralls' rapid growth had already resulted in the hiring of both a clerk and a sewer-inspector far sooner than originally planned. Now, despite the fact that the company was small, there were a large number of activities that could not be handled by Elaine alone.

It was now evident that, in both the sales and office areas, there were many activities where additional help was required. Elaine felt that some short-term investment would have to be made to facilitate orderly growth. There was some question in her mind about the sequence of needed additions and how the tasks and responsibilities should be dealt with once the additions were made. She also noted that despite the neat appearance of the organization chart (Figure 2), "everybody is still doing everything . . . we are not well organized."

At the present time only three people worked full-time for Coveralls and their responsibilities and duties were not as clearly delineated as the chart would suggest. Elaine, who managed the organization, also had direct responsibilities in accounting, purchasing, employee and contractor relations, design and sales. The clerk performed some bookkeeping duties, filing, office and clerical duties and prepared several reports, as well as handling packing and shipping when required. The inspector-sewer looked after production operations, cutting and sewing, inspection, inventories, quality control and packing and shipping. Two part-time people were also involved in sewing those items currently produced in the factory.

Figure 2

Computer
Coveralls
Planned
Organization

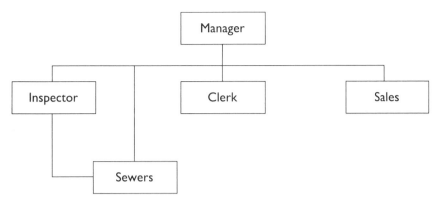

Some Present and Future Concerns

Short-term growth had exceeded expectations and major problems were arising with delivery, inventories, stockouts and cost control. The simple bookkeeping system designed at start-up was not providing adequate information for controlling the operation. Nor was it easy to determine where the priorities should be placed, since there was little information available for management.

The marketing approach had resulted in the company selling in both Canada and the US and in both dealer and mail-order channels. Whether to discontinue activities in some of these markets was a major issue, since Elaine felt that all might be jeopardized if service performance was not improved. Simply put, orders were exceeding capacity. Some decision had to be made about allocating output, increasing output or exiting from one or more of the market options to insure that future growth was not jeopardized. After early market successes, the decision to walk away from one or more of the market segments was proving very difficult. Both partners were reluctant to pull back from the market in any way since they felt that such a move would open the door to competitive products.

Production also posed problems. The choice to go "cottage industry" presented a real dilemma. It had provided a low-cost method of start-up without major fixed-cost commitments. However, it also prevented Coveralls from responding quickly to the unexpected sales that had emerged. Arthur Vasco was reluctant to invest in facilities and equipment for production but would consider it if this approach turned out to be the best solution to the problem. However, Elaine was not enthusiastic about making a significant investment, since it would delay the achievement of her personal objective of owning the business as soon as possible.

Mounting problems, an inability to solve the problems, inadequate information and control, and the many other loose ends associated with this growing business made the choices facing Elaine difficult.

Endnote   1.   Prior to obtaining a federal tax license, companies can do about $50 000 in sales. However, the tax must be paid by the manufacturer on all purchased materials.

Exhibit 1

Computer
Coveralls
Projected Sales
by Unit
1990–1992

	1st Quarter	2nd Quarter	3rd Quarter	4th Quarter
1990–1991				
Diskpak 3	150	500	750	750
Diskpak 5	250	750	1000	1000
Briefpak 3	100	250	350	500
Briefpak 5	150	300	400	750
Execpak 3	50	100	250	400
Execpak 5	75	150	350	500
1991–1992				
Diskpak 3	750	750	750	750
Diskpak 5	1000	1250	1500	1500
Briefpak 3	500	500	750	750
Briefpak 5	750	1000	1000	1250
Execpak 3	500	500	600	750
Execpak 5	750	750	1000	1000

Note: Quarters refer to the company's fiscal year. The first quarter of 1990 would be June, July and August 1990.

Exhibit 2		Diskpak	Briefpak	Execpak
Computer	Selling Price	$17.95	$24.95	$34.95
Coveralls	Less: Discounts	7.43	10.22	14.33
Product Costing	Factory Selling Price	10.52	14.73	20.63
	Less: Federal Sales Tax	1.36	1.91	2.68
	Net Selling Price	9.16	12.82	17.95
	Cost of Goods			
	Labour	2.40	3.03	3.78
	Material	1.12	1.62	3.17
	Overhead	1.20	1.51	1.89
	Total	4.72	6.16	8.84
	Gross Profit	4.44	6.66	9.11
	Selling & Administration	2.89	3.31	4.85
		$ 1.55	**$ 3.35**	**$ 4.26**

Exhibit 3

Computer Coveralls Projected Sales and Revenues 1990–1992

	1990					1991				
	1st Qtr.	2nd Qtr.	3rd Qtr.	4th Qtr.	1990 Total	1st Qtr.	2nd Qtr.	3rd Qtr.	4th Qtr.	1991 Total
Net Sales	10 950	26 106	38 360	50 794	126 210	57 420	62 243	75 620	80 486	275 769
Cost of Goods	5 149	12 382	18 184	23 916	59 631	27 010	29 258	35 554	37 794	129 616
Gross Profit	5 801	13 724	20 176	26 878	66 579	30 410	32 985	40 066	42 692	146 153
Expenses										
Sell & Admin.	3 225	7 668	11 231	14 823	36 947	16 657	18 101	21 956	23 348	80 062
Net Profit	**2 576**	**6 056**	**8 945**	**12 055**	**29 632**	**13 753**	**14 884**	**18 110**	**19 344**	**66 091**

Exhibit 4

Computer
Coveralls
Income
Statement
Summary
(5 Months–1990)

	January	February	March	April	May	Totals
Sales	2,975	5,640	11,580	20,644	30,765	71,604
Less Fed. Tax	0	0	0	0	2,738	2,738
Net Sales	2,975	5,640	11,580	20,644	28,027	68,866
Less Cost of Goods						30,571
Gross Profit						38,295
Sell & Admin.						11,462
Net Profit						**26,833**

Note: Federal Excise Applicable after $50,000 in Sales.

CASE 7-4

Kolapore Inc.*

In January 1986 Mr. Adriaan Demmers, president and sole employee of Kolapore Inc., a firm based in Guelph, Ontario, specializing in the importation, processing, and sale of high-quality souvenir spoons, was becoming increasingly frustrated with the pace at which his business was developing. Over a two-year period, Demmers had taken his idea of importing souvenir spoons from Holland to Canada to annual sales of nearly $30 000. He believed the potential existed for well over $100 000 in Canadian sales plus exports to the United States. This success to date had been a strain, however, on Demmers's limited financial resources and had not provided any compensation for the long hours invested. Demmers was beginning to question if he was ever going to have the major break-through that he had always believed was just around the corner.

Recently, Demmers had accepted a full-time position with another firm in an unrelated business. While Demmers realized that he could continue to operate Kolapore Inc., on a part-time basis, he wondered if he should face reality and simply fold up the business or try to sell it.

This case was prepared by Paul W. Beamish, Wilfrid Laurier University. Reprinted by permission, University of Western Ontario.

Alternatively, Demmers could not occasionally help wondering if he should be devoting himself full-time to Kolapore.

Background

In February/March 1984 Demmers conducted a feasibility study of starting a business to market souvenir spoons. His idea was to offer a high-quality product depicting landmarks, historic buildings, and other unique symbols of the area in which the spoons were to be sold.

There were numerous spoons on the market, but most tended to be for Canada or Ontario rather than local sites of interest and were generally poorly made and not visually appealing. The few quality spoons that did exist were priced in the $15–$40 range.

Sources of spoons were examined and quotations were received from firms in Canada, the United States, and the Netherlands. The search process for a country from which to source the spoons was a limited one and was settled quickly, thanks to Demmers's Dutch heritage, the existence of a well-recognized group of silversmiths in Schoonhoven, plus a particular company that already had over forty Canadian-specific dies as well as lower prices.

Demmers believed the key factors for success were a good quality product, the use of designs of local landmarks, and an eye-catching display. He felt displays should be located in a prominent position in retail stores because souvenir spoons are often bought on impulse.

As part of his feasibility study, Demmers conducted a market analysis (including customer and retailer surveys), a competitive analysis (both manufacturers and distributors), and developed an import plan, marketing plan, and financial projections (including projected break-even point and cash flows). Excerpts from this study follow.

Market Analysis   The market for souvenir spoons consists of several overlapping groups—primarily tourists and the gift market. There are also groups interested in spoons for more specialized purposes, such as church groups, service clubs, associations, and others. These are very specialized and for special occasions.

A random telephone survey of 50 people conducted in Guelph in March 1984 revealed that 78 percent owned souvenir spoons. Forty-six percent of those people had purchased the spoons themselves, while 54 percent had received them as gifts. In total, almost 25 percent of the people in the sample collected souvenir spoons or had a rack on which to hang them. Retailers indicated that sales occurred primarily during the summer months and at Christmas time. Twelve retail outlets were visited to obtain information regarding quality, sales, and prices. Background on a selection of these retailers is summarized in Exhibit 1.

There was a high awareness of souvenir spoons in the market, but the product quality was generally at the low end of the market. For example, rough edges on the bowls were common, and the crests on the spoons were often crooked. In fact, one manufacturer's spoon had a picture of Kitchener City Hall that was out of focus and off-centre. (Terms concerning souvenir spoons are explained in Exhibit 2.)

Often, a limited variety of spoons was available, and few of the spoons were of local points of interest, even though these were the ones that were most in demand. One retailer noted that of a total of 140 spoons sold in 1983, 106 were one variety, a spoon with a relief design in plastic of a Conestoga wagon. This was the only unique spoon Demmers found in the area.

There was no advertising for souvenir spoons due to the nature of the product and the lack of identification with a particular brand.

Souvenir spoons appeared to be a low priority in many producing companies, with little marketing effort made to push the products. Even the packaging was of poor quality; often, boxes were not supplied for gift wrapping.

The sale of spoons was viewed as seasonal by some retailers. In many instances, point-of-purchase displays were removed once the summer rush was over.

Spoons were not prominently displayed in most stores, yet they are largely an impulse item. In several stores they were kept in drawers and taken out only when requested.

Competitive Analysis   Souvenir spoons essentially serve two customer functions: as gifts or commemoratives. They can be used as gifts for family, friends, or for special occasions such as Christmas. They can also serve as a commemorative token of a visit somewhere or of a special anniversary; for example, the province of Ontario's 200th aniversary. They can be either functional (used for coffee or teaspoons) or decorative (hung in a spoon rack or put in a cabinet).

Competition comes from all other gift items and all other souvenir items in approximately the same price range.

Demmers identified 11 companies that distributed souvenir spoons in the southwestern Ontario area and gathered what data he could—much of it anecdotal—on each. This process provided encouragement for Demmers to proceed. Background on these suppliers is summarized in Exhibit 3.

Southwestern Ontario contained a number of large urban areas, including Toronto (over 2 million people), Hamilton/Burlington, Kitchener/ Waterloo, and London, with over 300 000 people in each, plus many smaller cities such as Guelph. Guelph was located roughly in the centre of the triangle formed by Toronto, Waterloo, and Burlington and was within an hour's drive of each.

Importing   To import goods into Canada on a regular basis in amounts over $800, an importer number was required. This was available from Revenue Canada, Customs and Excise. Requirements for customs were an advise notice from the shipper and a customs invoice. These were available in office supply stores. A customs tariff number and commodity code were also required to complete the customs B3 form.

Souvenir spoons of either sterling silver or silver plate were listed in the customs tariff under number 42902-1. The Netherlands has Most Favoured Nation status, so the duty was 20.3 percent. On top of the cost of the merchandise (excluding transportation and insurance but including duty) there was a further 10 percent excise tax and 9 percent federal sales tax.

A customs broker could be hired to look after the clearing of goods through customs. Rates were approximately $41 plus $3.60 for every thousand dollars of value, duty included.

Insurance on a shipment of less than $10 000 cost a fixed fee of about $150 with insurance brokers. This could be reduced if insurance was taken on a yearly basis, based on the expected value of imports over the year. Freight forwarders charged approximately $2 per kilo regardless of the total weight of the shipment.

On small shipments such as spoons, the importing could be easily handled without help. The product could be sent by airmail and insured with the post office. It could also be sent to a small city like Guelph rather than Toronto, and this avoided the busy Toronto customs office and possible delays of several days. The customs office in Guelph could clear the goods the same day they arrived.

Marketing Plan   The marketing plan is presented in schematic form in Figure 1.

Product   The proposed souvenir spoons would be a high-quality product with detailed dies made to give them a relief design far superior to any competitive spoons (except for those retailing in the $30 range). These

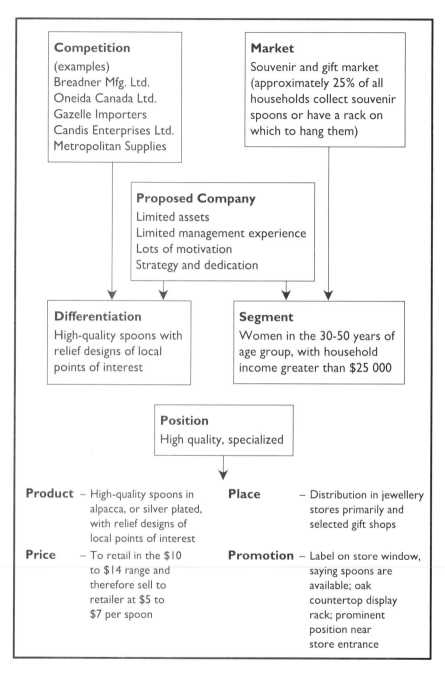

Figure 1

Kolapore Inc.
Marketing Plan

Competition
(examples)
Breadner Mfg. Ltd.
Oneida Canada Ltd.
Gazelle Importers
Candis Enterprises Ltd.
Metropolitan Supplies

Market
Souvenir and gift market
(approximately 25% of all
households collect souvenir
spoons or have a rack on
which to hang them)

Proposed Company
Limited assets
Limited management experience
Lots of motivation
Strategy and dedication

Differentiation
High-quality spoons with
relief designs of local
points of interest

Segment
Women in the 30-50 years of
age group, with household
income greater than $25 000

Position
High quality, specialized

Product – High-quality spoons in
alpacca, or silver plated,
with relief designs of
local points of interest

Price – To retail in the $10
to $14 range and
therefore sell to
retailer at $5 to
$7 per spoon

Place – Distribution in jewellery
stores primarily and
selected gift shops

Promotion – Label on store window,
saying spoons are
available; oak
countertop display
rack; prominent
position near
store entrance

spoons are available in silver plate and alpacca, which makes them similar to jewellery.

Designs would be of specific points of interest. In the Kitchener-Waterloo area, for example, possible subjects would include Seagram Museum, Schneider House, Doon Pioneer Village, university crests, and city crests. Kitchener-Waterloo would be printed under the picture, also in relief in the metal, along with the title of the particular picture.

Price Points

$2.25	—Metropolitan Supplies: nickel plated
$4.50–$6	—Breadner Manufacturing: rhodium plated and silver plated
	Candis Enterprises
	Gazelle Importers
$7–$8	—Oneida or Commemorative: simple designs with engraved insignia. Appear to be made of a silver alloy.
$10–$14	—Proposed price range for retail
	Quality comparable to $30 spoons, but silver content is lower
	Detailed designs of local landmarks
	Variety of six to ten spoons in each market
$30 and up	—Breadner
	Sterling silver
	Fine workmanship
	Very limited variety of designs

Place　Because souvenir spoons are purchased on impulse, locations with high traffic are essential. Jewellery stores and gift stores in malls and tourist areas are probably most suitable in this respect.

Due to the price range proposed and the quality of the merchandise, the quality and image of the store has to be appropriate. This would eliminate discount jewellery stores and cheap souvenir shops for the aforementioned reasons. Secondly, it would not please higher-end retailers if the same spoons were sold for less in the same area and would likely restrict distribution in the appropriate channels.

Jewellery stores are perceived by many people as selling expensive, luxury items that are not part of one's everyday needs. For this reason, it would be helpful for these stores to have a window display.

Promotion　Each retail location would carry a minimum product line of six varieties of spoons: one with a Canadian theme, one with a provincial theme, and at least four spoons with designs of local landmarks or points of interest.

The packaging would be suitable for gift wrapping, so would probably consist of a small box with a clear plastic cover.

Each retail location would have an oak countertop display rack. There would be a relatively high cost to the displays initially, but they would attract attention and convey the quality of the spoons. Different sizes could be made, depending on the number of spoons for a particular market.

Because souvenir spoons are primarily an impulse purchase, location in the store is important; the spoons should be near the entrance or in a window display. This is something that can be controlled only by persuading the retailer that this would increase the turnover and consequently his profits.

Finance   Contribution margin per spoon has been calculated using the most conservative numbers and at a wholesale price of $3.50. Typically, retailers would mark prices up by 100 percent (see Table 1). The contribution margins worked out to $2.05 on alpacca spoons and $1.50 on silver-plated spoons.

The break-even point, assuming costs of $25 250 per year and a contribution margin of $2.05, would be a sales volume of 12 317 spoons with sales value of $43 110 (see Table 2). Assuming the spoons would be

Table 1		**Alpaca**	**Silver Plate**
Kolapore Inc. Forecast Variable Costs and Margins of Spoons	Quote by Dutch manufacturer, Zilverfabriek (1 guilder = $0.43 Cdn.)	2.20 guilders	3.10 guilders
	Factory cost in $Cdn.	$0.95	$1.33
	Duty @ 20.3%	.19	.27
	Cost duty included	$1.14	$1.60
	Federal sales tax @ 9%	.10	.14
	Federal excise tax @ 10%	.11	.16
	Freight and insurance	.10	.10
	Cost	$1.45	$2.00
	Contribution margin	$2.05 to $3.55	$1.50 to $3.00
	Cost to retailer	3.50 to 5.00	3.50 to 5.00
	Retailer markup	3.50 to 5.00	3.50 to 5.00
	Retail price	7.00 to 10.00*	7.00 to 10.00

* These prices are lower than originally forecast due to Demmers's recognition that a retail price of $10 to $14 was too high.

Table 2	Distribution costs (transportation)	$ 4,000
Kolapore Inc.	Rent expense (work from home)	—
Forecast	Salary	15,000
Break-Even	Office supply costs (including telephone)	1,000
Point	Inventory costs	1,000
	Merchandising expenses (displays and boxes)	3,000
	Investment in dies (10 @ $125 each)	1,250
	Total fixed costs	$25,250

$25,250/$1.50 = 16,833 spoons
$25,250/$2.05 = 12,317 spoons
$25,250/$3.00 = 8,416 spoons

introduced in the Toronto market and distribution obtained in 100 retail locations, this means sales of 124 spoons per store.

Upon graduating from a university business school in April 1984, Demmers planned to devote his efforts to Kolapore. He felt that while there could be a short-term financial drain, his cash balance would be positive at the end of the second month of operation (see Exhibit 4).

Subsequent Events

Soon after graduating in April, it became clear to Demmers that Kolapore was not going to realize his forecast sales of $28 000 by September 1984. Due to delays in shipments from Holland and difficulty in obtaining distribution in Canada, sales were only $1830 over the summer. A number of assumptions in the original feasibility study (as described in the first section) had proven incorrect:

1. The number of dies ultimately required (each of which cost $125) was not going to be 10 but closer to 50.
2. The federal sales tax rate had increased to 10 percent from 9 percent.
3. Duty was payable on the dies themselves as well as on the spoons, at the rate of 20.3 percent excise tax plus federal sales tax.
4. Delivery time for new dies was closer to six months than the forecast ten to twelve weeks. (The artist had been ill for several months.) Several orders were cancelled during this period as a result.
5. Packaging costs per spoon were closer to 32¢ per unit than the estimated 10¢.

6. Distribution had been difficult because the large chain stores which dominated the market all had established suppliers.

7. The target market was not nearly as upscale as originally envisioned. Although Kolapore's spoons were readily identifiable as being of superior quality, most customers would only pay a maximum of $7–$8 retail for any spoon. Demmers had estimated the total Canadian souvenir spoon market at about $1.5 million annually. Within that, a very small portion was for sterling silver (where Demmers could not compete), about $450 000 was at the $7 retail price point where Demmers was selling (some of his competitors were promoting similar or poorer quality spoons at the same price), with the balance of the market reserved for lower priced, lower quality spoons.

The goal of 100 stores by September 1984 was still a long way off.

Demmers had also discovered that the chain stores plan all their buying from six to twelve months in advance. Because many of the spoons he had designed did not arrive until September 1984, this meant that he missed much of the tourist season (and nearly all of the Christmas market).

On the positive side, the Dutch guilder had depreciated relative to the Canadian dollar. In September 1984 it cost 39¢ Canadian for one guilder rather than 43¢ as forecast. In addition, delivery times for spoons from existing dies required three to four weeks rather than the expected four to six weeks, and the cost of display cases was only about $16 each. These were made of plastic rather than the originally envisioned oak.

Although Kolapore was showing a negative cash balance at the end of August 1984 (see Exhibit 5), sales began to improve in September (see Exhibit 6), growing to nearly $16 000 by the end of the first full year of operation (see Exhibits 7 and 8 for financial statements). A financial loss of $1800 was incurred for the first year of operation, and this took no account of the countless hours Demmers had invested.

Since the business was not yet self-supporting, in September 1984 Demmers began to look for other sources of income.

Between September 1984 and January 1986 Demmers worked for five months in a fibreglass factory, acquired a house in Guelph in which he was able to live and to rent out rooms, sold Bruce Trail calendars on a commission basis, worked at organizing and selling several ski tours (which did not take place), and opened an ice-cream store in a regional resort area (Wasaga Beach). Due to a low volume of traffic, this latter venture in the summer of 1985 resulted in an $8000 loss. In the fall of 1985 Demmers accepted a position as production manager for a weekly newspaper in Guelph.

By this time, Demmers was selling direct to retailers in twenty towns and cities in Ontario and through five chains: Simpsons and United Cigar Stores and, to a much smaller extent, Eaton's, Birks, and Best Wishes. Other chains such as The Bay, Sears, and Woolco had been approached but so far without success. Demmers was hoping to find time to approach the buyers at K-mart, Zeller's, Consumer's Distributing, Robinson's, Woodwards, and others.

Kolapore spoons were sold in Simpsons stores from Windsor, Ontario, to Halifax, Nova Scotia, and in eighteen United Cigar Store locations in southern Ontario. Four months after Demmers's first delivery to the chain outlets in the summer of 1985, about half the stores were sold out of Kolapore spoons. Neither chain would reorder stock partway through the year.

To sell direct in some of the smaller cities, Demmers's practice had been to drive or walk through the main shopping areas, stopping at jewellery stores or other likely retail outlets. If he was unable to meet with the store owner, he would usually leave a sample and a letter with some information (see Exhibit 9 for a copy of the letter). Demmers's experience had been that unless he personally met with the right person—which sometimes took three or more visits—no sales would occur. When he was able to meet with the owner, his success rate was over 70 percent. To sell direct in larger centres such as Toronto (where he had forty customers), Demmers had focused his efforts on hotel gift shops. Having established these customers, he could now visit all forty customers in Toronto personally in two to three days.

By year end, Demmers had access to a pool of eighty-nine Canadian-specific dies. Demmers's supplier in Holland had forty-six dies in stock that another Canadian from western Canada had had designed. Spoons based on these dies were no longer being sold anywhere as far as Demmers cound tell.

For the most part Demmers was selling spoons based on his own designs. (For those spoons which Demmers had had designed, he had exclusive rights in Canada.) In less than two years he had forty-three more dies made up (see Exhibit 10 for a complete list). In some cases Demmers had asked a particular company/group to pay the cost of the dies; in others, such as for universities, he had built the die cost into his price for the first shipment; while in others he had simply gone ahead on his own with the hope that he could achieve sufficient sales to justify the investment.

There was a wide variability in the sales level associated with each spoon. Sales of his best-seller—the Toronto skyline, which depicted major buildings and the CN Tower—were about 1,000 spoons a year. Dem-

1. Metro Zoo
2. CN Tower
3. Casa Loma
4. Royal Ontario Museum (ROM)
5. Black Creek Pioneer Village
6. Art Gallery of Ontario (AGO)
7. Canada's Wonderland
8. Ontario Place
9. The Ontario Science Centre

mers's second-best-selling spoon in Toronto was Casa Loma, about 300 a year. (For a list of some of the major tourist sites in Toronto, see Table 3). This spoon had quickly sold out on site in ten days. However, the buyer had been unwilling to order more partway through the year. Spoons with other Toronto designs were selling less than fifty units a year.

By December 1985 inventories had increased and Kolapore Inc. was still showing a small loss (see Table 4). Any gains from changes in the rate of import duty on spoons (20.3% in 1984 to 18.4% in 1986) had been negated by changes in federal sales tax (9% in 1984 to 11% in 1986) and exchange rates. The fluctuating Dutch guilder was at a two-year high relative to the Canadian dollar. From a March 1984 value of 43¢ Canadian, the guilder had declined to 36¢ in February 1985 and climbed to 50¢ by

Table 4

Kolapore Inc.
Statement of
Income
Eight Months[a]
Ending
November 30,
1985 (unaudited)

Sales	$21,000
Cost of sales:	
Inventory at beginning of year	2,873
Purchases	12,000
Duty and freight	3,500
Dies	1,950
	20,323
Less: Inventory at end of year	5,000
Cost of sales	15,323
Gross profit	5,677
Expenses	6,500
Net profit (loss) for the year to date	$ (823)

[a] Annual sales expected to be $30,000

December 1985. During the past eight months, partially due to these exchange fluctuations, Demmers had also arranged for the spoons to be silver plated at a cost of 40¢ each in Ontario. This had resulted in a saving of 15¢ a spoon (which varied with the exchange rate). More significantly, because many spoons were purchased as souvenirs of Canada, by adding sufficient value by silver plating in Canada the imported product no longer had to be legally stamped "Made in Holland." In fact, the packaging could now be marked "Made in Canada." Demmers was quite optimistic regarding the implications of this change because a number of potential store buyers had rejected his line because it did not say "Made in Canada." Demmers's supplier, however, was upset with the change.

Meanwhile, the feedback he was receiving from many of his customers was positive—in most cases they were selling more of his spoons than any other brand. Some customers, in fact, had inquired about other products. Since he had so far not experienced any competitive reactions to his spoons, Demmers was thinking of investigating the possibility of adding ashtrays, letter openers, key chains, lapel pins, and bottle openers to the product line in 1986 if he stayed in business. Each one of these products could have a crest attached to it. These crests would have to be the same as those used on the spoons and would thus utilize the dies to a greater extent. The landed costs per metal crest from the same supplier would be 85¢. Demmers contemplated attaching these crests himself onto products supplied by Canadian manufacturers. However, initial investigations had revealed no obvious economical second product line.

Demmers also planned to phase out alpaca imports; all products would now be silver plated. In fact, Demmers was also wondering if he should acquire the equipment and materials in order to do this silver plating and polishing.

With no lack of ideas, many of the original frustrations nonetheless remained. The buyers at major chains such as Eaton's and Simpsons had changed once again, and because they did not use an automatic reorder system, new appointments had to be arranged. This was as difficult as ever. Also, Demmers still had not been able to draw anything from the firm for his efforts. These factors, coupled with his lack of cash and the demands of his new full-time position, had left Demmers uncertain as to what he should do next. With the spring buying season approaching—when Demmers would normally visit potential buyers—he realized that his decision regarding the future of Kolapore could not be postponed much longer.

Exhibit 1

Kolapore Inc.
Survey of Spoons
Carried by Local
Retailers in
Guelph
and Kitchener–
Waterloo Region

- A Taste of Europe–Delicatessen & Gift Store,
  Guelph Eaton Centre
  A selection of spoons from Holland with Dutch designs
  One with the Canadian coat of arms, which looked good
  Rhodium-plated spoons: $5.98 per spoon
  Well displayed at front of store

- Eaton's–Guelph Eaton Centre
  Breadner spoons with maple leaf or Canadian flag and "Guelph" stamped in
    the bowl
  Rhodium plated: $4.98
  No display and hard to find

- Pequenat Jewellers–Wyndham Street, Guelph
  Carry Candis spoons, which look cheap and do not sell very well
  $4.98
  Poorly displayed

- Smith & Son, Jewellers–Wyndham Street, Guelph
  Do not carry souvenir spoons because they are not in line with the store's
    image. They often get requests for them.

- Franks Jewellers–King Street, Waterloo
  Carry Breadner spoons with the Waterloo coat of arms
  Rhodium-plated spoons: $4.50 per spoon
  Not on display but kept in drawer
  Sell fewer than 12 per year

- Copper Creek–Waterloo Square Mall, Waterloo
  Candis spoons: $5 each

- Birks–King Centre, Kitchener
  Carry Oneida and Breadner spoons
  Rhodium-plated spoons for $5.98
  Oneida spoons were $8.95 and looked like a silver alloy
  Sterling silver Breadner spoons for $31.95
  Displayed in a spoon rack, looked good
  Birks regency spoons with crest of each province, $12.50

- Eaton's–Market Square, Kitchener
  Breadner spoons, two types for Canada only
  Rhodium plated: $4.98

- Young's Jewellers–King Street, Kitchener
  Rhodium-plated Breadner spoons, $4.50 each

- Walters Jewellers
  Against chain policy to carry souvenir spoons because of poor quality and
    low turnover

Exhibit I
(cont'd)

Survey of Spoons

• Peoples Jewellers
  Do not carry souvenir spoons

• Engels Gift Shop–King Street, Kitchener
  Carry Breadner, Oneida, Gazelle, and Metropolitan
  Altogether about 20 varieties
  Well displayed near entrance of store; prices range from $2.25 for
      Metropolitan spoons to $7.98 for Oneida spoons
  Saleslady said they sell hundreds every year, mostly in the summer

Exhibit 2

Terms
Concerning
Souvenir Spoons

Crest	– Emblem, either metal, plastic, or enamel that is affixed to a standard spoon.
Picture spoon	– Spoon with a picture under plastic which is heat-moulded to the spoon.
Relief design	– Spoon with an engraving or picture, which is moulded into the metal of the spoon.
Enamel	– Opaque substance similar to glass in composition.
Plated	– Thin layer of metal put on by electrolysis.
Rhodium plated	– Shiny "jeweller's metal," which does not tarnish (no silver content).
Silver plated	– Silver covering on another metal (such as steel).
Sterling silver	– Alloy of 92.5% silver and 7.5% copper, nickel, and zinc.
Alpacca	– Alloy of 82% copper and 18% nickel.

Exhibit 3

Souvenir Spoon
Suppliers

Breadner Manufacturing Ltd.

Breadner appears to have national market distribution and includes two major retailers, Birks and Eaton's. According to some of the store managers interviewed, their sales of souvenir spoons in each location was low. Several retailers also expressed dissatisfaction with the Breadner line because of the slow turnover. Typically, there was a basic design for the spoon, which did not change except for a different crest glued on for the different locale.

Breadner has been in the jewellery business since 1900 and has a plant in Hull, Quebec. They manufacture to order various types of pins, medals, and advertising specialties but advised Demmers that in general they use their entire output of souvenir spoons for their own sales.

They have many varieties of spoons in their catalogue and an established distribution system across the country. Demmers recognized the possibility that they could upgrade their selection in a short time to compete directly with his intended selection of spoons.

Typical retail prices for Breadner spoons were $4.50 and up, the cost to the retailer being $2.25 and up. Breadner's high-end sterling silver spoons were available at Birks for $31.95, with the cost to Birks estimated at about $15 per spoon. Both rhodium-plated and silver-plated spoons were available, but rhodium-plated was more common.

Candis Enterprises Ltd.

Candis is located in Willowdale, Ontario. This company has good distribution in gift shops (for example, the 650-outlet United Cigar Store chain) and in some jewellery stores. They have a line of rhodium-plated spoons marketed under the MaR-VEL name and silver-plated spoons under the Candis name.

Their strategy appears to be one of putting out a large variety of spoons for each place in which they sell. However, the quality seems to be toward the low end: many of the spoons have rough edges on the bowls and there is no detail in the dies.

Wholesale cost ranges from $2 per spoon for a rhodium-plated picture spoon to $3.25 for a silver-plated spoon with a five-colour ceramic crest.

Metropolitan Supplies Ltd.

Metropolitan Supplies is located in Toronto and distributes its goods across Canada primarily to gift shops and souvenir shops in tourist areas. This company deals with all sorts of souvenirs and novelty items. They have a large selection of spoons, each of which can be crested to suit the buyer. The quality of the spoons is at the low end. Prices range from 55¢ per spoon (wholesale) for iron- and nickel-plated spoons to $2 per spoon for silver-plated ones.

Gazelle Importers and Distributors

Gazelle Importers and Distributors is located in Grimsby, Ontario. They originally imported spoons from Holland but later manufactured in Ontario. Their spoons are sold under the Gazelle name. They retail for $5.95 and,

Exhibit 3
(cont'd)

Souvenir Spoon
Suppliers

therefore, presumably cost the retailer about $3. Spoons have designs for Ontario and Canada but nothing local. Quality seems about the same as Breadner's less expensive line.

Oneida Canada Ltd.

Oneida is located in Niagara Falls, Ontario, and is a division of Oneida Ltd. in the United States. The Niagara Falls plant manufactures stainless steel and silver-plate flatware. Their product is distributed in several jewellery stores including Birks and gift shops. The quality is better than any other spoons except Breadner's sterling spoons. Prices are also somewhat higher, with a retail price of $7.98, giving a probable cost to the retailer of about $4 per spoon. There is little variety. All spoons come in one design with a different engraving in the top of the spoon.

Commemorative Spoons

This firm is located in Ottawa and sells spoons in the $6.95–$8.95 range. They have three basic designs (supplied by Oneida). They have large accounts with Simpsons and Cara and frequently deal with clubs for whom they make up special spoons for fund-raising.

Hunnisett and Edmonds

This is a distribution company that specializes in selling to card shops and variety stores. They use a somewhat unique packaging system—selling via fly-top displays of twelve spoons.

Parsons-Steiner

This firm is located in Toronto. The quality of the product is low. Retail prices range from $1.99 to $5.98. Spoons tend to be picture spoons, and the least expensive ones appear to be made of cast iron with a decal attached.

Boma

This company is located in Vancouver. The product quality is very good. Spoons are made out of pewter with designs of such things as totem poles. Retail prices range from $10 to $20.

Aalco Souvenirs

Located in Vancouver, this company carries over 300 "three-dimensional" models of spoons. They are made in Canada and are nickel plated with a white gold flash. Aalco's products are distributed across Canada. They also carry other souvenir items such as bells, bottle openers, key chains, lapel pins, and charms. Prices for spoons range from $2.50 to $3 each.

Souvenir Canada

Located in Downsview, Ontario, and operating throughout Canada and the United States, this company carries spoons with plastic decals, key chains, bottle openers, bells, lapel pins, mugs, plates, glasses, clothing, and special promotional items. They have been in business for about ten years and use standardized spoons with crests attached. Retail price per spoon is $3.

Exhibit 4

Kolapore Inc. Forecast Cash Flow, May–August 1984

	May	June	July	August
Cash	$3,000	$ (750)	$1,000	$ 7,500
Disbursements:				
Moulds	1,250	–	–	–
Purchases	–	7,250	–	7,250
Promotion expenses	2,000	1,000	–	–
Car expenses	500	500	500	500
Total disbursements	3,750	8,750	500	7,750
Net cash	(750)	(9,500)	500	(250)
Receipts:				
Accounts receivable	–	10,500	7,000	10,500
Cash balance (to be borrowed) Terms n/30	$ (750)	$1,000	$7,500	$10,250

Exhibit 5

Kolapore Inc. Actual Cash Flow, 1984

	May	June	July	August
Cash	$2,600	$1,000	$ 950	$ 530
Disbursements:				
Purchases	1,000	550	870	1,460
Expenses	1,000	80	300	300
Total disbursements	2,000	630	1,170	1,760
Net cash	600	370	(220)	(1,230)
Receipts:				
Accounts receivable	400	580	750	1,100
Cash balance	$1,000	$ 950	$ 530	$ (130)

Exhibit 6

Kolapore Inc. Actual Sales, 1984–1985

May	$ 400
June	580
July	750
August	1,100
September	2,600
October	2,540
November	1,500
December	1,400
January–March	4,923

Exhibit 7

Kolapore Inc.
Balance Sheet
as at March 31,
1985
(unaudited)

Current Assets:

Cash	$1,708
Accounts receivable	1,763
Inventory	2,873
Total current assets	$6,344
Incorporation expense	466
Total assets	$6,810

Current Liabilities:

Accounts payable and accruals	$ 268
Due to shareholder	8,342
Total liabilities	$8,610

Shareholders' Equity:

Retained earnings (deficit)	(1,800)
Total liabilities and shareholders' equity	$6,810

Notice to reader: These financial statements have been compiled solely for tax purposes. I have not audited, reviewed, or otherwise attempted to verify their accuracy or completeness.

Guelph, Ontario
May 2, 1985

Chartered Accountant

Exhibit 8

Kolapore Inc.
Statement of
Income
Year Ended
March 31, 1985
(unaudited)

Sales	$15,793

Cost of sales:

Inventory at beginning of year	—
Purchases	8,453
Duty and freight	2,288
Dies	3,034
	13,775
Less: Inventory at end of year	2,873
Cost of sales	10,902
Gross profit	4,891

Expenses:

Office	657
Samples	582
Auto expenses	1,137

**Exhibit 8
(cont'd)**

Statement of
Income

Car allowance	3,900
Bank interest and charges	139
Advertising	26
Accounting	250
Total expenses	6,691
Net profit (loss) for the year	$(1,800)

Notes:

1. Significant accounting policies:
   Kolapore Inc. is a company incorporated under the laws of Ontario on April 6, 1984, and is primarily engaged in the importing and selling of souvenir spoons. The accounting policies are in accordance with generally accepted accounting principles.
   Inventory is valued at lower of cost or net realizable value.
   Incorporation expense is not amortized.
2. Due to shareholder is noninterest bearing and payable on demand.

Exhibit 9

Kolapore Inc.
Letter of
Introduction

Kolapore Inc.
P.O. Box 361
Guelph, Ontario
N1H 6K5

Dear

Kolapore Inc. would like to offer you the opportunity to have your own design on a spoon made up in metal relief; for example, a logo, coat of arms, crest, building, or whatever you would like.

There is always a large market for souvenir spoons of unique design, and high quality Kolapore Collection Spoons fit this category extremely well and are priced very competitively.

The spoons are available in silver plate at $3.50 per spoon. This price includes a gift box, federal sales tax, and shipping.

The minimum order is 100 spoons to get a new design made up, and there is also a one-time die charge of $125.00 to help offset the cost of making the new die. Delivery time is approximately three months if a die has to be made up; subsequent orders will take four to six weeks.

The dies for Kolapore Collection Spoons are made by master craftsmen in Schoonhoven, Holland, the silversmith capital of the world. The spoons themselves are made in Canada. As a result, the quality of the spoons is exceptional and recognized by the consumer at a glance.

I trust that this is sufficient information. I look forward to hearing from you. If you have any questions or concerns, please don't hesitate to contact me. Thank you for your time and consideration.

Sincerely,

Adriaan Demmers
President

Exhibit 10

Kolapore Inc.
Collection
Spoons—
Designs Available

Canada:

Deer
Elk
Caribou
Cougar
Mountain goat
Moose
Bighorn sheep
Grizzly bear
Salmon
Coast Indian
Indian
Coat of arms
Mountie
Maple leaf

Province of Nova Scotia:

Bluenose (schooner)

Province of Quebec:

Montreal, skyline
Montreal, Olympic Stadium

Province of Ontario:

√ Trillium
√ Windsor, Ambassador Bridge
√ Sarnia, Bluewater Bridge
√ Chatham, St. Joseph's Church
√ London, Storybook Gardens
√ Woodstock, Old Town Hall
√ Stratford, swan
√ Kitchener, Schneider Haus
√ Waterloo, The Seagram Museum
√ Waterloo County, Mennonite
     horse and buggy
√ Elora, Mill Street
√ Guelph, Church of Our Lady
√ Guelph, Credit Union
   Guelph, St. Joseph's Hospital
√ Kitchener-Waterloo, Oktoberfest
√ Hamilton, Dundurn Castle
√ St. Catharines, Old Court House
√ Niagara Falls, Falls,
     Brock Monument, and
     Maid of the Mist

**University and community
college crests/coats of arms:**

√ Wilfrid Laurier
√ Waterloo
√ Carleton
√ Guelph
√ York
√ Western
√ Windsor
√ McMaster
√ Brock
√ Fanshawe
√ Humber

Province of Alberta:

Banff, Mount Norquay
Banff, Mount Rundle
Banff, Banff Springs Hotel
Calgary, bronco rider
Edmonton, Klondike Mike
Wild Rose (flower)
Oil derrick
Jasper
Jasper sky tram

Province of British Columbia:

Coat of arms
Prince George
Victoria, Parliament buildings
Victoria, lamp post
Victoria, Empress Hotel
Nanaimo, Bastion
Dogwood (flower)
Totem pole
Kermode Terrace
Smithers
Northlander Rogers Pass, bear
Northlander Rogers Pass, house
Kelowna, The Ogopogo
Okanagan, The Ogopogo
Vancouver, Grouse Mountain/
     skyride/chalet
Vancouver, Grouse Mountain
     skyride

Exhibit 10
(cont'd)

Designs Available

Acton, Leathertown
   (hide with buildings)
√ Toronto, skyline
√ Toronto, City Hall
√ Toronto, St. Lawrence Market
√ Toronto, Casa Loma
√ Kingston, City Hall
√ Ottawa, Parliament buildings
√ Collingwood, Town Hall
√ Owen Sound, City crest

Vancouver, Grouse Mountain
   skyride/cabin
Vancouver, Cleveland Dam
Vancouver, The Lions
Vancouver, The Lions Gate Bridge

Yukon Territory:

Coat of arms
Gold panner

Note: Check marks denote those made up on Demmers's initiative.

CASE 7-5

Eclipse Golf Ltd.

"I'm sorry, but I'm only authorized to wait until Monday for your answer." After hearing this comment, Sean Hall left the lawyer's office. He had just been offered $10 000 for his 4000 shares in Eclipse Golf Limited (Eclipse), a company with a unique state-of-the-art process that guaranteed perfect replication and matching between golf clubs. The offer came from Irene Sakellis, wife of the founder of the company. The product had been well accepted by better golfers and sales had increased 350 percent over the past two years.

Hall had paid $2000 for 1000 of his shares two years earlier and received the other 3000 for services rendered. He knew that taking the offer would give him a substantial return on investment but he was not sure if the $10 000 was the full value of the shares. Since the shares were not traded on any exchange, their value could not be determined by market forces. Hall was playing successfully on the PGA tour and he did not need the money in its own right, but he felt that there was a principle involved, since he had helped get the company on its feet.

This case was prepared by David C. Porter, Research Assistant, under the direction of Professor David C. Shaw. Reprinted by permission—University of Western Ontario.

Precision Machine

John Sakellis, the principal shareholder in Eclipse, had emigrated from Yugoslavia with his wife in 1946. In spite of language problems and a shortage of money, John was persistent and finally found a job using his knowledge of machining. He was a hard worker and very skillful, and within a few years became the person that everyone consulted on difficult or complex jobs. He was very proud of his accomplishments and enjoyed his job, but his main goal had always been to own his own company. In 1964, Sakellis realized his ambition and started Precision Machine Co. Ltd. (Precision), an aerospace/aircraft parts machining company, located in Malton, Ontario, five miles from Lester B. Pearson International Airport. Contracts were not easily found, but after several months Precision won its first contract with De Havilland Aircraft. The quality of its products, along with competitive prices, ensured that Precision never again had difficulty winning contracts.

The company's reputation grew and by 1978 it was considered one of the top three or four machining companies in North America. Precision developed the reputation of being able to build parts that no other company could build. This was possible because Sakellis and his vice president, Ray Summers, designed and built many of Precision's machines to their own exacting specifications. Their equipment was always in the forefront of technology and Sakellis and Summers were constantly testing new ideas and designs to increase quality or decrease production times.

In mid-1978, Sakellis decided to step down as president of Precision and leave the business to his son Maurie, who had worked part-time for Precision for several years and was about to complete his degree in chemical engineering. Sakellis felt that Maurie could continue to learn the business under Summers, who was to become president. By the time Summers retired, Maurie would have the knowledge necessary to manage Precision.

With retirement in mind, Sakellis started playing more of his favourite sport, golf. On one of his weekend outings Sakellis met a "master" club builder from a major North American golf club company. After hearing of Sakellis's machining background, the club builder invited him for a tour of the Canadian facilities. Although he never mentioned it during the tour, Sakellis could not believe how inefficient and inaccurate the whole process was, and he was sure he could devise a far better method. Just to be cautious, he decided to check other golf manufacturing facilities and found the same manufacturing problems. He knew it would be difficult to design machines that would accurately reproduce golf club heads because the heads would have to be cut on several planes at the same time. He thought that this complexity might be the reason why no one else had attempted production of this type before, but building the machines would only be the beginning of the problem. Finding proper iron castings, wood turnings, shafts, grips and other supplies to meet the same high standards would not be easy either. The entire golf business seemed to survive on marketing alone and few if any of the internationally published claims and advertisements for golf equipment had any basis in physical fact. Sakellis was also worried about suggesting that his product would be superior to the already so-called "perfect" clubs currently on the market, since the perfect matching of golf clubs had been claimed by the golf industry for many years. Sakellis knew these claims to be untrue, but how could a small Canadian company dispute the statements of sporting giants such as Wilson, MacGregor and Ben Hogan? Ping, a small golf club manufacturing company based in Southern California, had managed to overcome the odds, but it had taken ten years to do so and was considered one of the "lucky" ones.

The Golf Club

By June 1979, Sakellis had successfully designed and built several numerically controlled machines capable of accurately machining both iron and wood golf club heads. Even though the prototypes were perfect from an engineering standpoint, Sakellis thought that the clubs were not aesthetically pleasing so he sought out a prominent Canadian tour player to correct the appearance of the clubs and to test several metal alloys in order to find that elusive quality golfers call "feel." Sean Hall was the professional approached and he agreed to help finish the product in exchange for shares in the company.

It took the better part of a year to complete testing and designing, but when the club was finally ready, everyone was confident it would take the market by storm. Hall believed the clubs would give him a two shot advantage over the rest of the tour field, but, more importantly, he felt that the ability to replace broken clubs with exact duplicates, so that no retraining period was required, was virtually priceless. The confidence in the superiority of the clubs exhibited by all those involved in their production led Sakellis to suggest the name *The Golf Club*, with the slogan, "undoubtedly the finest available on the market."

Eclipse

Sakellis decided to call the new golf club company Eclipse Golf Limited. He also decided to restructure the management of both his businesses and have Summers take charge of the golf machining sections. He put his son-in-law, Derrick Kouzounas, who had an M.B.A. from a well-known eastern business school, in charge of Precision and put Maurie in charge of marketing the golf clubs. Sakellis then was free to oversee both companies in an unofficial capacity, leaving time to continue designing, redesigning and building better equipment.

The clubs were introduced at the Canadian Professional Golfers' Association's fall buying show in October of 1979. Sakellis and Maurie decided to introduce the product at a price near the lower end of what consumers would consider were comparable products, as shown in Table 1. Sales were slow at first mainly because of lack of funds for advertising and the difficulty of overcoming the "Canadian product" stigma.

By the end of 1983, Eclipse had secured a small niche in the Canadian market and had entered several foreign markets, such as West Germany, Spain, and Australia. But there had been some problems. Everyone involved with the running of Eclipse found golf professionals difficult to understand. They seemed to come to the annual buying shows simply to have a good time with some old friends. It was not unusual to have several pros visit the Eclipse booth partially or even totally inebriated. Senior management could not understand why sales had not increased more rapidly. In the aerospace industry, all a manufacturer had to do was produce a superior product at competitive prices, send out a prototype, and then watch the orders roll in. This method did not seem to work in

Table 1		
Eclipse Golf	Walter Hagen	$450
Limited	Wilson Staff	495
Wholesale Prices	Ben Hogan	508
for Top Line	THE GOLF CLUB	516
Golf Sets[1]	Dunlop Maxfli Australian Blade	525
(as of 1982)	Ram Tour Grind	550
	Spalding XL-4	580
	Titleist Tour Model	669
	MacGregor Nicklaus Muirfield	795[2]
	Ping	822
	Sounder	853

[1] All prices were for 11-piece sets, 3 laminated woods and 8 irons.

[2] Available in solid persimmon woods only.

Source: Manufacturer's wholesale price catalogs.

the golf business. Various reasons for this difficulty were discussed, but the one Eclipse management kept returning to was that golf professionals were more interested in selling something easily, rather than working at selling the best. Everyone thought that if the golf pros were properly educated, it would only be a matter of time until they recognized the quality of the product and started to purchase in larger quantities. In any case, management believed that sales had climbed to a point where entry into the US and Japanese markets seemed possible for the summer of 1984. The American market was huge in comparison to all other markets and even a 0.1 percent market share would double Eclipse's total sales volume. Exhibits 1 and 2 show income and balance sheets for Eclipse for the years 1980 to 1983.

The Share Situation

In Eclipse's early years funds were scarce. Sakellis was totally against public financing, either debt or equity, but was willing, in special cases, to issue small numbers of shares to employees as payment beyond their regular earnings. Sakellis himself worked long hours for virtually no pay, since he was drawing a pension from Precision. Eclipse was housed in the same building as Precision and Precision equipment and labour were used when available to keep Eclipse's costs to a minimum.

A total of 16 000 of the 20 000 authorized shares had been issued. Sakellis and his wife, who had worked as a bookkeeper, owned 3000 shares each. Maurie owned 3000, Hall owned 4000 and the remaining 3000 were distributed among other employees, mostly to Summers. Sakellis was interested in repurchasing Hall's shares and those of the employees because of his desire to have the company completely family-owned. Hall was currently on the Board of Directors because of the number of shares he held, but believed his position was really a token gesture since he was rarely consulted on decisions other than product testing.

Hall knew he had little time to make his decision on whether to accept the $10 000 for his 4000 shares. He had dabbled in the stock market for several years and was quite capable of reading financial statements. He thought that other information would be necessary to make his decisions and proceeded to gather the facts shown in Exhibit 3.

Hall had been friends with the Sakellis family for a number of years and did not want to create any animosity. On the other hand, he wanted to be treated fairly for his involvement in Eclipse and his contribution to the company's success. If worse came to worst, he was not against hiring a lawyer to increase his chances of receiving fair value for his shares.

Exhibit 1		1983	1982	1981
Eclipse Golf	Sales	$ 522,904	$366,036	$ 148,447
Limited	Gov't Grants	4,169	8,230	12,714
Income	Gross Revenue	527,073	374,266	161,161
Statement	Cost of Sales	326,126	209,961	85,674
for the years				
ended	Operating Profit	200,947	164,305	75,487
1981–1983				
(unaudited)	Expenses:			
	Office wages	57,304	55,109	42,348
	Accounting & legal	914	1,325	3,760
	Travel	3,617	2,992	4,327
	Rent	6,998	6,426	6,006
	Insurance	7,436	7,436	7,436
	Advertising*	21,215	19,196	38,111
	Repair & Maintenance	6,312	5,604	5,143
	R & D	15,900	11,400	8,866
	Interest	5,248	13,319	7,745
	Office Supplies	964	978	1,004
	Telephone	826	711	787
	Depreciation	14,411	12,124	11,361
	Miscellaneous	319	425	531
	Total Expenses	141,464	137,045	137,425
	Net Profit Before Tax	59,483	27,260	(61,938)
	Tax	9,376	1,192	(12,410)
	Net Profit	**$ 50,107**	**$ 26,068**	**$(49,528)**

---

* Includes cost of CPGA buying shows held annually in five cities across Canada.

Exhibit 2		1983	1982	1981
Eclipse Golf Limited Balance Sheet as at December 31, 1981–1983 (unaudited)	**Assets**			
	Cash	$ 4,756	$ 5,112	$ 11,406
	Accounts receivable	94,053	64,307	28,939
	Inventory	76,158	54,639	40,517
	Total current assets	174,967	124,058	80,862
	Equipment, cost less accumulated depreciation	202,169	248,568	242,875
	Total assets	$377,136	$372,626	$323,737
	Liabilities			
	Bank loan	$ 42,244	$ 88,196	$ 67,193
	Accounts payable	17,245	16,890	15,072
	Total current liabilities	59,489	105,086	82,265
	Loans from shareholders	275,000	275,000	275,000
	Capital stock (16,000 issued, 20,000 authorized)	16,000	16,000	16,000
	Retained earnings	26,647	(23,460)	(49,528)
	Total Liabilities and Equity	$377,136	$372,626	$323,737

Exhibit 3		
Eclipse Golf Limited Selected Statistics	Long-Term Government Bond Yield	12.73%[1]
	T-Bill Rate	9.24%[1]
	TSE Composite P/E	22.41 times[1]
	Consumer Products P/E	11.48 times[1]

Company		Sales	EPS	Div	Price[2]	High[3]	Low
Cooper	82	$66,883,000	$1.08	–	$ 3.38	$ 4.00	$2.25
	81	66,988,000	(.24)	–		4.13	2.50
Irwin	82	88,639,000	.88	$.15	11.00	15.25	6.38
	81	60,787,000	.41	.10		8.88	2.00

[1] Statistics as of December 31, 1983.

[2] Share Price as of December 31, 1982.

[3] High and low share price for year specified.

Old Country Furniture A (OCF)

Carl Barth had operated a small furniture manufacturing plant in the Kingston, Ontario area for almost 15 years. Producing a limited line of early Canadian furniture, the company had grown to sales of over $2 million per year and employed 30 full-time plant employees by 1988.

Since 1982, Barth's company had experienced a rapid increase in sales. Recently, however, profits had declined and, while the deterioration was not yet drastic, it had become a matter of concern. Although sales had increased overall, direct furniture sales had shown only small increases, despite a buoyant market. A number of marketing initiatives had done little to improve the trend. Barth's main concern was the rising number of competitors in the area, and the slightly larger firms from the Toronto and western Ontario area who were selling through eastern Ontario dealers. The competition was further heightened in his market by a number of small, and in some cases well equipped, individuals who produced furniture out of home workshops on a part-time basis.

Background

After working for small furniture builders and refinishing shops around Ontario, Carl Barth made the decision to start his own business in 1975. He returned to the Kingston area and opened a small shop in a building behind his home. The building had been used as a machine shed and was easily modified for woodworking. A year later Barth made the decision to move into larger quarters and to manufacture early Canadian furniture reproductions. There was a rich history with respect to early Canadian furniture in eastern Ontario, and Barth felt there was a market for copies of period furniture. Early in the process of setting up Old Country Furniture (OCF) Barth recognized the need to make three significant changes in his designs. First, he would downsize the furniture to fit the smaller rooms typical of modern houses and apartments. Second, he would add new functions to otherwise decorative pieces (for example, designing traditional pieces to accommodate stereos and television sets). Finally, he decided to create new pieces for use as wall units, book cases etc., using period designs.

The business grew rapidly. Old Country Furniture began by selling direct from the factory, but by 1978 the factory showroom space was needed for production and the store was moved to leased space in a downtown retail market. Since 1979, Barth had added two additional outlets, one in Cornwall and a second in Ottawa. More recently, he had looked at space in the Toronto area with the thought that retail space in that market would provide the sales necessary to reverse current profit trends and fill unused plant capacity.

The Furniture Industry

Located primarily in Quebec and Ontario, the furniture industry employed almost 55 000 people and generated 2 billion dollars in annual revenues. Despite some rationalization, and more expected because of the Canada-USA Free Trade Agreement, the industry was characterized by small companies. The average company employed 30 people, had sales of less than $1 million in 1987, and produced very limited lines for local and regional markets. Few of the smaller companies had a national image and most who sold to the larger retail merchants did so on a contract basis, often for private branding. Sales for most were garnered at the major furniture shows, leaving many of the small firms that could not afford this exposure without adequate or extensive distribution.

Typically, companies specialized in one or more types of furniture. These included: case goods, upholstered goods, metal furniture, some miscellaneous categories of furniture, and household furnishings such as lamps. The market for these products was divided into several categories, including household, office and business, industrial, and church furnishings. Within the household group, furniture was further divided into bedroom, dining room, living room, etc. Furniture was also classified according to general style. These classifications included colonial, Danish modern, art deco, French provincial, shaker, etc. Within these groupings, the styles took the names of some of the designers who down through history had developed pieces which continued to be popular with furniture buyers. There were also a large number of Ontario and Quebec furniture manufacturers producing a wide variety of early Canadian pine furniture.

At best, the furniture industry is evolutionary. While some segments have introduced automated computer-controlled equipment, most companies in the business remained labour intensive using traditional equipment and skills. There was a growing use of veneers, plywoods, particle board, and a variety of new fastening equipment to speed up assembly. As well, specialized equipment had been developed for the use of large-volume producers. But, for the most part, the production of furniture had remained unchanged. Packaging, handling, storage, and delivery technologies had improved to a degree, but relatively speaking, for small- and medium-sized producers, furniture making was a low technology industry.

With the population of Canada centred in Quebec and Ontario, most Canadian furniture was manufactured and sold in these provinces. Imported furniture from both Europe and the US was a significant market factor, although foreign producers focused on specialty markets. For example, IKEA sold knockdown furniture (KD) in modern, simple designs, while some Italian producers sold very expensive and elaborate furniture featuring hand carving and painstaking finishes. Major US furniture producers tended to export expensive high-end furniture into Canada. This was expected to change as the Free Trade Agreement came into full effect.

Old Country Furniture

OCF had evolved in a way that was typical of the furniture industry. Some ideas such as direct selling were part of the original approach; wholesaling, custom work and sales to the hospitality industry had all been added to fill capacity. Most of the markets had been developed around the production interests of the company. Only recently had marketing, and more specifically retailing, received special attention. It had become apparent to Barth that OCF could not maintain stable sales at a level of $2 million or more without increased marketing support. This recognition, and the reluctance of the wholesale trade to support OCF products at the retail level, suggested to Barth that increased efforts to build the OCF retail group would lead to new and more profitable growth.

The OCF Product Concept

Normally, a customer would select pieces from the showroom display and place a deposit on the order. The pieces were then produced, finished to order, and delivered in six to eight weeks. While OCF produced a wide range of products, design was not an issue. Carl Barth selected pieces from various early Canadian antique collections and simply copied them, altering dimensions but maintaining the integrity of the original design. The products were produced from several native Canadian woods including pine, oak, cherry and elm. Each piece was finished with a hand rubbed oil application (lacquer finishes were available on request). Production runs were relatively short and for the most part the factory delivered to order. As well as direct sales through company outlets, OCF furniture was wholesaled to a number of retailers in non-competing areas. Beyond the case goods (wooden furniture for the bedroom, living room and dining room) manufactured for household consumption, OCF produced furniture and fixtures, again in an early Canadian motif, for the restaurant trade. This market was served through a Toronto agent who represented a number of non-competing manufacturers. And finally, the company had produced a variety of wooden items, including furniture, furniture in kit form and parts for other manufacturers and retailers.

OCF Marketing

OCF served three different markets and each required a different approach. The markets included:

1. Household furniture,
2. Restaurant furniture, and
3. Wooden products, kits etc.

Household furniture was distributed through one of three channels. Retail sales were made through three retail outlets owned and operated by OCF. These were located in Kingston, Cornwall, and Ottawa. Wholesale furniture was sold to other retailers for resale in their respective markets. Much of this was sold by Barth. Custom furniture, based on customer drawing and specifications, was sold from the factory.

Restaurant furniture was handled by a Toronto agent and designer. These orders were for chairs, tables, booth seating and serving pieces. OCF had also produced beds, tables and desks and dressers for hotel and motel chains which used an early Canadian motif.

Wooden products, including turned parts and small furniture kits, were produced for a variety of customers. Since most of these products required only the machining operations, they were useful in filling machine capacity, which exceeded assembly capacity in the OCF plant. One customer had accounted for over $150 000 in sales of the miscellaneous products group. Table 1 presents a breakdown of factory sales.

OCF Retail Operations

Retail operations were managed by Katherine Parker, who was responsible for the three retail stores and recently had been visiting some of OCF's wholesale customers. Initially Parker had operated out of the Kingston retail store, but as the job grew she had returned to an office in the plant and hired a new store manager.

Table I

OCF Factory/Retail Sales Breakdown

	1988	1987	1986	1985	1984
Sales–Factory	$1,987,000	$1,764,000	$1,540,200	$1,390,340	$1,120,100
Wholesale	557,400	459,600	392,400	370,100	254,400
Retail	790,600	727,320	652,117	602,460	567,379
Institutional	533,400	451,000	256,000	242,000	186,000
Miscellaneous	105,600	126,080	239,683	175,780	112,321
	1,987,000	1,764,000	1,540,200	1,390,340	1,120,100
Retail Sales	1,340,000	1,276,000	1,124,340	1,004,100	978,240
Less Cost of Goods	790,600	727,320	652,117	602,460	567,379
Gross Margin	$ 549,400	$ 548,680	$ 472,223	$ 401,640	$ 410,861

Retail sales had grown slowly since passing the $1 million mark in 1985, in spite of the fact that furniture markets had been extremely buoyant. Parker had made a number of proposals to increase sales and these were yet to be discussed. Both Ottawa and Kingston had shown steady growth, while sales in Cornwall were erratic. Parker's review of the activities in Cornwall had not shown any specific reasons for the fluctuations. Now that she had a fully trained manager in Kingston, she intended to spend some time in Cornwall to see if some improvements could be made in the sales levels. Table 2 presents OCF's retail sales by outlet for the five-year period 1984–1988.

Table 2

OCF Retail Sales By Location*

Location	1988	1987	1986	1985	1984
Kingston	562,640	491,540	435,780	391,500	372,900
Cornwall	233,460	346,537	289,560	234,600	264,100
Ottawa	543,800	437,923	399,000	378,200	341,240
Total Sales	**1,339,900**	**1,276,000**	**1,124,340**	**1,004,300**	**978,240**

---

* The retail operations are discussed in detail in Old Country Furniture (B).

New Products

New products planned for the furniture line included wall units, bookcases, and a line of specialty tables and mirrors. As well, OCF was considering the addition of products such as cutting boards, cheese boards, breadboards, spoon racks, coat racks, hall trees and other small wood items to round out the retail store inventories. Barth felt that some of these items would allow the use of wood that was now going to scrap. He had to assess this involvement carefully, however, since many small producers of giftware had specialized in these products and, as a result, were extremely competitive. The option of buying these products from other producers was also under consideration.

As well, the company was considering a limited line of upholstered products. Currently, most of the upholstered work was for the restaurant furniture market and it was contracted out. As this work grew, Barth believed that one or two people could be employed as upholsterers. OCF would then be able to offer some upholstered furniture to fill out its lines. Frames for chairs, couches, settees and other upholstered pieces could be purchased from frame makers and finished to a variety of customer specifications at OCF.

OCF Financial

OCF had been profitable in every year since its inception. The company was somewhat unique in that Carl Barth had been able to finance OCF's operations and growth from personal funds. OCF had therefore never borrowed from any lending institutions. In fact, Barth had an aversion to borrowing, often mentioning what had happened to a number of his competitors during the high interest days in the early 1980s when rates soared beyond 20 percent. It was no longer clear, however, that he could afford to personally finance some of the expansions currently being considered.

Barth's attitude toward financial performance was limited to the bottom line, and as long as OCF was profitable he did not intend to make major changes. While there was some concern with declining profits (as a percentage of sales), it was not urgent and, according to Barth, increased direct sales were the answer. In his own words, he was mainly a cabinet-maker interested in quality and service; he believed that attention to product and production would keep the company profitable in the long run. His growing attachment to company-owned retail outlets reflected his dedication to quality and value. He believed that his own outlets could do a better job of conveying OCF's concern for these two elements than an outlet that handled a variety of products and was mainly concerned with volume. More often than not, any discussion of financial or cost issues resulted in a production solution, since Barth saw the factory-retail concept as the only way for quality producers to transmit their story into the marketplace. Exhibit I presents income statements for the OCF operations from 1984 through 1988.

OCF Operations

For several years Joe Shelton had assisted Carl Barth in running the factory. Barth looked after the design, the production planning, and general supervision of plant employees. Shelton had specific responsibilities for machining operations, but supervised the whole factory during Barth's frequent absences.

The factory was divided into four areas which included: breakout and machining; assembly; finishing; and shipping and inventory. There was some overlap, and cabinetmakers who worked in assembly usually did machining operations when assigned to custom work. Parts for direct sale were completed in the machining department and moved directly to finishing or shipping. Machined parts for furniture were moved to assembly, and from there to inventory to await finishing instructions. Typically about 50 percent of an assembly lot had been pre-sold by the time it was assembled, and these pieces moved to finishing and shipping for distribution. Most wholesale orders were shipped upon completion, although OCF might produce a quantity of which half could be shipped immediately, with the balance to be shipped within 30 days.

Alternately, OCF might machine the full order, holding half of it in a parts inventory and assembling the balance for later shipment. All furniture parts were machined in economic order quantities. Figure I presents a factory layout of the OCF Kingston Plant.

Machining (MD) The machining department was responsible for all machine operations except finish sanding. Typically, this involved rough cutting, planing, finish cutting, drilling, routing, turning, dovetailing and rough sanding. The parts were then stacked on a pallet and moved to in-process inventory awaiting their removal to assembly. Major equipment such as the automatic lathe and the wide-belt sander were scheduled, since they were used for special orders apart from the regular runs. Most other equipment was available without prescheduling.

Joe Shelton managed the area. His skills in machining and the selection of material were important in keeping scrap and subsequent labour costs

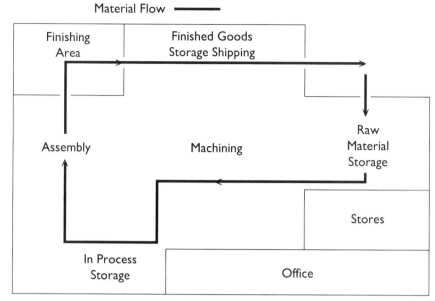

Figure 1

OCF
Factory Layout
of the
Kingston Plant

Material Flow ━━━━

Finishing Area	Finished Goods Storage Shipping	
Assembly	Machining	Raw Material Storage
In Process Storage		Stores
	Office	

in line. He was a working supervisor, assisting his people as well as machining orders when time was available. He was also skilled at machine set-up, and even where he did not do the set-up he would check the work, especially when longer runs were involved.

Much of the standard scrap estimated as part of the quote or production order was taken in machining, although no records were kept to compare actual with standard.

Assembly (AD)   Assembly at OCF was handled by cabinetmakers and apprentices under the supervision of a cabinetmaker. Assembly included finish sanding, fitting and the assembly of parts. All of these operations were performed at a workbench with the assistance of power and hand tools. The cabinetmakers were responsible for the quality of their own work, and where faults were detected the pieces were returned for repair. On occasion, each qualified cabinetmaker was assigned to custom work. Here the cabinetmaker took a drawing and participated with Barth in the layout and estimating of the order. If the order was received, the cabinetmaker performed all of the operations except finishing.

Finishing (FD)   Two finishing processes were employed at OCF. Most non-OCF customers requested stain with a lacquer finish, while OCF retail stores used hand-rubbed oil stains. Each process was priced at the same level, and according to Barth the costs were similar.

The finishing area was equipped with two ventilated spray booths, a large room for staining and oil finishes, and a storage area where the pieces were allowed to dry prior to shipment. Three to four people worked in the various finishing areas depending on the scheduled work load.

Material Control (MCD) Two full-time people and a part-time person handled the material control area. Here they were responsible for raw materials, supplies, parts inventories, assembled pieces, and finished goods and delivery. Inventory control and shipping were the major responsibilities. Purchasing was handled by making requests of Barth who would issue the purchase orders, usually in writing, sometimes verbally. Copies of orders and quotes for custom work or parts were sent to MCD. Inventory was set aside for the orders, or ordered if required. If it was necessary to order materials or parts, this information was conveyed to Barth and deliveries confirmed, with purchase delivery times taken into consideration. For quoted orders, inventory was designated and if the order was not confirmed, the designation was removed. If designated materials were required for other confirmed orders, Barth was advised and he decided if additional materials should be ordered to insure that quoted delivery times could be met. Inventories were totalled monthly, deleting materials used according to the production schedule and adding on the basis of supplier deliveries. Physical inventory was taken annually for the purposes of the year-end statement.

All prices were quoted f.o.b. the factory (i.e., the cost of delivery was extra). Some customers picked up orders using their own trucks, but many used the delivery service of OCF. It was priced below the costs incurred by most customers, and certainly below commercial trucking services. However, to get these prices (15 percent of the order value or a minimum charge for small orders), customers had to accept delivery schedules set by OCF. OCF in turn was able to offer competitive delivery prices by arranging full loads in both directions from the Kingston plant. Furniture and parts were hauled one way, while parts and supplies were picked up and returned to the plant. Typically, the company truck was in Toronto once a week and Montreal every second week. Other deliveries and pick-ups were scheduled as required. The factory delivered orders for retail stores when the time was available; otherwise the outlets used local cartage firms for home delivery.

Table 3	Total Employees	30			
OCF	Total Hours	30×2000		$=$	60,000
Factory Labour	Less:				
Rate	Indirect employees	5×2000	$=$	10,000	
	Vacations & holiday	$17 \times 30 \times 8 =$		4,000	
	Personal time	$25 \times 50 \times 3 =$		3,750	
	Material handling	$25 \times 50 \times 4 =$		5,000	
	Maintenance			2,200	
	Miscellaneous			860	
				25,810	25,810
	Direct Labour Hours				34,190
	Labour Costs	$272,780			
	Overhead Costs	210,340			
	Total	483,120			
	Factory Rate	$483,120/34,190 = \$14.13$/hour			

Labour and Overhead Costs

OCF employed 30 people full-time in Kingston. Of these, six (including Joe Shelton) performed indirect labour amounting to approximately 11 000 hours annually. Those activities classified as indirect labour included maintenance, clean-up, material handling, delivery, and other jobs around the plant not directly associated with furniture manufacture. The remaining 24 people were classified as direct labour.

The factory labour rate was calculated as shown in Table 3. This rate ($14.13) was used for estimating the standard costs of production runs. Custom work was priced at a factory rate of $20 per direct labour hour.

OCF Support Functions

As Carl Barth had managed the company since its inception, many of the support activities in personnel, finance and accounting were structured around his knowledge of the firm. Since he knew all of the employees on a first name basis, he felt little need for extensive personnel files. Financial statements, accounting records and other internal information had been developed to meet the needs of "outsiders" and Barth made little use of the information included in the various reports to government and other agencies.

However, recent additions to the retail operations and the accounting area had resulted in an increased need for internal information. As well, Barth was finding it increasingly difficult to make all of the decisions, particularly since he was away from the plant on a regular basis. Barth's accountant had suggested on several occasions that he would have to formalize some of the internal reports in order that others in the organization could function effectively. It was becoming apparent to everyone, including Barth, that his currently planned expansions were going to make the whole issue of his personal control a major problem.

Accounting and Control

Cheryl Oleawitz had worked as office manager and bookkeeper for OCF for almost nine years. She used a Nebb's one-write bookkeeping system (two parts—sales/payroll). The system had been in use for about five years and had been reasonably satisfactory for the first three or four years. Only recently had there been some difficulties, most of which arose from the establishment of the retail division. In addition, Barth had been requesting information about sales, costs, expenses and breakdowns related to retail sales, custom sales, institutional sales and miscellaneous products. She had provided the necessary information but much of it had been based on her best estimates of which costs and expenses were associated with which sales. The system she was using was not designed for this type of analysis. Barth had asked her to suggest some changes and at the time had made her aware of some of the company changes that might occur, including the new retail organization, and the possibility of one or two new stores in Toronto.

Oleawitz thought that separate systems should be set up for OCF manufacturing and OCF retail. Parker felt that each retail outlet should have a separate accounting system, or at least a system that would permit store managers and the division manager to deal with the costs and revenues of each unit. She felt this was essential if unit performance was to be tied to manager performance assessment. There certainly was a need to have more details within the retail division and Parker thought this would require separate books for each store. Even if all the books were kept in Kingston, it would be necessary to keep separate figures for each retail outlet. (Her proposals for the retail division are set forth in OCF (B).)

Finally, Oleawitz expressed a need for some help in setting up a cost system for the manufacturing division. The basic documents for collecting information were in place and being used in the factory, but so far these cost sheets were not being used as part of the accounting system.

Each time a part, piece of furniture, etc. was to be produced, the job was quoted on a standard form. The form included a drawing or sketch followed by a job estimate, containing estimates for materials, scrap, labour, overhead, and profit. This estimate became the standard cost base for the particular product. For production items such as the furniture line, it was used with each new run; for custom work it was used for the specific order, both for the quotation and the measurement of costs in the factory. These forms were checked only intermittently. When Barth felt that a particular job was taking longer than he thought reasonable, he would check the standard cost record; however, little action was taken and few of the estimates were reviewed. It was evident that the main purpose of the estimate was to establish a price, but this, too, was often altered to meet competitive market needs.

Budgets and forecasts had not been used on a regular basis, although they were prepared for new projects such as the opening of new retail outlets. Once a year labour rates and overhead rates were adjusted, and all new estimates were then based upon the revised rates. Prices on the wholesale furniture price list were adjusted from time to time, and this triggered an automatic change in the retail price lists. To date no forecasts or budgets had been prepared for the retail outlets, although Parker had asked for help in this area for the 1990 budget year.

Payrolls for the factory and the retail stores were prepared every two weeks. Barth had adopted a policy of paying for 40 hours per week on the understanding that hours missed would be made up at the convenience of company and employee. Most factory employees had 20 to 40 hours banked against a "rainy day." This policy, proposed by the employees, allowed payrolls to be made out in advance. During the months of June through September, the plant went to a four-day (10 hours/day) week. Barth closed the plant in July, giving all employees a two week vacation. Employees entitled to more than two weeks were allowed to take the additional days at any time during the year.

Barth had estimated company benefits at 15 percent of payroll. This figure included worker's compensation, Canada Pension Plan, Unemployment Insurance, Blue Cross Medical, and Life Insurance. He was firmly attached to the 15 percent figure, and for the last five years had committed the surplus to Registered Retirement Savings Plan contributions for each employee with a minimum of one year's service. The company would estimate the surplus and divide it by the number of employees willing to make matching RRSP contributions. The employees agreed to invest in a five-year investment certificate to qualify for the company's contribution. As part of this process Barth employed a tax consultant to help employees fill out their income tax forms, and most employees were convinced to buy and keep the RRSPs. The company did not have a pension plan or profit sharing. Barth was ready to proceed with profit sharing, but again the profit sharing contributions would be made to the RRSP fund since he was concerned about retirement benefits and felt that the company was too small to have a pension plan.

OCF retained an accountant to provide an audit of the accounts, and from time to time assist in the preparation of projections and financial statements for outside use by the bank and other groups involved directly or indirectly with OCF.

OCF Organization

The organizational functions such as hiring, employee relations, employee programs, etc. were handled by Barth and the accounting manager. When pressed to define his organization, particularly in view of his planned expansion, Barth produced a tentative outline (see Figure 2) of what he thought would be reasonable. At an earlier date he had given a partial organization chart to Parker when he appointed her manager of the retail operations. The sketch had been prepared after a discussion with an advisor. It resulted from some questions about Barth's role and what he might need in the way of management help.

Figure 2

OCF Organization Chart

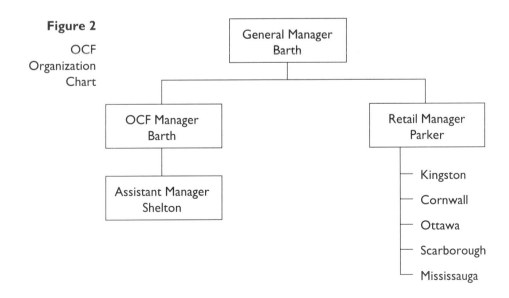

Although he had produced this outline of a prospective organizational structure, Barth expressed some discomfort with the degree of formalization suggested by the approach. He did realize, however, that unless the functions were kept separate, it would be difficult to talk meaningfully about performance and responsibility.

Organizational activities such as wage, salary and benefits administration were handled by Barth on an *ad hoc* basis. The factory had five labour categories with different rates. Apprentices were paid minimum wage to start, with increases every six months until they became cabinetmakers. The labour categories were as follows:

1. Cabinetmaker,
2. Finisher,
3. Machinist,
4. General Labour (Shipping/Delivery), and
5. Apprentice

The rates were the same for all individuals in a category regardless of age and experience. An additional hourly amount was paid to those designated as lead hands, but currently there were none so assigned. Shelton, the assistant manager, was paid a salary.

Present Situation

Commenting on the current situation, Barth noted:

> I would like to handle all of our furniture sales through company owned outlets. It would facilitate planning at the plant and with five to ten outlets we could develop some marketing impact for our product line. In the long term, direct marketing would give us more control and if the volume can be increased, we can expect better profits at all levels of the organization.

Exhibit I

OCF Income Statement June 1, 1984–May 31, 1988

	1988	1987	1986	1985	1984
Gross Sales	$1,987,000	$1,764,000	$1,540,200	$1,390,340	$1,120,100
Less excise tax	160,947	139,356	126,296	105,666	88,488
Net Sales	1,826,053	1,624,644	1,413,904	1,284,674	1,031,612
Cost of Goods Manufactured					
Beginning Inventory	638,470	704,230	582,460	520,450	444,680
Materials	457,890	389,915	325,198	282,628	206,322
Labour	438,253	357,422	296,920	269,268	202,322
Factory overhead	292,168	243,697	212,086	205,548	165,068
Less End Inventory	(657,240)	(638,470)	(704,230)	(583,460)	(520,450)
Cost of Goods	1,169,541	1,056,794	712,434	694,434	497,942
Operating Profits	656,512	567,850	701,470	590,240	533,670
Expenses–Administrative					
Wages & salaries	221,400	198,600	174,200	160,780	159,020
Benefits	12,000	12,000	12,000	8,000	8,000
Cleaning & maintenance	3,700	1,280	1,020	760	592
Telephone	33,210	29,790	26,130	24,117	23,853
Professional	5,400	3,100	2,560	2,290	1,756
Insurance	12,600	8,400	7,200	3,600	2,700
Travel	7,900	5,400	4,860	2,450	1,970
Taxes	7,640	6,970	6,450	5,890	5,579
Depreciation	4,470	5,610	5,230	3,400	3,290
Miscellaneous	2,980	1,256	1,462	1,520	980
Total	311,300	272,406	241,112	212,807	207,740
Expenses–Selling					
Wages & benefits	69,400	62,700	56,700	52,980	48,240
Commissions	6,000	6,000	6,000	3,200	3,200
Advertising	17,900	12,670	9,800	8,950	5,240
Travel	18,900	15,600	12,720	8,960	7,430
Shipping (net)	12,200	10,980	8,800	6,940	6,450
Telephone	7,600	7,600	5,960	6,590	3,490
Insurance	7,100	5,129	4,473	3,290	2,150
Depreciation	7,200	5,400	3,680	3,780	2,060
Miscellaneous	1,390	1,270	1,310	710	560
Total	147,690	127,349	109,443	95,400	78,820
Total Expenses	458,990	399,755	350,555	308,207	286,560
Net Profits (pre-tax)	197,522	168,095	350,915	282,033	247,110
Taxes	39,504	33,619	70,183	56,407	49,422
Net Earnings	$ 158,018	$ 134,476	$ 280,732	$ 225,626	$ 197,688

Old Country Furniture B (OCF)

Carl Barth had operated a small furniture manufacturing plant in the Kingston Ontario area for almost 15 years. Producing a limited line of early Canadian furniture, the company had grown to sales of almost $2 million in 1988. It employed 30 full-time plant employees and operated three retail outlets in eastern Ontario.

Old Country Furniture (OCF) produced and marketed furniture through both wholesale and retail channels. As well as three company-owned retail outlets, OCF supplied, on a wholesale basis, 12 to 15 retailers in Toronto, Burlington, Hamilton, Kitchener and St. Catharines. The furniture pieces shipped to these outlets were also early Canadian reproductions but differed from those used by the three captive retail outlets. None of the dealers was exclusive to OCF.

In addition to the furniture lines, OCF also made institutional furniture (primarily tables, chairs and serving pieces for restaurants), furniture kits, and furniture parts. The kits and parts were sold to a variety of customers, although in 1987 60 percent of the kits and parts went to one customer.

Old Country Furniture

Located in Kingston Ontario, OCF produced furniture for the wholesale and retail trade from a well equipped plant. Since its inception, OCF had used a factory-direct selling concept, although it had also produced for the wholesale trade using unsold production capacity. To pursue the factory-direct approach remained a major part of its strategy. To this end OCF operated three retail outlets, one each in Kingston, Cornwall, and Ottawa. Carl Barth was now considering additional retail outlets for the Toronto area and had surveyed several locations looking for the right spot.

Katherine Parker, manager of the retail operations, was responsible for the three retail stores. Parker joined OCF in mid-1988 when Barth realized that trying to run the plant, visit with wholesale and industrial customers, and supervise the retail stores was just too much to handle. Parker had been hired to manage the Kingston store, but shortly after joining OCF, Barth made her manager of retail operations and, until the end of 1988, she held both jobs. Effective January 1, 1989 she had assumed

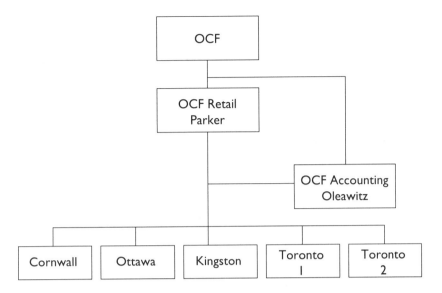

Figure 1
OCF
Retail Division
Organization
Chart

her new job; however, it was not until June 1, 1989 that Parker and Barth put together an organization chart and decided on her responsibilities (see Figure 1).

In part, the reorganization was prompted by the performance of the retail outlets. Despite reasonably good sales levels, the stores were only marginally profitable. The new Ottawa store had grown rapidly but profits had declined in 1988. Parker believed there were other problems that distorted retail performance. These included everything from the way the bookkeeping was done to the product line featured in the retail outlets.

In March 1989, Barth asked Parker to begin gathering some information on opening a Toronto outlet. He provided her with the information he had, including a list of his contacts. He asked that she prepare a proposal for opening one, perhaps two, retail stores in the Toronto area. He targeted August 1, 1989 as an opening date.

Retail Operations—(OCFR)

Retail sales had grown slowly since passing the $1 million mark in 1984, despite the fact that furniture markets had been extremely buoyant. Barth felt that the major reason lay in the fact that he didn't have the time to run the retail stores and really had not hired anyone to do the job. As a result, each of the stores drifted without coordination and without much marketing effort. Changing managers, little control or guidance, and a lack of focus left the retail stores without direction.

Product Line

OCF had purposely positioned its product lines at the upper end of the early Canadian offerings. Because of the large number of small producers located in eastern Ontario, most of whom competed on price, OCF made a conscious decision to produce high-quality, high-priced furniture.

OCFR carried two relatively complete lines: the Durham County and the Renfrew County, as well as different pieces selected from various antiques owned by Barth or some of the local museums. These pieces were not sold to the wholesalers and thus were exclusive to OCFR outlets. From time to time, pieces produced for wholesalers were overrun, and these were marketed by the retail division. These pieces were usually specialty items and did not compete with other items in the retail line.

Until early in 1989 the retail stores handled only furniture produced by OCF. In March of 1989 Parker convinced Barth to try some giftware and furniture accessories as part of the retail inventories. These had been successful and Parker was proposing that these items be included in each of the retail stores. She thought it was particularly important since all of the outlets were in high-traffic areas and could benefit from impulse, gift, and special-occasion buying. She believed that giftware and accessories could eventually account for 25 to 40 percent of retail sales, at least in the high-traffic outlets.

Support Services

Most of the support services required by OCFR were provided by OCF out of Kingston. Payroll was handled by Cheryl Oleawitz, as were other bookkeeping functions. Employee hours were submitted each Monday and the payroll was completed and cheques issued every second Friday. Retail employees were always one week behind and, while this caused some difficulties for new employees, it was not generally of much concern.

Sales invoices were written in four parts. Copy 1 went to the customer, copies 2 and 3 remained with the store until the sale was complete. Copy 3 was then forwarded to the OCF accounting office. Copy 4 was sent to the OCFR office at the time of sale. Various summaries were made in the store and at the OCFR office.

Employee records were maintained at OCF, as were all permanent records of the retail operation. OCF did not provide any financial feedback on retail performance beyond a monthly and cumulative expense summary. These figures were compared with a total budget for the retail group as a whole. Parker had to extract figures from various documents to get any idea of the expenses and revenues on a store-by-store basis. The whole process of performance measurement at the retail level depended on a summary of data provided to OCF. Because the bookkeeper at OCF was too busy to provide the information, Parker had to run the figures herself if she wanted even an incomplete picture.

Outlets

Since assuming the manager's job, Parker had made a number of proposals to increase sales and these were yet to be discussed. Ottawa, in particular, posed some special problems since the store was located in a high-traffic mall. It was Parker's feeling that the location would never be profitable unless the store added gift items to the furniture offerings. Traffic in the mall was good, but the lack of small-ticket items resulted in many "lookers" and few "buyers." As well, traffic counts past the store were increasing while traffic into the store was decreasing. It seemed evident to Parker that the inventories in each store should be tailored to suit local needs, with OCF products forming the core. To date, only OCF products were featured in each of the stores, although Parker's experiments in the Kingston store suggested that a variety of items could be sold profitably and might, if properly selected, make a significant contribution to the fixed costs of the retail outlet. Since Barth had little or no interest in giftware and accessories, these were not a part of the retail inventory. Table I shows sales figures from each outlet for the years 1984 through 1988.

Both Kingston and Ottawa had shown sales declines in 1988 as compared to 1987. Cornwall, the smallest of the three stores, registered a small increase. All three stores had managers that had been on the job less than a year. Because the bookkeeping and record keeping were done at the OCF office (costs were allocated under office expenses), few details could be sorted out by retail location. Parker had requested and received

Table I

OCF Retail Sales by Outlet

	1988	1987	1986	1985	1984
Kingston	$ 562,640	$ 491,540	$ 435,780	$ 391,500	$ 372,900
Cornwall	233,460	346,537	289,560	234,600	264,100
Ottawa	543,800	437,923	399,000	378,200	341,240
Total Sales	**$1,339,900**	**$1,276,000**	**$1,124,340**	**$1,004,300**	**$ 978,240**

income statements for each of the locations, but beyond the sales and cost of goods figures, there was very little useful information. Parker knew that some of the expenses had been divided up in an arbitrary fashion. Since Barth had never paid a great deal of attention to the retail outlets, figures on the performance of each store had not been part of his management approach. There was no doubt in Parker's mind that good management, at the retail level, would require more attention to the details of each outlet and better coordination of the group as a whole. In her opinion, the managers of each store would need more autonomy if they were to successfully tailor their stores to the needs of each retail area.

Kingston   Located in a restored downtown mall, the Kingston store benefited from a long involvement by OCF and Barth in the Kingston area. Word-of-mouth advertising and location had always been important to the store. Recently, some advertising had been undertaken to attract Kingston customers to shop downtown, and to attract customers from the surrounding areas to shop in Kingston. About 50 percent of the advertising expenditures had been part of "downtown" and mall promotions. These commitments were made by Barth, who felt it necessary that his company have a public presence. He chose the retail operation as a vehicle for this involvement, feeling it could benefit most from these expenditures.

The Kingston retail store employed a full-time working manager and three part-time employees. The store, closed on Sundays and Mondays, was open 10 a.m. to 6 p.m., Tuesday to Thursday and Saturdays and until 9 p.m. on Friday. Along with the other stores in the group, it displayed a full line of OCF products. Customers placed orders for furniture, specifying one of five stain colours and the wood of their choice (most of the pieces were offered in pine, oak and cherry). Delivery required from five to eight weeks depending on factory orders and inventory. A deposit of 10 to 20 percent was made and the furniture was delivered upon completion. Deliveries in Kingston were handled by the factory, and a small charge was paid by the store to OCF for the service.

Parker had experimented, successfully she thought, with giftware and accessories since January 1, 1989. Sales of these non-OCF goods during the first six months of 1989 were $51 200. Gross profit on these goods was 49 percent, about 6 percent higher than on furniture sales. As well, Parker felt that these goods increased the traffic-to-sales ratio by providing small-ticket items to people who would otherwise not buy. Having moved to a downtown location, the store could now benefit from these products.

Kingston was a city of approximately 60 000 people. Among other things, it had one of Ontario's oldest universities, a significant industrial base, a large hospital and medical facilities associated with the university, and a large prison installation. The city was noted for a stable economy and a relatively high average disposable income. As one of the older cities in Ontario, it had a long tradition with early Canadian furniture, and many of the pieces typical of the area had both British and American influences, arriving in Canada with the Loyalists.

Cornwall   The Cornwall store, opened in March 1985, had grown steadily. Prior to the store's existence, Barth had attended flea markets, home shows and fall fairs in the Cornwall area. Sales from these undertakings led Barth to believe that a Cornwall location could be viable.

The store was located in downtown Cornwall and, as with all OCFR outlets, sold only furniture. The turn-of-the-century building, owned by Barth, had three storeys with office tenants occupying the second and third floors. It had shown steady sales growth, although the total sales were below Barth's expectations. Parker's review of the activities in Cornwall had not shown any specific reasons for the low volume. Now that she had a fully trained manager in Kingston, she intended to spend some time in Cornwall to see if improvements could be made in the sales levels.

Cornwall was a city of 48 000 people in a market area approximating 120 000. It was located on Highway 401, almost at the Quebec/Ontario border, and approximately equidistant between Kingston and Montreal. Although some industrialization was present, the major economic thrust was tourism related to the St Lawrence Seaway and the vacation areas close to the city. Cornwall was approximately one hour from Ottawa.

As with Kingston, Cornwall was a part of the early Loyalist and Canadian traditions. Furniture making had been a part of its history, and the restoration of old homes and furniture helped create a knowledge about, and a market for, early Canadian reproductions. Although close to the Quebec border, the traditions were very much English Loyalist in the city, with the French Canadian influences evident in the surrounding countryside. As with the other outlets, shipments from the factory were made weekly. These were delivered locally by a contracted service after the customer had been contacted and delivery arranged. Until recently the store had handled only furniture; however, it was now experimenting with accessories and gifts.

The store had a manager and two part-time employees. It was open Tuesday to Saturday 10 to 6, except Friday, when the hours were 10 to 9. There was no requirement to be open any particular hours, and the

Tuesday-Saturday choice suited the operation and the customers. Located in the downtown area, it experienced high traffic patterns during office hours. As with other stores, the manager felt that a broader line would be helpful as a means of generating more traffic.

Ottawa The Ottawa store was the first OCF retail outlet in a mall location. It was smaller than either Kingston or Cornwall but, because of the location, traffic counts were much higher. As well, lease costs were much higher, but Barth felt that advertising costs could be reduced because of mall-generated traffic. Parker was less sure that this would work for big-ticket items like furniture. A traffic survey indicated that there were many who entered the store looking for small items. A furniture purchase was usually planned and was seldom made by casual shoppers, who tended to use the mall for a wide range of shopping needs.

Ottawa faced different problems than the other two outlets. The mall lease required that all stores stay open when the mall was open. Currently the hours were Monday to Wednesday 10 to 6, Thursday and Friday 10 to 9, and Saturday 9 to 6. To meet these requirements, the store employed two full-time and three part-time employees. As part of the mall association, the store contributed to advertising and mall event funds as part of the agreement. This represented about half of the store's advertising budget.

As part of Parker's practical research, the store had stocked a few gift items in May and June 1989. Sales had been brisk, prompting the managers to suggest that this was the only way the store could benefit from mall traffic. Parker felt that in order to improve sales it was essential that the store stock be expanded to include small goods, gifts and accessories. These sales involved very few incremental expenses. The only increase would be inventory investment of approximately $10–12 000, which Parker thought could be turned three to six times a year. By her rough estimates, these sales could make Ottawa a profitable operation, and the increased traffic would benefit furniture sales.

Ottawa was Canada's national capital and a city of 310 000 people. The market area could draw on almost twice that number. With its stable economy, high-income levels and large tourist traffic, it was a growing and attractive market. Competition was stiff, with many small companies producing and marketing early Canadian furniture. As well, surrounding Ottawa was a large area of cottages and ski-lodges which provided an additional market for OCF products.

Retail Pricing

OCFR priced at suggested retail on all OCF furniture. Giftware and accessories were priced at 100 percent over wholesale. Sales, clearances, and specials reduced the average markup on both furniture and accessories. Since there was no furniture inventory except showroom pieces, "sales" were used only when showroom stock was to be replaced. From time to time, when OCF was producing tables and chairs for the wholesale trade, extra units would be run and these sold as package specials out of the retail stores.

OCFR offered two distinct furniture lines. Prices on each line were competitive with similar products in all three markets now served. Barth felt that OCF's lines represented good value. Exhibit 1 presents the retail price list in effect at July 1, 1989.

The Toronto Market

"The largest, fastest growing and most competitive market in Canada, that's Toronto. And that is why we want to be in it," said Carl Barth. "Of course, there are other reasons. We are in Toronto weekly, so shipping from the plant to a retail store can be done on a contribution basis. Also, we would like to increase our total volume and in the process replace our current wholesale trade with more profitable retail sales."

Prior to Parker's appointment to the manager's job in OCFR, Barth had done some work in the Toronto area looking for a new store location and visiting some of the competitors. He had seen locations in downtown Toronto, North York, Scarborough and Mississauga. All of these locations were in malls; however, only the North York location was in an enclosed mall similar to that of Ottawa. Lease rates in all were high compared to the existing stores, but Barth expected this difference. The North York location included a fixed lease price or a percentage of sales, the greater amount to be the lease rate. The others were quoted on the basis of a five-year net/net lease. OCFR would have to pay utilities and tax increases.

Traffic counts were taken at all locations and apart from North York, all were about the same. The Mississauga and Scarborough locations were in large residential areas, and both were close to new residential construction projects. North York had the highest counts, but this was an established mall and there were a large number of stores which shared these consumers. Parker was convinced that the counts were a small part of the total picture, since furniture was a major purchase. She believed that people would search out alternatives if they were aware of the various outlets handling lines of interest. Before completing her recommendations to Barth, she would undertake to gather as much information as possible and present it as part of a business plan for the retail operation.

Barth was convinced that prices would have to be higher in the Toronto area to cover the higher space and labour costs. Parker, on the other hand, thought that the competition would result in lower prices and could only be recovered through higher volumes. She believed that additional high-volume items (tables, chairs and beds) would have to be added to the line.

Some General Observations

Parker had a number of ideas she felt would improve the retail operation. Gifts and accessories should be added to all stores. Additional pieces oriented to cottage and summer homes would provide OCFR with access to some untapped markets in all three existing retail areas. These items could be stocked on a seasonal basis. She also thought that each store should have at least two full-time employees to lessen the impact of turnovers and provide a more knowledgeable sales force for the outlets.

Advertising and promotion activities should be centralized in order that a more professional approach could be taken. Part of the budget (which was mostly *ad hoc* at this time) could be allocated to meet local needs, and part to the advertising of store-wide activities (seasonal sales and special events). By coordinating these activities, artwork and media rates would be lower because longer contract commitments offered substantial savings. She also thought that increased coordination would allow the stores to take full advantage of the factory's characteristics and production efficiencies. Since tables and chairs could benefit from long production runs, special sales (spring and fall) could be built around these opportunities. Finally, Parker felt that there would have to be improvements in reporting and control. She admitted that the figures currently available on each outlet were not accurate and, while overall these figures might be useful to OCF, they did not provide her with many tools for pinpointing specific problems in the outlets.

Parker had discussed these and other problems with Barth and it was agreed that she would set out her ideas for the retail division as part of the study, and report on the Toronto store proposals. They agreed that her report on Toronto would reflect change proposals for the whole retail division. Parker wanted to see the marketing and operations of the retail division freed up from the manufacturing operations. In her mind, this meant that the retail division would have to stand on its own, produce a profit, and meet other objectives that were relevant to the retail group. She thought if OCFR had a coherent strategy it would provide acceptable returns, although she knew there was a slight possibility this might lead to OCFR buying furniture from other suppliers. Even if an exclusive agreement were a central part of OCFR, this would not alter the retail division's need to find effective ways to respond to market needs independently of OCF.

Furniture Pieces	Suggested Retail Prices–Net*		
	Pine*	Oak	Cherry
Dining Room Pieces			
Tables			
Pedestal			
36"	329	378	411
38"	339	390	424
40"	349	401	436
42"	359	413	449
Trestle			
Four	419	482	524
Five	439	505	549
Six	459	528	574
Seven	479	551	599
Eight	499	574	624
Extension			
Four	449	516	561
Five	469	539	586
Six	489	562	611
Seven	509	585	636
Eight	529	608	661
Chairs			
Chicken Coop–Side	89		
—Arm	109		
Low Arrowback–Side	89		
—Arm	109		
High Arrowback–Side	109	125	136
—Arm	139	160	174
Ladderback–Side	99	114	124
Ladderback–Arm	139	160	174
Gunstock–Side	119	137	149
Windsor–Side	149	171	186
—Arm	229	263	286
Rocker–Arrowback	229		

Exhibit 1

OCFR Retail Price List (July 1, 1989)

Exhibit 1 (cont'd)

OCFR Retail Price List

Furniture Pieces	Suggested Retail Prices–Net*		
	Pine*	Oak	Cherry
Sideboards			
Durham County	429	493	536
w/Hutch	759	873	949
Renfrew County	529	608	661
w/Hutch	999	1149	1249
Serving Table			
Renfrew County	229	263	286
Bedroom			
Beds			
Cannonball–Single	379	436	474
–Double	429	493	536
–Queen	479	551	599
–King	529	608	661
Spindle–Double	459	528	574
–Queen	499	574	624
Dressers			
Durham County	399	459	499
Renfrew County	429	493	536
Wash Stand			
Durham County	229	263	286
Armoire			
Durham County	799	919	999
Renfrew County	999	1149	1249
Blanket Boxes			
PreConfederation	199	229	249
Napanee	299	344	374
Benches			
Bucket Bench	149	171	186
Deacon's Bench	279	321	349
Desks			
Secretary	799	919	999
Kneehole	499	574	624
Lawyers	1299	1494	1624
Miscellaneous			
Rocking Cradle	229	263	286
Single Commode	189	217	236
Double Commode	249	286	311
Night Table–Durham	199	229	249
Night Table–Renfrew	269	309	336
Bar Stool	99	114	124
Console Table	149	171	186

Exhibit 1 (cont'd)

OCFR Retail Price List

Furniture Pieces	Suggested Retail Prices–Net*		
	Pine*	**Oak**	**Cherry**
Corner Cupboard–Open	599	689	749
Straight Bench–3 ft.	99	114	124
–4 ft.	119	137	149
Coffee Table–Durham	189	217	236
–Renfrew	249	286	311
Folding Table	329	378	411
Rustic Kitchen Table	289	332	361
Shaker Series			
Shaker Table–6 ft.	349		
–8 ft.	379		
Shaker Ladderback–Side	79		
–Arm	129		
Shaker Hutch	529		
Shaker Hanging Cupboard	199		
Shaker Pegboards–3	39		
–4	49		
–5	59		
–6	69		
–7	79		
–8	89		
Mirrors			
Cathedral	199	228.85	248.75
Round	159	182.85	198.75
Window	199	228.85	248.75

Note: Retail Prices Include FST.
Wholesale Price = Retail less 45%
Tax Exempt with License Only—Wholesale less 10.7%
Wholesale × 12/112 = 10.7% (FST)

Old Country Furniture C

Carl Barth had operated a small furniture manufacturing plant in the Kingston Ontario area for almost 15 years. Producing a limited line of early Canadian furniture, the company had grown to sales of over $2 million in 1988 and employed 30 full-time plant employees. Ontario Country Furniture (OCF) produced and marketed furniture through both wholesale and retail channels. As well as three company-owned retail outlets, OCF supplied, on a wholesale basis, 12 to 15 retailers in Toronto, Burlington, Hamilton, Kitchener and St. Catharines. The furniture pieces supplied to these outlets were also early Canadian reproductions but differed from those used by the three captive retail outlets. None of the dealers was exclusive to OCF.

In addition to the furniture lines OCF also produced institutional furniture, primarily tables, chairs and serving pieces for restaurants, furniture kits and furniture parts. The kits and parts were sold to a variety of customers, although in 1987 60 percent of the kits and parts went to one customer.

Background

While looking for retail space in the Toronto area, Barth was contacted by Ken Dorad, the owner of Craftsman's World (CW). CW was a small franchisor which provided kits, tools, equipment and other supplies for woodworkers and hobbyists. CW consisted of a company-owned retail outlet (Markham) and twelve franchises located across Canada. Barth knew Dorad from previous dealings. In fact, CW had been one of OCF's largest customers, although OCF had not done much with them recently, primarily because Barth had become very unhappy with the time CW took to pay its account. However, Barth did speak to Dorad while in Toronto and was told CW was for sale. Dorad felt that the CW operation was a good fit for OCF. For its part OCF could use the sales, and since most of the CW product line did not require assembly, it was a chance to use surplus machining capacity without hiring additional people.

Barth agreed to meet with Dorad to discuss a possible purchase arrangement. Before meeting he asked that Dorad forward some information to his Kingston office. The information was to include some company background, statements, franchise information and other relevant documents. Once this information was in hand Barth agreed to meet Dorad for some preliminary discussions.

While Barth was not sure he wanted to get involved with CW, he was confident that OCF could improve the product line and the image of CW.

Franchises and Franchising

In 1981, franchising sales were estimated at approximately $376 billion, about one-third of all retail sales in Canada and the United States. One thousand to 1200 different franchisors were operating over 25 000 franchise units in Canada. About 70 percent of franchise units are franchisee operated with the remaining units operated by franchisors.[1]

There are a variety of approaches to franchising and not all are successful. Many use a business-format approach providing business plans, location services, marketing strategy, and operating plans. As well, the franchisor will provide training, operating systems, and detailed operating manuals and instructions. Most insist that operators follow their rules. Many use periodic on-site inspections and standard reporting to insure that the integrity of the franchise concept is maintained. Dress codes, quality standards for product and service, facility decor, head office reporting and accounting systems are spelled out in most agreements. Advertising and promotional packages are provided by the franchisor (usually paid for by a franchisee contribution).

While there are no definitive figures, it is generally thought that franchise operations are more successful than most small business startups. This is certainly true for the top 100 franchises in the marketplace. But with this success comes a number of requirements that may not suit all who are interested in owning their own business. Regimentation is an important factor, since many who enter small business seek the freedom of self direction. As well, franchises often require a major investment, major borrowing, and a commitment to personally manage the business.

Since most of Canada (except Alberta) has few regulations governing franchise operations and franchisor reporting, the new franchisee should be prepared to ask a lot of questions, talk to other franchisees, and pay for professional advice before making an investment.

Craftsman's World

Ken Dorad had always been interested in wood and woodworking as a hobby and, when he sold the family business, he decided to make a business of his hobby. It was his impression that many people shared his woodworking interests but, because most had little space and could not invest in proper equipment, their interests were never pursued. Further, the move to apartment living and the growing amount of leisure time meant that hobbies, along with various other recreational activities, were growing in popularity. Dorad had checked with local school boards and community colleges and found that courses in woodworking were always oversubscribed. As a result of this information and some additional market research performed by a government-sponsored small business consulting service, Dorad started Craftsman's World in Markham, Ontario in 1983.

Dorad began the operation of Craftsman's World by leasing space in a small industrial mall. At this location he sold tools, equipment, furniture kits, finishing supplies, and miscellaneous items such as hardware and glue for the woodworking enthusiast. As well, he taught classes in woodworking. During certain hours of the day, he rented his facilities (hand tools, equipment, and work space) on an hourly basis to those who wanted to build furniture but couldn't afford the cost or space to acquire their own.

The concept proved extremely popular and Dorad eventually kept the facility open from 8:00 am to 11:00 pm. There were even requests for 24-hour service, particularly by shift workers, but Dorad wasn't sure that extended hours would be profitable.

As well as the local hobbyists, the facility attracted a number of people who were interested in starting similar businesses. This led to queries about franchising. Since the business had grown in a rather haphazard way Dorad had never thought about franchising, but his success with the Markham location led him to believe that it might be worth considering.

Before arriving at his version of the Craftsman's World concept, Dorad had consulted with a number of business associates who had experience operating franchises. Some were in the fast-food business; others included an equipment rental operation, a travel agency and an automobile rental business. While each was different, they shared several factors. These included site location, training, well documented operations manuals, and turnkey set-up and information/control systems that provided the operator with timely and detailed information on the performance of his or her franchise. Often, at least in some of the larger franchises, the information included operating comparisons with similar franchises. On the other hand, each differed in cost, other up-front and royalty/license payments, degree of operating control, decor and facilities control, and control over marketing and product service offerings. Some franchises allowed for adjustments to suit local conditions; most, however, maintained strict control, feeling that consistency of operation was central to customer confidence. Dorad was not sure if any or all of these factors applied to CW franchises.

After a year of working on the Craftsman's World concept, Dorad was ready to franchise. He began by moving his present operation to new quarters in the same industrial complex. The new space was designed to act as a model for the future franchise operations. He would test new products, and develop marketing programs and business systems in order that the franchises could be operated effectively.

Craftsman's World—The Concept

Based on his market research and almost three years' experience, Dorad developed a concept of Craftsman's World. Basically it involved a total service for woodworking enthusiasts. CW sold parts, kits, supplies, tools, and furniture designs. As well, it provided training in the use of equipment and tools, woodworking and finishing skills. Tools, equipment and space were rented on an hourly basis. The classroom and shop facilities were supervised by a skilled craftsman.

Franchising

Dorad decided to franchise his concept as a way of getting rapid growth. Although he could have opened several outlets, managing them would have been a problem. He was convinced that owner-managed franchises would provide the kind of approach he felt essential to the success of this kind of craft organization. He wanted the franchise relationship to be a simple arrangement, one that either party could cancel with appropriate notice. He hired a lawyer to draw up the agreement and this was the Franchise Contract that was in place for the present franchisees.

Questioned by Barth about the document, Dorad was quick to admit that the Franchise Contract was not typical of most franchise agreements. There were few restrictions on, or requirements of, the franchisee, and there were few services provided by the franchisor. Dorad felt that the supplier/buyer arrangement meant that there was an acceptable level of dependence by both franchisor and franchisee to make the relationship work. Dorad also felt that as small business people attempted to run a business, the needs of each location would be different and they were in the best position to adjust to community markets. He had thought that the restrictions were more than adequate to insure that the Craftsman's World concept would be profitable for franchisee and franchisor. Without this mutual profitability, more detailed rules would fail anyway. (A list of the major points of the Franchise Contract are set forth in Exhibit 1.)

Barth's quick perusal of the Franchise Contract suggested that it would be difficult to build a tight franchise setup with a contract so lacking in details, but he knew little about franchising so would ask some questions about it later. Dorad made the point that the strength of any franchise agreement lay largely in the ability of the franchisor to provide a package that made the franchisee profitable. He felt that OCF had the skills to do that for Craftsman's World.

Markham Operations

The Markham facility had been established to serve several roles in the CW system. First, it was to be used as part of the franchise sales approach. It was to represent a model for new franchise operations. As well, it was used to test new products and services, and it was to function as a "stand alone" store which should be profitable as a CW franchise. Finally, it was used to test market programs and, more recently, the control system that was to be offered to all existing and new franchises early in 1990.

Facilities

CW's Markham location occupied approximately 420 square metres of industrial mall space. (See Exhibit 2.) This space was divided into three general areas, including a retail area with office space, a classroom area, and the workshop area. The classroom could accommodate approximately 15 people while the shop could handle 30 people, although there were always some bottleneck operations.

Since the store was company-owned, it was run by a manager with woodworking skills. While it was not always easily separated from the parent organization, Markham was expected to operate like a franchise. Exhibit 3 provides a summary of revenues and purchases, while Exhibit 4 presents income statements for the Markham store.

Early Operations

Early in the franchise development process Dorad was approached by a number of people seeking information about a franchise. These indications of interest prompted him to move on his franchise ideas long before the vague outline of a franchise concept was firmly translated into sound operating guidelines. As a result, the first franchises operated pretty much around each owner's idea of what Craftsman's World was all about, and this produced the inconsistencies that were to plague the operation later.

Since Dorad had not secured an adequate supply of kit products, many of the franchises purchased these items elsewhere. This was also true of tools, supplies, and raw materials. Purchases of this nature were proscribed by even the early agreements, but the franchisees claimed the need to buy elsewhere to satisfy customer needs. Dorad did not actively pursue these infractions. He rationalized that in the short term he simply did not have the supply issue well in hand. He felt that he could regain control in this area as time passed. The opportunity to open additional franchise units had been too compelling to resist, and as a result, 9 of the 12 franchise units operated with major departures from his final franchise concept.

Control over accounting and reporting procedures was also a serious problem resulting in a loss of revenues. Also, the marketing techniques employed by some of the units departed radically from Dorad's suggestions, although here, too, he admitted that his interest in this area had been a low priority at the outset. His attempts to gain control in some of these areas had not been effective despite the fact that he could point to the last three franchises (all written under a tighter agreement) as much more successful than the first nine. He knew however, that this comparison was not totally valid since sales at the original units included some goods purchased outside the organization.

These inconsistencies were now causing problems with the sale of new franchises. As of October 1988 CW had not entered into a new franchise arrangement for over seven months, despite intensive advertising in major Canadian newspapers. The advertising produced enquiries but Dorad had not been able to close the deals. This suggested, in part at least, that the problems in the system were both evident, and of major concern to new prospects.

These were some of the problems that arose from Barth's discussion with Dorad. Of course, Dorad felt that most of these difficulties could be corrected by someone who wished to make the concept work. He felt that his other business interests made it difficult to spend the time required to manage CW properly. He also felt one of the key issues impeding good franchise relations was the lack of product choices available to the franchisees and he was sure Barth's background, and OCF's reputation for quality products, would insure franchise loyalty in a way that controls could never do. Barth was less sure, but the proposal was interesting inasmuch as it could provide sales, which would utilize currently idle plant time.

Business for Sale

Barth left Dorad indicating that he would seriously consider the possibility of acquiring the business, but before the discussions proceeded he would need more information. Dorad promised to have his accountant forward operating statements. As well, he would send copies of the current franchise agreement and other information he felt would assist Barth in his assessment of the CW proposal. Among the materials forwarded by Dorad were those shown in Exhibits 3 to 7.

In addition, Dorad sent a detailed letter outlining his terms and conditions for the sale. He noted that he was open to variations in the offer but the $75 000 purchase price was firm. (See Exhibit 8.) As well, Dorad offered to sell the Markham location for $200 000, or he would continue to operate it until a suitable buyer could be found. He stressed the idea that the Markham franchise could be used as a "flagship" in the sale of other franchises, as well as providing an operating base for trying out new product and marketing ideas, and new systems for control and cost effectiveness within the franchise organization.

There were a number of things to consider beyond the direct contribution of CW to the sales of OCF. The fit between OCF and CW was important. The current situation among franchisees and their relationship with CW was certainly of interest, and of course, the potential for expansion of the franchise system was important. (A list of existing franchises is included as Exhibit 9.) While the price for the franchise operation was not out of line, Barth was interested in the future potential of the operation, since it would consume time that could be used in other ways to improve OCF's performance.

Upon receipt of the information from Dorad, Barth called CW's accountant and requested further details on the Markham franchise. (See Exhibit 10.) He was particularly interested in the expenses of the operation. As well, he requested some typical reports from the franchisees in other locations. He was informed that the franchise reports were not part of the accounting activities carried out for CW, and that these would have to be acquired directly from Dorad.

Endnote   1.   Russell M. Knight, "The Independence of the Franchisee Entrepreneur," *Journal of Small Business Management* (Morgantown, WV: Bureau of Business Research, West Virginia University). See also Ian McGugan, "So You Wanna Buy A Franchise," *Financial Post Moneywise*, August 1989, pp. 42–51.

Exhibit 1

Craftsman's
World
Franchise
Contract
Summary of
Key Points

Facilities

– All facilities will meet the design specifications provided by CW Inc.
– Changes and alterations to facilities must be approved prior to implementation by CW Inc.

Location
– CW Inc. will assist the franchisee in finding an acceptable location. All locations must be approved
– Design and layouts will be provided by CW Inc. The cost of revisions will be borne by the franchisee

Franchise Services

Products
– All products sold by the franchisee must be purchased from CW Inc., or from a supplier approved by CW Inc.

Services
– All franchisees will use paperwork and computer systems purchased from CW Inc. or from suppliers approved by CW Inc.
– Advertising and Promotion used by the franchisee must be approved by CW Inc. if it is to be approved for cooperative advertising contributions.

Franchisor Obligations

– Advertising and promotion will be supplied to the franchisee by the franchisor
– The franchisor agrees to provide the full range of products specified in the agreement
– The franchisor agrees to provide the business systems (designs and software) to the franchisee. Hardware, forms and other consumables will be purchased from CW Inc.

Franchisee Obligations

– The franchisee agrees to carry such insurance as is specified in the agreement
– The franchisee agrees to accept all goods from the franchisor as consignments owned by the franchisor until paid for by the franchisee. The franchisee will not use franchisor property as collateral for loans and or other forms of financing.
– The franchisee agrees to sell all products and services at prices approved by CW Inc.

Exhibit 2

Typical
Craftsman's
World
Franchise
Layout

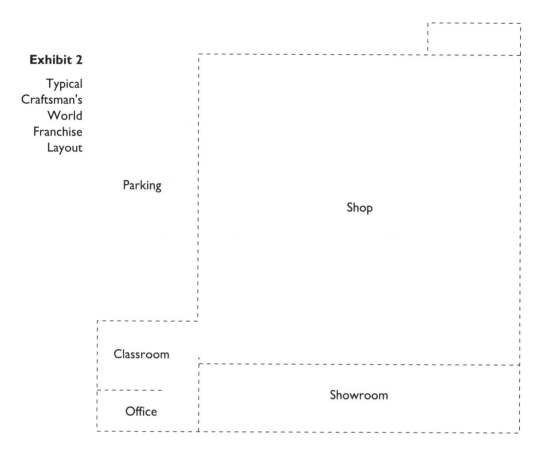

Parking

Shop

Classroom

Office

Showroom

Parking

Exhibit 3

Craftsman's World Markham Franchise Unit Financial Report Summary

		1985	1986	1987	1988
Purchases from Franchisor					
	Tools & supplies	15,887	19,929	21,780	26,530
	Sized wood	4,766	5,861	7,824	9,780
	Kits, parts, etc.	76,770	81,256	97,549	137,080
	Hardware	7,626	9,026	14,230	1,954
	Plans	234	272	340	440
	Miscellaneous	964	1,159	1,067	1,254
Totals		106,247	117,503	142,790	177,038

Exhibit 3	Income Statement—Markham				
(cont'd)	December 31, 1985–1988				

Income Statements

Revenues					
Sales materials	133,871	153,929	188,483	228,379
Classroom activities	16,450	19,345	21,220	24,230
Rentals	59,780	72,434	86,590	91,220
Miscellaneous	11,234	14,568	17,666	21,322
	221,335	260,276	313,959	365,151
Less Promotion Fee	6,640	7,808	9,419	10,955
	214,695	252,468	304,540	354,196
Less Franchise Fee	2,147	2,525	3,045	3,542
Operating Revenue	212,548	249,943	301,495	350,655

Exhibit 4

Craftsman's World Markham Ontario Franchise Income Statements December 31, 1985 to December 31, 1988

	1985	1986	1987	1988
Operating Revenue	212,548	249,943	301,495	350,655
Cost of goods	42,839	46,179	54,660	63,946
	169,709	203,764	246,835	286,708
Expenses				
Wages & benefits	98,554	120,232	143,315	168,481
Rent	12,000	12,000	14,800	14,800
Heat, power etc.	8,940	9,210	10,900	11,420
Telephone	1,240	1,090	1,420	1,640
Professional	2,210	2,410	3,440	2,460
Taxes	860	2,890	3,460	4,510
Depreciation	5,440	6,540	7,210	7,720
Advertising	3,960	5,240	3,980	7,640
Travel	3,164	3,470	4,020	3,860
Shipping	2,490	1,780	1,960	2,110
Miscellaneous	2,370	2,410	1,980	2,105
Total Expenses	141,228	167,272	196,485	226,746
Net Profit (pre-tax)	28,481	36,492	50,350	59,962
Taxes	5,696	7,298	10,070	11,992
Net Earnings	**22,785**	**29,194**	**40,280**	**47,970**

Exhibit 5		1984	1985	1986	1987	1988
Craftsman's World Income Statements December 31, 1984 to December 31, 1988	**Revenue**					
	Sales	434,620	505,892	650,404	693,595	766,920
	Cost of Goods	312,926	356,654	453,332	498,695	552,949
	Gross Profit	121,694	149,238	197,072	194,900	213,971
	Royalties*	20,059	23,349	30,019	32,012	35,396
	Gross Profit	141,753	172,587	227,091	226,912	249,367
	Expenses**					
	Wages & salaries	54,600	61,290	67,670	87,920	102,440
	Benefits	8,190	9,194	10,151	13,188	15,366
	Advertising	3,460	5,370	8,900	11,900	15,900
	Promotional	4,450	7,980	11,240	12,460	15,970
	Travel	32,370	41,230	39,720	34,560	36,590
	Telephone	4,870	5,990	7,420	8,960	9,670
	Professional	5,480	5,690	6,440	7,920	8,560
	Office	14,600	15,600	17,200	19,840	22,540
	Insurance	3,124	3,367	4,050	4,240	4,420
	Bad Debts	650	1,390	0	3,460	6,920
	Memberships	450	1,270	1,420	1,560	1,580
	Shipping	2,160	3,020	3,240	2,980	4,010
	Depreciation	6,720	7,680	8,800	9,830	7,960
	Miscellaneous	3,220	3,428	4,120	3,250	3,650
	Total Expenses	144,344	172,499	190,371	222,068	255,576
	Net Profit	−2,591	88	36,720	4,844	−6,209

Notes

  * 3% of Franchise Sales

** Expenses related to the establishment of a new franchise are charged against the franchise fee account. In addition, advertising done in support of the franchisee is paid for from a special account. Contributions to this account are based on 1% of the gross sales by the franchisee and a $3500 one time payment from the franchise fee.

Exhibit 6

Revenues from Sale of Franchises

Craftsman's
World
Franchise Fee
Account

Franchise Units	Unit Price	Total Revenue
100–105 (6)	25,000	150,000
106–108 (3)	30,000	90,000
109–111 (3)	40,000	120,000
		360,000
Bank Loan (12/31/1988)		27,440
		387,440

Less: Franchise Related Expenses		
Advertising	42,000	
Professional	24,000	
Development costs	50,000	
Inventory & equipment	190,000	
Training costs	30,000	
Design/Development	26,000	
Travel	20,580	
Loan Interest	3,440	
Miscellaneous	2,100	
	388,120	388,120
		−680

Bracketed figures indicate the number of franchise units in the group.

Exhibit 7

Craftsman's
World
Franchisee
Purchase
Accounts

	1985	1986	1987	1988	1989
Franchise Sales–Total	434,620	505,892	650,404	693,595	766,920
By product group					
Tools and supplies	73,040	89,654	94,350	99,670	103,450
Sized wood	21,342	19,874	24,351	31,488	36,270
Kits, parts etc.	305,670	359,560	479,340	502,540	560,500
Hardware	32,000	31,900	45,290	50,980	56,750
Plans	560	740	1,120	1,290	1,450
Miscellaneous	2,008	4,164	5,953	7,627	8,500
Totals	**434,620**	**505,892**	**650,404**	**693,595**	**766,920**

Note: 1989 figures are projected.

Exhibit 8

CW Letter,
Terms and
Conditions

Craftsman's World
1024 Kinney Road
Scarborough, Ontario
M5W 1E2

March 12, 1989

Mr. C. Barth
President,
Old Country Furniture
34 Heather Circle
Kingston, Canada

Dear Carl,

As discussed when last we met, I have enclosed the statements and information. No doubt, if your interest proceeds beyond the initial stage, you will require additional information on both Craftsman's World and its franchise operations. My accountants, lawyer and staff are available to answer your questions and I have instructed them to do so if the need arises.

As to price, I am interested in selling both Craftsman's World ($75,000) and the Markham franchise ($200,000) although I would continue to operate the franchise until another buyer was found if the acquisition of that operation was not part of your plans.

One small matter I would call to your attention. If you are to sell additional franchises, develop and test market new products, develop control and reporting systems etc., you will need a franchisee operation to try out your proposed changes and ideas before making them part of the larger operation. The Markham operation has served well in that role in the past and I offer it as part of the package although it is not essential that it be sold now, or to Old Country Furniture. One final item, that will be confirmed when our accountants complete their work, is the existence of a bank loan for $27,440 which is secured by inventory and accounts receivable. Obviously, if we are to strike a deal, the details of our balance sheet will be required and these will be on the table if we proceed beyond these preliminary discussions.

I look forward to your comments and, if I can provide additional information, please call on me.

Sincerely,

Ken Dorad, President

Exhibit 9	**Number**	**Location**	**Projected Franchises**	
Craftsman's	000	Markham, Ontario	112	Scarborough, Ontario
World	100	Kingston, Ontario	113	Dorval, Quebec
Franchise	101	Halifax, Nova Scotia	114	Victoria, B.C.
Locations	102	Ottawa, Ontario	115	Saskatoon, Sask.
	103	Windsor, Ontario	116	Hamilton, Ontario
	104	Montreal, Quebec	117	Burlington, Ontario
	105	Kitchener, Ontario	118	Calgary, Alberta
	106	Barrie, Ontario	119	Quebec, Quebec
	107	Winnipeg, Manitoba	120	Guelph, Ontario
	108	Vancouver, B.C.	121	London, Ontario
	109	Edmonton, Alberta	122	Sarnia, Ontario
	110	Regina, Saskatchewan	123	St. Catharines, Ontario
	111	Mississauga, Ontario	124	Brandon, Manitoba

Exhibit 10

Letter–
Consultant
Services

Old Country Furniture
34 Heather Circle
Kingston, Canada
March 22, 1990

Mr. J. Tonnelli
Tonnelli Associates
Barrie, Ontario

Dear Jim

As you know from our earlier conversations I have been approached to buy a small franchise organization called Craftsman's World. I have received some information and have been promised more, but frankly, I have neither the time nor skills to handle a preliminary assessment. I would appreciate it if you would undertake a study of the situation for me in order to determine if we should proceed beyond the preliminary phase.

While there are, at least in my mind, some serious shortcomings in the present operation of Craftsman's World (I am sure these will be evident in your assessment), I am particularly interested in your ideas about how the whole set-up could be improved if we were to get involved. Currently, franchisee relations are tenuous. However, I believe it is mainly a matter of poor franchisor support, too few products and promotional ideas, ineffective controls and reporting, and too little coordination by the franchisor. Of course, if these were improved there would have to be a payoff for both the franchisee and the franchisor. I believe the opportunity exists for some substantial improvement.

As well, my brief talks with Dorad indicate a very poorly organized operation in Markham. It would not be unrealistic to expect that the franchises would

**Exhibit 10
(cont'd)**

Letter

be much better if they could depend on head office for systems support. There are a number of areas that need attention and I hope, through your study, that you can identify these and make some suggestions about how this operation might be an attractive addition to our current business.

One final point. You will note that Dorad has discussed the matter of fit with Old Country Furniture. While this is important in the final decision, I am much more interested in Craftsman's World as a going concern, profitable or potentially profitable on its own. If, beyond that, it can contribute to profits elsewhere in the organization then it becomes more attractive. I am sure there is a substantial opportunity for both tighter control and better information through the installation of a computer and some improved systems, and this is certainly an area where your skills will come in handy. At present Dorad does most of this work by hand and, as a result, there is very little interaction between head office and the franchisee. It is my impression that constant contact with the franchisee is essential, since he or she is being asked to pay ongoing fees and expects to see some tangible evidence that these are buying something of value to their operation.

Certainly some study of the financial materials and records at CW's head office is important. As well, I think it would be worthwhile to meet with one or two of the older franchises to get some kind of picture from their side. I am sure we can get Dorad's approval for such discussions if you think it worthwhile.

I am sorry to put you under the gun once again, but I am sitting on an offer to lease retail space in Toronto and must make a decision on that shortly. Since I am prepared to open one or two new retail outlets and acquire Craftsman's World, if justified, your study will be important in my deliberations. No doubt acting on both will strain our organization once again. Before I move I would like an objective assessment of Craftsman's World and its potential as part of our organization.

You will note in Dorad's letter that he will make additional information available if required. If you need to get some more data I will be happy to call, however, it is my preference that we proceed with our initial assessment without further contact. I feel we may gain in any negotiations if we proceed quickly and without any further indications of interest until we are ready to move. Of course, if the information you need were to be crucial it could be obtained. As to balance sheet evaluations, these can be done later as part of the detailed negotiations. No doubt there will be many minor details and adjustments during that process and certainly any offer we make would be tied to some degree to asset evaluations.

Sincerely,

Carl Barth, President
encl.

CHAPTER

8

Other Issues in Small Enterprise Management

Introduction

Small business, like all business, is faced with a variety of situations that do not fit easily into functional or organizational discussions. Issues such as the role of entrepreneurship, women in business, and the management of time cut across all of the activities of small business managers and small businesses. The objective of this chapter is to discuss these topics in greater depth.

The Entrepreneurs

Recently, the entrepreneur, the entrepreneurial approach, and the entrepreneurial spirit have received a great deal of attention. And while some would limit its use to small business situations, others speak of entrepreneurship as a particular way of managing in organizations of all sizes. Peters and Waterman, in *The Search for Excellence*, set down eight characteristics that were important to America's best run businesses; many see all of these activities as characteristic of a management with entrepreneurial flair.

1. Emphasize a bias for action,
2. Be close to the customer,
3. Provide autonomy and entrepreneurship,
4. Achieve productivity through people,
5. Have a hands-on, value-driven operation,
6. Stick to one's knitting,
7. Utilize simple form—lean staff,
8. Apply simultaneous loose-tight controls.[1]

Whatever the definition, it seems clear that entrepreneurship involves an understanding of risks and risk-taking, and a willingness to take those risks, or encourage others to do so, where the potential returns justify it. Entrepreneurial firms exhibit a flair for innovation, through a different product, a different process or a different way of marketing existing products and services. It would also appear that company size is not a factor in using the entrepreneurial approach since the companies studied by Peters and Waterman were all part of the *Fortune* 500.

What is an entrepreneur? Are all new businesses started by entrepreneurs? Certainly, if risk is the key issue, most small business startups are entrepreneurial since most will fail. Are those who start corner variety stores entrepreneurial? Are they only entrepreneurial if the concept is different? Or, is a cornerstore operation entrepreneurial only when the owner is able to franchise the concept to others? And are those who invest money in the franchise operation entrepreneurs? The literature on entrepreneurs and entrepreneurship is not much help in finding answers to these questions. Unfortunately, the term entrepreneur has become part of the jargon; it is much more fashionable to be an entrepreneur than simply an individual investing in a new business. Copetas notes in his article "The Selling of the Entrepreneur, 1986" that:

> Almost overnight, "entrepreneur" has become a sweeping snap, crackle, mom-and-pop catchall, a trendy metaphor that takes in rules, values, lifestyles and attitudes. Entrepreneurship now means anything that is better than it was before, a synonym for achievement, quality, and taste. It is a source of power and money, a touchstone for creativity, a way to excitement and fame. Business schools now teach it, sociologists study it, and politicians

left and right lay claim to having fostered it. Hucksters steal it shamelessly to sell their products. Before long so much meaning will have been piled on the back of this one word that it may collapse of its own weight. Myth will give way to meaninglessness. And the entrepreneur will once again be out of fashion, unworshipped and unchic.[2]

Too often we read about entrepreneurship as something distinct and different from management in small business. Drucker, a noted management theorist, believes that while enthusiasm and inspiration may be key factors in entrepreneurship, it is mainly a matter of discipline. He frames it as another aspect of the manager's task when he says:

> management is the new technology (rather than any specific new science or invention) that is making the American economy into an entrepreneurial economy. It is also about to make America into an entrepreneurial society . . . . Entrepreneurship requires above all application of the basic concepts, the basic techne of management to new problems and new opportunities.[3]

Kaplan also believes that good management and entrepreneurship are compatible. He notes that:

> Recent celebrations of entrepreneurship have confused what management is and what entrepreneurs need. . . . Most unfortunate is the notion that seems to have taken hold that entrepreneurship and management are in opposition to each other.[4]

His concerns strike a sensitive note when one considers how many entrepreneurs do not make it beyond the good idea and the enthusiasm.

Startup Entrepreneurship

Most successful entrepreneurs simply make common ideas pay off through hard work. No doubt some very uncommon ideas are promoted successfully by entrepreneurs but, for the most part, it is the willingness to take the risk, coupled with hard work, that characterize startup entrepreneurship. In other words, to paraphrase Thomas Edison, entrepreneurship is made up of 2 percent inspiration and 98 percent perspiration. The uniqueness of the product or service may be far less important than the process by which successful entrepreneurs put new products and services into the marketplace. Ray Kroc did not have a unique product when he started McDonald's. In fact, in Kroc's own words, he sold the "sizzle" not the steak. Brown, in *The Entrepreneur's Guide*, stresses the importance of marketing skills, but points out that the fragility of the new firm makes "avoiding the wrong market . . . more important for the new venture than selecting the right one."[5] All new businesses are characterized by risk; what seems to characterize entrepreneurial ventures is that the risk is undertaken in pursuit of an innovative product or process (either production or marketing).

Management Entrepreneurship

For some, management entrepreneurship is a contradiction in terms. But for many corporate managers, instilling an entrepreneurial spirit into their organizations is both a realistic and a necessary undertaking. For them, entrepreneurship represents an organizational approach based on the principle that owners (and self-interest) can achieve the best results. It is an attempt by small and large companies to let competent people implement their own ideas in the belief that competence, the freedom to respond quickly to change, and the motivation to succeed will produce results.

Most of the evidence in support of this approach is anecdotal, typically found in the memoirs of those that have succeeded. Its appeal stems largely from the view that competent managers, given room to manoeuvre, will be more productive than would be possible within a bureaucratic organization.

Some contend that true entrepreneurs are hardly ever good managers. They claim that the entrepreneurial role is to nurture new product and business ideas, but once the business is in place profits and growth will depend on management skills. The high failure rate for new businesses supports this belief, particularly since Dun and Bradstreet statistics consistently reveal that the main causes of business failure are managerial incompetence and insufficient management experience.[6] High interest and financing costs are also among the major reasons for small business bankruptcies as we enter the 1990s.

However, there is another side to this issue. Just as entrepreneurship can exist without management, management can stifle or eliminate a small firm's interest in innovation and risk, effectively removing the entrepreneurial role in the company. The secret may lie in achieving management growth without losing entrepreneurial flair. Figure 8-1 superimposes evolving entrepreneurship on the phases of small business development.

If a growing business is to retain its entrepreneurial flair, its entrepreneurship must evolve from individual to collective entrepreneurship. As Robert

Figure 8-1

Management and
Entrepreneurship

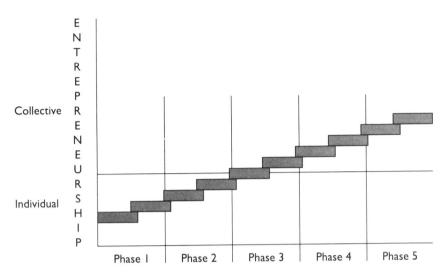

Reich notes: "Innovation must become both continuous and collective. And that requires embracing a new ideal: collective entrepreneurship."[7] Reich states that

> Competitive advantage today comes from continuous innovation and refinement of a variety of ideas that spread throughout the organization. The entrepreneurial organization is both experience-based and decentralized, so that every advance builds on every previous advance, and everyone in the company has the opportunity and capacity to participate. . . . In this paradigm, entrepreneurship isn't the sole province of the company's founder or its top managers. Rather it is a capability and an attitude that is diffused throughout the company.[8]

It is this ability to involve others in the entrepreneurial role that Peters and Waterman see in America's best run companies.[9] Even in the small businesses we are dealing with there is a need to foster an ongoing entrepreneurial involvement so that, as the need for management grows, the organization remains supportive of entrepreneurial activity. As valuable information and expertise are dispersed throughout the organization, top management solves fewer problems; it creates an environment in which people can identify and solve problems on their own.

Not all new businesses are entrepreneurial, nor are those which begin as entrepreneurial ventures likely to continue in that mode unless there is support for the continued innovation that made them entrepreneurial in the first place.

Other businesses, which may not have been innovative at startup may become entrepreneurial as they grow into phase 3 and phase 5 companies.[10] This type of evolution occurs only when owner-managers and general managers provide the organizational support needed to spur innovation, rather than rigidly adhering to the rules which pervade many traditional hierarchical organizations. Reich notes that[11]

> For managers, this path [collective entrepreneurship] means continually retraining employees for more complex tasks, automating in ways that cut routine tasks and enhance worker flexibility and creativity; diffusing responsibility for innovation; taking seriously labor's concern for job security and giving workers a stake in improved productivity through profit linked bonuses and stock plans.

> For workers, this path means accepting flexible job classifications and work rules, agreeing to wage rates linked to profits and productivity improvements; and generally taking greater responsibility for the soundness and efficiency of the enterprise.

> Under collective entrepreneurship, all those associated with the company become partners in its future.

Women in Business

Under Roosevelt's New Deal, work was offered to the unemployed on the following basis:

- Men $5.00 per day
- Women $3.00 per day

And those who ran programs hired very few women.[12] This is not ancient history; current statistics indicate that women, on average, still earn approximately 65 to 70 percent of the wages paid to men. But there are changes underway that may eventually alter the job balance. In the college and university systems half or more of the students are women. Corporations are promoting more women to higher paying jobs. But more important, the labour pools are providing more women to promote, and legislation and public opinion are providing the impetus to do so. Seniority, job rules, and plain old discrimination continue to slow the process in many organizations.

Women Entrepreneurs

Women are responsible for over half of the small business startups between 1981 and 1986. In this area, where there are few barriers to entry, women entrepreneurs have been able to destroy a lot of the conveniently held myths about women in business. Jensen notes that in the last decade the number of women starting their own businesses increased by 43 percent, while the number of men in the same role increased only 9.8 percent. She concludes that

> In retrospect, it was inevitable. When there are large numbers of highly educated, highly motivated women moving into business with high expectations—something has to give. When old prejudices give, these women move up in corporations and contribute needed skills. When the prejudices won't give, these women do not sit still and feel sorry for themselves; they do something about it.

> "I'll show them" is becoming as big a motivator for women as it has been for some men in the past. The woman a company won't promote today is turning up as their competitor of tomorrow.[13]

But Ellen Wojahn, writing in *INC*, suggests that most of the women represented in the growth statistics are in

> . . . microbusinesses that are going to stay small. . . . They aren't out to build the biggest companies, and they are not doing it to stroke their egos. Mostly these women are just trying to support themselves, to bring balance to their lives in ways that the corporate world can't. And won't. They are out to redefine work, not to restructure the economy. What they are doing has more to do with self employment than enterprise. . . . there is powerful evidence that women go into business for different reasons than men.[14]

Although they may go into business for different reasons than men, the rules by which women entrepreneurs or corporate executives must play the game are not much different from those faced by men in similar situations. But many of the conditions surrounding the rules are different. If successful entrepreneurs and executives benefit from mentors, then most women are at a distinct disadvantage. "Cronyism," "the old boys' network" and "school ties" are not in place for women in business. Furthermore, early education continues to expose boys to sports, competition and winning and losing—all important ingredients in risk-taking. Jensen makes the point that

> Learning to take risks is one of the most important lessons available from

sports. This is not an innate skill, or something that comes from male hormones. Confidence in taking risks comes from frequent practice and from familiarity with all the possible consequences—and, in the process, learning that the answer to failure is to pick yourself up and try again . . .[15]

Young girls, on the other hand, are encouraged to play games of sharing, taking turns not risks. Losing, for them, has different meanings and implications. The focus is on nurturing, cooperation, and sharing, terms that many men are now recognizing and accepting under the rubric of "Japanese management." The woman entrepreneur has been characterized by her pragmatism, patience, attention to detail, and perhaps most notably her capacity to seek out and make effective use of advice.

However, there is an absence of empirical research to support the notion that women entrepreneurs as a group are somehow distinct. Based on her 1986 study, Lois Stevenson reported that

> While there appear to be some differences between male and female entrepreneurs, are they truly sex-based differences? While it is true that women as a class of entrepreneurs have had a shorter history, perhaps it is the length of time in business that accounts more for "differences" than the sex of the owner.[16]

We share this assessment, and would argue that the prescriptions for successful small business management described in this text apply equally to female and male entrepreneurs. Certainly women managers tend to adopt a different management style, but the problems they encounter, the resources they must manage, and the managerial functions they must undertake are largely the same as those faced by their male counterparts.[17]

In learning how to cope in business, women may have acquired traditional "male skills" in addition to equally essential "female skills," making the range of activities in which they can function effectively much broader than those available to their male counterparts. "She is acting like a woman" may change from an unthinking put-down to a recognition that major achievements in the workplace may result from managers who bring a different perspective to the job of managing.

Legal Structures

The law provides a number of forms of organization that both new and existing businesses must consider. Each has specific requirements and particular advantages and disadvantages. While there are other possibilities, the basic legal forms are:

1. single or sole proprietorships,
2. partnerships, and
3. corporations.

Sole Proprietorships

A sole proprietorship is defined as a business owned by one person, with the business and that person being one in the eyes of the law. The proprietor provides the capital, owns the assets and assumes the liabilities. The owner is responsible for company debts, and assumes all of the risks associated with company losses.

Startup in this form is a simple matter, requiring only that the proprietor complete such registrations and obtain such licenses as are required in the particular business jurisdiction. The advantages and disadvantages of proprietorships are summarized in Figure 8-2.

Figure 8-2

Advantages and Disadvantages of Proprietorships

Advantages

1. Organizational simplicity and minimal setup costs
2. Decision-making autonomy
3. Few legal restrictions
4. Procedures for establishing the business are simple and straightforward

Disadvantages

1. Limited number of external sources of funding
2. Company ceases to exist with death of owner
3. Unlimited liability

Partnerships

Usually defined as "an association of two or more persons to carry on as co-owners of a business for profit," partnerships require a formal partnership agreement. The agreement should specify authority, rights and duties (including limits) of each partner, and the distribution of profits and losses, and might also include special arrangements for each partner (remuneration, service commitments, interest on capital investment, drawings, etc.). Advantages and disadvantages of the partnership form are summarized in Figure 8-3.

Figure 8-3

Advantages and Disadvantages of Partnerships

Advantages	Disadvantages
1. Larger talent pool	1. Limited number of external sources of capital
2. Pooling of partners' financial resources leads to a larger capital base	2. Limited company life
3. Procedures for establishing the business are simple and straightforward	3. Unlimited liability
	4. Possibility of disagreements, since each partner is legally bound by the actions of the other

Incorporation

While the corporate form is not restricted to larger firms, there are a number of reasons why larger firms opt for incorporation.

The advantages and disadvantages of incorporation are listed in Figure 8-4. When considering the question of whether or not to incorporate, the entrepreneur must pay close attention to the treatment of the business for income tax purposes. The taxation question is anything but straightforward and, contrary to popular belief, there are not necessarily a host of tax deductions available once the company is incorporated.

The most frequently cited tax advantage for the incorporated small enterprise pertains to the favourable rates of taxation accorded to Canadian controlled private corporations: the basic federal income-tax rate (applied to the first $200 000 of annual taxable income) is only 12 percent, whereas proprietorship and partnership income is taxed directly in the hands of the owner at marginal rates of 17 percent to 29 percent. Given that the owner will typically be an employee of the company, he can also obtain employee benefits (e.g., insurance coverage, club memberships, interest-free loans) that would not be available in a proprietorship or partnership. He will also have the option of electing to take income from the business in the form of a salary or as dividends. Finally, many provinces provide attractive tax concessions for business startups if the venture is incorporated.[18]

A number of other, more specific, benefits could be added to the list. However, it should be recognized that for the small enterprise that is still approaching a break-even level of operations, incorporation is seldom appro-

Figure 8-4	**Advantages**	**Disadvantages**
Advantages and Disadvantages of Incorporation	1. Limited liability for shareholders (although given that lenders often insist on personal guarantees supported by the entrepreneur's assets, this advantage may be more apparent than real)	1. Government regulation and time consuming reporting requirements to various outside bodies
	2. The company is considered a separate legal entity and can therefore continue to operate indefinitely	2. Legal and other expenses associated with incorporation
	3. Ownership can be transferred through the sale of common shares	3. Prescribed procedures (e.g., board of directors' meetings, governing bylaws) can impinge on management's flexibility
	4. Greater selection of external sources of funding	

priate from a tax standpoint. Indeed, there are some distinct advantages associated with the unincorporated form; for instance, any losses incurred from operations can be applied as a tax deduction against other income the proprietor may have; incorporated businesses do not have this flexibility.

Halpern provides a rather succinct summary of this topic:

> Many of the provisions of the Income Tax Act reduce the tax incentives for a small business to incorporate. These . . . include the addition of a dividend distribution tax and the possibility for unincorporated businesses to put family members on the payroll. It is still difficult, however, to generalize on the attractiveness of incorporation.[19]

Time Management

Time management has received much attention in the business press. Courses, time managers, to-do lists, appointment calendars, software, and a proliferation of other tools and approaches constantly remind managers of the importance of time. In many cases, time is even more important in small businesses, since individual jobs are fragmented and the need to establish priorities is critical. Robert Dorney suggests that

> Time management is more about management than about time. Writing everything down in a planner or diary may inspire a feeling of ineffable virtue and even well-being. But if you're tracking activities you shouldn't be involved in at all, you aren't managing your time.[20]

However, he also suggests that

> Unless you keep records, it is easy to think you are managing, planning, organizing and setting goals when in fact you may be spending most of your time putting out fires . . . [21]

Establishing Priorities

One of the key components to time management is the establishment of clear priorities. In most situations there will not be adequate time to perform all of the activities faced by individual managers. Without priorities, time will be spent on activities with limited payoffs. Or, alternatively, all activities will receive limited attention, resulting in a poor allocation of management resources. With priorities clearly established, time can be allocated to those activities the individual considers important to the overall objectives of the firm. Other important but lower priority activities can be delegated, and some activities will be rescheduled or cancelled; good time managers make sure that key priorities are not among the latter items.

Budgeting Your Time

Most time management concepts require that the individual set long-term objectives and budget time for their achievement. Ideally this precludes, or at least lessens, the possibility that key long-term objectives will be superseded by the pressures of shorter-term requirements. As with company objectives, time management objectives can provide both direction and a basis for action. Among the key long-term objectives that should be included in your time management activities are:

1. Planning,
2. Personal development, and
3. Professional development.

Analysis of Time Use

Consultants, lawyers, accountants, and other professionals who sell time *must* keep track of how they spend their working hours. But other managers will find a record of the actual use of their time important for performance measurement, as well as for future planning and time allocation. Most time management tools provide for the following time management activities:

1. Appointments;
2. A to-do list (including calls to be made, reports and letters to be written, and activities to arrange);
3. A record of time use;
4. Expenses;
5. Weekly/monthly/yearly appointments; and
6. A contact list: names/titles/addresses/phone numbers.

While printed forms and expensive time managers are currently very popular, they are neither essential nor necessarily the best way for all managers to manage time. Some keep simple notebooks for each day's entries, a list of suppliers' names and telephone numbers, and notes that will be used in the course of their business day; others use computer programs (PIMs, personal information managers) such as Sidekick, Arriba, Metro, and Desk Power. Finally, many business people and professionals are using pocket-sized electronic organizers that offer as much as 256 000 bytes of random access memory for appointments, telephone and fax numbers, memos and calculations.

Time Management—The Future

We have dealt primarily with time management in a personal context, where the focus is on better and more effective use of management time. But beyond this personal perspective on time management has emerged a new focus on time as a company resource which must be managed along with raw materials, equipment, people, and money. This approach spawned just-in-time inventory management, drastic reductions in the time spent on design and development projects, and flexible manufacturing and response systems.

George Stalk points out that

Today's new generation companies compete with flexible manufacturing and rapid response systems, expanding variety and increasing innovation. A company that builds its strategy on this system is a more powerful competitor than one with a strategy based on low wages, scale or focus. . . . In contrast, strategies based on the cycle of flexible manufacturing, rapid response, expanding variety, and increasing innovation are time based. Factories are close to the customers they serve. Organization structures enable fast responses rather than low costs and control. Companies concentrate on reducing if not eliminating delays and using their response advantages to attract the most profitable customers.[22]

Currently, this focus on time-based strategy is used primarily by bigger companies, but it is beginning to affect small suppliers, and will ultimately affect all businesses. Fortunately for many entrepreneurs and small business managers, a time-based strategy is a natural fit for small firms. Properly managed, this approach can reduce inventories, minimize development and production lead times, and reduce some of the uncertainties of long-range and market planning. Companies that can bring out new products faster than their competitors and shorten the time between product conception and product delivery enjoy significant competitive advantages. But these advantages don't just happen because a firm is entrepreneurial or small. Again, Stalk notes

The best competitors, the most successful ones, know how to keep moving and always stay on the cutting edge. . . . Today, time is on the cutting edge.[23]

Microcomputers in Small Business Management

Most experts believe that during the 1990s there will be explosive growth in the use of microcomputers by small businesses. Declining unit costs of computers, the wide variety of small business applications they offer, and the potential access to timely, low-cost decision-making information portend well for small business computing. Making people more effective, and business more cost-effective, will provide the impetus; easy-to-use hardware and software will make the change possible, and relatively painless.

Unfortunately, the people who sell and write about microcomputers are interested mainly in the latest developments, many of which exceed the needs of their small customers. Too often, small business buyers are oversold, buying capacity and features that go well beyond their present and future needs.

Systems Hardware

Increased processing capacity continues to attract large users, but most small businesses find that mature platforms such as the XT and AT (and the clones)

meet their needs. As well, the mature equipment has extensive competition and is priced accordingly. In many cases, hardware costs are far lower than the costs of software and of the training necessary to use the equipment.

Systems Software

Several systems are available to small business buyers, but DOS continues to dominate the microcomputer industry. It provides an adequate system base for small business software development, and while new systems (OS/2 and Unix) provide some advantages for future software development, their proprietary nature means less competition and higher costs without any significant benefits for the average user.

Applications Software

There are literally thousands of applications software packages, although only a few qualify as best sellers. Such names as WordPerfect, Word, Lotus, Excel, dBase, and RBase dominate software offerings. Added to these general programs is a growing list of more specialized software dealing with project management, time management, accounting, financial analysis, inventory control, desktop publishing, and graphics.

Most small business applications require one or more of the following applications packages:

1. Word processing,
2. Worksheets (spreadsheets),
3. Data base management,
4. Project management,
5. Personal information managers,
6. Accounting software, and
7. Inventory software

There are many competing products in each of these categories and most can do a respectable job of processing small business data requirements. However, to make an appropriate decision, buyers must be clear on their present and future needs to insure that the applications packages can meet essential requirements. Ease of use, vendor support, software features and equipment requirements can vary from package to package.

Buying a Computer System

Gellman,[24] among others, has provided a detailed checklist for those in the market for a computer. (See Figure 8-5.) However, much of what he suggests applies to the purchase of mini- or mainframe computers. With the advent of the microcomputer, some of the traditional concerns are disappearing. Many

Figure 8-5

A Buyer's Guide to Small Business Computers

1. Take an introductory computer course or read a book on small business (computers).
2. Invest in independent consulting advice.
3. Determine the potential benefits your organization can obtain from electronic data processing (EDP).
4. Examine your existing systems and their deficiencies.
5. Estimate your current (and future) information needs.
6. Estimate your current costs.
7. Prepare and send out requests for a (systems) proposal.
8. Consider feasibility questions:
   Will it work?
   Will it pay?
   Will we use it?
   Will it cause adverse effects?
9. Avoid potential risks:
   Availability of proper personnel;
   Availability of proper programs;
   Continued support of software;
   Expendability of the equipment;
   Security of computer installation;
   Security of files and programs;
   Availability of a disaster recovery plan;
   Adequate formal management and personnel discipline.
10. Deal carefully with suppliers:
   Get everything in writing;
   See a realistic demonstration;
   Check suppliers' references;
   Negotiate a contract.
11. Develop and follow an implementation plan:
   Form a conversion and installation team;
   Involve top management;
   Plan your conversion carefully;
   Emphasize careful system testing.

Source: Harvey S. Gellman, *A Buyer's Guide to Small Business Computers* (Toronto: CIPS, 1979), p. 12.

buyers forgo maintenance contracts, buy without the involvement of consultants, and design their own systems using popular applications packages.

Social Responsibility and the Small Business[25]

Today, business enterprises of all sizes are under closer scrutiny than ever before as management finds itself responding to the needs of not only common shareholders, but also employees, creditors, customers, regulatory bodies, special interest groups, and the public at large. As many managers have discovered, these stakeholders have become quite adept at publicizing their concerns and protecting their particular interests.

While the issue of social responsibility may be of limited significance for a great number of small enterprises, particularly proprietorships, partnerships, and privately held companies, it does emerge as an important consideration for many businesses in the later stages of development.

In general, companies can develop a reputation for social responsibility by following certain steps:

1. Conducting an ongoing assessment of the expectations of the wide constituency to which the company is accountable;
2. Developing policies and implementing specific programs designed to meet these standards of corporate behaviour; and
3. Integrating these activities into the company's day-to-day operations.

Whether an enterprise responds to the pressures for greater social accountability by way of external activities (e.g., active concern for ecology) or internal initiatives (e.g., employee safety standards, equal employment opportunity programs), it is essential that management first overcome the perception that socially responsible management may somehow be financially detrimental to the firm. The weight of public opinion suggests that companies that are successful in developing a reputation for integrity, ethical behaviour, and responsibility to society, may also expect to find a good deal of support in their particular business market. The benefits may not necessarily be realized in the short term, but a number of researchers have concluded that companies with high ethical standards are often more profitable in their respective industries. For most small businesses this reputation is cultivated within a relatively confined market area.

Once management has defined the scope and nature of the organization's obligations, a set of criteria (e.g., plant safety; compliance with industry regulations; prompt response to customer complaints; recruitment and hiring of minorities) can be established and measurement procedures formulated. In a general sense, the following commentary from 1973 is still quite applicable today:

> Many of the costs associated with social responsibility are marginal, out of proportion to all the time and talent that have gone into arguing about them. Behaving responsibly often means no more or less than acting humanely, treating employees and customers with consideration, avoiding ineptitude and blunders, cultivating a sharp eye for the important little things, and knowing how to spend where the returns are high. In this sense, responsibility can accomplish a lot with relatively small cost.[26]

Regardless of their particular circumstance or level of authority, those in managerial positions of any kind would do well to take guidance from the words of business writer A.B. Carroll: "Moral issues in management are not isolated and distinct from traditional business decision making but rather are right smack in the middle of it. Therefore, moral competence is an integral part of managerial competence."[27]

Summary

This chapter is devoted to a discussion of a number of diverse small business issues that can be pivotal to the success of the enterprise at any phase. At one time or another almost every entrepreneur will have to deal with at least one of the following questions:

- Would my business benefit from the computerization of certain procedures?
- Are there special issues to consider in cultivating *female entrepreneurship*?
- Why do there never seem to be enough hours in the work day and how can I use my time more efficiently?
- Is socially responsive behaviour a reasonable expectation for the small enterprise? What steps can the organization take in order to become more accountable to society as a whole?
- What factors should be considered before deciding to incorporate the business?

Since these issues rarely lend themselves to definitive answers, we have avoided treating them as such. Rather, the basic objective of this chapter has been to outline their main elements, while providing some general insights into how the small business owner can approach these different questions.

List of Key Words

Business Ethics	Social Responsibility
Collective Entrepreneurship	Startup Entrepreneurship
Limited Company	Systems Hardware
Microcomputers	Taxation
Partnerships	Time Management
Proprietorships	Women Entrepreneurs
Software	

Questions for Discussion

1. How does *startup entrepreneurship* differ from *management entrepreneurship*?

2. An entrepreneur is considering the incorporation of her two-year-old proprietorship and has asked for your advice. She has been told that by incorporating the business she can limit her personal liability for any debts incurred by the company.

   This operation has yet to generate a profit and the owner receives substantial income from outside contract work. Does incorporation seem to be appropriate in this case?

3. It has been argued that a major part of the challenge for any small business with a reasonably large employee complement lies in the manager's ability to instill an *entrepreneurial attitude* in these individuals. The ideal would seem to be a group of employees who are imaginative and enthusiastic, take initiative, seek challenges, and function well as part of a team.

   What steps can the small business manager take to create an atmosphere which is conducive to this entrepreneurial spirit?

Selected Readings

Allen, David N. and S. Rahman, "Small Business Incubators: A Positive Environment for Entrepreneurship," *Journal of Small Business Management*, 23, no. 3 (July 1985), pp. 12–22.

Belcourt, Monica, "Sociological Factors Associated with Female Entrepreneurship," *Journal of Small Business and Entrepreneurship*, 4, no. 3 (Winter 1986/87), pp. 22–31.

Belfall, Donald, "Acquiring Packaged Software: Buyer Beware!" *CMA Magazine*, September–October, 1986, pp. 51–55.

Blanchard, Kenneth and Norman Vincent Peale, *The Power of Ethical Management*, New York, N.Y.: Ballantyne Books, 1988.

Brandt, Steven C., *Entrepreneuring in Established Companies: Managing Toward the Year 2000*. Homewood, IL: Dow Jones Irwin, 1986.

Brockhaus, R.H., "Entrepreneur Folklore," *Journal of Small Business Management*, 25, no. 3, pp. 1–6.

Certified General Accountants Association of Ontario, *How to Conduct a Meeting*, Toronto, Ont.: 1990.

Gartner, William D., "What Are We Talking About When We Talk About Entrepreneurship?" *Journal of Business Venturing*, 5, no. 1 (January 1990), pp. 15–28.

Ginsberg, Art, and Ann Duckholtz, "Are Entrepreneurs a Breed Apart?" *Journal of General Management*, 15, no. 2 (Winter 1989), pp. 32–40.

Goffee, Robert and Richard Scase, *Women in Charge: The Experiences of Female Entrepreneurs*. Boston, MA: Allen & Unwin, 1985.

Gray, Douglas A. and Dianna Lynn Gray, *The Complete Canadian Small Business Guide*. Toronto, Ont.: McGraw-Hill Ryerson, 1988.

Hisrich, Robert D., "The Woman Entrepreneur: Characteristics, Skills, Problems and Prescriptions for Success," in *The Art and Science of Entrepreneurship*. Cambridge, MA: Ballinger Publishing Company, 1986, pp. 61–84.

Hisrich, Robert D. and Candida G. Brush, *The Woman Entrepreneur: Starting, Financing and Managing a Successful New Business*. Toronto, Ont: D.C. Heath, 1986.

Hornaday, J.A. and J. Aboud, "Characteristics of Successful Entrepreneurs," *Personnel Psychology*, 24, 1971, pp. 141–53.

Korasik, Myron S., "Selecting a Small Business Computer," *Harvard Business Review*, 62 (January–February 1984), pp. 26–30.

Litton, Monica, *Women Mean Business: Successful Strategies for Starting Your Own Business*. Toronto, Ont.: Key Porter Books, 1987.

Masters, Robert and Roberta Meier, "Sex Differences and Risk Taking Propensity in Entrepreneurs," *Journal of Small Business Management*, 26, no. 1 (January 1988), pp. 31–35.

Pinchot, G., *Intrapreneurship*. New York, N.Y.: Harper & Row, 1985.

Ronstadt, R.G., *Entrepreneurship: Text, Cases and Notes*. Dover, MA: Lord Publishing, 1984.

Sexton, D.L. and N.B. Bowman, "Validation of a Personality Index: Comparison of Psychological Characteristics of Female Entrepreneurs, Managers, Entrepreneurial Students, and Business Students," *Frontiers of Entrepreneurial Research*. Wellesley, MA.: Babson College, 1986.

Stroup, Margaret A., Ralph Neubert and J.W. Anderson Jr., "Doing Good, Doing Better: Two Views of Social Responsibility," *Business Horizons*, March–April 1987, pp. 22–25.

Endnotes

1. Thomas J. Peters and Robert H. Waterman, *In Search of Excellence: Lessons From America's Best Run Companies* (New York, NY: Harper and Row, 1982).

2. A. Craig Copetas, "The Selling of the Entrepreneur, 1986," *INC.* (March 1986), p. 34.

3. Peter Drucker, *Innovation and Entrepreneurship: Practice and Principles* (New York: Harper and Row, 1985), p. 17.

4. Roger Kaplan, "Entrepreneurship Reconsidered: The Antimanagement Bias." *The Harvard Business Review*, May–June 1987, pp. 84–89.

5. Deaver Brown, *The Entrepreneur's Guide* (New York, NY: Ballantyne, 1980), p. 21.

6. According to 1984 statistics, these two factors were responsible for 95 percent of business failures. See *The Canadian Business Failure Record* (Toronto: Dun and Bradstreet Canada Limited, 1985), p. 3.

7. Robert B. Reich, "Entrepreneurship Reconsidered: The Team as Hero," *Harvard Business Review*, May–June 1987, p. 80.

8. *Ibid.*, p. 80.

9. Peters and Waterman, *In Search of Excellence: Lessons from America's Best Run Companies*.

10. The act of innovating in an entrepreneurial sense inside large organizations has been called "intrapreneuring." See Roger Kaplan, "Entrepreneurship Reconsidered" pp. 84–89. He states that "Innovation within existing companies has now gained the accolade 'intrapreneurship.' "

11. Reich, *"Entrepreneurship Reconsidered: The Team as Hero,"* p. 83.

12. Allen H. Neuharth, *Confessions of an SOB* (New York: Doubleday, 1989). A quick appraisal of the many books of the "how I did it" genre currently in print indicates that few of these successful men ever had high profile women as part of their business activities. In that sense Neuharth is a refreshing change. It is particularly encouraging to note that his performance

expectations were extremely high for all of his management group, males and females.

13. Marlene Jensen, *Women Who Want to be Boss* (Garden City, NY: Doubleday and Company, 1987), p. 6.

14. Ellen Wojahn, "Why There Aren't More Women in This Magazine," *INC.*, July 1986, p. 47.

15. Jensen, *Women Who Want to be Boss*, p. 12.

16. Lois Stevenson, "Against all Odds: The Entrepreneurship of Women," *Journal of Small Business Management*, October 1986, p. 35.

17. In her study of female entrepreneurship, Lavoie [see Dina Lavoie, "A New Era for Female Entrepreneurship in the 80's" *Journal of Small Business*, 2, no. 3 (Winter 1985–86), 34–35] identifies three types of women entrepreneurs: the sponsored entrepreneur, the young college-educated entrepreneur, and the social entrepreneur. Again, this author argues that any conclusions about differences between male and female entrepreneurs would be premature until there are a reasonable number of comparable companies vis-á-vis industry sector, size, year of startup, age of founder, etc.

18. *Financial Post*, January 2, 1989, p. 10.

19. Paul Halpern, J.F. Weston, and Eugene Brigham, *Canadian Managerial Finance*, 3rd. ed. (Toronto: Holt Rinehart and Winston of Canada Limited, 1988), p. 37.

20. Robert C. Dorney, "Making Time to Manage," *Harvard Business Review*, January–February, 1988, p. 39.

21. *Ibid.*, p. 39.

22. George Stalk, Jr. "Time—The Next Source of Competitive Advantage," *Harvard Business Review*, July–August 1988, p. 45.

23. *Ibid.*, p. 21.

24. Harvey S. Gellman, *A Buyer's Guide to Small Business Computers* (Toronto: The Canadian Information Processing Society, 1979), p. 12.

25. Adapted from J.T. Zinger, "Stand Up and Be Accountable," *CGA Magazine*, 24, no. 8 (August 1990), pp. 49–53.

26. G. Burck, "The Hazards of Corporate Responsibility," *Fortune*, June 1973, pp. 114–17, 214–18.

27. A.B. Carroll, "In Search of the Moral Manager," *Business Horizons*, March–April, 1987, pp. 14–18.

2

The Functional Aspects of Small Business Management

C H A P T E R

9

The Environment and General Management for Small Business

Introduction

While the need for a general manager in the small firm often does not emerge until phase five, many general management "functions" must be dealt with earlier in the firm's growth. Two broad activities usually define the role of the general manager in a small business. These are:

1. Managing the firm's relationship with its external environment, and

2. Organizing and coordinating the internal tradeoffs that must be made to allocate scarce resources to the firm's various activities.

Although related, these responsibilities differ in that the general manager has limited or no control over the external environment, and thus his involvement is limited to reading the direction, the type, and the timing of projected changes in an effort to provide guidelines for allocating and managing internal resources effectively. Seldom, at least for small businesses, will the actions of the firm affect change in its external environment.

As the firm grows, it has more fixed commitments, making a quick response to environmental change both more difficult and more expensive. Predicting environmental change becomes progressively more important as the firm faces the tradeoffs between long-term investments in increased organizational efficiency (capital investment in people, equipment and inventories, etc.) and the need for a flexible response to changing environmental conditions.

The major internal role of the general manager is one of acquiring and allocating resources to meet the needs of the target environment, and measuring the performance of employees as they coordinate their respective functional activities in the pursuit of company objectives.

Hence the major roles of the general manager in the small business can be summarized as:

1. environmental scanning and assessment,
2. resource acquisition and allocation, and
3. performance measurement and control.

The general management process has many steps, all of which are interrelated and which arise largely out of the necessity to coordinate the needs of the growing firm. These activities, properly handled, have both an action component and a communications component that are essential for effective performance within the firm.

Usually, the general management role involves all or part of the following activities:

1. strategy formulation (direction)
   a. environmental scanning
   b. goal setting
   c. strategic planning
2. strategy implementation (action)
   a. operational planning
   b. motivating action
   c. measurement and control

We present a simplified model of the small business general management process (Figure 9-1). Our purpose is to identify the key factors, and to discuss them as part of a process that can be managed in the small firm.[1]

Figure 9-1

A Small Business
General
Management Model

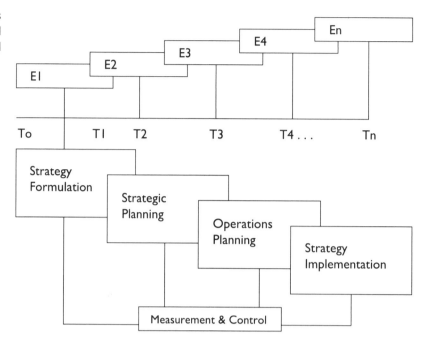

The Environment

Strategy Formulation

For most small business managers, strategy can be a simple statement about how the firm will allocate its resources over time to achieve some stated objectives. It requires that management have clearly stated objectives, a well defined environment (for small businesses, a product/market definition), and a clear understanding of both the present and future resources available to the firm.

Environmental Scanning

Adequate environmental scanning is important, for several reasons. First, the business environment changes over time, as Figure 9-1 suggests, and since few companies control their business environment, intelligent response to change depends on adequate information. Second, good scanning can assist in the development of meaningful and manageable objectives. And finally, good scanning allows for the testing of strategic options as the firm goes about the business of finding and developing an effective business strategy.

Figure 9-2

Environmental
Scanning—
Assessing Risks
and
Opportunities

Strategic Option:	Risks	Opportunities
Political		
Economic Competition Market		
Social		
Technological		

While there are different approaches to the development of a manageable method of environmental scanning, the one most often used involves an assessment of environmental risks and opportunities. Figure 9-2 presents an analytical format for assessing the political, economic, social, and technological risks and opportunities associated with a particular strategy.[2]

Choice of Environmental Segment

At a minimum, the chosen environment must be capable of supporting the stated objectives. For example, it would be difficult (although not impossible) to set a growth objective of 15 percent per year in a market environment which was declining at the rate of 15 percent. The small business strategist should be seeking to place the firm in the environmental segment that permits the achievement of company objectives with the fewest risks and the most attractive opportunities. It is important to note that companies *must* respond to environmental conditions, and that once a particular competitive environment is chosen, management effectiveness will be determined by the way available internal resources are managed.

Setting Objectives

Objectives are usually set to meet the needs of stakeholders. Chief among these are shareholders, but even in small businesses they are not alone in determining realistic objectives. Employees, lenders, suppliers, and customers will have significant input into the setting of objectives. Thus, among the first and most important tasks facing the general manager is one of defining an environment where company objectives can be met.

Figure 9-3

Company
Resources—
Assessing
Strengths and
Weaknesses

Strategic Option:	Strengths	Weaknesses
Marketing		
Operations		
Personnel		
Finance		
Control		
General Management		

Assessing Company Resources

If strategy describes how the firm will use its resources to achieve its objectives, then management must have a complete understanding of available resources and how these can be managed to exploit environmental opportunities. One of the most common tools for making this assessment is a company strength and weakness analysis. Figure 9-3 presents a format for making this assessment. In this analysis, the small business manager is seeking a strategy that will produce the greatest number of strengths and the fewest weaknesses. It is important to note that in the internal setting, the manager can exercise significant control over the type and timing of resources at her disposal.

Defining a Business Strategy

There are many strategy definitions, but we will use a simple concept of strategy formulation that fits our small business focus. Strategy, then, is a process of

allocating resources over time to achieve stated objectives in the defined competitive environment.

For most small businesses the key environmental factor is economic and its working environment is usually defined in "product/market" terms. Most theoretical discussions of the business environment include some variation of the PEST (Political, Economic, Social, and Technological) framework. For many small businesses, political, social, and some technological issues are seen as parameters or boundary conditions and their management is left to small business associations and lobby groups.

Few strategy statements are complete in the sense that they detail all of the components and how they will be managed. These details are part of strategic planning.

Strategic Planning

In the main, the vehicle for articulating strategy is the strategic plan. Here, the details and timing for acquiring resources and allocating these resources to the various functional activities of the firm are set forth. The strategic plan should set out detailed objectives and environmental descriptions (products, services, and markets), and resource allocations (equipment, people, and money) in sufficient detail that functional managers can develop detailed operating plans for their respective functional activities. In general, the strategic plan provides both direction and parameters to guide in the development of operating plans for the firm. The time frame for strategic plans is typically three to five years, usually determined by movement in the environment and the nature of resources available to the firm. While the strategic plan must be monitored, review and changes in the plan are periodic.

Implementing a Business Strategy

Implementing a business strategy involves the general manager and the functional managers in those day-to-day business activities essential to meeting the needs of the broad strategic plan.

Operating Plans

Operating plans spell out how functional activities such as marketing, operations, personnel, finance, and accounting will be organized to meet the needs of the strategic plan and overall objectives. While the major thrust of strategic planning is to provide direction for the firm, the operating plan provides guidelines for action. It should spell out specific activities, the people who will perform them, when they will be performed, and the performance measures that will be used to assess these activities. Typically, the course of action must be constantly reviewed and revised in light of the success, or lack of success, of functional activities.

Motivating Action

In the final analysis, action must be taken by managers through people. To provide motivation, the manager must communicate expectations, provide and adjust direction, and respond to performance deviations from plan. This requires leadership and an ability to balance the needs of the company and of its employees with the kind of sensitivity that engenders commitment to the long-term interests of the firm. (These topics are further developed in Chapter 12.)

Measurement, Feedback, and Control

Finally, if objectives are to be met (resource acquisition is often dependent on this factor), performance in key areas must be measured to provide a basis for adjusting day-to-day activities. It is unrealistic to expect that all will go according to plan. In an attempt to minimize deviations good and timely performance information is essential. As the firm grows (and moves from phase 1 to phase 5) and managers retreat from the direct activities of the workplace, measurement, feedback, and control become progressively more important.

Selected Readings

Curtis, David A., *Strategic Planning for Smaller Businesses*, Toronto, Ont.: Lexington Books, 1983.

Murray, John, "A Concept of Entrepreneurial Strategy," *Strategic Management Journal*, 5, no. 1, pp. 1–13.

Nagel, Arie, "Strategy Formulation for the Smaller Firm: A Practical Approach," *Long Range Planning*, 14, no. 4 (August 1981), pp. 115–110.

Perrigo, A.E.B., "Developing Corporate Strategy for Small Business," *Journal of Business Policy*, 3, no. 4, 1974.

Porter, Michael E., *Competitive Strategy: Techniques for Analyzing Industries and Competitors*. New York, N.Y.: Free Press, 1980.

———, *Competitive Advantage: Creating and Sustaining Superior Performance*. New York, N.Y.: Free Press, 1985.

Endnotes 1.   This is not meant to be a complete strategy model but rather a simplification to provide a manageable small business approach to the strategy formulation and implementation process. Fry and Killing have taken an approach they call the "Diamond-E" drill which consists of the following steps:

1. Define the relevant environment: using a specific time horizon, identify the relevant elements of demand, competition, supply, capital and government policy.

2. Assess the environment: forecast the evolution of the critical environmental forces, and evaluate the key success factors for operating within them.

3. Evaluate the proposed strategy: determine the strategy's consistency with the projected environmental conditions.

4. Take action: confirm the strategy if your forecasts look good. Otherwise, pinpoint needed changes, and recycle the analysis.

To develop the strategic idea, Fry and Killing suggest four further steps:

1. Identify performance trends (how well is the firm meeting the goals it has set for itself?)

2. Set the strategic agenda (based on the organization's performance trend, does it want to seek new opportunities or diagnose and solve problems?)

3. Analyze the current strategy (identify the strategy, run your Diamond-E drill, and then consider a "no change scenario": what will happen if no part of the strategy is altered?)

4. Make your strategic choice (develop options, and decide how to proceed. By now, your analysis should have turned up several options, which should all be checked with the Diamond-E drill)

Reproduced with permission from *Ideas for Managers*, National Centre for Management Research and Development, University of Western Ontario and Telemedia, 1, no. 4, pp. 2–3.

2. For most small businesses, assessing the political, social, and to some degree the technological dimensions of the environment they populate is a matter of depending on and using small business organizations and lobby groups. These tend to inform, as well as lobby for, environmental (industry and market) conditions suitable for their small business members.

CHAPTER

10

Marketing Management for Small Business

Introduction

Marketing is a central concern for small businesses. Before embarking upon her venture, a prospective proprietor needs to determine whether there is a demand for the product that she hopes to sell. She must be convinced that there will be purchasers in the marketplace who will buy her offering at a particular price, and that she can access these would-be buyers. Moreover, the forecasted sales must be deemed sufficient to support the new venture. Once the small business is established, strong demand continues to be vital. The business may face the prospect of competitive and even superior offerings which undermine its sales revenues. This prospect is particularly threatening to the small business offering a single product within a limited market.

Besides marketing its product, a small business may have to market itself (in particular, its objectives and business plan) to bankers, government agencies, suppliers, and even employees. Because of the close identification of the owner-operator or owner-manager with the organization, he will have to sell his personal strengths. Moreover, the small business that is entering a market must differentiate itself from its competitors and build up loyalty through the goodwill generated by various marketing activities.

Many small enterprises fail to undertake effective advertising, pay very little attention to distribution or packaging, and never develop a clear idea of who comprises their target market. In the following discussion, we review some of the basic principles of marketing, and attempt to relate them to the small business context.

Fundamental Marketing Issues

In cases where the small business owner has developed a new product, marketing often comes as an afterthought to the creative process. In other instances, the small business owner is responding to an expressed demand, and the marketplace is uppermost in her mind. But regardless of the extent to which the firm is market-oriented, there are certain issues to consider before developing a marketing program. These issues can be framed as questions:

- *What* are the perceived benefits of the product?
- *Who* is the target market(s)? Is it comprised of more than one distinct subgroup or segment?
- *How* can the firm satisfy the needs of each subgroup in the served market?

For the established organization wishing to enlarge its presence in the marketplace, there are further, related questions:

- How can we increase the usage/loyalty of existing users?
- How can we convert non-users?
- How can we gain sales from our competitors?
- Are there segments not currently served that might be attracted to the product?
- What modifications to the product, or to the current marketing activities, would be required to appeal to these segments?

Building Demand for the Product

The initial step in devising a marketing program is an appraisal of the product—the good or service—that the firm is trying to sell. Are people aware of this product? Are they knowledgeable about its benefits? Or does the firm have to create generic or primary demand for the product as well as a demand for its particular offering? For example, when esthetics services were first introduced into smaller urban areas, most people did not know what was meant by "esthetics." Therefore, before any particular esthetics establishment could hope to succeed, it was necessary to build primary demand for these services—to educate potential clients about what these services involve and their associated benefits. Sometimes, too, firms encourage users to associate a product with benefits that go well beyond its physical attributes. For instance, ice cream has been marketed not merely as a tasty frozen dessert but as a novelty item associated with fun and excitement.

A successful product will usually attract competitors. Consequently, a basic objective of marketing is to distinguish the product being offered from substitutes so that potential users recognize some desirable difference, whether in the product itself (such as packaging or price) or in its ancillary services.

Identifying the Market

There are two generic markets that the small business may consider: the consumer market and the industrial/organizational market (including government). Each requires thorough research before the product is launched, and careful monitoring during the ongoing marketing program. Even more effort is required if the small business owner decides to enter the consumer or industrial/organizational market in another country.

The Consumer Market   The consumer market may be analyzed in terms of its demographic characteristics (e.g., age, place of residence, education, occupation, income); lifestyle characteristics (e.g., activities, interests, opinions, personality traits, media habits); and purchasing characteristics (why are people motivated to buy? when do they buy? where? and in what quantity?).

The Industrial/Organizational Market   The second type of market is the industrial/organizational market, broadly comprised of companies, institutions, and the government. Purchases are often made by a buying group or committee, with experience in the product category and in weighing competitive offerings in terms of such purchase criteria as price, quality, capability to manufacture to specification, speed of manufacture and delivery, dependability of supply, and after-sale service. The selling task generally requires considerable technical knowledge. In the manufacturing sector, demand for a product used as a component in the production of another is often derived from demand for the final product: this in turn may be affected by factors such as product obsolescence, the economy, and government policy.

The Export Market   The export market entails crossing a national boundary to sell into one of the above two categories of markets. The organization must contend with the regulations of a foreign country, and in many cases, with very different ways of doing business. Careful research is required before initiating an export venture. Often it is essential to retain specialists with expertise in such areas as trade financing, international law, and export insurance.

Segmentation and the Target Market   Normally the small business proprietor, working with limited resources, must concentrate his marketing efforts on a particular group within the chosen market. Segmenting the market and then focusing on one or more chosen segments allows the small firm to align its product to the needs of that segment, to price it at a level that the segment finds acceptable, to make it readily available to the selected segment, and to emphasize benefits valued by the segment through its various promotional activities. The *marketing mix* (Product, Price, Promotion and Place) can be harmonized for a greater overall impact.

Meeting Needs

The product offered by the firm should be geared to some specific need of the target market. This is a fundamental principle of marketing, vital to ensuring demand for the product. The need to identify, and satisfy, a need on the part of the user explains why so much effort is devoted to test marketing a product with a representative sample of the target market. In practical terms, a product policy based on an awareness of desired quality level, the depth and breadth of the product line, packaging, after-sale service, and warranties can foster loyalty to a particular product. However, in order to gain acceptance, it is critical that the product satisfy some specific need of the user.

As suggested earlier, a successful (or even potentially successful) product will soon inspire competitive offerings. To survive and prosper in this competitive arena, many smaller firms choose to serve a niche in the marketplace, and achieve a relatively sustainable competitive advantage by staying "close to the customer." A niche strategy calls for the firm to specialize in some respect (e.g., customized products). The objective is to cater to the needs of a particular segment that is of negligible interest to the major players in that industry, and yet sufficient in size and purchasing power to be profitable. Through close attention to customer needs and an emphasis on good customer relations, a small firm with such a strategy can create a barrier to entry which dissuades would-be competitors. Since the small business is typically free from the constraints that characterize the bureaucratic organization, a strong "service" orientation can be easily developed.

The Marketing Plan

The small business person may be deterred from engaging in marketing activities, either because she cannot find the time to design and implement a marketing plan or because she deems it unnecessary (implying that the product will sell itself, presumably through favourable word-of-mouth). In virtually all cases, however, the small business will benefit from a carefully developed marketing plan that specifies how the firm will achieve some anticipated level of sales over some particular time interval. A marketing plan should be an integral part of the firm's ongoing planning process. The resulting document should lay out *what* will be done by *whom, when,* and *at what cost,* taking into account the small firm's constraints in both working capital and time. For instance, given a skeletal workforce, there is limited time to devote to promotional activities and personal selling.

The Marketing Mix

Figure 10-1 depicts the components of the marketing mix. These are product, price, place (the channel or method of distribution), and promotion (activities to communicate information to and/or promote the product to those influential in the purchase decision).

Product   Products in the consumer market are often broadly categorized as convenience goods, shopping goods, or specialty goods, with different marketing tactics associated with each category.

Convenience goods are those purchased with a minimum of effort—necessities, and unplanned or emergency purchases. Products which primarily

Figure 10-1

The Marketing Mix

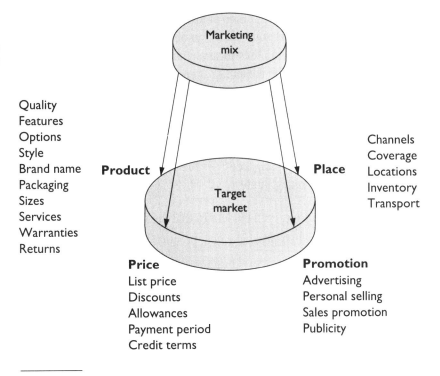

Quality
Features
Options
Style
Brand name **Product**
Packaging
Sizes
Services
Warranties
Returns

Place
Channels
Coverage
Locations
Inventory
Transport

Price
List price
Discounts
Allowances
Payment period
Credit terms

Promotion
Advertising
Personal selling
Sales promotion
Publicity

Source   Kotler, McDougall & Armstrong, *Marketing* Toronto, Ont.:
         Prentice-Hall Canada Inc.,1988, p. 41. Reprinted with Permission.

fall within this category are usually made readily accessible to consumers, with impulse purchases encouraged by point-of-purchase displays. Within a certain range, the purchaser tends to be insensitive to price.

Shopping goods are purchased only after comparative shopping. If price is not the first consideration, competing products may be compared on quality and style; they will almost certainly be compared on price if they seem otherwise equivalent. In a retail outlet such products are normally adjacent to one another so as to aid comparison (for the same reason, competing stores may be located in close proximity). Advertising messages normally attempt to differentiate a given product from its competitors on some aspect of value. Packaging is often an important element here, and for many companies is essential to the differentiation of their product. Examples include the colour and design of a retailer's packages and bags, or the standard layout favoured by certain fast-food franchises.

Specialty goods are goods which provide benefits of sufficient value to the user to engender brand or product loyalty. The consumer is willing to go to considerable effort and expense to obtain these products. Therefore, within a certain tolerance, neither location nor price is an important factor in the purchase decision; the consumer merely needs to be made aware of where to obtain the product.

The concept of the **Product Life Cycle** (PLC) captures the notion that products come on the market (introductory stage), move into a growth stage as awareness and acceptance increase, plateau in a mature stage when sales become level, and finally fade (decline stage). Each stage of the PLC requires a different marketing strategy, as will be discussed later.

Price There are certain guidelines that the small business proprietor should keep in mind when pricing a new product:

1. Establish an overall image for the product, taking quality into consideration;
2. Establish specific product costs; and
3. Establish the level of demand for the product, the level of competition, and the anticipated price sensitivity in the trading area, taking the local economy into account.

There are several generally accepted approaches to product pricing. New owners of small businesses, inexperienced in making pricing decisions, often choose to be *price takers* (following the pricing policy of competitors). Yet a number of alternative approaches are possible, depending on the firm's objectives.

Demand-based pricing uses the price sensitivity of the purchaser as the chief determinant in setting the final price. For purchasers of convenience and specialty products in the consumer market, or of industrial products with no direct competitor, price may not be a major concern. Existing price levels can provide a useful indicator to the small business owner. With a product new to the market, one pricing option is *skim pricing*, applicable during the introductory and early growth phase. This involves charging a premium price for the product. Those willing to pay the price must perceive the product to offer superior benefits relative to substitute products. Skim pricing makes sense only under certain conditions: when demand is deemed sufficient at the higher price; when the costs of producing a small volume without economies of scale do not negate the advantage of a premium price (sales volumes will be relatively low); when the product's quality and image are compatible with the higher price; and when competitors cannot easily enter the market at a lower price. On the other hand, if the object is to gain market share as fast as possible, then *penetration pricing*, with a low initial price, will maximize sales (often at the expense of per unit profitability). This practice invites large-volume production which may permit even lower prices in future, and thus discourage the entry of competitors.

Cost-based pricing takes into account the costs incurred in bringing the product to the consumer, and then adds a percentage markup to reflect the profit objective of the firm. This type of pricing is primarily associated with industrial products and professional services. A variant is *rate of return pricing*, which is based on the company's investment in the product. A rule of thumb that is sometimes applied to certain consumer packaged goods is one third for production, one third for promotion, and one third for profit.

A third major approach to price setting is **competitive pricing**, where a firm's prices are synchronized with those of competitors; taking relative quality into account, prices are set at par, higher, or lower. If there is no meaningful difference between one product offer and another, the premise is that the prices must match (imitative pricing).

Pricing practices may also be affected by a variety of other external considerations. For instance, the retail price will reflect the conventional markup by wholesalers for that type of product, and also the conventional markup at retail. If the product is to get support from the wholesaler and the retailer equivalent to that accorded similar products, the markups must normally be on a par or better. Industry associations and trade journals will provide information on retail markups. Obtaining information about wholesale markups is more difficult because strong competition prevails among firms vying for wholesalers to push their particular offering. Manufacturers commonly offer promotional allowances at both the wholesale (e.g., special price discounts and payment terms) and retail levels (e.g., co-operative advertising; specialized in-store promotions and displays).

Alternatively, price levels can be affected by the need to build sales by increasing store traffic. This often leads to *loss leader pricing* (pricing below cost for a temporary period) on some selected products known to appeal to a wide cross-section of potential purchasers. The goal is to lure more buyers onto the premises in the hope that they will purchase high markup items as well as the loss leader.

Place   The "distribution channel" comprises all those firms or individuals who take title, or assist in transferring title, to a product as it moves from producer to end user. The small business owner needs to evaluate the different options, which vary from direct selling (e.g., mail order, door-to-door) to selling through one or more intermediaries, including selling agents hired by small producers unable to afford their own sales force. For example, a startup business in the process of manufacturing 400 bicycle carrying racks designed specifically for compact cars chose to determine the best distribution method by placing the product on a trial basis in a local department store and in two specialty sporting goods outlets, and by advertising for mail-order purchase in a major cycling magazine. After a three-month period, the costs and revenues were determined for each alternative, which provided the company with valuable information in selecting its preferred distribution method.

In general, standard products distributed over a wide geographic area are best suited to an indirect/long channel through which goods move from manufacturer to wholesaler/agent to retailer to end user. Non-standard or perishable goods entering a geographically concentrated market are better distributed directly or through a short channel.

Small producers generally face formidable constraints with respect both to production and to selling capability. Consequently, they often elect to distribute through some narrow channel (e.g., selling miniature appliances, suitable for dormitories, only to colleges and universities), and frequently in a restricted geographical area. Further, an upmarket product (high quality/ high price) may dictate a niche strategy whereby a limited number of dealers are given exclusive rights to distribute the product. It is important that the elements of the marketing mix, including the distribution channel, be carefully orchestrated to support the desired product image.

Promotion   For a small enterprise, the promotion component of the marketing mix has a number of possible dimensions, each of which is explained below.

1. Advertising   Since many small enterprises serve a limited market area, the choice of medium or type of advertising must be made carefully. What are the media habits of the target market? How large is the area served by the particular establishment? Is the product one that needs to be displayed visually, thus requiring a pictorial medium? Or is there a lot of factual information related to the product, hence suggesting a print medium? Small organizations may use the media generally used by large organizations: television, radio, newspaper, magazines, billboards, and direct mail. In small cities the local radio, television, or newspaper may cover the market of the small firm very well. On the other hand, the reach of the medium may extend well beyond the trading area of the particular firm, at which point impact has to be balanced against cost effectiveness. Billboards are most effective when used near the actual location of the firm. While subject to the fate of most "junk mail," direct advertising has the advantage of being selective in its coverage, less expensive and more flexible than most other forms of advertising, and subject to measurement of its effectiveness. To succeed, the communication vehicle must have visual appeal, must be easy to understand, and should be appropriate to the image of the business.

Many small businesses prefer lower cost devices designed to reach a limited target market. These include specialty advertising (distribution of such items as matchpads, pencils, ballpoint pens, calendars, telephone pads, shopping bags); public transit posters; yellow pages; catalogues; and handout leaflets. Handbills distributed over a three to four block radius may generate awareness in a highly cost effective manner for businesses with a localized clientele. Yellow-page advertising is recommended only when the firm is dealing in shopping goods or has a market wherein customers may be looking for a firm which is first contacted by telephone.

Conventional wisdom suggests that advertising is most needed at the front end of the product life cycle in order to build awareness, and that it can taper off in the mature stage. The very legitimate question "How well did the advertising work?" is bound to come up, particularly given the budgetary constraints of many small organizations. To determine the effectiveness of a specific print vehicle, one can include a coupon to be redeemed at the time of purchase. Similarly, one can place separate identifying marks in an ad which appears in two places, again asking the purchaser to exchange the ad for a special price or prize. To appraise the impact of a specific advertisement, one technique used in retailing establishments is to advertise one item in one ad only, but have no reference to the item on the sales floor. The number of requests that follow can then be counted. On a different level, to evaluate the effectiveness of advertising in general, one method is to omit advertising for intermittent periods and then to monitor the effect on sales.

2. Sales Promotions Sales promotion activities are directed at a more restricted audience than is advertising and can include point-of-purchase displays, coupons and discounts, trade shows and exhibitions, and contests.

The use of sales promotion (in particular, sampling, small size packages, and price adjustments to induce trial) is most important in the early stage of product launch, and during the mature stage. By the time a product reaches maturity, price competition is often rampant among otherwise non-differentiated competing products.

3. Public Relations and Publicity   Public relations can be very important in promoting not only a particular product, but also the business itself. Sponsorship of a community sports team or a cultural event, for instance, can enhance public awareness of the business. Public relations activities combine with customer services and customer relations to build goodwill. The adoption of a uniform is often an effective way of developing the firm's public image. Public relations activities also generate publicity in the form of public interest news stories, which can be considered free advertising. Publicity can also be generated when the product is innovative or unique in some respect. Although the impact on sales is more attenuated than that of direct promotional activities, the potential of public relations activities and publicity should not be overlooked.

4. Personal Selling   While advertising and some sales promotion can generate interest in the product, personal selling is often crucial in achieving actual sales. Many small businesses will be heavily involved in personal selling, often directly to the end user. Clearly the most demanding task of selling involves obtaining orders—the task of finding prospective customers and then trying to persuade them to purchase the firm's product. Salespeople will need to be trained in product knowledge, and also in selling skills. Another aspect of selling is order-taking: recording the customer's order once the decision to purchase has been made. For the sake of good customer relations it is important to have an order control system in place even in the smallest organization, and to have the requisite inventory or service capability available to meet demand. As the business grows, the order control system is often one of the first areas to become automated, not only because of its complexity, but because failure to fill orders promptly and accurately generates ill will among both customers and salespeople. Another key element is after-sales service. Ascertaining that what the customer receives matches expectations helps foster subsequent patronage and may generate the most powerful form of advertising—word-of-mouth.

Developing a Marketing Program

The Product Life Cycle offers a useful framework within which to develop a marketing program. Critical to the success of this program is knowledge of where the product is in its life cycle. Identifying the position of the product in the PLC can provide a general perspective on the type of support needed. The specific blend of techniques to employ is then a function of the nature of the product, the business setting, the organization's resources, and the marketer's skill.

In the introductory stage of its life cycle, the major objective of the firm is to build awareness and induce trial. Choosing a restricted geographical area into which to launch the product can make it easier to create awareness on the part of the target market. Advertising can increase name recognition for the product and/or company, and can highlight particular benefits to which the target market is likely to respond. Promotion can take the form of coupons or samples, in-store promotions, and public demonstrations. As an example, fitness centres or indoor racquet clubs will often make free guest passes available. Trial is encouraged if information about the product is readily available and easy to understand, and if the product can be purchased in small quantities with a minimum of financial or social risk. For items requiring a greater financial outlay, risk may also be reduced through assistance at the time of installation, and by guarantees or warranties.

Note that the startup expenses needed for these and other sales activities, coupled with the research and development expenses needed to bring the product to market, normally exceed the sales revenues generated by the product during this stage, and often continue to do so well into the growth stage.

The small business person who is attempting to launch a new product within the consumer market should be aware that only a few persons within the potential target market will adopt the product at its outset. The rate of adoption is significantly affected by the product itself. If a clear advantage is perceived relative to other existing offers, and if this advantage is conspicuous or can be easily communicated, the rate of adoption will be accelerated. On the other hand, if the product is complex and hence difficult to understand and/or describe, the rate of adoption will be impeded. This problem may be partially resolved through use of the product in a setting which entails minimal risk, as for instance exposure to personal computers in a classroom or business office.

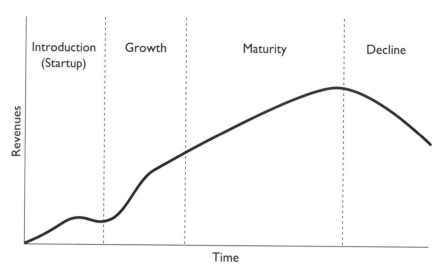

Figure 10-2

The Product Life Cycle

Introduction (Startup) | Growth | Maturity | Decline

Revenues

Time

In the growth stage, the product continues to require heavy advertising and sales support in order to ensure that the upward slope depicted in Figure 10-2 is as steep and as high as possible. There are two basic goals:

1. to get current users to use more of the product, perhaps through offering **price deals** or presenting new uses for the product, or
2. to find new users, often by directing sales efforts to previously untapped market segments and perhaps other geographic areas.

To maintain growth for as long as possible, or to create a resurgence of growth when sales flatten, companies often modify the format in which the product is presented, or emphasize new uses for the product. Admittedly, the influence of the small enterprise in this regard is generally minimal.

In the mature stage, there will likely be a number of competitive look-alikes. Often the challenge at the retail level will be to maintain shelf facings, display space, and even continued access to the outlets themselves through a robust level of sales. At this stage, a certain amount of **maintenance advertising** is necessary, but the emphasis is often on promotions which affect price. Many firms rely on **deals** (discounts or more product at the same price) to maintain sales volume. Dealing, rather than outright price cutting, allows the price to drop temporarily without altering the purchaser's perception of product quality. The product in this stage is frequently generating profits that can be used to support some newly launched product. A corollary of the life cycle concept is that new products are necessary to replace those which in due course will decline.

In the decline stage, product support expenditures are normally limited, and products are often retired from the market before sales fade entirely. For some products this stage arrives in very short order. Fads, such as the hula hoop, move through the entire cycle with great speed. Alternatively, the 'first out' of a new product may soon be surpassed by followers, as occurred with the original electric knife. On the other hand, certain long lived products, such as Procter and Gamble's Tide laundry detergent, face no foreseeable decline. Also, production of parts and add-ons for some products, particularly those representing a sizeable investment, often continues for goodwill reasons after the core product has been eclipsed.

Market Research Activities

Information Needs

Entrepreneurs often rely on gut feel rather than hard facts when making decisions. Yet even the fledgling enterprise needs sound information concerning the nature and size of the prospective market, and competitive conditions. As the organization continues in operation, many aspects of its environment can change. Throughout its existence it will need to make accurate assessments of user wants, the size of its market, competitive factors, and the impact of technological developments. The manager may need to gather information as to the viability and potential of new product concepts or promotions. In new or very small organizations, funds for expenditures in information are normally limited. But no organization can operate without some basic facts and figures.

There are two types of information external to the enterprise: primary and secondary. Primary sources (e.g., interviews, statistical data) furnish information directly. Secondary sources (e.g., newspaper and magazine articles, trade association reports; business directories; government studies) report, and frequently interpret, information gathered from primary sources.

As the organization evolves, it will also develop internal sources of information such as financial documents, letters from customers, inventory turnover reports, and sales reports. Information on the sales and profitability of product lines should also be available. Eventually it may possess a reasonably sophisticated management information system (MIS) which calls for systematic collection of data, which is then reported in a structured fashion.

Conducting Market Research

There are several steps in conducting market research. The first involves defining the problem and determining, as precisely as possible, the information required to address the problem. It may well be that the needed information is already available in-house (e.g., customer and supplier reports) or can be obtained from secondary sources such as local libraries or government offices. Most local libraries have excellent indexes to newspapers and periodicals. Most also have, at minimum, the current Statistics Canada publication, *Catalogue*, which provides toll-free numbers to regional reference centres. The local telephone directory can be a valuable source of information about competitors and suppliers in the trading area.

If primary research is required it is important to formulate specific goals, establish a schedule, and set up a budget. Since many small business owners know little of sampling procedures, questionnaire design or statistical analysis, and hence lack the skills to conduct surveys, one expedient solution is to approach the small business consulting unit of a local college or university. Under certain circumstances, the small organization may wish to engage a market research firm.

The Survey   If the small organization decides to proceed on its own, several elements must be considered:

- the sample population to be surveyed,
- the sampling method to be used,
- the survey method, and
- the analytical procedures to be used.

The Sample   The group to be surveyed is called the population; because of cost and time considerations, it is normal practice to survey a representative sample from the total population. The size of the sample is determined by cost and time considerations, and by the level of statistical accuracy required.

The Sampling Method   There are a number of methods of selecting a sample; the choice is often dictated by the sophistication and accuracy required by the study. The ideal approach is random sampling, whereby every member of the population has an equal chance of being selected. If the sample is selected on a geographical basis, city blocks, wards, or census tracts may be surveyed.

The Survey Method   The three most common survey methods are mail, telephone, and personal interview. The method selected will be influenced by the goals of the survey, accessibility of the sample population, and cost considerations. Mail surveys can cover a wide geographic area, and permit highly accurate sampling. However, this approach takes longer than the other two, and tends to produce the lowest response rate. Telephone surveys are ideal when information is needed quickly. The response rate and the amount of detailed information that can be collected is highest with personal interviews, but this method is costly, time-consuming, and requires a high level of expertise.

The Questionnaire   Once the sample and survey methods have been decided, a questionnaire is generally prepared. It is critical that the questions be clearly worded, and as brief as possible. The purpose of the survey should be described, and the least sensitive questions asked first. Questions may range from "Yes/No" questions, easy to understand and answer, through multiple choice, to evaluative questions that employ a scale (e.g., -3 to $+3$). Open-ended questions, in which the respondent gives her own views, are common in personal interviews. However, it is important to design the questionnaire so that it is easy to tabulate the data, and it is essential to pretest the questionnaire for ambiguities.

Analyzing and Interpreting Data   Depending on how the data will be used, totals, percentages, and perhaps cross-tabulations may serve the intended purpose. More sophisticated quantitative analysis will be beyond the in-house capability of most small businesses.

Test Markets

Many small enterprises make effective use of test marketing: the testing of new products on a small sample of potential consumers, or the evaluation of a promotional campaign, product, price or name. In many cases a representative body of opinion is solicited from a panel recruited for this purpose. The goal is to avoid a marketing disaster when the final launch of the product or campaign takes place. If the test market indicates failure, at least it is on a small scale and corrections can be made before entering the overall market.

Market Research Companies

Because market research draws on a number of sciences and requires expertise, it is sometimes wise to hire professionals. Many companies seem willing to risk $100 000 on a product but balk at spending $10 000 on research to find out whether it has a market. Research houses usually employ a collection of design, testing, and statistical experts who are equipped with state-of-the-art technology and processing equipment. They can design questionnaires, select samples, test questionnaires, conduct focus groups, and prepare a detailed set of recommendations. Costs vary, but even the most modest budget can afford to buy some expertise and advice.

Selected Readings

Aaker, David A. and George S. Day, *Marketing Research*. 2nd. ed. New York, N.Y.: Wiley, 1983.

Blake, Gary and Robert Bly, *How to Promote Your Own Business*. Scarborough, Ont.: Canadian Small Business Institute, 1990.

Byers, Gerald L. and Harry E. Teckert, *Marketing for Small Business: What It Is and Why You Need It*. Toronto, Ont: MacMillan, 1980.

Dean, Saneha L., *How to Advertise: A Handbook for Small Business*. Vancouver, B.C.: International Self-Counsel Press, 1985.

Gray, Ernest, *Profitable Methods for Small Business Advertising*. Toronto, Ont.: John Wiley & Sons Canada Limited, 1985.

Kao, Raymond, *Entrepreneurship and Enterprise Development*. Toronto, Ont: Holt, Rinehart and Winston of Canada Limited, 1989, pp. 177–193.

Kotler, Philip, Gordon McDougall, and Gary Armstrong, *Marketing*. Scarborough, Ont.: Prentice-Hall Canada, 1988.

Luck, David J. and Ronald S. Rubin, *Marketing Research*. 7th. ed. Scarborough, Ont.: Prentice-Hall Canada, 1987.

Monty, Vivienne, *The Canadian Small Business Handbook*, Toronto, Ont.: CCH Canada Limited, 1985, pp. 63–70.

Withers, Jean and Carol Vipperman, *Marketing Your Service; A Planning Guide for Small Business*. Vancouver, B.C.: International Self-Counsel Press Ltd, 1987.

11

Operations Management and The Small Business

Introduction

Operations management involves activities directly related to the production and delivery of products (goods and services) to the customer. To satisfy customer expectations the product must be of acceptable quality, delivered on time, and sold at a competitive price. To meet these demands, operations managers must control the process (people, equipment, and materials), the quality of inputs and outputs (quality control over materials, suppliers and process), the timing of outputs (arrival of materials, production scheduling, and delivery to the customer), while assuring that the cost of these activities allows the business to make a profit on the sale. Whether the business produces parts for the auto industry, drycleans clothes, or delivers food to a high school cafeteria, the basic elements of production/operations management are similar:

1. Managing equipment and processes,
2. Managing materials, and
3. Managing people.

Operations management is generally subdivided in this fashion as a matter of convenience. In reality, the firm must coordinate these different elements in order to deliver products that satisfy user needs through some mix of quality, cost effectiveness, and timeliness.

The product offered usually dictates the parameters within which the production system can be designed. However, the operations strategy chosen by the firm determines *how* the space within those parameters is exploited. Operations decisions are influenced by a combination of internal and external factors. The decision by a restaurant to offer a wide menu choice determines the type of equipment it will need, whether it will make or buy certain foods, and whether service will be its main focus.

The *production* process transforms inputs (equipment, labour, and materials) through processing (including assembly) into outputs to meet market needs. In most cases a variety of process designs can be used to structure the production/operations system. However, costs and cost control, quality and quality control, delivery, and in fact each of the dimensions of production, are inextricably linked. Decisions about one affect the others.

Managing the Equipment and the Process

Traditionally, the processes of production have been classified three ways: continuous process (oil refineries, chemical plants, and automobile assembly), job shop process (machine shop, furniture manufacture, and steel fabrication), and project management process (construction of large buildings, pipelines, and architectural design). But few processes fall neatly into one category or another. For example, in the fabrication of non-ferrous tubing, the early operations (extrusion and breakdown drawing) common to all products in the plant approximate a continuous process, while later operations (finish drawing, annealing, straightening, bending, and fabrication) are specific to the product and approximate job shop processing. The process design that best fits the needs of the business is determined by such factors as the volumes to be produced, the feasibility of storing the product, and the set-up costs associated with equipment changeovers.

Continuous Process

In continuous process operations all products in the plant proceed through a similar set of operations. Continuous processing requires large markets, few product variations, a balancing of line capacity, buffer inventories to smooth production flows, and preventive maintenance to minimize equipment breakdowns which can shut down the whole line.

Job Shop Process

The job shop process provides greater manufacturing flexibility and more customer oriented product variations than continuous process operations. This approach uses a variety of sequences to facilitate different product requirements, and is bound to customer requirements and short-term sales. A variety of in-process and finished goods inventories smooth production flows and customer deliveries.

Project Management

Characterized by large projects, each unique, this approach can be totally or partially customized to best meet the needs of the project. Project management is suitable for long time-horizons, unique operations, and specially designed cost systems.

Major investment in design, materials equipment, and human resources characterizes the project management process. Consulting firms, general contractors, and research labs are all examples of organizations that depend to a large degree on project work. Day-to-day controls are often nonmonetary (hours billed, yards of concrete used), and overall cost summaries are measured against estimates and bids. Scheduling is critical to insure that large investments in equipment and labour can be efficiently utilized. And finally, project management depends largely on subcontractors, and significant penalties are often imposed for late completion.

Each process is designed to serve or meet different needs. While the determination of process design is dictated to some extent by market choices, the choice of production process can also dictate the market conditions essential to make the system and the business work.

Despite these divisions, most production processes are mixed to some extent to allow for both the production and the cost benefits of continuous processing, and the market benefits of differentiation, which may require job shop processing. In some cases these processes are carried out in separate facilities that may even be separately owned. More and more, production processes, even those that are distinctly separate, are being managed as part of an integrated total, giving rise to new forms of design, quality control, transportation systems, just-in-time delivery, and shared information systems.

Production Management

Irrespective of the type of production process chosen, there are a number of activities that are common. In this section, rather than engaging in a comprehensive discussion of the production management function, we briefly outline the issues of particular significance to the small business person.

Product Design and Engineering

Most products are designed to perform specific functions. However, if they are to be successful in the marketplace, product designs must also consider consumer expectations that go beyond simple function. As well, product design must balance cost effectiveness with quality, safety, and process limitations. Product designers must consider such factors as environmental concerns, and customer desires for status and uniqueness, without losing sight of the need to make a profit. It is worth noting that while Henry Ford made his reputation by producing large numbers of low-cost, similarly designed cars, the assembly-line process he popularized has evolved to the point where it offers hundreds of option choices to meet the needs of the market, while retaining the benefits of a mass production process.

Consumer advocates, government intervention, and product liability suits are just a few of the factors that constrain product designers. Improved information and communications in the marketplace, as well as government regulations (such as engine performance in the auto industry and research and testing requirements in the food and drug industries) provide both guidelines and constraints for product designers.

Process Design

Process designers are constantly confronted with the need to balance production efficiency with the need for product differentiation. As well, significant parts of the process may be performed off-site by suppliers or subcontractors, making quality specifications, cost considerations and delivery requirements important aspects of process design.

Process designers must also compare the benefits of equipment and technology with the costs of inventories, product design restrictions, and market compromises in an effort to find a balance between product appeal and profitability. Often, the equation must also include new requirements to improve quality, reduce scrap and costs, and improve the environmental friendliness of the processes.

Equipment Maintenance and Replacement

Equipment management (acquiring, operating, maintaining, and replacing equipment) is an important function in the production/operations setting. New technologies may produce better quality, lower costs and quicker processing but often these must be traded off against higher maintenance, tighter scheduling, increased skill requirements, expensive training, and sophisticated control systems. The decision to buy particular equipment may have significant market, delivery, and inventory implications. Such changes can involve shiftwork, extensive use of overtime, and significantly increased layoffs if production outputs and market requirements are out of phase.

Capital budgeting analysis and review, quality requirements, maintenance costs, and capacity planning are all factors in managing equipment and processes. Competitive pressures, buyer expectations (cost, quality, and delivery) and labour costs all contribute significantly to equipment management decisions. Computer-aided design, computer-aided manufacturing, process control and other technologies make the management, maintenance, and replacement of equipment a complex subject.

Preventive Maintenance

As production processes become more integrated, both internally and externally, the importance of preventive maintenance increases. Increased inventories, high-cost shutdowns, and increased quality costs are some of the significant factors which give rise to this concern. Failure to deliver on time may influence buyers to look elsewhere for reliable supply.

Facility Location and Layout

The location decision involves a number of considerations: the cost of shipping raw materials vs the cost of shipping finished goods, labour supply, supplier services, and the cost of serviced land and facilities. With the increased emphasis on inventory control, just-in-time deliveries, and quality control, access to efficient and cost effective transportation systems may be essential. Local tax structures, and the availability of community services (schools, recreation facilities, housing, and shopping) may be critical in providing adequate labour skills.

With the rising costs of energy and labour, plant design and layout for efficient operations are important to the cost structure. Cutting down on handling and in-process storage minimizes inventory as well as quality and safety costs.

Quality Control

Early in its development, quality control was viewed by many production managers as another barrier to efficient production. Few saw it as a way to cut costs, improve performance, and provide increased customer satisfaction. Even quality control people, in their role as "process police," failed to grasp their potential. Often the seller's processes took precedence over the particular needs of the customer. Rarely was much attention given to the internal payoffs to be derived from quality control programs. Limited warranties, replacement goods, and repair were used in lieu of tight control. It was the Japanese (who borrowed the early QC techniques from North American producers) who recognized the cost savings that might accrue from detailed attention to quality design and production. Savings in inventory, delivery, repair, and replacement costs all improved as a result, along with customer satisfaction. The Japanese focus on quality and their management style made quality everyone's job. It has become ingrained in the process as much as the equipment, materials, and labour that go into producing the products of the firm. In an article on quality, Geoffrey Rowan noted that:

> "[defects] can cost a thousand times more to fix if the defective part makes it out the back door than if it is caught early. . . . That extra cost is compounded by customer dissatisfaction, potential loss of business, damage to reputation and damage to employee morale."[1]

Quality Circles

While statistical quality control and inspection continue to be a part of the quality control process, there has been a shift to making each employee responsible for the product he produces. The growth of quality circles—small teams of workers and supervisors which focus on improved quality and efficiency through improved communication and employee involvement—has become a cornerstone of production processes around the world.[2] As the small enterprise adds more employees, the quality circle option should be seriously considered, in order to give employees a greater stake in the outcome of their particular tasks.

Time Study and Production Standards

Establishing "standards," whether by time study, statistical sampling, or in some other fashion, provides the basis for a wide variety of operations activities.

Determining budgets, costs, delivery schedules, the need for new equipment, and the return on investment for prospective expansion or process improvement all require standards inputs. Performance to plan (units produced to units projected) uses production standards as a base measure and often acts as an integral activity within the planning/control cycle in each of the five phases of small business development.

Health and Safety

Accident prevention, safety in the work place and the health of the workforce have become important issues for businesses of all sizes. Rising health costs, as well as the costs of compensation for work place accidents, contribute to increased product costs. Job design, training, and a genuine interest in safety in the work place can affect costs both directly (through reduced compensation premiums and less time lost), and indirectly (through improved employee morale and efficiency).

Scheduling

In most operations the effective use of equipment, labour, and materials requires some significant attention to production scheduling. Efficient scheduling can minimize inventory costs, reduce equipment and labour inefficiency, and minimize late shipments.

On-time deliveries have traditionally been dependent on production planning, efficient scheduling, and the judicious use of in-process and finished goods inventories. The emergence of just-in-time (JIT) delivery has put pressure on efficient process management, since the customer expects delivery only as the items are required; the buyer also expects the resultant cost savings from this process to be reflected in lower supplier prices.

In an article on JIT Patricia Lush notes that:

Within the plant, just-in-time (JIT) production works to make your customer's first operation just a step away from your last operation . . . you don't produce the part until your customer is ready for it.

JIT eliminates the need for warehousing and saves hours of material handling time. Quality improves dramatically: less handling means less damage. Adding it all up, the savings can be enormous.

But the implementation is far from simple: it requires spending months— or years—reorganizing your operations. You need to know your systems thoroughly and to streamline them. You need to establish an effective program of preventive maintenance. And suppliers and customers need to talk to each other, regularly and at length.

JIT involves a complex combination of predicting what your needs will be and then firming the actual order closer and closer to the actual delivery date.[3]

Purchasing

In general, purchasing has been associated with the procurement of the right material, in the proper quantity, and at the best price. Hence, this activity was traditionally involved with prices and volume discounts on raw materials and some assembled parts. However, even in small organizations, purchasing departments now must deal with complex technologies and tight quality specifications, and delivery schedules. In some companies the purchasing function may be part of the organization's material control activities; in others, material control is part of the purchasing function. Either way, the tasks of material control include a list of complex activities.

1. Specifications: developing the material or product specifications essential to obtaining supplier bids. These could include specifications for design, quality, packaging, and delivery.
2. Sourcing: developing supply sources that can meet purchase specifications at competitive prices and deliver on schedule. Since many firms are reducing supplier numbers, the typical purchasing department must constantly evaluate the performance of its suppliers.
3. Inventory management (raw materials, in-process and finished goods): determining how much to buy, when to buy, and how much to stock as inventory.

The growing integration of supplier processes with buyer processes has made good supplier relations critical to the success of the firm's operations. Where alternate suppliers once provided price and delivery protection to the buyer, firms now often commit themselves to one or two reliable suppliers. Communications about costs, quality, and delivery are an integral part of the supplier relationship.

Industrial purchasers use a formula which balances the cost of purchasing (issuing the purchase order) with the costs of carrying the inventory (handling, storing, insuring, and maintenance). The point at which the order is placed (re-order point) is determined by supplier lead-times and projected use.

While the order quantities and order points can be easily calculated,[4] their effective use requires careful monitoring of product sales, supplier lead-times, changing production schedules, packaging and transportation constraints, and price changes. These changes will affect in-process and finished goods inventories, requiring a constant monitoring of the variables that affect material purchases and flows in the firm.

Retail Purchasing

Retail purchasers (buyers) face a variety of opportunities and problems in managing purchases and inventories. Buyers stocking a small retail food store can usually replace inventory quickly and to the extent that the goods are staples, orders can be based on past experience. A different problem arises where the buyer has an opportunity to buy items at substantial discounts for quantity orders. Here, purchasing must coordinate the buying process with sales, advertising, and promotion to insure that the goods move quickly and profitably. Inventory turnover, the allocation of shelf space and the coordination of weekly advertising are an integral part of the buying process.

At the other end of the spectrum, the buyer of fashion goods faces another kind of decision process. Often this buyer must order goods three to six months before they will be delivered. Overbuying can result in costly price reductions and sales discounts. Short ordering will also result in lost sales, since the designers and producers are busy producing items for the next selling season. In many cases retail buyers also sell the products, thereby integrating the purchase-sell process in an effort to minimize the risks often inherent in retail selling. In between these extremes, the buying process must be tailored to the retailer's needs.

Selected Readings

Schonberger, Richard J., "Some Observations on the Advantages and Implementation Issues of Just-in-time Production Systems," *Journal of Operations Management*, 3, no. 1 (November 1982), pp. 1–11.

Walleigh, R.C. "What's Your Excuse for Not Using J.I.T.?," *Harvard Business Review*, March–April 1986, pp. 38–54.

Endnotes

1. Geoffrey Rowan, "Quality Goes to the Top of Many Agendas," *Globe and Mail*, February 20, 1990, p. B1.

2. See Olga Crocker, Cyril Charney, and Johnny Sik Leung Chiu, *Quality Circles: A Guide to Participation and Productivity* (Toronto: Methuen, 1984).

3. Patricia Lush, "Just in Time Pays Off for Auto Sector," *Globe and Mail*, February 21, 1990, pp. B1 & B4.

4. The Economic Order Quantity (EOQ) formula is provided below:

$$EOQ = \sqrt{\frac{2AB}{c}}$$

where A = projected annual usage in dollars
      B = cost of issuing a purchase order in dollars
      c = annual carrying costs (including storage, handling, insurance, etc.) per unit.

For a concise comparison of the EOQ methodology to the just-in-time approach, see: R.J. Schonberger and M.J. Schniederhans, "Reinventing Inventory Control," *Interface*, May–June 1984, pp. 76–83.

12

Human Resource Management in the Small Organization

Introduction

This chapter reviews the three key areas of human resource management: managing change, managing people, and personnel management.

Implementing strategies at all levels of the organization, big or small, requires that people be organized in ways which permit the achievement of objectives. Also, competent people need to be recruited to fill key jobs in the organization, and these people must be motivated to achieve organization objectives. After all of the planning is complete, and the facilities and equipment are in place, the accomplishment of goals depends on people working effectively with people. This task, difficult at the best of times, becomes even more challenging when the organization is confronted with the ongoing change evident in most small businesses. Finding a workable balance between the economic needs of the firm and the social needs of its people is a major management concern. In small firms few jobs are easily defined, responsibilities are blurred, and often change to meet pressing needs, and most of the authority is held by the owner, at least until the firm reaches phase 5.

Managing Change

Managing change presents problems for all firms, large and small. First, the need for change is usually dictated by forces outside of the firm and resistance to these pressures often wastes valuable energy that could be used to facilitate change. Pressures from market, competition, government regulations, and consumer groups generate both opportunities for change and constraints on small business operations. Internally, change tends to create resistance, and if handled poorly can cause instability, insecurity, and confusion. Why does the resistance emerge? Hirschavitz[1] provides us with some insights:

- Change is perceived as a threat to economic security.
- Change introduces uncertainty and inconvenience.
- Individuals feel a sense of loss when required to give up familiar ways.
- Change is perceived as a threat to the competence or status of individuals.
- Change entails a shift in personal relationships.
- Change is unanticipated and/or unexplained.

Knowing in advance that change is necessary, and approaching the need to change in an open and informative manner can ease the resistance. Again, Hirschavitz provides some general guidelines for making change less threatening:

- Tell those involved the reasons for the change.
- Involve those affected in the design of the change process.
- Be especially sensitive to their needs for reassurance and recognition during this process.
- Provide help in learning new tasks, new roles and the establishment of new relationships.
- Be available for discussions and questions.
- Encourage discussion and participation in the change process.
- Be sensitive to the need for patience and clarification.
- Be positive about the change process.

Lawrence provides another perspective by suggesting that resistance to change should not be automatically regarded as an obstacle. "Instead it can be best thought of as a useful red flag—a signal that something is wrong. . . Therefore, when resistance appears, it is time to listen carefully to find out what the trouble is."[2]

Most managements, in their choice of product or service, tie the company to a changing environment. This choice dictates both the need for, and the rate of change faced by, the firm. The conflict between facilities that grow old and inefficient, equipment that quickly becomes obsolete and people who become comfortable with the status quo, makes the effective management of change extremely important to the success and survival of most companies. The discomfort precipitated by the prospect of change often arises when the business is striving to make a profit, since postponing change may be the only way to control costs in the short term. Unfortunately, the longer essential changes are delayed, the more costly and upsetting will be the process when it is finally undertaken.

Change takes several forms and each requires different responses. Gradual change permits a kind of internal evolution and adjustment; equipment can be replaced, facilities upgraded, and people retrained. Rapid change, on the other hand, requires the ability to move quickly, and the organization should be geared to meeting new challenges. People should be involved in the change process, making it an integral part of the small business strategy. Finally, turbulent or unpredictable change (the type often facing entrepreneurs) poses special problems. Planning is difficult, and the ability of the business organization to "re-invent itself" on short notice is essential.

Entrepreneurs face special problems in managing change since, for most, change and survival are inextricably linked. The benefits of rational organization, and the payoffs from some planning are viewed as less important than total commitment and unbounded enthusiasm. It is often said that others will tell the entrepreneur why it can't be done while he is busy doing it. But this commitment is not always shared by others in the entrepreneurial organization. If the organization is growing, the entrepreneurial manager will have to bridge the gaps and face the problems of uncertainty and resistance created by change.

Managing People

While the relationship between productivity and good relations with employees can be complex, the advantage of good human relations in the firm is widely recognized. At the very least, employees must have a firm grasp of what is expected of them, clearly understand company procedures, and have the opportunity to participate in the development of objectives. Beyond these givens, Gellerman notes that:

> The new approach to human relations does not consist of a set of techniques for handling people but of an analytic approach to understanding them. Precisely because the behaviour of people can be understood, and because the manager does not have to be a psychologist or a human relations expert to understand it, . . . human relations are manageable.[3]

For entrepreneurs and small business managers, this approach is useful, in that it is not necessarily tied to formal organizational structures, benefit packages, job security, and many of the other elements usually comprised in discussions about managing people.

Entrepreneurs and managers often make assumptions about employee interest and commitment based on their personal experience. And equally often they are surprised when these assumptions prove faulty. Building a strong organization requires a matrix of strengths to insure that the firm can meet the variety of challenges faced by all small businesses. Kao[4] suggests that the team needs three strengths for growth: entrepreneurial, technical, and administrative. Building an organization that ensures a balance among these strengths is not always easy, since ownership and ability to perform the variety of tasks necessary do not always coincide.

Organization Design

The organization structure is usually designed to provide an effective medium for coordinating the firm's skills and resources in meeting company objectives. While an efficient organizational structure is important to the success of the company, it is mainly a vehicle for action, and must be adapted both to withstand external pressures and to meet the internal human needs of the organization. In small companies the organization is not neatly defined. Authority and responsibility are not easily delineated or shared, and hence not easily portrayed. Job definitions, if they exist, must be flexible to meet changing situations, and the organization structure must facilitate effective informal communication. In many small companies performing the essential tasks at any given point in time requires a flexibility that defies many of the recommended approaches to personnel management. Perhaps the most important role of the organization in the entrepreneurial firm is that of ensuring communication and involvement. Too often, the benefits of formal structures are more than offset by their resistance to change that may be absolutely essential to the entrepreneur and the small business manager.

There are many questions to be answered when designing an organization. How should operations be divided? By product lines? By functions? By geographical locations? Lawrence and Lorsch suggest there is no definitive answer, and have developed a contingency theory of organization based on the following premises:

1. There is no one best way to organize, and
2. One form of organization may be better than another, depending upon the environmental factors and the firm's situation.[5]

Earlier, we discussed the importance of establishing goals and objectives for the business. Ensuring that these objectives are communicated to all members of the organization provides a starting point for organizational action. However, the structures and people must be capable of responding to these guidelines; the effectiveness of the company's employees can be very much dependent on a responsive organization structure that enables personnel to perform their duties efficiently by providing support, direction, and motivation.

What seems clear is that the organization cannot be developed in isolation. It will flow from the strategic choice and must reflect both the competitive pressures of the environment and the objectives of the firm. Most organization theorists deal with organization structures using terms such as responsibility, authority, and accountability, but these distinctions, at least in a formal sense, go beyond what is essential in small business. In small companies, where job descriptions not only encompass a wide variety of activities but can also change dramatically over time, the development of conventional structures can impede growth and effectiveness.

Leadership

The way managers choose to relate to the people they work with (their management style), has become an important facet of management effectiveness. McGregor[6] has suggested that management style is determined by the assumptions of the manager about human behaviour. He claimed that traditional management approaches frustrate the needs of most employees by assuming that:

1. They dislike work and will avoid it if at all possible.

2. This dislike for work requires that they be directed, controlled, and coerced by threats of punishment in order to get the effort required to achieve the organization's goals.

3. These individuals accept this treatment to avoid responsibility and gain security.

McGregor called this approach "Theory X" and suggested that managers who made these assumptions were underestimating and underutilizing the capacity of their subordinates. "Theory Y," he argued, was a more appropriate assessment of people. It was based on the opposite assumptions:

1. Expending physical and mental energy is a natural activity at both work and play;

2. People will practice self-direction and self-control to meet objectives to which they are committed;

3. Accepting objectives is a function of the rewards associated with achievement;

4. Under acceptable conditions people learn and accept responsibility;

5. A large part of the population can practice imagination and creativity in solving organizational problems; and

6. Many job situations underutilize the intellectual potential of the job holder.

McGregor's views were not presented as leadership strategies but rather as assumptions about people that might broaden the base for developing a management style.

Blake and Mouton suggest a range of five management styles based on the manager's concerns for task and people (see Fig. 12-1). These positions (1-1, 1-9, 5-5, 9-1, and 9-9) suggest a variety of management styles without offering an optimum model).[7] Other studies conclude that a successful style may depend on the social structure, the situation, the leader, and the followers.[8] Management beliefs and assumptions about coercion, threats, punishment, and direction may be inappropriate and counterproductive.[9] Such assumptions about what motivates employees can impede effective communication and focus employee attention on the reward-punishment system.

Typically, effective leaders are able to define goals that not only meet the needs of the organization but with which others in the organization can identify. The nature of leadership is to stimulate and direct the efforts of others in the

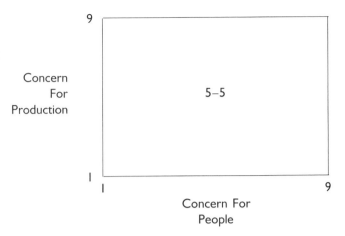

Figure 12-1

The Managerial Grid

Concern For Production

5–5

Concern For People

pursuit of organization objectives. There is an important distinction to be made between leadership and management. Leaders exhibit the ability to shape the attitudes and behaviour of others in both formal and informal situations; management involves the formal tasks of decision-making.

Communication

Management, in all organizations, must develop and maintain adequate communications to ensure that limited resources are used effectively. This is particularly true in small organizations where formal communications and the structural distinctions that support them are blurred or non-existent. Communication facilitates interaction, and establishes and maintains relationships in the organization. Communications are used to inform, to persuade, to initiate action, and to facilitate social interaction. Three major channels of communication exist in most organizations. These include: formal, informal, and implicit. Formal communications include the official or sanctioned channels. Informal channels consist of rumours, gossip, and speculation; these are often referred to as the "grapevine." Implicit channels include the folklore of the organization—its traditions and norms—and act more as an information filter than a channel.

The list below outlines the more common causes of ineffective communication by small business owners:

1. A failure to understand the backgrounds of those with whom they communicate.

2. A lack of appreciation for the atmosphere into which communications are placed.
3. A failure to understand the full range of meanings attached to the words, symbols, and actions that make up communications.
4. A failure to understand that people hear and see what they expect to hear and see.

There are several ways to alleviate these communication problems and managers need to be constantly aware of ways they can improve or prevent distortions in communications. These include:

1. Inviting and using feedback;
2. Using personal communications and informal channels as much as possible;
3. Confirming important oral messages in writing; and
4. Ensuring that management actions are consistent with management communications.

Motivation

People join organizations to satisfy needs and wants, and these needs and wants play a significant role in determining organizational behaviour. From the organization's point of view, role behaviour can be utilized to achieve objectives; for the individual, role behaviour satisfies personal needs. Small business managers must maintain a balance between these two goals.

Motivation in an organizational setting can be defined as the willingness of the individual to respond to the organization's requirements. Highly motivated employees are more likely to perform well in the organization, although there are a variety of factors that play a part in this relationship. And since needs and perceptions provide the basis for an individual's motivation, management attention is critical. Sutermeister[10] has observed that:

> A highly stable set of needs can be the standard on which perceptions are based . . . an individual may tend to perceive situations in a manner conducive to his needs and disregard anything that does not support his need fulfillment.

The proprietor has a vested interest in encouraging superior performance. Many small business owners promote a family atmosphere in their firms and at the same time tailor formal rewards to the specific employee. The latter can include bonuses, pay raises, or increased responsibility. As suggested in the earlier section on leadership, employees, particularly those at the managerial level, often welcome advancement and additional challenge.

Personalizing the reward system is a highly productive approach as long as these rewards are perceived by other employees to be fair. As the business grows, however, the distance between the owner and the workforce normally increases, and personal contact between the owner and employees may become infrequent. One response to this attenuation of the original relationship between employer and employees is to build a team approach into the company operating practices.

Incorporating an employee suggestion system with appropriate follow-up encourages reforms and innovations that can build both loyalty and profits. While perhaps not directly motivational, this device fosters satisfaction within the work place, which can contribute to low absenteeism and turnover. Rewards may be bestowed for ideas leading to improvements directly related to the firm's profitability. Because of its flexibility, the small organization has a distinct advantage over larger organizations that, if properly applied, can engender strong employee loyalty. This advantage can be brought to bear in the area of work-related fringe benefits such as flexible hours, job sharing, and job rotation. The factors and forces affecting behaviour are among the most important issues facing management and the organization.

Personnel Management

Introduction
The calibre of the small organization's personnel can enhance significantly both its efficiency and its image. Good customer relations, built up over time by friendly, efficient service, can furnish the business with a major competitive advantage. Further, the enterprise's reputation in its community may be determined to a large degree by the attitudes of its employees.

Personnel Plans and Policies
Prior to hiring a new employee, it is essential to define the task(s) to be performed, and the personal characteristics and expertise needed to do so. If the organization is entering a transition phase (phases 2 and 4), facing a

reorganization within phases 3 and 5, or starting up in phases 3 or 5, then it will be necessary to develop a personnel plan. This plan must include an organizational structure and a set of personnel policies. (Organizational structure was discussed earlier in this chapter.) All jobs within the firm must be defined within the context of the organizational structure, with clear lines of authority between levels. It is important that each employee report to only one supervisor. Also, the number of people for whom each supervisor is directly responsible (span of supervision) must be appropriate, given the complexity of the task, the experience of the subordinates, and the degree of coordination needed. After determining where each particular job fits within the organizational structure, the next step is to prepare a job specification, normally comprised of a job description, the associated personal requirements, the conditions of work, and salary range. The description explains briefly what tasks are to be performed, how, and why. Based on this information, the job requirements set out the skills, abilities, educational qualifications, and, when relevant, the physical characteristics needed to do the job. Depending on the size of the firm, the job specifications may be included in an employee policy manual. The job description can also be used in the performance appraisal process.

The next step is to develop personnel policies. The extent to which these are formalized and recorded will vary with the size of the organization; in a small firm with a closely knit workforce, it may not be necessary to develop a formal policy manual. To the extent that policies are codified, it is important to recognize that they may require revision in the course of operations. The primary purpose of the policy manual is to prevent ambiguity on important issues, thus avoiding misunderstanding and/or conflict in the work place. The manual also plays an important role in introducing new employees to company procedures, expectations, and benefits. It typically covers:

1. Duties, responsibilities, and reporting lines for the employees of the organization;

2. Working conditions, including hours of work, holiday entitlements, and overtime provisions;

3. Employee benefits such as employee discounts, bonuses, profit sharing, medical or dental insurance plans;

4. Payroll practices such as date of payment, time periods, and reviews of pay levels; and

5. Grievance procedures.

Hiring

Recruiting Once the personnel plan has been developed, the next step is to recruit potential employees. In the more evolved small business, some positions may be filled from within. If a current employee has the qualifications and interest, promoting from within is often the preferable course of action since it generally raises employee morale and acts as a motivator. If no suitable internal candidate exists, the small business may look to firms in the same industry for prospective employees in order to reduce training costs.

Quite often the entrepreneur is guilty of bringing acquaintances on board, in some cases even as partners, without first determining whether the individual really meets the particular needs of the business.

Screening Screening applicants for the job involves a number of key activities. For instance, the employment interview can be an important screening tool, particularly for jobs where the appearance, communication ability, and interpersonal skills of the employee are important. In the phase 5 organization the immediate supervisor would normally conduct the interview. Preset topics and guidelines for the discussion help to focus the interview and facilitate comparisons between applicants. An important element of the interview that is sometimes overlooked is an open period for questions from the candidate; the nature of these questions can provide some valuable insights into character. In addition, one is generally well advised to closely check business and personal references. Finally, the prospective employees may be asked to demonstrate proficiency in a particular skill, trade, or craft. Normally, however, the small business owner lacks the background to administer some of the sophisticated tests (e.g., vocational interest, aptitude, personality) used by personnel experts in larger organizations. Unless the tests are quite straightforward, the owner should consider retaining the services of a personnel agency.

Training

In most small businesses training is provided on the job. Where the tasks are fairly routine, another worker may be assigned to work closely with the new recruit. In some work situations (e.g., tax preparation service) the employee may be encouraged to take formal courses at an educational institution. Other businesses (e.g., real estate agencies) rely on periodic seminars conducted by outside experts.

Many small business employers designate a probationary period of three to six months, according to the time required to learn the job. Upon successful completion of the probationary period, the new recruit attains the status of a permanent employee, and may also receive a pay increase.

Remuneration

To some extent the perceived benefits of working in a small, and frequently more flexible, organization may compensate for the higher salary an employee might earn in a large organization, particularly if the employee shares some of the owner's enthusiasm for the business's prospects. By and large, however, the small business owner is under pressure to offer competitive salaries, and/or commissions (if applicable), and to provide at least basic fringe benefits (e.g., insurance plans). Some small business employers, more often at the phase 5 level, arrange profit-sharing agreements with key employees, or develop stock dividend or stock option plans. The latter are clearly most attractive if the stock is publicly traded. However, these programs are occasionally used by private companies as well.

Employee records in the small organization should include a file for each individual containing the employee's original application, work record, performance appraisal reports, and salary level, and will certainly entail payroll related records.

As an employer, the small business owner must make certain prescribed deductions, including income tax, and remit these as well as the employer's share of the Canada Pension Plan and Unemployment Insurance to Revenue Canada. Each province also requires that the employer pay Workers' Compensation to protect the earnings of employees who suffer permanent or temporary disablement due to a job-related accident or disease.

Unionization and the Small Organization

The majority of small businesses are not unionized. As the firm grows into a phase 5 organization, however, and as the employees become further removed from the owner, the possibility of the workforce becoming certified increases.

Small businesses in certain industries may be required to hire unionized employees. In this situation both the employer and the union must comply with the regulations of the provincial Labour Relations Act. Some typical aspects of collective bargaining that may affect the small business owner are the following:

- Both parties must meet and bargain in good faith. However, an employer does not have to reveal company data that he prefers to keep confidential;

- The collective agreement is required to deal with wages, benefits, and working conditions, and employers and unions are bound to the terms and conditions of the collective agreement;
- What is not specified as an employee right is deemed to be a management right;
- Disputes concerning interpretation of the agreement must be resolved by an arbitrator; and
- The owner cannot discriminate against an employee for union involvement.

Conclusion

Human resource management is a complex and critical small business function. Getting the most out of your people is of the utmost importance: few small enterprises can afford unproductive employees or inefficient personnel procedures. This chapter provides the small business manager with a broad overview of the various aspects of managing change, managing people, and personnel management. This discussion is intended to give the small business person the tools of human resource management that are most applicable to the small organization.

Selected Readings

Coward, Laurence E., *Mercer Handbook of Canadian Pension and Welfare Plans.* 8th ed. Don Mills, Ont.: C.C.H. Canada Ltd., 1984.

Dolan, Shimon L. and Randall S. Schuler, *Personnel and Human Resource Management in Canada.* New York: West Pub., 1987.

Drache, Arthur, "Life Insurance Can Save A Small Business," *The Financial Post*, April 2, 1990, p. 21.

Kindal, Alva F. and James Gatza, "Positive Program for Performance Appraisal," *Harvard Business Review*, 41 no. 6 (November–December 1963), pp. 153–167.

McClelland, David C., "An Advocate of Power," *International Management*, July 1975, pp. 27–29.

Mukhopadhyay, A.K. and S. Pendse, "Profit Sharing in Small Business: An Analysis of Risk and Incentive Efforts," *American Journal of Small Business*, 7, no. 4 (April–June, 1983), pp. 31–37.

Werther, William B., Keith Davis, Hermann F. Schwind, Hari Das, and Frederick C. Minor, Jr. *Canadian Personnel Management and Human Resources*. 2d. ed. Toronto: McGraw Hill Ryerson, 1985.

Endnotes

1. Ralph Hirschavitz, "The Human Side of Managing Transition," *Personnel*, 51, no. 3 (May–June, 1974), pp. 8–17.

2. Paul R. Lawrence, "How to Deal with Resistance to Change," *Harvard Business Review*, January–February 1969, pp. 4–12.

3. Saul W. Gellerman, *The Management of Human Relations* (New York, N.Y.: Holt, Rinehart and Winston, 1966), p. 3.

4. Raymond W. Y. Kao, *Small Business Management: A Strategic Emphasis*. (Toronto, Ontario: Holt Rinehart and Winston of Canada, Limited, 1981), p. 219.

5. Paul R. Lawrence and Jay W. Lorsch, *Organizational Environment: Managing Differentiation and Integration* (Boston, MA: Graduate School of Business, Harvard University, 1967). See also F.E. Kast and J.E. Rosenweig, *Contingency Views of Organization and Management* (Chicago, IL: Science Research Associates, 1973).

6. Douglas McGregor, *The Human Side of Enterprise* (New York, NY: McGraw-Hill Book Company, 1960), pp. 33–35, 45–49. See also W.J. Reddin, "The Tri-Dimensional Grid," *Training and Development Journal*, July 1964, wherein Reddin proposes a *theory z* dimension to management assumptions concerning motivation.

7. Robert R. Blake and Jane Mouton, *The New Managerial Grid* (Houston, TX: Gulf Publishing Company, 1978), p. 11.

8. See for example, P. Hershey and K.H. Blanchard, "Life Cycle Theory of Leadership," *Training and Development Journal*, May, 1969, pp. 26–34; Claude L. Graeff, "The Situational Leadership Theory: A Critical View," *Academy of Management Review*, 8, no. 2 (1983), pp. 285–91; F.E. Fiedler, *A Theory of Leadership Effectiveness* (New York, N.Y.: McGraw-Hill, 1967); Fredrick Hertzberg, "One More Time: How Do You Motivate Employees?" *Harvard Business Review*, January–February 1968, pp. 53–62.

9. Douglas McGregor, "An Uneasy Look at Performance Appraisal," *Harvard Business Review*, September–October 1972, pp. 133–34.

10. Robert A. Sutermeister, *People and Productivity* (New York, NY: McGraw-Hill, 1963).

13

Financial Management for the Small Business

Introduction

While many activities can fall within the definition of financial management, there is general agreement that the finance function concerns itself with the acquisition of funds and the allocation of these funds within the organization. Typical issues that must be addressed include:

- How much will it cost to operate the business this year?
- Should we be exploring cost reduction/new equipment/market expansion opportunities? What are the incremental costs/benefits of such opportunities?
- How much cash flow can we expect the company to generate in the near term? Over the long term?
- How much external financing will be needed? What are the alternative sources? Should we be utilizing a greater proportion of long-term funding? Are we taking on too much debt?

Financial management as a discipline encompasses a variety of issues. However, certain aspects of finance tend to be more crucial at the small business level. This chapter will outline the essential elements of finance from the small business perspective and provide a description of some of the basic techniques of financial management and how these are utilized as decision-making tools.

Assessing the Company's Financial Condition

Before giving consideration to which outside funding sources to approach, it is important, regardless of the company's phase of development, that the owner have a clear picture of the amount, nature, and timing of the required monies. This is achieved by developing a month-by-month cash-flow forecast using projected income statements and balance sheets (ideally for the next two or three years, depending on the volatility of the industry and the company's previous performance, if applicable). As discussed in Chapter 3, such forecasts play an integral role in the business planning process, inasmuch as managers are obliged to think through their future plans and deal with the financial implications of their business decisions. It is not the purpose of this text to serve as a primer in the area of financial statement preparation and interpretation. Rather, our focus is on the valuable role that various financial techniques can play in ensuring that the small business person has a clear understanding of how the business is performing and can make informed judgements with respect to fundamentals such as wage increases, new equipment purchases, or expanding inventories.

The Cash Budget

The cash-flow forecast or cash budget is one of the key financial planning tools. It is prepared as a supplement to the projected income statement (which indicates the level of expenses associated with the business's various operating and marketing activities), and balance sheet (which provides a picture of the asset investments required to support the expected revenues). The cash-flow forecast breaks these plans down into cash receipts and disbursements, thereby allowing one to anticipate cash shortfalls, reconsider the advisability of taking available discounts for early purchases of supplies and materials, determine the feasibility of putting down large cash payments on equipment and/or vehicle purchases, and classify funding needs as temporary or long term.

Figure 13-1 outlines a standard cash budget format; the disbursement items will, of course, vary from industry to industry. Despite the obvious simplicity of this document, it is only as good as the quality of the projections that underlie it. When *reviewed* on a monthly basis, the cash budget can act as

Figure 13-1

The Cash Budget

	Month											
	1	2	3	4	5	6	7	8	9	10	11	12

A.   Cash (beginning of month) (E + F)

Cash Inflows:
   Cash sales
   Collection of receivables
   Proceeds of capital loans

B.   Total Receipts

Cash Outflows:
   Material (cash payments)
   Accounts payable payments
   Wages (including owner)
   Delivery and automotive
   Tax payments
   Telephone
   Postage
   Supplies
   Professional fees
   Utilities
   Repairs & maintenance
   Advertising
   Commissions
   Employee benefits
   Rent
   Insurance premiums
   Interest
   Loan repayment

C.   Total Disbursements

D.   Monthly Cash Flow (B − C)

E.   Cumulative Cash Position (A + D)

F.   Required Bank Credit

a valuable warning device: for instance, as the cash position of the organization deteriorates, the owner can determine where the variations from plan are occurring (e.g., slow inventory turnover, a high proportion of credit sales, heavy overtime or subcontractor costs) and possibly take corrective action.

Financial Ratios

We assume that the reader has some basic grounding in computing financial ratios. More often than not, the small enterprise does not use these ratios effectively. The first step is to understand what these figures are measuring. Figure 13-2 provides a useful framework for categorizing the more common financial ratios.

Because small enterprises generally operate with limited liquidity, working capital is quite often of immediate concern. Inventories typically represent a high proportion of assets[1]; also, accounts receivable are often allowed to build up as the company uses a liberal credit policy to attract business. On the other side of the ledger, trade credit from suppliers, and, to a certain extent, bank lines of credit are used to support these investments in current assets. Dependable short-term funding sources are the lifeblood of most small organizations. This support enables the company to pay its ongoing obligations, such as rent, utilities, payroll and taxes, while inventories are converted into sales and credit sales are subsequently collected. The working capital ratios listed in Figure 13-2 will provide a picture of the company's ability to meet its current liabilities and more importantly, an assessment of how efficiently the different

Figure 13-2 Standard Financial Ratios	**I**	**Working Capital Ratios**	
		Current Ratio	Acid Test Ratio (Quick Ratio)
		Cash/Current Assets	Age of Accounts Receivable
		Inventory Turnover	Age of Accounts Payable
	II	**Measures of Financial Capacity**	
		Debt/Assets	Interest Coverage
		Debt/Equity	Cash-Flow Coverage
	III	**Profitability Ratios**	
		Gross Margin	Return on Assets
		Net Profit/Sales	Return on Equity

working-capital components are being managed. Figure 13-3 outlines the cash-flow cycle described above, focusing on working-capital items and excluding longer-term sources and uses of cash.

Financial capacity is the ability to borrow funds, and is directly linked to how well the small enterprise manages its cash-flow cycle. Companies that fail to monitor the number of days between the time that they must pay for goods and services and the time that they in turn are paid by their own customers often find themselves using outside credit extensively. Thus cash flow is hampered, interest costs escalate and financial capacity ratios deteriorate. In order to survive the early phases of development it is important to recognize the hazards of overstocking inventories or granting credit to questionable clients, given that the business can become overly dependent on short-term debt as a result. If accounts payable are being delayed, suppliers will eventually react by limiting shipments or insisting on C.O.D. terms. All lenders, whether they are providing long-term financing or simply trade credit, must see evidence of an adequate cushion of equity in the business as well as the ability to meet principal and interest commitments. The financial ratios listed in Figure 13-2 let the owner evaluate how the enterprise is performing along a number of dimensions. The value of these measures lies not so much in their significance to outsiders (e.g., lenders and prospective investors) as in their usefulness to the manager in determining what areas are in need of her attention.

Two final points are worth noting. First, the various ratios are interrelated, and inferior numbers in several ratios may in fact be attributed to a single facet of the business. Slow-moving inventories in a product line, for instance, can be responsible for a poor inventory turnover, greater need for short-term bank credit (which affects financial capacity), and reduced profitability due to

Figure 13-3

The Cash-Flow Cycle

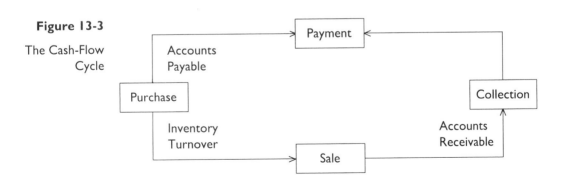

high interest costs. Second, the manager must have a reliable yardstick against which to compare these ratios. Ideally, industry averages should be the base for comparison, but for small businesses, many of which are privately held, such data are quite difficult to obtain. Historical data are generally a reliable gauge of current performance, assuming the company has not dramatically changed its product/market focus or adopted different accounting procedures (e.g., inventory costing or depreciation policies). The third possible frame of reference for evaluating financial ratios is comparison to budget. The essentials of budgeting will be examined in Chapter 14; however, a well formulated forecast of financial performance can often be the most appropriate vehicle for determining which ratios are satisfactory and which require improvement. By answering questions such as the following, the small business person can pinpoint specific areas of weakness, focus on those areas which are deemed crucial to the firm's survival, and perhaps even gain some insights into the effectiveness of the financial planning and budgeting process:

- Are gross margins at a reasonable level?
- Is our average investment in inventories too high or low, given our sales levels?
- Are the sales for each market area growing at the rate we anticipated?
- Is the company capable of generating the level of cash flow needed to service projected borrowings?

Managing Credit and Collections

Most working capital lenders routinely require an aged listing of the small business's accounts receivable. This report (for an example, see Figure 13-4) can be a useful monitoring device, given that the accounts are categorized according to age of invoice (less than 30 days, 30 to 60 days, 60 to 90 days, over 90 days) thus showing at a glance where the problems lie. Of course, collecting accounts receivable is never a pleasant task, but it tends to be an area that poorly run companies overlook.[2] This is one function where the adage "time is of the essence" directly applies; from a practical standpoint it is imperative that the company use *systematic* follow-up procedures—for example, a reminder notice mailed after 10 days past due, a phone call five to seven days later, a second phone call four or five days after that, followed by a personal visit to the customer if feasible. Once the delinquency has

Figure 13-4

Statement of accounts receivable

Date: _____

at _____ 19 _____

_____
(Name of Company)

Name of Debtors	Total (Omit Cents)	Current	31–60 Days	61–90 Days	Over 90 Days & Holdbacks	Remarks
1. Sub totals $						
2. *Aggregate of accounts under $ ____ $						
3. *Number of Accs. ____	No.	No.	No.	No.	No.	
4. TOTALS $						
Percentage	100%	%	%	%	%	
Total last statement dated ____ $						
DATE						
Percentage	100%	%	%	%	%	

The undersigned submits the foregoing to be a true statement of accounts receivable.

_____
Signature of Customer

Source: *Starting a Small Business in Ontario*, 1981 (Ministry of Industry & Tourism), p. 28.

exceeded a certain reasonable time period, then it is quite likely that the customer is taking advantage of your credit to satisfy other needs, or simply lacks the financial resources to meet your payment. Future dealings can be put on a C.O.D. basis; however, one still has to deal with the outstanding balance. At this stage the independent business person needs to consider more drastic steps—either legal action or assigning the account to a collection agency. While collection agencies are quite proficient at getting results, they charge from 20 to 50 percent of the amount collected.

Also, there must be clear responsibility for collections within the organization. In the early stages of development, the entrepreneur is of course oriented towards developing market opportunities and expanding volume. She cannot be expected to put much emphasis on collecting accounts receivable, which may conflict with her primary mission. However, as soon as the organization has a reasonable complement of full-time employees, it is important that one of them be assigned responsibility for credit and collections. In any enterprise, maximizing return on investment is a key financial objective; entrepreneurs have a tendency to focus their attention on the numerator and fail to recognize the importance of keeping the "asset base" (i.e., the investment) in line.

The nature of a company's collection task can to a certain degree be attributed to its credit policy. It is a fact of life for most small enterprises that the credit policy they adopt will be governed by the traditions of that industry. For instance, if most of its competitors sell on 2/15, net 60 terms, a new company will not consider C.O.D. or even net 30 terms. Some competitors provide a longer credit period in an attempt to attract more business, but such a decision should not be taken without a clear understanding of the extra administrative and collection efforts that can be expected to result.

Many small enterprises routinely offer discounts for early payment in an effort to accelerate collections, but this policy is not without cost. The following formula is used to determine the percentage cost associated with a particular discount policy.

$$(\text{Discount \%}) \times (365)/(\text{full term days—discount period})$$

For instance, terms of "3/10, net 45" will provide the buyer who takes advantage of the discount with an annual saving of 31.28 percent.

In addition to its credit terms and its approach to collections, the small business can also use credit standards as a means of establishing its overall credit policy. Setting a credit standard simply entails deciding the degree of risk the company is prepared to assume in granting trade credit to its customers. The tradeoff implicit in liberalizing one's credit policy is illustrated by the example in Figure 13-5. This decision will be influenced by factors such as the aggressiveness of the marketing effort and the financial health of the industry. The implementation of a minimum credit standard is achieved by assessing the financial status (i.e., "capacity to repay"), as well as the credit record (i.e., "willingness to repay") of buyers, and extending credit to those

	Benefits	Costs
Figure 13-5		
Analysis of a Change in Credit Policy	Contribution generated by new sales	Incremental bad debts
		Incremental credit Department expenses
		Incremental carrying costs–receivables
		Incremental carrying costs–other working capital (e.g., inventories)

Example

A small distribution company is evaluating the extension of credit to a new group of customers. Although these customers will provide $50,000 in additional sales, 10 percent of the sales are expected to be uncollectable. There will also be $4,000 in incremental administrative and collection expenses.

Variable production and marketing costs represent 68 percent of sales and the average collection period is 90 days. The company will be obliged to invest an additional $6,500 in other working capital to support the new sales volume.

Should the company extend credit to these customers, assuming that it has a 10 percent pre-tax opportunity cost?

Solution

Incremental Contribution: .32 × $50,000 =		$16,000
Less:		
Extra Bad Debt Expense: .10 × $50,000 =	$ 5,000	
Incremental Credit Dept. Expenses:	4,000	
Carrying Costs: New A/R ($50,000/365) × (90) × .10 =	1,233	
Extra Inventories (6,500 × .10) =	650	
Total Costs	$10,883	10,883
Net Benefit		**$ 5,117**

accounts which meet a minimum level of creditworthiness. The data base compiled by credit reporting agencies such as Dun & Bradstreet can act as a useful source of information for purposes of assessing a new customer's willingness to repay.

Credit policies should be constantly reviewed as conditions change. Credit decisions must be consistent with the credit standards that have been set, and collection procedures must ensure that overdue accounts do not go unattended, needlessly tying up badly needed capital.

Marginal Analysis

Two forms of marginal analysis are widely used, particularly in business startups, where product and service pricing and volume of output are critical factors. These are:

1. Breakeven analysis, and
2. Contribution analysis.

Breakeven Analysis A surprising number of business startups proceed with no clear idea of how many units have to be sold in order to break even. When launching a new enterprise, proposing an automation program, or contemplating the addition of a new product line or service, an important first step is to determine what constitutes a reasonable price and cost structure, and compute how many units will have to be sold to reach a breakeven level of operations. For example, with a price level of $25 per unit, variable unit production and selling costs of $14, and fixed overhead totalling $154 000 per year, the breakeven point would be 14 000 units:

$$\frac{\$154\,000}{(\$25-\$14)} = \frac{\$154\,000}{(\$11)} = 14\,000 \text{ units}$$

Breakeven analysis is a straightforward means of assessing the viability of a new venture. However, it is highly sensitive to the price, unit cost, and fixed cost estimates, and therefore should be used as only a first step. This analysis can serve as an effective screening mechanism. If, in the foregoing example, the total demand for this product or service was estimated at only 40 000 units and there were several competitors, then it is quite likely that the entrepreneur would abandon the idea, given the prospect of having to achieve a 35 percent market share to break even.

Contribution Analysis   The notion of classifying all costs as fixed or variable also underlies the technique known as contribution analysis. Thus, in the preceding example, $11 is the unit contribution: for every unit sold, $11 remains after deducting the direct costs of preparing that unit for sale. In contribution analysis, it is not the total cost ($25), but rather the $14 in direct costs, that is used for decision-making, since the latter are the only costs that disappear if that particular product or service is dropped.

By evaluating new proposals or even departmental performance on a contribution basis only the costs directly attributable to that proposal or department are taken into account. The utility of this process is based on the premise that for a short period, additional sales can be added profitably to normal sales volume, even at prices too low to cover a proportionate share of fixed overhead. Returning once again to our example, even if the unit variable costs were estimated at $24, the decision would be to proceed with the proposal since it still promises a positive contribution.

While contribution analysis can be a valuable financial tool, there are a number of caveats to bear in mind. The first is that no business can survive by making decisions that continually presume that 100 percent of fixed overhead will be borne by existing activities. Too often, growth is seen as the solution to all problems facing the small enterprise, even though the hazards of ill conceived growth are well documented. Unfortunately, marginal analysis can contribute to this emphasis on growth. Second, cost behaviour patterns are sufficiently complex in practice that it is somewhat misleading to neatly define every cost item as either fixed or variable. Over the long run, no costs are truly fixed; rather than being regarded as fixed *per se*, they can be thought of as overhead items that vary in the long run with the level of activity.[3]

Funding Sources for Small Business

This section addresses two of the major shortcomings of entrepreneurs in the area of financial management: inadequate knowledge of the available sources of funding and a failure to understand lenders' information requirements and the terms and conditions of commercial loans.

Small businesses, unlike their larger counterparts, generally raise their capital in an unorganized market and tend to rely heavily on debt. Bank financing plays a dominant role in the funding of most small enterprises, whether they are owner-operated, owner-managed or approaching a functional structure. Bank funds are supplemented by equity (supplied by the owner, friends and relatives, or venture capital firms) and various other forms of debt (including government lending programs, leasing arrangements, accounts receivable factoring, and loans from trust companies, specialized term lenders, finance companies, or insurance companies).

Differentiating Funding Needs and Finding the Right Source

Many entrepreneurs underestimate their external funding needs, particularly in the startup stage. As discussed earlier, this problem can be addressed through the preparation of a thorough business plan, and more specifically, a cash budget.

Confusion may also arise over the nature of the funding required. Outside funding can be subdivided into short-term financing and capital funding. The former includes trade credit from suppliers, and operating lines of credit, which are generally provided by chartered banks to cover inventory, accounts receivable, and other working-capital requirements. These credit lines fluctuate within a prescribed ceiling and are reviewed annually. Capital funding, on the other hand, pertains to a wide array of long-term uses, including the purchase of machinery, equipment, or vehicles, expansion of facilities or leasehold improvements, the acquisition of another company, or perhaps the buy-out of a partner or shareholder.

Ideally, one should strive to match the maturity of the funding with the nature of the expenditure. In this way,the equipment, property, etc. can pay for itself. However, many small business owners are guilty of abusing the availability of bank credit lines by using them for various long-term uses, thereby choking off short-term financial capacity and rendering the enterprise even more vulnerable to adverse economic trends. Capital expenditures should be funded by some combination of long-term debt (including financial leases) and equity derived either from earnings reinvested into the business or from additional investment by the owner. While the level of equity invested in the business is often seen by lenders as a true barometer of the owner's commitment, the entrepreneur naturally resists the sharing of control and profits that would be required by outside sources of equity. This dynamic helps to explain not only why small businesses are generally quite highly levered and particularly dependent on short term bank credit, but also why many owners choose not to have their company advance beyond a certain level; low financial capacity is every bit as restrictive to growth as low operating capacity.

The entrepreneur should try to appreciate the lender's perspective; small businesses, particularly those in the earlier phases of development, are perceived as risky propositions. Typically, collateral is inadequate, the company's planning and control systems are incomplete, and the costs of administering the loan are quite high in relation to the size of the loan. As a result, small business owners are generally expected to provide the lender with personal guarantees supported by pledges of personal assets such as real estate, automobiles, Canada Savings Bonds, or publicly traded securities.

Leasing Leasing can be an attractive means of acquiring vehicles, certain types of machinery, and even office equipment. For the business that must make large investments in fixed assets, leasing provides an opportunity to obtain these assets without having to make heavy cash outlays. In addition, many lease arrangements relieve the business owner from certain responsibilities by providing for insurance and maintenance. In certain industries where technological obsolescence can occur, leasing enables the user to avoid this risk, inasmuch as the final disposal value is of concern only to the lessor/owner. The interest cost implicit in a particular lease contract may be substantially less than the rate available on an equipment loan, simply because the leasing company will pass on to the lessee a portion of the tax savings it incurs by being able to depreciate the equipment or vehicles for tax purposes. For the startup operation that is generating little if any taxable income, the loss of the capital cost tax deduction is of little significance. Finally, since leasing packages are available from a wide array of manufacturers, commercial finance companies, term lending institutions, etc., the small business can use leasing as a means of gaining a secondary source of financing to supplement its bank loans.

Factoring Small manufacturers and wholesalers that wish to release cash tied up in receivables will sometimes turn to a factoring company. The function of these specialized institutions is to purchase accounts receivable and assume the risk of any subsequent bad debts. Also, the factor will serve as a credit department—investigating credit applications, invoicing clients, providing reporting services, and controlling collections. Factoring is relatively expensive, with the user paying a service fee of 1–2 percent of factored sales plus premium interest rates on any monies advanced before the account would normally be collected. However, the benefits to the small business can be substantial:

1. The entrepreneur can concentrate on the marketing and operating aspects of the business;
2. The company is relieved of slow-moving receivables and shielded from bad debt losses (note, however, that the factor will not agree to assume responsibility for all of the accounts); and
3. As sales increase, funding is available immediately and any loans from the factor will typically involve a higher lending ratio (for example 80 percent of approved receivables) than would be obtained through a chartered bank.

Factoring services are most appropriate for companies with a diversified client base, an average invoice amount of approximately $300, and a product that is not subject to repeated returns. While factoring does not enjoy a high profile in Canada, the advantages it offers to the growth oriented but cash-short small enterprise should be obvious.[4]

Government Programs   The array of government funding programs (both federal and provincial) can be overwhelming and the small business owner should have at least a general idea of which ones might apply to his operation. Figure 13-6 provides a representative list of government funding sources.

As noted in Chapter 1 (and elsewhere), the typical small business owner places a high value on independence and accordingly tends to be less than receptive to the idea of government grants, guarantees, or low interest loans. Others may be concerned about onerous documentation requirements, the relatively long time periods involved in obtaining government approval or the conditions upon which the funding might depend, such as the location of the business or creation of jobs.

Nonetheless, these programs have been put in place to fill perceived gaps in the financial system. For small enterprises, particularly those engaged in targeted activities such as manufacturing, tourism, or exports, government assistance presents a means of addressing the ever-present capital shortage problem.

Commercial Lenders: Information Requirements, Terms and Conditions
Small business lending has developed into a highly competitive market. Nonetheless, each of these institutions, whether a chartered bank, the Federal

Figure 13–6

Federal
Government
Assistance
Programs for
Small Business*

Federal Business Development Bank

Equity investments, loans, and/or loan guarantees to small enterprises that have been turned down by conventional lenders. Generally provides financing for purchase of land, buildings, and equipment, but working capital loans are also available. Very few loans are granted for amounts below $15,000. Interest rates may be slightly higher than those of chartered banks.

Small Business Loans Act

Loans up to $100,000 for the purchase of land or equipment or the modernization or purchase of buildings are provided by approved lenders (banks and certain trust companies, credit unions, caisses populaires, and insurance companies), and guaranteed by the Department of Finance. Working capital loans are excluded and the business's sales must not exceed $2 million. The interest rate is prime plus 1 percent and the maximum repayment term is 10 years.

Farm Credit Corporation

Low rate, long-term mortgage loans are provided to individual farmers and farming corporations to finance as much as 100 percent of land, equipment, or livestock purchases, permanent improvements, or refinancing programs.

Export Development Corporation

Supports export business through credit insurance, loans to foreign buyers, loan guarantees on behalf of foreign buyers, and purchases of promissory notes issued to Canadian exporters. The exported goods must have a Canadian content of at least 60 percent.

Industrial Research Assistance Program

Grants are made available to companies with fewer than 200 employees to finance projects that involve industrial research and show technological promise.

---

* For a complete listing of federally sponsored programs for small business, see: *ABC: Assistance to Business in Canada* (Ottawa: Ministry of State for Economic Development, 1986). In addition, each province offers several programs intended to assist small businesses to overcome their immediate financing hurdles, and facilitate easier access to private sources of capital.

Business Development Bank, an insurance company, a factoring company, or a specialized term lender, have fairly rigorous documentation requirements. The small business owner's chances of successfully obtaining the outside financing she requires is greatly enhanced if the following information is made available:

• The management background of the owners;

- Financial statements for the past two years and a projected income statement and monthly cash budget for the ensuing year;
- Details of any present debt obligations;
- Listing of major fixed assets, including age, original price, and resale value;
- Schedule of unfilled orders;
- Aged listing of accounts receivable (see Figure 13-4);
- Details of owner's life insurance coverage; and
- Description of internal reporting procedures (e.g., what reports are prepared and who receives them).

Once the financing is in place, few independent business owners take the time to keep their lender(s) informed of important developments. Every attempt should be made to institute the practice of providing standard financial reports to one's major creditors on a regular basis. Many organizations have been placed in a precarious financial position by lenders who, without an understanding of the company's situation and lacking up-to-date information on its current status, have taken precipitous action. This may range from refusing to honour a cheque presented by a key supplier, to demanding full repayment of outstanding loans or repossessing security.

It is useful for the entrepreneur to have a general understanding of the loan conditions that typically apply to small businesses. In addition to personal guarantees, the lender will generally require an assignment of fire and life insurance policies. If the loan is for working capital purposes, all receivables and inventories will be taken as collateral. Capital loans supported by fixed assets can be secured by chattel mortgages, the assignment of conditional sales contracts, realty mortgages, debentures, or the assignment of leasehold interest (if the borrower rents its premises).

In comparing different lending institutions, the small business owner is well advised to compare fee structures and payment terms. With respect to the latter, some lenders are prepared to provide longer amortization periods than others, allow for fairly flexible prepayment privileges, or schedule monthly principal payments according to the seasonality of the business. As far as fees are concerned, the small business owner must ensure that the combination of "commitment," "standby," "administration," or "negotiation" fees proposed by the lender are warranted and in line with the financial marketplace.

Finally, most term loans will include a set of "restrictive covenants" designed to protect the interest of the lender. These clauses are legally binding and may stipulate a minimum level of working capital, a limit on capital expenditures, the prohibition of any additional long-term debt from other sources, the retention of voting control by present owners(s), or a limit on dividends and/or management salaries. While the owner enjoys very little bargaining power, he must be satisfied that the proposed covenants will not compromise his ability to run the operation effectively.

The Venture Capital Market

The venture capital market provides funding to enterprises that offer higher than average growth potential, but do not qualify for conventional financing. Traditionally, venture capital funding has implied the purchase of common stock of a company whose shares are not publicly traded. Venture capital is quite often used in pre-startup or startup situations where the owner is prepared to give up a minority interest in the company in order to test the feasibility of the business idea or get the business up and running.

Venture capital activity over the years has broadened to encompass a wide range of scenarios where the business's required equity base exceeds the funding that can be supplied by the owner, and/or reinvested earnings:

- Development needs—the company is close to its breakeven point and is on the verge of generating profits but needs a cash infusion to support growth;
- Expansions—additional equity funding is required to allow for expansion into new markets or products;
- Turnarounds; and
- Buy-outs—the business may be well established but there is a new group of owners whose personal investment is only a small portion of the purchase price.

The common thread running through all of these situations is the fact that the probability of losses tends to be quite high and conventional commercial loan packages, whether arranged through a chartered bank, trust company, credit union/caisse populaire, finance company or government agency (such as the Federal Business Development Bank), are simply not appropriate. Not only are the forecasts of near-term cash flows inadequate to cover a standard repayment schedule, but also the level of assets is generally too low to provide the normal collateral requirements.

Venture capital should not be perceived as a convenient solution for the undercapitalized company. Even though the sources of venture capital are highly fragmented, as a group they are quite selective, only approving in the order of 2 percent of their applicants. It is not uncommon for a venture capitalist to specialize by industry, geographic location, or life-cycle stage.[5] Some are oriented towards high technology companies; others have a preference for buy-outs or turnarounds; and still others will only consider proposals exceeding the $1-million level.

In order to justify the degree of risk inherent in this market, these investors must see evidence of a certain distinctive competence, be it a technological edge, a pricing advantage attributable to production efficiencies, or perhaps access to an untapped market segment. Most venture capitalists are quick to point out that the quality of management is the key ingredient in any venture capital deal. A highly committed management team possessing diversified skills and familiar with the market in question is often more important than the product or service *per se*.

Another important consideration for the small business person is the ongoing reporting requirements of the venture capitalist and its subsequent involvement in the affairs of the company. It is not unusual for the venture capital firm to require quarterly financial statements, regular cash-flow forecasts and other budget information, and representation on the company's board of directors. In this way the investment can be closely monitored and the venture capitalist can participate in major decisions such as hiring, dividend policy, financing plans, and spending programs. While some entrepreneurs construe this as interference, many small enterprises have used this outside expertise quite effectively in areas such as the implementation of financial controls and the evaluation of new product ideas.

Venture capital funding may entail a wide range of financial arrangements, from a convertible debt or preferred stock vehicle supplemented by an option to purchase some of the company's common stock, to a straight purchase of a majority common share holding; however, it is still difficult to obtain venture capital for an amount less than $200 000, or greater than $2 million.

Given that the Canadian venture capital market is not particularly well developed, that few small businesses meet the requirements of venture capitalists, and that some which could qualify have no interest in sharing authority with outsiders, it is not surprising that venture capital plays only a minor role in the funding of small enterprises.

Reorganization and Liquidation

Certainly the notion of being prepared for and possibly guiding the small business through a receivership/reorganization or bankruptcy is anathema to the entrepreneur. Nonetheless, as outlined in Chapter 1, the casualty rates in this sector continue to be quite high. Also, small business owners that find their company in serious financial difficulty are seldom aware of the alternative actions they can take or the basic rights and obligations of borrowers and lenders (including suppliers of trade credit).

It is not our purpose to address the underlying causes of business failure; the text as a whole offers insights into how the hazards that confront small enterprises in the various phases of development might be avoided. Rather, what follows is an outline of the directions in which the faltering business can proceed, whether on its own initiative or at the behest of its creditors.

The Basic Dilemma: Liquidate or Reorganize?

There are varying degrees of financial distress and winding up the business may not be the most appropriate response.

Too many small business owners allow their organizations to be slowly overcome by financial problems, and wait for their creditors to dictate a course of action.

Figure 13-7 outlines the basic options available to a small business that is unable, at least temporarily, to cover its financial commitments. It is clear from this table that it is the company's future prospects that determine how the organization should be dealt with.

The balance of the chapter is devoted to an elaboration of the Figure 13-7 framework. Our discussion is designed to enhance the small business owner's ability to cope with a period of financial strain. From another perspective, an understanding of the fundamentals of bankruptcy and reorganization is quite valuable to the company that has extended trade credit to a failing enterprise.

Procedures Under the Bankruptcy Act

Insolvency pertains to a *financial* condition: the inability to meet maturing obligations as they fall due, or alternatively, when total liabilities exceed the value of realizable assets. Bankruptcy describes a *legal* condition and a

Figure 13-7

Liquidation vs. Reorganization (Comparative Issues)

Future Prospects	Strategy	Alternatives
Strong–financial problems deemed to be temporary	Financial reorganization	i) *Voluntary Settlement*–Persuade lenders to refinance ii) *Formal Proposal*–under section 32 of the Bankruptcy Act iii) *Receiver/ Manager*–operates company with the objective of selling as a going concern
Questionable–the most realistic scenario calls for continued marginal performance and ultimately failure	Liquidate assets	i) *Petitioned* into bankruptcy by creditors under section 25 of the Bankruptcy Act ii) *Voluntary Assignment* by debtor company. iii) *Receivership* (as empowered by a specific loan agreement) for purpose of liquidating assets iv) *Private Liquidation*

company can be insolvent without necessarily being bankrupt—these two terms are not interchangeable.

According to the terms of the Bankruptcy Act, creditors can petition the court to declare the debtor company bankrupt. In order for the petition to succeed, the creditors must prove that an "act of bankruptcy" was committed within the past six months.[6] On this basis, a receiving order is obtained, which permits the transfer of the company's assets to a court-appointed trustee. It is the duty of this licensed trustee to dispose of these assets for the benefit of the creditors. The claims of any "secured creditors' must be settled first, from the proceeds of the disposal of the encumbered assets. If there is any shortfall, the balance of the claim is classified as unsecured debt.

The Bankruptcy Act also provides for another, less expensive approach to liquidation: the voluntary assignment of assets by the insolvent company to a trustee, who has the same rights and responsibilities as outlined above. In certain instances, small enterprises that are unable to make satisfactory arrangements with their creditors will elect to file for an authorized assignment, rather than wait to be petitioned into bankruptcy. It is interesting to note that since this procedure is not under the jurisdiction of the courts, the trustee has somewhat greater flexibility in liquidating the assets. In addition, the trustee can commence his duties as soon as the debtor files its documents with the Official Receiver; involuntary bankruptcies, on the other hand, are more cumbersome and time consuming.[7] There is an important tradeoff here, insofar as bankruptcy proceedings carried out under a receiving order ("involuntary") provide the borrower with a full release from any liability and also protect the creditors from fraud.

As outlined in Figure 13-7, the Bankruptcy Act also affords protection for the financially strapped business that wishes to revise its debt commitments in an effort to avoid liquidation. In this situation, the insolvent business and a licenced trustee jointly draft a proposal for financial reorganization, which is submitted to the creditors. The specific arrangement may, for example, entail lower rates of interest, a longer amortization period and/or the forgiveness of a portion of the indebtedness. If the proposal is accepted by a least 51 percent of the creditors, representing at least 75 percent of the value of the claims, it is presented to the court, and if approved, *all* creditors are bound to the agreement.

In order to support such proposals, the creditor's evaluation of the small business must indicate that the value of the enterprise as a going concern exceeds its liquidation value. In the event that the creditors withhold their endorsement, the company is automatically declared bankrupt.

Other Courses of Action

A more direct way for the insolvent enterprise to stave off bankruptcy is through a voluntary settlement.

The process is similar to the proposal alternative already described, in that a plan is submitted to the creditors which might entail full payment over an extended time period (in which case the creditors will often demand tighter controls on the operation) or even a *pro rata* cash settlement.

While voluntary settlements allow the different parties to avoid legal proceedings, they depend on the cooperation of *all* the creditors. Should the small business owner find that he cannot obtain the required consensus, or should the company's future prospects deteriorate, the failure of the organization is likely.

To avoid the costs and formalities of a protracted bankruptcy proceeding, the business owner can consider a "private liquidation." Here, the company's assets are simply assigned to an administrator or agent who undertakes to dispose of them (possibly via an auction) and distribute the proceeds to the creditors. Again, this alternative is subject to the approval of all creditors and is generally only appropriate for those businesses with easily disposable assets and a limited number of lenders.

The final area to be addressed concerns receiverships. These can apply when a borrower defaults under a security instrument (such as a debenture or general security agreement), which empowers the secured creditor to appoint a receiver to take possession of the company's assets.[8] However, unlike the bankruptcy procedures discussed in the previous section, title to the assets remains with the company. Also, a trustee operating under the Bankruptcy Act rarely oversees the continued operation of the business, whereas a receivership proceeding can entail the hiring of a receiver-manager. The secured creditor will pursue this option when the business is considered worth salvaging. By definition, the receiver-manager assumes responsibility for the day-to-day activities of the company—supervising employees, maintaining links with suppliers and customers, completing work-in-process, and honouring existing contracts—while taking the corrective actions (reorganization of staff, refinement of internal control and information systems, renegotiation of loan terms) that are deemed necessary to ensure the organization's long-term survival. The objective is to sell the company as a going concern, which usually maximizes the selling price.

Alternatively, should the firm's financial difficulties prove to be insurmountable, a receiver will be appointed to sell off the business's assets in an orderly fashion. The role of the receiver in this instance would be quite similar to that of the licenced trustee operating under a receiving order or an authorized assignment; however, the receiver is not bound by a set of legal regulations and reports to only one secured creditor.

Summary

Many small business people find that financing the operation is one of their most difficult problems. While this chapter provides some insights into the various sources of small business funding, its primary theme is that financing problems are quite often only a symptom of more fundamental problems elsewhere in the organization: slow inventory turnover, improper pricing practices, poor credit/collection procedures. One needs to address these areas first, in order to ensure that the company's external funding needs are indeed warranted.

This chapter also provides some useful insights into the liquidation and reorganization area. If the activities of the company are well planned, its resources are organized in an efficient manner, management provides effective direction, and appropriate control mechanisms are in place, then the chances of financial distress should be minimal. Nonetheless, the inescapable fact is that the failure rates for small enterprises are inordinately high. As we have suggested, insolvency need not lead to shutting down the business. A clear understanding of the options presented here can be instrumental in dealing with the harsh realities of a small business insolvency.

Selected Readings

Buerger, James E. and Thomas A. Ulrich, "What's Important to a Small Business in Selecting a Financial Institution," *Journal of Commercial Bank Lending* (October 1986), pp. 3–9.

Del Grande, M. "Factoring, a Misunderstood Source of Financing," *CA Magazine*, June 1980, pp. 37–40.

Dipchand, Cecil R. and Roy E. George, "The Cost of Bankruptcy," *CA Magazine*, 110 (July 1977), pp. 28–30.

Equipment Leasing for Canadian Business, No. 5, RoyNat, Inc.

Fells, George, "Venture Capital in Canada—A Ten-Year Review," *Business Quarterly*, Spring 1984, pp. 70–77.

Gibson, Mary, "Financing for your Small Business," Part I, *CA Magazine*, 118, no. 2 (February 1985), 28–32; and Part II, *CA Magazine*, 118, no. 3 (March 1985), pp. 44–53.

Horsley, David, *et al*, *Government Assistance Programs in Canada*. Scarborough, Ont.: Canadian Small Business Institute, 1990.

Margel, Simon, *Successful Banking for Small Business*. Toronto, Ont.: Methuen Publications, 1984.

Partridge, J., "Venture Capital," *Canadian Business*, June, 1983, pp. 66–87.

Richards, V.D., and E.J. Laughlin, "A Cash Conversion Approach to Liquidity Analysis," *Financial Management*, Spring 1980, pp. 32–38.

The Money Comes in . . . Managing Credit and Receivables, No. 13, "Successful Business Management" Series. Toronto, Ont.: Hume Publishing Company Limited, 1986.

White, Jerry S., *Government Assistance for Canadian Business*. Don Mills, Ont.: Richard De Boo Publishers (loose leaf series updated 6 times per year).

Wichmann, Henry Jr. and Harold M. Nix, "Cost-Volume-Profit Analysis for Small Retailers and Service Businesses," *Cost and Management*, 58, no. 3 (May–June 1984), pp. 31–35.

Williamson, Iain, *Successful Small Business Financing in Canada*. Toronto, Ont.: Productive Publications, 1988.

Wilson, Bernard R., "Accentuate the Positive—The Role of the Licensed Trustee," ed. Paul Evans, *CA Magazine*, January 1980, pp. 58–59.

———. "Pass to the Receiver," *Canadian Banker & I.C.B. Review*, 87 (April 1980), pp. 18–20.

———. "Spotting the Danger Signals," *Canadian Banker & I.C.B. Review*, 86 (October 1979), pp. 30–33.

Endnotes

1. According to a study of small business financial data from 1975–1977 (see Larry Wynant, James Hatch and Mary Jane Grant, *Chartered Bank Financing of Small Business in Canada*, London, Ontario: School of Business, University of Western Ontario, 1982), for companies with total assets of less than $500,000 inventories represented 23.5 percent of assets, while companies in the $500,000 to $5 million range held on average 26.9 percent of their assets in the form of inventories.

2. Herbert N. Woodward, "Management Strategies for Small Companies," *Harvard Business Review* Jan–Feb. 1976, 54, no. 1, p. 119.

3. *Ibid.*, p. 114.

4. For a detailed discussion of factoring, see Roland Horst and J. Humphrey, "Note Factoring in Canada," University of Western Ontario, School of Business Administration, London, Ontario.

5. In Canada there are upwards of 600 venture capital organizations. Some of these (e.g., Innocan, Inc., Charterhouse Canada Ltd., and Helix Investments Ltd.) are private independents, while others (such as Scotia Capital Corp. Ltd., and Royal Bank Venture Capital Ltd.) are subsidiaries of financial institutions. In addition, a growing number of large corporations, including General Motors of Canada and Northern Telecom Ltd., have taken a position in this market, either directly or by forming limited partnerships with others. Finally, the federal government is active in this area primarily through the Federal

Business Development Bank, while provincial governments have established a variety of venture capital pools (Alberta's Vencap Equities Ltd., for example), as well as small business investment corporations designed to channel funds from various investors into eligible small businesses requiring start up or expansion equity. Ontario's Small Business Development Corporations Program and Quebec's *Société de placement dans l'entreprise Québécoise* are examples of the latter.

6. The most common of these are:
   - failure to meet maturing obligations;
   - notice to creditor(s) of suspension of payments;
   - fraudulent conveyance of assets to a third party;
   - failure to redeem goods repossessed under an execution order.

   For a complete listing of the acts of bankruptcy as set out in the legislation, see J.E. Smyth and D.A. Soberman, *The Law and Business Administration in Canada* (Scarborough: Prentice-Hall Canada Ltd., 1976), pp. 712–713.

7. Pending the official declaration of the company's bankruptcy through the issuance of a receiving order, the creditors usually request the courts appoint an *interim receiver* to manage the company's receipts and disbursements. Once the creditor's petition has been approved by the courts, a trustee, licenced by the Superintendent of Bankruptcy, takes control of the company. Beyond this point, the process (convening meetings of the creditors, proving their claims, appointing a board of inspectors, selling assets and distributing proceeds) is the same under an involuntary bankruptcy as it is for one initiated by the borrower.

8. While the creditor's security documentation may provide for the appointment of a "receiver" or "receiver-manager," the borrower has the right to contest this appointment. By resisting the installation of a private receiver, the borrower in effect forces the creditor to institute legal action in order to obtain a court order. If the insolvent firm is unsuccessful in its attempts to prevent issuance of the court order, then a court-appointed receiver is put in place.

   One of the benefits of this type of appointment is that, as with a receiving order issued under bankruptcy law, lawsuits cannot be launched against the borrower without the permission of the court.

CHAPTER

14

The Accounting Function and Small Business

Introduction

In general, the accounting function encompasses the recording, classifying and summarizing of the company's transactions. We assume that the reader is familiar with the accounting cycle, wherein a *journal* is used to list transactions in chronological order, these data are classified by being posted to the appropriate *ledger* (account), account balances are totalled periodically to ensure they are collectively in balance, and are used to produce end of period financial statements.

If a business is to run smoothly, its accounting system must provide managers with information that is relevant for their various needs. In a small enterprise these needs may be as general as "How much revenue was generated in each of the last two quarters?" or as specific as: "How much of the advertising budget remains unspent?" or "Was a particular invoice in fact paid within the prescribed discount period?"

Purposes

There are three general uses for accounting information:

1. To enable outside parties such as creditors, suppliers, and tax officials to interpret and analyze the activities of the company;
2. To plan and control routine operations; and
3. To support special decisions (e.g., capital expenditures, or to produce or purchase a particular component).[1]

Responsibility for developing documents and procedures to facilitate the firm's record keeping is normally handed over to a public accountant. Nonetheless, it is important that the small business person familiarize herself with the fundamentals of accounting so that she can contribute to the process. For most small businesses the success or failure of the "accounting system" is a function of the degree to which it has been designed to meet company and management needs. If this is to happen, the small business manager must take an active interest in this aspect of the business.

The accounting system should be designed to address such concerns as:

- Is the information being provided in an easily used form and will I have it on time?
- Does the system produce too much paper, thus contributing to information overload?
- Are there mechanisms in place to ensure that transactions are recorded correctly?
- Do the procedures provide for the proper authorization of certain transactions (e.g., granting a higher credit limit, approving salesforce travel expenses)?

Unfortunately, the use of accounting information within the small enterprise is generally very limited; many entrepreneurs use their accounting system only to respond to the needs of outsiders. However, few small businesses can afford to ignore the other uses of accounting information; indeed, in the interests of improved decision-making, and better control of the business, it is incumbent on small business managers to clearly define their information needs and insist that their particular system of reports and procedures delivers accordingly.

While financial data for external usage must be prepared according to generally accepted accounting principles[2], the rules governing accounting data used within the company (i.e., Management Accounting) are quite flexible, dictated largely by the particular needs of the business.

It should be evident that the planning and controlling functions, which are emphasized throughout this text, are very much dependent on the internal accounting system. Moreover, these planning and controlling activities should manifest themselves in an annual budget, which acts as a blueprint for the operations for the upcoming year.

The Budgeting Process

The Purpose of Budgeting

The budget quantifies the company's planning activities and, if properly implemented, gives planning the priority and sense of urgency that might otherwise be lacking. Certainly, budgeting should not be regarded solely as an accounting activity. It is the function of the accounting system, however, to assemble and organize the data that emerge from the budgeting process. As the enterprise grows, it becomes necessary for each of its units (personnel, sales, engineering, finance and administration, etc.) to prepare individual budgets in accordance with their estimated level of activity. While this exercise demands a certain commitment of time and effort on the part of the key people in the organization, the resultant benefits can be crucial to the well-being of the enterprise. These benefits include:

1. *Formalization of planning*: One is forced to look ahead and develop a realistic projection of future expectations (revenues, expenses, asset needs, etc.). This process entails an examination of external factors and enables the organization to anticipate potential problem areas.

2. *Communication of long-term objectives and coordination of internal activities*: Annual budget meetings allow the organization as a whole to reassess its overall direction and, by clarifying sub-goals, ensure that there is synchronization between the different activities and units. Of course, this particular aspect of budgeting is of greatest significance to the phase 4 or 5 company.

3. *Motivation*: If staff members participate in setting performance targets for their particular activities, they will be motivated to achieve

those goals and at the same time contribute to the overall objectives of the company.

4. *Control*: Budget figures provide a useful yardstick against which performance (department, project, individual) can be measured. It is essential to have explicit, agreed upon standards established in advance for each activity; otherwise actual results lack meaning and the utility of the budget as a feedback mechanism is compromised. Once the company implements its plans, a well-conceived budget acts as a control instrument, facilitating the comparison of "actual to standard" and enabling management to isolate any problem areas and take corrective action, if necessary. Small businesses sometimes find that due to unforeseen circumstances—for instance, a strike or lockout at a key supplier or a new branch-opening by a direct competitor—the original plan must be adjusted.

Implementing the Budget

Budgets are perceived by many as a threat and it is incumbent on the manager to avoid some of the common pitfalls associated with the budgeting process.[3] These include a failure to involve key individuals, the use of unduly complex procedures, and inadequate communication during the initial design of the budgeting system. Furthermore, employees must understand how the process will actually operate on an ongoing basis, and how it will benefit them.

Regardless of the size or structure of the organization, some degree of consensus is critical to the successful implementation of the budget; otherwise, it is reduced to little more than a pressure device. It is imperative that operating units are evaluated strictly on the basis of items that they control. Consider the following example:

A private, multi-faced recreation centre (consisting of a 36-hole golf course, 8 outdoor tennis courts, and an indoor facility with a running track, weight room, and swimming pool) operates as three separate divisions, each with its own manager. In February of each year the centre's director develops and distributes revenue and expense targets for each of the three divisions. These budgets act as yardsticks for evaluating the division managers, who can earn bonuses of up to 25 percent of their base salary if these objectives are surpassed by year end (December 31).

Managers receive no credit for "crossovers"; an existing golf member who decides to also join the fitness centre is considered to be a member of the golf division only, for purposes of totalling divisional revenues.

Joint expenses (e.g., property taxes, mortgage interest, or fire insurance) are allocated to the separate divisions according to their relative share of dollar revenue.

There are a number of problems inherent in this system. Not only does it rely on a top down process, but it results in decisions being made on the basis of uncontrollable costs. In addition, managers obviously have no incentive to promote crossover business. As a result, the interests of the organization as a whole will be subordinated to those of the individual divisions.

An in-depth treatment of financial planning and budgeting is beyond the scope of this text. However, it is worth noting that one of the most crucial aspects of developing budget targets is setting objectives that will be considered challenging, yet attainable. In addition, budgets tend to be viewed first and foremost as evaluation instruments, and unless this process is managed properly, the value of the budget as an information device will be outweighed by its reputation as a punitive tool.

Hence, in small organizations, the process itself can be as important as the outcome—broad participation is often a paramount concern.

Flexible Budgets

From an accounting standpoint, one of the most effective ways to address many of the concerns cited in the preceding section is to institute a set of "flexible budgets," which set out specific objectives for a range of possible levels of activity. While both the annual budget and cash flow forecast (see Chapter 13) are vital planning tools, they are designed to act as control mechanisms and should not be allowed to become an end in themselves. Flexible or variable budgets represent a straightforward means of counteracting the rigidity that can plague the budgeting system.

Variable budgets will typically yield budget yardsticks that remain fair, insofar as this process involves setting different performance standards for different levels of output. (See Figure 14-1 for a sample flexible budget.)

Accounting Procedures as Control Measures

Generally, the entrepreneur not only finds it difficult to set aside adequate time for the planning activities that underlie the budget, but is understandably more interested in working with his particular product or service. At all stages

		Projected	Volume	Levels
Figure 14-1		15,000	17,500	20,000
The Flexible Budget	**Budget Per Unit**			
Sales	$33	$495,000	577,500	660,000
Variable Costs				
Material	6.75			
Wages	10.50			
Variable overhead	3.35			
Sales commissions	1.65			
Variable selling expenses	1.15			
Delivery	.70			
Total Variable Costs	24.10	361,500	421,750	482,000
Contribution	$ 8.90	133,500	155,750	178,000
Total Fixed Costs (Mfg, Selling, Admin.)		135,500	135,500	135,500
Operating Profit		$ (2,000)	20,250	42,500

of business development, he must rely on the accounting system both to provide basic information needs and safeguard the assets of the business. Moreover, the independent business owner is often unaware of how existing accounting procedures could be improved to provide more reliable financial data and better protection of physical and financial resources. A well conceived accounting system can eliminate inefficiencies and shortcomings, such as those outlined below:

- Invoices are prepared by salespeople in the field, errors are not detected until a trial balance is run.
- Retail stock is controlled by visual inspection only, making it impossible to coordinate purchases of inventory.
- The responsibility for reconciling bank account balances and updating the accounts receivable journal is left to one individual, and there are suspicions that a lower payment is being recorded than was actually received.
- Supplies are frequently drawn out of storage without proper authorization; goods are sometimes shipped without checking the status of the customer's credit account.

This is only a partial listing of the problems that can develop as a result of accounting procedures that are poorly conceived or improperly implemented. Clearly, the interests of the small company are best served by an accounting system which provides for the following:

1. The clear separation of certain duties (e.g., preparation of purchase orders and authorization of subsequent invoices);
2. The design and utilization of appropriate documents (e.g., pre-numbered invoices and cheques, a cash disbursements journal); and
3. Strict adherence to prescribed procedures with respect to authorization of transactions and confirmation of record-keeping accuracy.

Automating the Accounting Information System

Within the small business sector, there are some companies, including many owner-operated firms, wherein the owner is able to keep informed of the business activities through relatively informal means. Clearly these operations would derive little if any benefit from detailed accounting procedures and reports. Nonetheless, accurate and timely information is often a prerequisite for efficient use of the enterprise's limited resources; as the organization develops, the accounting system must be revised and upgraded to keep pace with its development.

A manual system is often appropriate for the basic requirements—accounts receivable listings, income tax returns, payroll accounting, cash budgets, shipping, and invoicing—of the smallest businesses, including most proprietorships and partnerships. However, the option of computerizing the firms' accounting and administrative functions merits serious consideration if the following problems start to arise with any regularity:

- Key reports, such as monthly sales, accounts payable schedule, and updated "actual-budget" comparisons, are not being provided until two or three weeks after they should be;
- The present system is incapable of providing comprehensive inventory status reports or formal production schedules depicting uncompleted jobs, backorders, etc.;
- Management is unable to access reliable cost data on specific jobs, including materials used, waste produced, and labour requirements;

- The volume of daily transactions make it difficult to keep the account ledgers up to date; or
- Administrative staff are obliged to spend an inordinate proportion of their time on mundane, repetitive tasks such as government reports or routine form letters.

In general, businesses that depend on a number of different product lines, have departmentalized their operations, or are serving a number of geographic territories, find it beneficial to automate at least a part of their accounting system. While the computer itself will not solve the company's problems, it can be used for a number of diverse functions—word processing, standard financial analysis, access to data banks, engineering analysis and statistical analysis for special projects—in addition to the aforementioned accounting-oriented tasks, which are available in standard software packages (order entry, inventory control, payroll, accounts payable and receivable, etc.).

Assuming the company is of adequate size, has a reasonable number of potential computer applications, and can justify the associated costs, the installation of a computer system can yield a dramatic improvement in the flow of information within the organization. This issue is discussed in somewhat more detail in Chapter 8.

Conclusion

One of the primary themes of this chapter is the dependence of the small business on its accounting system. It is crucial that the proprietor understand how the accounting function can contribute to the efficiency of the organization. Too many small business people are derelict in this regard, operating on the premise that accounting duties simply involve record keeping for the benefit of outsiders and provide very little direct value to the business. Myriad problems can arise if the accounting procedures are not followed or the information needs of management are not being satisfied by the accounting system.

Finally, accounting activities provide essential tools for planning and controlling the small enterprise; but even the best designed routine procedures and reporting systems will be of little value if management is not committed to making them work. In addition, employees at all levels must not only understand how the accounting system functions, but must also be motivated to implement the various procedures. Participation and teamwork are as important to the accounting function as they are to the other aspects of operating a small business.

Selected Readings

Clute, R., "How Important is Accounting to Small Business Survival?," *Journal of Commercial Bank Lending*, January 1980, pp. 24–28.

Coltman, Michael M., *Financial Control for the Small Business*. Vancouver, B.C.: International Self-Counsel Press Ltd., 1984.

Cornish, Clive G., *Basic Accounting for the Small Business*. Vancouver, B.C.: International Self-Counsel Press Ltd., 1985.

Noble, Michael, T.K. Clarke and F.G. Crane, "A Small Business Information System," *Journal of Small Business and Entrepreneurship*, 6, no. 2 (Winter 1986–87), pp. 3–9.

Endnotes

1. The terminology used by Horngren for these three facets of accounting is widely recognized:

   Scorekeeping—Am I doing well or badly?
   Attention-directing—What problems should I look into?
   Problem Solving—Which is the best way of doing the job?

   See Charles T. Horngren, *Accounting for Management Control: An Introduction*, (Englewood Cliffs, N.J.: Prentice-Hall, Inc., 1974), pp. 4–5.

2. *CICA Handbook* (Toronto: The Canadian Institute of Chartered Accountants, 1988).

3. See Kenneth G. Koehler, "Budgeting Pays if You Do It Right," *CMA Magazine*, 60, no. 3 (May–June 1986), p. 12.

A

Note on the Use of the Case Method*

Many courses in Business Management are taught entirely or in part by what is known as the case method. Since for many people the use of the case method may be unfamiliar and will require the development of somewhat different study and work habits, this note has been prepared to assist those students in the transition to a different learning method.

---

* This note was prepared by Professor Dwight R. Ladd, University of New Hampshire, for classroom use. Used with permission.

Use of Cases in Teaching

Essentially, the use of the case method is based on the concept of learning by doing. There are many definitions of what management is, but all agree that its central activity is the analysis of data—quantitative and qualitative—and the making of decisions based on that analysis. The use of the case method in business education rests upon the assumption that an effective way of preparing for a business career is to learn to analyze data and to make decisions. The student in a case method course will make his own analysis and reach his own decision, and then in the classroom will participate in a collective analysis and decision-making process. The case method provides the student with simulated experience in analysis and decision-making.

There are, of course, other requirements for effective preparation for a business career. The student must have some working knowledge of various business instruments and institutions—the nature of a capital lease, provisions of the Canada Business Incorporations Act, for example. He must also be familiar with the process and techniques relevant to business, such as discounted cash flow or linear programming. The case method is not a particularly efficient way of teaching and learning about these institutions and processes. This is best done through the direct methods of readings and lecture-demonstrations. Consequently, a case course will usually require reading of texts, journal articles and the like, and will from time to time involve more or less formal lectures or demonstrations by the instructor. However, use of the case method does imply a basic focus on the use of data and substantive knowledge in decision-making, rather than on the gathering and manipulation of data and the study of institutions. The effective manager must understand the conceptual differences between payback and internal rate of return, for example, but he does not need to be an expert in the calculation of either of these methods. In a case course, the acquisition of substantive knowledge is secondary to analysis and decision and will not take place in the orderly, consistent manner characteristic of a course devoted to some specific process or technique.

It is perhaps unfortunate that the word "case" rather than a word such as "situation" was used in connection with business education, because it leads some to seek parallels with legal education. A law case is quite different from a business case, because in our legal system cases are, quite frequently, the law itself. Law cases establish precedents, and future decisions in similar situations will be based on past decisions. Business cases, on the other hand, do not establish precedents. (The purpose in studying business cases is not to learn specific answers to specific problems, but to become familiar with analysis and decision-making, with the process of arriving at answers rather than with answers themselves.) Legal cases are a principal basis of the law. Business cases are not the basis of business practice. On the other hand, there are many similarities among various classes of business problems and the study of a series of cases, should lead to some useful generalizations. Case courses will, from time to time, pause for the statement by class or professor, or both, of generalizations which may be drawn from discussions completed.

In the Classroom

A first experience with a case course generally requires development of new study habits for most students. Since classes involve discussion of cases by students, it is obvious that the effectiveness of the class depends upon the student's having studied the case beforehand. Unlike lecture courses, where one has no specific preparation for the lecture and where one may do assigned reading and review of lecture notes at irregular intervals, a case course requires regular preparation before each class.

Without prior preparation, a case discussion will have little value, for sitting through a discussion of a problem with which one is quite unfamiliar is likely to be a boring experience and is generally an educationally empty one. Nor can the discussion generally be captured and retained through notes, since it is extremely difficult to take useful notes on an active discussion in which several people are participating.

It should be apparent that a case course requires regular attendance. Since much of the learning anticipated by the course takes place during discussions, the student must be there in order to be involved in the learning experience. As noted earlier, a discussion cannot be effectively recorded in notes and, so much of what transpires in a case discussion is permanently lost to the student who is not present.

Case discussions, by definition, depend upon active participation by members of the class, but the extent to which an individual student should participate is less clear. Some instructors believe, and demand, that every student should regularly participate in class discussions. Other instructors feel that each student must decide for himself how he best learns, and that failure to participate in class discussions does not necessarily mean that the student is unprepared or uninvolved in the learning process. Experience seems to indicate that most students will benefit from active participation in classroom discussions. The fact that the student intends to participate generally will result in more careful preparation. Participation requires close attention to the progress of the discussion. (It also provides training in informal oral discourse—something which most of us need.) At the same time, it does not necessarily follow that the student who is constantly talking is learning. Listening effectively is as much a part of communication as is speaking effectively.

Regular attendance, faithful preparation before classes and, for most, participation in class discussions are requirements for effective learning through study of cases.

Preparation

There is no right way to study cases. Each student will eventually discover an approach which suits him best, and the following are simply some suggestions which may be useful at the start.

Basically, all case preparation has the same objective: to reach a decision about the issue or issues in the case in light of the facts given in the case and of the student's relevant knowledge. A full command of the facts in the cases is a critical element in the process and thus the case should be read carefully at least a couple of times. A first reading will give the general flavour of the situation and make possible preliminary identification of issues. Sometimes, there will be some guiding questions given at the end of the case. In any case, the student should always be alert for issues or problems which have not been identified. At least a second reading is generally required to insure full command of the facts. Part of a second reading should be a close analysis of quantitative data given in the case. As courses progress, the student will be learning many of the techniques of such analysis, so the fact that analyses may be rather superficial at the start should not be cause for dismay.

At this point, it is well to review all of the data and make sure that the issue or issues have been correctly stated. For example, the apparent issue in a case might be whether or not a supervisor is doing a good job, while the real problem is the basis being used for evaluation by his superior. Correct statement of the problem is often the most important part of decision-making.

When the issue is identified it is usually helpful to list all possible courses of action, and it should be remembered that not all of these will necessarily be stated in the case itself. For example, an ever-present alternative, not always stated, is to do nothing.

Once possible courses of action have been identified, a pro and con listing for each one is often helpful. Not infrequently, data in the case will be contradictory. For example, a person may say that he behaves in a certain way while the record of his actions given in the case indicates quite different behavior. A student's judgment about the validity of data must be utilized here and an objective of the whole educational process is the development of the student's powers of judgment. Once again, one should not be unduly disturbed about the apparent quality of one's judgment in early stages of a course.

On other occasions, some very desirable information may not be available. In these instances the student must make judgments on the basis of information available, though from time to time an appropriate "solution" may be to ask for more data. A careful assessment of the probable cost of getting the data is required to support such a conclusion, however.

After identification of possible actions and a weighing of the pros and cons of each, the final step in case analysis is to make a decision. In case analysis, as in real life, this is a step which most people like to avoid, but in terms of the educational experience it is the most important part of the whole process. Bear in mind that making a decision and jumping to a conclusion are not the same thing. Some of the great decisions of human history have, no doubt, been based on intuition and some successful administrators may well have uttered the legendary: "Don't confuse me with facts. I've made up my mind." However, virtually all decisions are made only after vigorous and logical analysis of all pertinent data and this is the way the student should proceed.

Finally, it is important to remember that only infrequently is there a "right" decision. A decision may appear to you to be "right" in light of your assessment and weighing of the facts. Another person may evaluate the same facts in another way and thus have a different "right" answer. Virtually every business decision involves both judgment and straightforward assessment of fact. Techniques for analysis and weighing concrete data can be taught effectively by lectures, demonstrations, readings and exercises. The important element of judgment apparently can be learned, if at all, only by making judgments about real situations. This is the purpose of the case method. As the late Professor Charles Gragg of Harvard put it in a well-known talk, the case method is used "because wisdom can't be told."

APPENDIX

B

A Business Plan Format

The role and importance of the business plan are discussed extensively in Chapter 3. Here we provide a general format for the business plan, which can be tailored to meet the needs of a specific business.

The business plan has become a critical document for most new business startups and for many small businesses seeking new financing, new stakeholder involvement or financial restructuring. Almost all lenders require one, and some government granting agencies and lenders provide for consultants to aid in their preparation and presentation. Despite the fact that many business plans are prepared by outsiders and may not include adequate involvement by the entrepreneur, they have become prerequisites to most new business discussions with lenders and stakeholders.

This presentation provides a guideline for business plan preparation. It recognizes several critical points:

1. Few entrepreneurs are skilled planners and even fewer find planning an agreeable activity.

2. Most entrepreneurs view the business plan as an activity required by others and thus something that must be done to get started. Often they see the activity as having little long-term value to the business.

3. With help, the entrepreneur is the person best equipped to prepare the business plan.

4. Significant inolvement in plan development best serves the entrepreneur when the time comes to present and defend the new business proposal.

There are a variety of views on what constitutes a business plan and whom it should serve. Some authors[1] see business plans as being designed for the user, and they define the user as the bank, venture capitalist or shareholder. Others,[2] ourselves among them, see all planning forms, including the business plan, as vehicles for determining direction and providing operating guidelines for the business in question. Business plans that are developed solely for bankers or venture capitalists provide little real help to the entrepreneur and may explain the entrepreneur's lack of interest and involvement in plan development, and the increasing involvement of outsiders in the process. This approach provides the banker with a format that is easy to read, but it should surprise no one to discover that such plans are quickly set aside by the entrepreneur once the financing is in place. Effective plans not only convince lenders to finance the proposal but should convince the lender that, if used, projected results will be achieved. Such plans require a high degree of entrepreneurial involvement. Bankers, venture capitalists and most shareholders have access to analytical resources and most likely will revise the entrepreneur's estimates depending on their assessment of the proposed product or service, and the ability of the entrepreneur to produce projected results.

This appendix and its associated software are designed to maximize the entrepreneur's input into the business plan while minimizing the planning skills essentials to its completion. Those involved in the development and writing of business plans use proven formats including computer software developed for this purpose.[3] Universities and community colleges provide courses designed to aid in business plan development, as do some Chambers of Commerce and the Federal Business Development Bank. As well, there are a large number of private courses offered by consultants and accounting firms.

While business plans come in a variety of formats, most include a standard set of topics. Of course, depending on the business, certain parts of the plan will require special attention. High technology products or services require some special attention to the needs of research and design, while service proposals may need increased emphasis on the availability of labour and training skills. Copyrights, trademarks, and patents are key factors in other proposals.

It is important for the entrepreneur to recognize that the figures (projected income statements and cash-flow projections) can be easily adjusted by the reader if the business proposal is not well thought out. Often adjustments are made to the financial projections simply because they overstate the potential evident in other areas of the plan. Where the plan is vague, these adjustments are almost certain to be made as part of the risk evaluation process. Uncertainty will cost the entrepreneur.

The Business Plan

While business plan formats vary in emphasis, most cover the areas common to many small businesses. Typically, business plans include information under most of the following headings. Not all business plans require coverage or comment on all of the items in this list.

- Letter of Transmittal
- Title Page
- Table of Contents
- Fact Sheet and Executive Summary
- The Plan
    - The Product or Service
        - Feasibility Study
    - The Company
        - The Entrepreneur
    - The Industry
        - Economic Considerations
        - Competition
        - Environment
    - Marketing
        - Market Description
            - Market Trends
            - Competitive Product/Service Offerings

- Marketing Strategy
    - Market/Sales/Distribution Approach
    - Pricing
    - Advertising/Promotion
- Operations
    - Site/Location/Layout
    - Facilities/Equipment
    - Engineering/Design
    - Labour
    - Process/Production Planning
    - Purchasing/Material Control
    - Quality Control
    - Delivery
- Personnel/Skills
    - Training
    - Safety
    - Personnel Records
- Management
    - The Management Group
    - Outside Support/Advisors/Consultants
- Financial Plan
    - Projected Financial Statements
        - Income Statement
        - Balance Sheet
        - Cash Flow Projections
        - Break-Even Analysis
- Support Services/Plan
    - Bookkeeping/Accounting Systems
    - Information Systems
- Ongoing Planning Activities

Appendices
- Technical Data
    - Product/Service Design Specifications
    - Plant/Office Layouts
- Market Research Data
- Customer/Supplier Lists
- Legal Documents
- Other Support Materials

–Personnel Dossiers/Management Profiles
–Consulting/Advisory Contacts and Reports

Business Plan Software*

The BUS-PLAN software is simple to use and focuses on inputs from the entrepreneur. It is designed in two parts (see Figure B-1):

Figure B-1

BUS-PLAN -
Software Modules

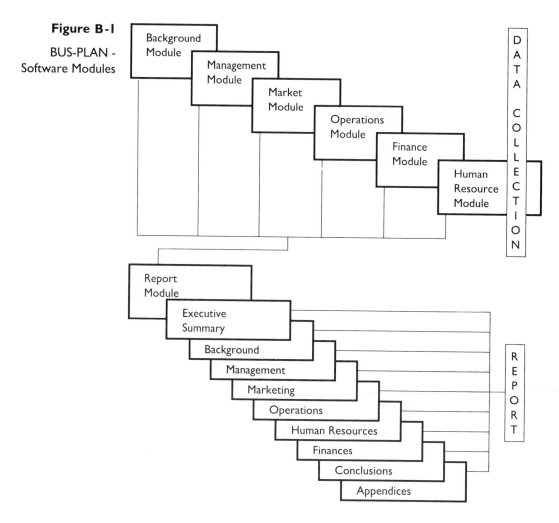

* For instructors adopting this text, the software described here is available from Prentice-Hall Canada. It is written using dBASE III+ and can be copied for use with the cases in *ENTREPRENEURSHIP AND SMALL BUSINESS DEVELOPMENT: TEXT AND CASES.*

1. Data collection module, and
2. Report module.

It consists of a series of questions, the answers to which are then used to develop a business plan. The format produced by the dBASE software can be enhanced later by using any one of several word processors. Instructions for using the dBASE software are included in this appendix.

Note all of the questions posed by the Business Plan software need to be answered. Nor does all of the space provided in the program have to be used. On the other hand, if further explanations are required, additions can be made when the plan in enhanced using word processing capabilities.

Each screen includes explanations for its use and instructions for progressing through the module sequence. Additional instructions accompany the software diskette.

Using BUS-PLAN

BUS-PLAN has been written using dBASE III + and must be invoked using that software.

1. To start, type: dBase.
2. In dBase, type <ESC> to exit the ASSIST menus and obtain a dot prompt.
3. At the dot prompt type .DO BUSPLAN

At the command .DO BUSPLAN, dBase will produce screen 1. Type enter/ return to produce Screen 2.

Screen 1

```
BBB   U  U   SSS        PPP  L      A   N   N
B  B  U  U   S          P P  L     A A  NN  N
BBB   U  U   SSS   = = = PPP  L     A   A N N N
B  B  U  U      S        P    L    AAAAA N  NN
BBB   UUUU   SSS         P   LLLL  A   A N   N
            PERSONAL  BUSINESS  PLANNER
```

Screen 2 provides the program menu and a starting point for the development of your business plan. Main Menu choice 1 provides the business plan

Screen 2

```
┌─────────────────────────────────────────────────┐
│                   MAIN MENU                     │
├─────────────────────────────────────────────────┤
│        1. BEGIN/CONTINUE BUSINESS PLAN          │
│        2. PRINT                                 │
│        3. EXIT TO dBASE                         │
│        4. CLEAR ALL MEMORY                      │
│        CHOICE? : 1:                             │
└─────────────────────────────────────────────────┘
```

modules. To start, continue, or revise an existing business plan use choice 1. Choice 2, the print module, will produce a hard copy of all or part of the business plan, or an outline of the business plan modules and the questions contained in each.

Choice 3, "return," exits the BUS-PLAN program and returns the user to dBASE. To exit dBASE at this point, type .QUIT at the dot prompt. Information entered in BUS-PLAN is retained for future use or updates. Choice 4 clears BUS-PLAN (you will be asked to confirm the choice) for use with new information. **PLEASE NOTE THAT CHOICE 4 DELETES ALL DATA.**

The Module Menu follows from Choice 1 in the Main Menu. The user can begin with any of the Module Menu choices and continue the process in any sequence. To produce a complete business plan each choice in the Module Menu must be used, although some questions may be excluded. Experience suggests that progressing from Choice 1 through Choice 5 is the best approach for the inexperienced user.

Screen 3

```
┌─────────────────────────────────────────────────┐
│                  MODULE MENU                    │
├─────────────────────────────────────────────────┤
│           1. GOALS                              │
│           2. MARKETING                          │
│           3. OPERATIONS                         │
│           4. PERSONNEL                          │
│           5. FINANCIAL                          │
│           6. RETURN TO MAIN MENU                │
│           CHOICE? : 1:                          │
└─────────────────────────────────────────────────┘
```

The screens that are part of each module contain explanations for the completion of module questions, and instructions for progressing from screen to screen, and module to module. Read the information on each screen carefully before proceeding. If the questions cannot be answered you may progress to the next screen and return later to provide missing data.

Screen 4 presents a typical screen from the BUS-PLAN program. In most cases, concise answers are encouraged. Where required, these answers can be expanded in your word processor.

Screen 4

GOALS: BEGIN	BUS-PLAN

Please enter the following general company information
Title of Plan:
Company Name:
Address:
City/Prov
Contact
Date

Additional information and instructions are provided with the BUS-PLAN software package.

Endnotes

1. See, for example, Raymond Kao, *Entrepreneurship and Enterprise Development* (Toronto: Holt Rinehart and Winston of Canada, Limited, 1989), p. 60.

2. See, for example, Donald L. Sexton and Phillip Van Auken, "A Longitudinal Study of Small Business Strategic Planning," *Journal of Small Business Management*, January 1985, 23, no. 1, pp. 1–6. See also Fred L. Fry and Charles R. Stoner, "Business Plans: Two Major Types," *Journal of Small Business Management*, January 1985, 23, no. 1, pp. 7–15. Fry and Stoner speak of working plans and investment plans as serving different purposes and different audiences.

3. See for example *VenturePlan*, from Venture Software Inc., 222 Third Street, Cambridge, MA., USA, 02142.

Index

formal, 19
information, 15, 112, 172, 174, 217, 218
marketing assistance, 222

T

Take-off, 19
Takeover(s), 211
    artists, 16
Tax,
    concession(s), 336
    corporate, 336
    income, 336
Technology, 112, 211, 219
Thain, 17, 18
The Perfect Pace, 9
The Second Cup, 61
Theatre(s), 55
    centres, 55
Tim Horton's, 221
Time, 20, 53, 58, 59, 108, 111, 112, 213, 214, 215, 217,
    218, 220, 327, 344
    management, 337–340
    manager, 339
Trademark, 61
Transition, 23, 28, 110, 174, 213, 214, 215, 217, 219,
    220, 221
    phases, 12, 17, 18, 19, 20, 21–22, 210–223; *See also*
        Development phases
    planning, 213–214, 217–218, 219, 220
        decision(s), 215, 220
        management, 212, 213, 214, 217, 218, 220,
        221
Turnkey operation, 61

U

Unionization, 396–397
Uniqueness, 329

Unix, 341
Upper Canada Brewing Company, 175

V

Van Auben, 30
Variance(s), 111, 178
Venture(s), 32, 34, 54; *See also* Capital
    capital, 35, 174
        market, 415–417
    capitalists, 33
    initiation, 32
    new, 175, 330
Vesper, 16
Vertical integration, 179
Vozikis, 39
Vulnerability, 54, 219, 221, 222

W

Waterman, 327, 328, 331
Weakness(es), 37, 39, 57, 58, 175, 222
    competitor, 109
Wholesaling, 177
Wojahn, 333
Women
    discrimination against, 332
    entrepreneur(s), 334
    in business, 327, 332–334, 344
    manager(s), 334
Word, 341
Wordperfect, 341
Workforce, 172; *See also* Employees, Personnel
    builder(s), 16
Working plan(s), 28, 29, 33, 37, 39
    implementation, 39–40

X

XT(computers), 340